Lone Star Blue and Gray

Lone Star Blue and Gray

Essays on Texas in the Civil War

Edited and with an introduction by

Ralph A. Wooster

Texas State Historical Association

Austin

Library of Congress Cataloging-in-Publication Data

Lone Star Blue and Gray : essays on Texas in the Civil War / edited and with an
    introduction by Ralph A. Wooster.
        p.   cm.—(Fred H. and Ella Mae Moore Texas history reprint series)
    Includes bibliographical references and index.
    ISBN 0-87611-152-5 (alk. paper)
        1. Texas—history—Civil War, 1861–1865. I. Wooster, Ralph A. II. Texas
    State Historical Association. III. Series.
E580.9.L66
973.7'464—dc20   95-38254
                                                                                                            CIP

Cover: Carte de visite of unidentified officer by J. H. Normand, coloring by Julio Pardonneau, Matanzas, Cuba, ca. 1865. This is one of the very few extant wartime photographs that includes an actual Confederate flag as part of the view. The flag is believed to be that of a blockade runner, and the man possibly is an officer of one of the blockade runners that frequented the Cuba-Texas coastal route in 1864–1865. *Courtesy Lawrence T. Jones III.*

Contents

Introduction

Ralph A. Wooster

In the 1850s a series of events focusing on the expansion of slavery in the national territories divided the northern and southern sections of the United States. Increasing numbers of northerners, convinced of the evils of chattel slavery, were determined to halt its expansion. Southerners, most of whom believed in state rights, argued that the Federal government had no right to interfere with slavery and looked for ways to expand it.

The 1860 election of Republican Abraham Lincoln as President of the United States on a platform opposing any expansion of slavery convinced many southerners that separation from the Union was the only means of preserving their way of life. In the winter of 1860–1861 seven states of the lower South seceded from the Union. South Carolina, the most radical southern state, was the first to take action. In mid-December her state convention passed an ordinance of secession by a unamious vote. In early January, Mississippi, Florida, and Alabama followed, with Georgia and Louisiana joining them a month later.

Texas was the last state in the lower South to secede. A state convention, meeting in late January 1861, adopted an ordinance of secession subject to ratification by the state's voters. In February Texans approved the ordinance by a three to one margin. The state convention then moved to join Texas with other seceding states in the Confederate States of America.

With these actions Texas and other slaveholding states began a four-year struggle for recognition as a sovereign nation. The war that followed as Americans fought one another over the preservation of the Union and the independence of the Confederacy was one of the bloodiest conflicts in modern history. Between the firing on Fort Sumter in April 1861 and the final collapse of the Confederacy in late spring 1865, more than six hundred thousand Americans died. Thousands of others were wounded or disabled.

Although a frontier state, Texas played a significant role in the American Civil War. Over seventy thousand Texans fought for the Confederacy. Another two thousand served in the Union army. Scarcely a household in the state was unaffected as mothers and wives assumed new roles in managing farms and plantations while husbands and sons were away at war. The increasing effectiveness of the Union naval blockade along the Texas coastline interrupted the shipment of cotton and grains from the state and interfered with the importation of various commodities. Union invaders were repulsed at Corpus Christi, Laredo, Port Lavaca, and Sabine Pass, but Galveston, Indianola, and Brownsville were occupied by Federal troops.[1]

Texans were divided by the war. While the majority of citizens favored and supported the Confederacy, a sizeable minority, including some of the state's most influential leaders such as Governor Houston, former Governor Elisha M. Pease, Congressman A. J. Hamilton, District Judge Edmund J. Davis, and state legislators James W. Throckmorton, John Hancock, Ben Epperson, and George Whitmore, opposed secession. Some of these Texas unionists came to support the Confederate cause but others, notably A. J. Hamilton and Edmund J. Davis, never accepted secession and worked actively to preserve the Union.[2]

---

1. Because of the loss of many Confederate records at the end of the war it is impossible to determine the exact number of Texans who served in Confederate and state forces during the conflict. In November 1863, Governor Francis R. Lubbock reported to the Texas legislature that ninety thousand Texans were in the military at that time, but this figure seems high. Stephen B. Oates, who has studied enrollment figures carefully, believes that eighty-eight thousand Texans, fifty-eight thousand in the cavalry and thirty thousand in the infantry and artillery, served in the military during the war. See Oates, "Texas Under the Secessionists," *Southwestern Historical Quarterly*, LXVII (Oct., 1963), 187. Dudley G. Wooten, *A Comprehensive History of Texas, 1685 to 1897* (Dallas: William G. Scarff, 1898), II, 571, calculated that 89,500 Texans served in Confederate and state forces. Robert P. Felgar, "Texas in the War for Southern Independence, 1861–1865" (Ph.D. diss., University of Texas, 1935), 106, estimated that sixty thousand Texans served in the Confederate army. Archie P. McDonald, in *A Nation of Sovereign States: Secession and War in the Confederacy*, Journal of Confederate History Series, Vol. X (Murfreesboro, Tenn.: Southern Heritage Press, 1994), 87, believes that sixty to seventy thousand Texans served in the military during the war.

2. In addition to the articles by Claude Elliott and Frank Smyrl in this volume see James Marten, *Texas Divided: Loyalty and Dissent in the Lone Star State, 1856–1874* (Lexington: University Press of

Unionist sentiment in Texas was strongest among the Germans of central Texas and the settlers in the counties along the Red River. Even in these areas there was division, however. Several German counties turned in heavy majorities for secession and hundreds of Germans served in the Confederate army. In the Red River counties voters rejected secession, but Colonel William Cocke Young, himself a unionist, recruited a military unit in the area that served with distinction in the Confederate army as the Eleventh Texas Cavalry.[3]

Texans fought in every major battle of the Civil War except First Manassas and Chancellorsville. They fought in New Mexico Territory, Maryland, Pennsylvania and every state of the Confederacy (including Kentucky and Missouri) except Florida. They battled the enemy in the hills and mountains of Arkansas, Missouri, and Indian Territory, along the banks of the Mississippi, Tennessee, Cumberland, Arkansas, Red, James, and York Rivers, in the bluegrass of Kentucky, in the red clay of Georgia, and in the pine forests and bayous of Louisiana. They recaptured Galveston from enemy occupiers and drove invaders away from other Texas seaports. They played a major role in defeating Nathaniel P. Banks in the Red River campaign and helped turn back Frederick Steele in his drive into southern Arkansas. The first surrender of United States troops in the war occurred in San Antonio two months before the firing on Fort Sumter when Ben McCulloch convinced Union Brigadier General David Twiggs to turn over all Federal property in Texas. The last battle of the Civil War was fought at Palmetto Ranch near Brownsville a month after Robert E. Lee had surrendered at Appomattox Courthouse.[4]

Kentucky, 1990); Elliott, *Leathercoat: The Life of James W. Throckmorton* (San Antonio: Standard Printing Co., 1938); Smyrl, "Unionism in Texas, 1856–1861," *Southwestern Historical Quarterly,* LXVIII (Oct., 1964), 172–195; Ralph A. Wooster, "Ben H. Epperson: East Texas Lawyer, Legislator, and Civic Leader," *East Texas Historical Journal,* V (Mar., 1967), 29–42; Randolph B. Campbell, "George W. Whitmore: East Texas Unionist," ibid., XXVIII (Spring, 1990), 17–28; John L. Waller, *Colossal Hamilton of Texas: A Biography of Andrew Jackson Hamilton* (El Paso: Texas Western Press, 1968); and Ronald N. Gray, "Edmund J. Davis: Radical Republican and Reconstruction Governor of Texas" (Ph.D. diss., Texas Tech University, 1976).

3. Terry G. Jordan, *German Seed in Texas Soil: Immigrant Farmers in Nineteenth-Century Texas* (Austin: University of Texas Press, 1966), 182–185; Ella Lonn, *Foreigners in the Confederacy* (Chapel Hill: University of North Carolina Press, 1940), 123–126, 193–194, 500–501; Richard B. McCaslin, *Tainted Breeze: The Great Hanging at Gainesville, Texas, 1862* (Baton Rouge: Louisiana State University Press, 1994), 41–48; Richard B. McCaslin, "Conditional Confederates: The Eleventh Texas Cavalry West of the Mississippi River," *Military History of the Southwest,* XXI (Spring, 1991), 87–99.

4. There were several Texans, including Tom Lubbock, Benjamin Terry, and Tom Goree, at the battle of First Manassas. They had come to Richmond in early summer 1861 to inquire as to Confederate military needs. All three served as volunteer aides on the staff of Brigadier General James Longstreet at First Manassas. Goree remained on Longstreet's staff for the duration of the war. Terry

In the course of the war Texans distinguished themselves on various battle fronts. Two of the Confederacy's eight full generals, Albert Sidney Johnston and John Bell Hood, were Texans. Johnston, considered one of America's finest soldiers, was a native of Kentucky but served in the army of the Texas Republic and lived in Texas for two decades prior to the Civil War. When the Civil War began he resigned his commission in the United States Army and was appointed commander of the Confederate western department. His untimely death at Shiloh while commanding Southern forces was a major blow to the Confederacy. Hood, like Johnston a native of Kentucky, was stationed in Texas prior to the war and considered it his adopted home. Early in the war he became commander of three Texas regiments that came to be known as Hood's Texas Brigade, one of the most famous of all Civil War military units.[5]

In addition to Johnston and Hood, thirty-five other Texans served as general officers in the Confederate army. Two, John A. Wharton and Thomas Rosser, attained the rank of major general; the other thirty-three were brigadier generals. Among these Ben McCulloch, Matthew D. Ector, Hiram Granbury, Tom Green, John Gregg, Sam Maxey and Lawrence Sullivan Ross were the most prominent. Ten of the thirty-seven Texas general officers died during the war; Granbury, Green, Gregg, Johnston, McCulloch, Horace Randal, and William R. Scurry on the field of battle; John A. Wharton in an altercation with fellow Texas officer George W. Baylor; and Joseph L. Hogg and Allison Nelson from disease.[6]

---

and Lubbock returned to Texas to organize the Eighth Texas Cavalry, which became known as Terry's Texas Rangers. Terry was killed in fighting in Kentucky in December 1861 and Lubbock died from natural causes the following month. Harold B. Simpson, *Hood's Texas Brigade: Lee's Grenadier Guard* (Waco: Texian Press, 1970), 41, 48.

The First Texas Infantry, which later was part of Hood's Brigade, arrived in Richmond in mid-July but too late to participate in the battle at First Manassas. The brigade took part in all the other major battles in the East except Chancellorsville. As part of Longstreet's Corps it was on detached duty in the Suffolk area of Virginia when this battle was fought. Simpson, ibid., 224–234. Texans fought in all the major campaigns in the Trans-Appalachian and Trans-Mississippi regions as well as in Georgia and the Carolinas.

5. For Johnston and Hood see Charles P. Roland, *Albert Sidney Johnston: Soldier of Three Republics* (Austin: University of Texas Press, 1964); John Bell Hood, *Advance and Retreat: Personal Experiences in the United States and Confederate States Armies* (New Orleans: G. T. Beauregard, Published for Hood Orphan Memorial Fund, 1880); John P. Dyer, *The Gallant Hood* (Indianapolis: Bobbs-Merrill Co., 1950), and Richard M. McMurray, *John Bell Hood and the War for Southern Independence* (Lexington: University Press of Kentucky, 1982).

6. There is some disagreement as to the exact number of general officers from Texas in the Confederate army. I have used the names given in Marcus J. Wright (comp.), *Texas in the War, 1861–1865,* ed. Harold B. Simpson (Hillsboro: Hill Junior College Press, 1965), 3–18. This varies

Hood's Brigade was the only Texas military unit to serve with Robert E. Lee's Army of Northern Virginia during the war. The brigade, consisting of the First, Fourth, and Fifth Texas Infantry and the Eighteenth Georgia (later replaced by the Third Arkansas), distinguished itself in fighting in Virginia and Tennessee, particularly in the battles of Gaines Mill, Sharpsburg, Gettysburg, Chickamauga, and the Wilderness. Its casualty rates were high. The First Texas sustained 82.3 percent losses at Sharpsburg, the highest of any regiment in a single engagement in the Civil War. The Fourth and Fifth Texas also suffered heavy casualties. Of the 5,300 men who served in the brigade during the war only 617 were with the brigade when Lee's army surrendered at Appomattox.[7]

Hood's Brigade was highly regarded by General Lee. The Brigade's finest hour may have been in the Wilderness campaign of 1864 when the Texans drove back the enemy while Lee looked on approvingly. It was on this occasion that the Virginian remarked "Texans always move them," a tribute to the Brigade's many successes in battle.[8]

Terry's Texas Rangers was another well-known Texas military unit. Recruited in central and coastal Texas by wealthy Brazoria planter Benjamin F. Terry, the Rangers, officially the Eighth Texas Cavalry, fought in all the major campaigns

slightly from Ezra J. Warner, *Generals in Gray; Lives of Confederate Commanders* (Baton Rouge: Louisiana State University Press, 1959). Warner does not include A. P. Bagby, Xavier B. Debray, Wilburn H. King, Hinche P. Mabry, Horace Randal, and A. W. Terrell. He does note that Bagby, Debray, King, Randal, and Terrell were assigned as general officers in the Trans-Mississippi department but not appointed by President Davis. Ibid., 351–352. Warner fails to mention Hinche P. Mabry of Jefferson, described by Wright and Simpson, *Texas in the War*, 86, as "promoted to brigade general by E. Kirby Smith sometime in 1864 . . . but never confirmed by Jefferson Davis or the Confederate Senate." Wright and Simpson do not include James P. Major, a native of Missouri who commanded a Texas cavalry brigade in Louisiana, but he is included in the list of Texas general officers by Richard M. McMurray, *Two Great Rebel Armies: An Essay in Confederate Military History* (Chapel Hill: University of North Carolina Press, 1989), 163–164.

Thomas L. Rosser, a major general in Lee's army, was more closely identified with his native Virginia than Texas. He is often listed among generals from that state. His family migrated to Texas in the 1840s, however, and his appointment to West Point was from Texas. He is listed as a Texas officer in Wright and Simpson, *Texas in the War*, 15, 92. Both Tom Green and Sam Maxey were recommended by their commanders for promotion to major general but neither promotion was ever approved by the President and the Senate. Warner, *Generals in Gray*, 117–118, 216.

7. The definitive account of the Texas Brigade is by Harold B. Simpson: *Hood's Texas Brigade in Poetry and Song* (Waco: Texian Press, 1968); *Hood's Texas Brigade: Lee's Grenadier Guard* (Waco: Texian Press, 1970); *Hood's Texas Brigade in Reunion and Memory* (Waco: Texian Press, 1974); and *Hood's Texas Brigade: A Compendium* (Waco: Texian Press, 1977).

8. R. C., "Texans Always Move Them," *The Land We Love*, V (1868), 481–486; Gordon C. Rhea, *The Battle of the Wilderness, May 5–6, 1864* (Baton Rouge: Louisiana State University Press, 1994), 299–302; Gary Gallagher (ed.), *Fighting for the Confederacy: The Personal Recollections of General Edward Porter Alexander* (Chapel Hill: University of North Carolina Press, 1989), 358.

in Kentucky, Tennessee, Georgia, and the Carolinas, including the battles at Perryville, Shiloh, Murfreesboro, Chickamauga, and Bentonville. Terry himself was killed near Woodsonville, Kentucky, in December 1861, but the Rangers, subsequently commanded by John A. Wharton and later Tom Harrison and Gustave Cooke, continued to carry Terry's name. With a reputation for boldness and daring, the Rangers were known for their fearlessness in the attack, preferring the six-shooter and double-barreled shotgun to the cavalry saber.[9]

Ross's Cavalry Brigade, Granbury's Infantry Brigade, and Ector's Infantry Brigade were other Texas units particularly noted for their fighting skills. Ross's Brigade, consisting of the Third, Sixth, Ninth, and Twenty-Seventh Texas Cavalry, played a major role in the Mississippi campaigns of 1863–1864 and in the fighting around Atlanta in 1864. Granbury's Brigade, consisting of five Texas regiments commanded by Waco lawyer-county judge Hiram Granbury, distinguished itself fighting in northern Georgia and Tennessee in 1864. Ector's Brigade, made up of four Texas regiments and units from Alabama, Mississippi, and North Carolina, also fought in these campaigns. The Brigade commander, Matthew D. Ector, was a Rusk county lawyer and state legislator who, like Nathan Bedford Forrest, enlisted as a private when the war began and rose to the rank of general officer.[10]

Walker's Division, which distinguished itself in the Arkansas and Louisiana campaigns of 1863 and 1864, was the largest Texas unit in the Civil War. With the exception of its commander, Major General John G. Walker, a Missourian who earlier served with Lee's army in Virginia in 1862, the division was an all-

---

9. Among the various accounts of the Eighth Texas Cavalry are L. B. Giles, *Terry's Rangers* (Austin: Pemberton Press, 1967); C. C. Jeffries, *Terry's Rangers* (New York: Vantage Press, 1961); J. K. P. Blackburn, "Reminiscences of the Terry Rangers," *Southwestern Historical Quarterly,* XXII (July–Oct., 1918), 38–77, 143–179; Thomas W. Cutrer (ed.), "'We Are Stern and Resolved': The Civil War Letters of John Wesley Rabb, Terry's Texas Rangers," ibid., XCI (Oct., 1987), 185–226; Robert W. Williams and Ralph A. Wooster (eds.), "With Terry's Texas Rangers: Letters of Dunbar Affleck," *Civil War History,* IX (Sept., 1963), 299–319; and H. J. H. Rugeley (ed.), *Batchelor-Turner Letters, 1861–1864, Written by Two of Terry's Texas Rangers* (Austin: Steck Company, 1961).

10. See Homer L. Kerr (ed.), *Fighting With Ross' Texas Cavalry Brigade, C.S.A.: The Diary of George L. Griscom, Adjutant, 9th Texas Cavalry Regiment* (Hillsboro: Hill Junior College Press), 1976; Judy Watson (ed.), *Confederate From East Texas: The Civil War Letters of James Monroe Watson* (Quanah: Nortex Press, 1968); Douglas Hale, *The Third Texas Cavalry in the Civil War* (Norman: University of Oklahoma Pres, 1993); Norman Brown (ed.), *One of Cleburne's Command: The Civil War Reminiscences and Diary of Capt. Samuel T. Foster, Granbury's Texas Brigade, CSA* (Austin: University of Texas Press, 1980); James M. McCaffrey, *This Band of Heroes: Granbury's Texas Brigade, C. S. A.* (Austin: Eakin Press, 1985); Peter Cozzens, *This Terrible Sound: The Battle of Chickamauga* (Urbana: University of Illinois Press, 1992), 135; and Clement A. Evans (ed.), *Confederate Military History* (12 vols.; Atlanta: Confederate Publishing Company, 1899), XI, 185.

Texas unit. Known as "Walker's Greyhounds" because of its extensive and rapid marches, the division numbered among its members a former governor of the state, Colonel Edward Clark of the Fourteenth Texas Infantry, and two future governors, Colonel O. M. Roberts of the Eleventh Texas Infantry and Colonel Richard B. Hubbard of the Twenty-Second Texas Infantry.[11]

Other Texas military units that served with distinction included Polignac's Brigade, an infantry brigade made up of Texans led by a French aristocrat, Camille Armand Jules Marie, Prince de Polignac; the Second Texas Infantry, a regiment first commanded by John Moore and later by William P. Rogers and Ashbel Smith; and Waul's Legion, consisting of several infantry companies and cavalry and artillery detachments recruited and commanded by Washington County planter Thomas Waul. These Texans served principally in Louisiana and Mississippi; Polignac's Brigade taking part in the Red River campaign, the Second Infantry in the battles of Shiloh, Corinth, and Vicksburg, and Waul's Legion in the battle and siege of Vicksburg.[12]

Few Texas military units saw service as varied as the cavalry regiments that made up the Sibley Brigade. Commanded by Brigadier General Henry H. Sibley in the New Mexico campaign, the brigade, consisting of the Fourth, Fifth, and Seventh Texas Cavalry, defeated Federal troops at Valverde and Glorieta Pass before being forced to retreat back into Texas. Units of the brigade later participated in the Confederate recapture of Galveston on January 1, 1863. In early 1863 they were transferred to Louisiana, where they helped stop Major General William B. Franklin's advance in the bayou country. Departmental chief Richard Taylor removed Sibley from command and replaced him with Texan Tom Green, who had served as Sibley's deputy in New Mexico. Under

---

11. The most complete account of Walker's Division is J. P. Blessington, *The Campaigns of Walker's Texas Division* (1875; reprint, Austin: State House Press, 1994). See also Norman D. Brown (ed.), *Journey to Pleasant Hill: The Civil War Letters of Captain Elijah P. Petty, Walker's Texas Division, C.S.A.* (San Antonio: Institute of Texas Cultures, 1982); Thomas W. Cutrer (ed.), "'An Experience in Soldier's Life': The Civil War Letter of Volney Ellis Adjutant, Twelfth Texas Infantry, Walker's Texas Division, C. S. A.," *Military History of the Southwest*, XXII (Fall, 1992), 109–172; and Thomas W. Cutrer (ed.), "'Bully for Flournoy's Regiment, We Are Some Pumkins, You'll Bet': The Civil War Letters of Virgil Sullivan Rabb, Captain 'I,' Sixteenth Texas Infantry, C. S. A.," ibid., XIX (Fall, 1989), 161–190; XX (Spring, 1990), 61–96.

12. See Alwyn Barr, *Polignac's Texas Brigade* (Houston: Texas Gulf Coast Historical Association Publication Series, 1964); Joseph E. Chance, *The Second Texas Infantry: From Shiloh to Vicksburg* (Austin: Eakin Press, 1984); Laura Simmons, "Waul's Legion From Texas to Mississippi," *Texana*, VII (Spring, 1969), 1–16; Wayne Flynt, "The Texas Legion at Vicksburg," *East Texas Historical Journal*, XVII (Spring, 1979), 60–67.

Green's leadership the brigade took part in the successful Confederate efforts to block Nathaniel P. Banks's move up the Red River in 1864.[13]

The most famous small Texas military unit was Company F, First Texas Heavy Artillery, better known as the Davis Guards. Made up of Irishmen recruited in Houston, the Davis Guards participated in several coastal operations early in the war but gained their greatest fame for the heroic defense of Sabine Pass in September 1863. Commanded by Lieutenant Richard W. Dowling that day, the Guards, consisting of forty-three men, defeated a major Union invasion force of some four thousand men and four gunboats in one of the war's most brilliant actions. For their gallantry the guards were praised by Major General John B. Magruder, Confederate President Jefferson Davis, and the Confederate Congress, and a special medal was given to every member of the company.[14]

The war affected the lives of all Texans, not just those in uniform. Although Texas suffered less than most other Confederate states, many adjustments in life-style were made necessary by the war. The Union naval blockade, while never totally effective, resulted in shortages of many commodities, especially coffee, medicine, clothing, shoes, and farm tools. The shortage of coffee was particularly felt by Texans. Colonel Arthur Fremantle, a British visitor to Texas during the war, noted that the loss of coffee was a matter of serious concern and observed that Texans exercised their ingenuity in devising substitutes. While traveling in East Texas he was served a mixture called "Confederate coffee" made of rye, meal, Indian corn, and sweet potatoes. Eliza McHatton-Ripley, a refugee from Louisiana living in Texas, noted that Texans drank a variety of substitutes including peanuts, sweet potatoes, rye, beans, peas, and cornmeal. "All of them were wretched imitations," she wrote, "though gulped down, when chilly and tired for lack of anything better." The family of Mathilda Doebbler Gruen, a young German Texan, used parched rye and wheat as a coffee substitute.[15]

---

13. Theo. Noel, *A Campaign From Santa Fe to the Mississippi: Being a History of the Old Sibley Brigade* (Shreveport: News Printing Establishment, 1865); Martin Hardwick Hall, *Sibley's New Mexico Campaign* (Austin: University of Texas Press, 1960); Odie B. Faulk, *General Tom Green: Fightin' Texan* (Waco: Texian Press, 1963); T. Michael Parrish, *Richard Taylor: Soldier Prince of Dixie* (Chapel Hill: University of North Carolina Press, 1992).

14. Andrew Forest Muir, "Dick Dowling and the Battle of Sabine Pass," *Civil War History,* IV (Dec., 1958), 399–428; Stewart Sifakis, *Compendium of the Confederate Armies: Texas* (New York: Facts on File, 1995), 9.

15. Arthur James L. Fremantle, *The Fremantle Diary: Being the Journal of Lieutenant Colonel Arthur James Lyon Fremantle, Coldstream Guards, on His Three Months in the Southern States,* ed. Walter Lord (reprint; Boston: Little, Brown, 1954), 62; Eliza McHatton Ripley, *From Flag to Flag: A Woman's Adventures and Experiences in the South during the War, in Mexico, and in Cuba* (New York: D. Appleton and Co., 1896), 101; Jo Ella Powell Exley (ed.), *Texas Tears and Texas Sunshine: Voices of Frontier Women* (College Station: Texas A&M University Press, 1985), 113.

Trade with Mexico enabled Texans to avoid some of the hardships suffered in other southern states. In exchange for cotton Texans received military supplies, medicines, dry goods, and other commodities. Matamoros, on the Rio Grande across from Brownsville, and Bagdad, a small seaport village thirty miles downriver, became centers of the overland trade from Texas as hundreds of vessels from Europe and the United States engaged in a flourishing business.[16]

Even though Texans were more fortunate than other Southerners in being able to trade with Mexico, the war brought many changes. Wartime needs stimulated industries already established and encouraged development of new ones. The promotion of manufacturing was one of the responsibilities of the Texas State Military Board, created in 1862. Under its direction a percussion cap factory and a cannon foundry were established at Austin. A textile mill constructed at the state penitentiary at Huntsville produced nearly three million yards of cotton and wool during the war. Major ordnance works were built at Tyler, Bastrop, Galveston, Houston, Rusk, and San Antonio. The Confederate quartermaster department operated facilities at Austin, Houston, Huntsville, Jefferson, Mount Prairie, San Antonio, and Tyler. Shipyards were built at Goose Creek and Beaumont for the construction and repair of naval vessels.[17]

Texas women often assumed new roles during the war. Although some, such as Martha Gaffney, Rebecca Hagerty, and Sarah Devereux, had managed farms and plantations before the war, other Texas women performed these tasks for the first time while their husbands and sons were in the army. Some Texas women entered professions formerly reserved for men, such as teaching. Others worked in hospitals and sickwards; made sheets, pillow cases and bandages; and assisted servicemen and their families with food, shelter, and clothing. One Texas woman, Sophie Coffee Butts Porter, obtained information about enemy troop movements and rode twenty-five miles to warn the Confederates, earning

---

16. The most complete account of the trade through Mexico is James W. Daddysman, *The Matamoros Trade: Confederate Commerce, Diplomacy, and Intrigue* (Newark, Delaware: University of Delaware Press, 1984). See also Robert W. Delaney, "Matamoros, Port for Texas During the Civil War," *Southwestern Historical Quarterly,* LVIII (Apr., 1955), 473–487; Ronnie C. Tyler, "Cotton on the Border," ibid., LXXIII (Apr., 1970), 456–477; Mitchell Smith, "The 'Neutral' Matamoros Trade, 1861–1865," *Southwest Review,* XXXVII (Autumn, 1952), 319–324; and Fredericka Meiners, "The Texas Border Cotton Trade, 1862–1863," *Civil War History,* XXIII (Dec., 1977), 293–306.

17. Charles W. Ramsdell, "The Texas State Military Board, 1862–1865," *Southwestern Historical Quarterly,* XXVII (Apr., 1924), 253–275; William A. Albaugh III, *Tyler, Texas: C. S. A.* (Harrisburg, Pa.: Stackpole Company, 1958), 11–12, 20–26, 270–271; Bill Winsor, *Texas In the Confederacy: Military Installations, Economy, and People* (Hillsboro: Hill Junior College Press, 1978), 41–43; James L. Nichols, *The Confederate Quartermaster in the Trans-Mississippi* (Austin: University of Texas Press, 1964), 88–89.

her the nickname "Paul Revere of the Civil War." Sally Scull, a horse trader before the war, became a gunrunner during the conflict. She freighted cotton to the Rio Grande, where she exchanged it for weapons and ammunition for the Confederacy.[18]

Many Texas women experienced loneliness caused by separation from their husbands and sweethearts as the war continued. For those women living on the frontier there was the added concern of Indian raids or attacks by Jayhawkers or marauders. An Indian raid in Cooke county in 1863 resulted in the death and capture of a dozen women and children. For other Texas women there was the sadness and despair that came with the news that a loved one had been killed on the field of battle or died from wounds or disease while in a hospital or prison camp.[19]

The Civil War and Lincoln's Emancipation Proclamation ultimately meant the end of slavery in Texas and the other southern states. During the war itself most Texas slaves continued working on farms and plantations as they had before the war. There were no major slave rebellions during the conflict and although some slaves ran away the number did not increase dramatically. The comparative security of Texas from enemy invasion caused many Louisiana and Arkansas planters to "refugee" their slaves in Texas for the duration of the war.[20]

The most serious disruption of slave life in Civil War Texas came from impressment by the military. Under Confederate law military commanders could

---

18. Katherine G. Goodwin, "'A Woman's Curosity': Martha Gaffney and Cotton Planting on the Texas Frontier," *East Texas Historical Journal,* XXIV (Fall, 1986), 4–17; Judith N. McArthur, "Myth, Reality, and Anomaly: The Complex World of Rebecca Hagerty," ibid., XXIV (Fall, 1986), 18–32; Joleene Maddox Snider, "Sarah Devereux: A Study in Southern Femininity," *Southwestern Historical Quarterly,* XCVII (Jan., 1994), 498–502; Drew Gilpin Faust, *Southern Stories: Slaveholders in Peace and War* (Columbia: University of Missouri Press, 1992), 174–192; Elizabeth Silverthorne, *Plantation Life in Texas* (College Station: Texas A&M University Press, 1986), 198–199; Mary Elizabeth Massey, *Bonnet Brigades* (New York: Alfred A. Knopf, 1966), 79–108; Annie Doom Pickrell, *Pioneer Women in Texas* (Austin: E. L. Steck, 1929), 202; and Ruthe Winegarten, *Texas Women: A Pictorial History from Indians to Astronauts* (Austin: Eakin Press, 1986), 28.

19. James Wilson Nichols, *Now You Can Hear My Horn: The Journal of James Wilson Nichols,* ed. Catherine W. McDowell (Austin: University of Texas Press, 1968), 151–154; Exley, *Texas Tears and Texas Sunshine,* 146–147; David Paul Smith, "Frontier Defense and the Cooke County Raid, 1863," *West Texas Historical Association Year Book,* LXIV (Oct., 1988), 39–41; D. S. Howell, "Along the Texas Frontier During the Civil War," ibid., XIII (Oct., 1937), 85–86; Davis Bitton (ed.), *Reminiscences and Civil War Letters of Levi Lamoni Wight: Life in a Mormon Splinter Colony on the Texas Frontier* (Salt Lake City: University of Utah Press, 1970), 142–143, 158–160; Seymour Connor (ed.), *Dear America: Some Letters of Orange Cicero and Mary America (Aiken) Connor* (Austin: Pemberton Press, 1971), 39–40, 53–54, 73–76, 87.

20. Marten, *Texas Divided,* 107–113; Randolph B. Campbell, *An Empire for Slavery: The Peculiar Institution in Texas, 1821–1865* (Baton Rouge: Louisiana State University Press, 1989), 231–233, 243–244.

impress private property, including slaves, for public service. General John B. Magruder, commander of the Texas district, impressed hundreds of slaves in building a stockade to enclose Federal prisoners of war near Tyler, in fortifying Sabine Pass, and in preparing defenses on the San Bernard River and Caney Creek. While Magruder's actions were necessary for Texas's defense, they were seldom popular with slaves or slaveowners. Although the owners received compensation, the absence of slaves interfered with normal plantation work. Too, the owners and slaves complained that slaves were not properly cared for while under military control.[21]

News of military defeats in Georgia, Tennessee, and Virginia in late 1864 and early 1865 convinced many Texans that the war was lost. Lee's surrender at Appomattox Courthouse in April 1865, followed by that of Joe Johnston in North Carolina, made further resistance appear futile. Texan John S. Ford defeated Union invaders at Palmetto Ranch near Brownsville in May 1865 in the last battle of the war. From captured prisoners Ford learned that Confederate forces elsewhere had surrendered. Although Generals Edmund Kirby Smith, head of the Trans-Mississippi department, and John B. Magruder, commander of the Texas district, attempted to rally forces in Texas, many soldiers, realizing the war was over, headed for home. On June 2, 1865, Smith and Magruder surrendered their commands to Union officals at Galveston.

The story of Texas participation in the American Civil War has been treated in various accounts. Some of the most thorough studies have appeared in essays published in historical journals. The present work has been prepared in the belief that readers would welcome a compilation of such essays in a single volume. In selecting the essays for inclusion the compiler has attempted to provide a broad coverage so that most aspects of Texas's role in the war are discussed. A brief introduction to each article is provided, as well as suggestions for additional reading.

Unsurprisingly, the majority of the essays appeared first in the *Southwestern Historical Quarterly,* the premier journal for Texas history. Other articles in this volume were first published in *Civil War History, East Texas Historical Journal, Military History of the Southwest,* and *Texana.* The compiler wishes to thank the editors of these journals for their generous permission to reprint these essays. Special thanks go also to Ron Tyler, director of the Texas State Historical Association, and George Ward, managing editor of the *Southwestern Historical Quarterly,* for their encouragement and assistance in the publication of this volume. Photographic consultant Lawrence T. Jones III has been most generous with his time, advice, and the contents of his extensive collection of photographs.

---

21. Campbell, *Empire for Slavery,* 234–239.

Sixth-plate daguerreotype of Sam Houston, ca. 1859. *Courtesy Archives Division, Texas State Library.*

Texas and the Riddle of Secession

WALTER L. BUENGER*

The sectional controversies that divided northerners and southerners in the late 1840s and 1850s concerned Texans but did not assume the importance felt in the older states. The expansion of cotton and grain production, the Mexican War, the New Mexico boundary dispute, settlement of the public debt, western exploration, and Indian problems occupied the attention of most citizens in the fifteen years between statehood and Lincoln's election as President. The population of the state was growing rapidly, opportunities for economic advancement were abundant, and most Texans were optimistic about the future.

Prior to Lincoln's election a majority of Texans seemed to support the Union which they had worked so hard to join in 1845, but three months later they voted to secede. In the following essay, Walter L. Buenger, professor of history at Texas A&M University, describes the process by which Texans came to support separation. "Understanding secession," he argues, "requires envisioning the nature of unionist and secessionist sentiment" in the state. Secession, he believes, was continuation of the search for a union "which would achieve all the goals and purposes of a nation of Americans." Texans did not lose their nationalism in becoming secessionists; "they refocused that nationalism on the Confederacy instead of the United States."

* Walter L. Buenger, "Texas and the Riddle of Secession," *Southwestern Historical Quarterly,* LXXXVII (Oct., 1983), 151–182.

For more on Buenger's views see his Secession and the Union in Texas *(Austin: University of Texas Press, 1984) and* "Secession Revisited: The Texas Experience," Civil War History, *XXX (Dec., 1984), 293–315.*

Secession remains a mystifying puzzle, a puzzle whose solution in 1861 was a bloody civil war and a puzzle whose solution in our time still defies rational explanation. From the end of the American Revolution until the start of the Civil War, the United States survived a series of intensely bitter internal disputes. Yet within the span of a few months in the winter of 1860–1861 the nation split apart, and a civil war soon began that resulted in over one million casualties. In Texas, secession seemed all the more improbable. Texans had continually asked to become part of the Union from 1836 to 1845. Their precarious position on the southwestern frontier reminded them daily of the value of belonging to a large and powerful nation. Prosperity seemed to preclude a political upheaval in 1860. The burgeoning trade in cotton, hides, and sugar flowing out of the commercial centers of Texas gave promise of making it one of the richest states in the Union. Slavery, while a major part of the social and economic life in some regions of Texas, was almost absent in other regions, and, except for Tennessee and Arkansas, Texas slaves made up the smallest percentage of the total population of any state in the Confederacy. Reflecting its position on the border of the South, politics in Texas on the eve of secession was dominated not by militant secessionists or unionists but by more moderate folk, who wanted to preserve the Union and the status quo if the costs of such action were not too high. At no time before 1860 did these moderates, who comprised a clear majority of the electorate, move persistently and urgently away from their comfortable middle ground. Nonetheless, before the firing on Fort Sumter changed the political question to either defending one's home or defecting to the enemy in defense of principle, Texans voted to secede by a three-to-one margin.[1]

---

1. For the election returns in the secession referendum see Joe T. Timmons, "The Referendum in Texas on the Ordinance of Secession, February 23, 1861: The Vote," *East Texas Historical Journal* (*ETHJ*), XI (Fall, 1973), 12–28. On the population of the southern states and Civil War casualty figures see E[verette] B. Long, *The Civil War Day by Day: An Almanac, 1861–1865* (New York, 1971), 701, 702, 709–712. For evidence that the vast majority of Texas voters clustered around the political center see Francis Richard Lubbock, *Six Decades in Texas; or, Memoirs of Francis Richard Lubbock, Governor of Texas in War Time, 1861–63. A Personal Experience in Business, War, and Politics,* ed. C[adwell] W. Rains (Austin, 1900), 179–313; *Standard* (Clarksville), Aug. 6, 13, 20, Nov. 5, Dec. 17, 1859, Oct. 13, 20, 27, 1860, Jan. 19, 26, 1861; *True Issue* (La Grange), Aug. 6, 13, 1859, Jan. 10, 17, 24, 1861. On the economic boom in Texas see Lewis Cecil Gray, *History of Agriculture in the Southern United States to 1860* (2 vols.; Washington, D.C., 1933), II, 905–907; Raymond E. White, "Cotton Ginning in Texas to 1861," *Southwestern Historical Quarterly* (*SHQ*), LXI (Oct., 1957), 257–269; Vera Lea Dugus, "Texas Industry, 1860–1880," ibid., LIX (Oct., 1955), 151–157.

At least four distinct explanations have been offered for the secession of Texas. In 1863 James P. Newcomb, a Texas unionist who had fled north, summed up the opinion of many contemporary observers of secession when he published his *Sketch of Secession Times in Texas.* Newcomb attributed secession to a conspiracy led by a handful of radical and self-serving Texans who duped the public into believing slavery and southern rights could only be preserved by secession. Ever since, the tendency to ascribe secession to a small band of plotters or, depending upon one's point of view, a group of vigilant patriots, has been a persistent theme in secession studies.[2] In the early twentieth century, troubled by secession in Texas, Charles William Ramsdell put forward a second interpretation. In his essay on "The Frontier and Secession," Ramsdell argued that not only did its frontier environment make Texas different from other southern states, but that in some ways the state's peculiar local conditions and pragmatic concerns created an impetus for secession. According to Ramsdell, not just concern for slavery but also bitter resentment of the federal government's failure to provide adequate protection from Indian attack caused frontiersmen to accept secession.[3] In the 1950s, following the lead of Avery O. Craven, interpreters of secession in Texas examined the growth of southern nationalism, based on common institutions and customs or on a common

2. James P. Newcomb, *Sketch of Secession Times in Texas and Journal of Travel from Texas through Mexico to California, including a History of the "Rox Colony"* (San Francisco, 1863), 1–12. On Newcomb see Dale A. Somers, "James P. Newcomb: The Making of a Radical," *SHQ,* LXXII (Apr., 1969), 449–469; Roy Sylvan Dunn, "The KGC in Texas, 1860–1861," ibid., LXX (Apr., 1967), 543–573. For other contemporaries who believed secession to be the work of conspirators and demagogues see J[ohn] T. Sprague, *The Treachery in Texas, the Secession of Texas, and the Arrest of the United States Officers and Soldiers Serving in Texas* (New York, 1862); Sam Houston, "Speech at Brenham," Mar. 31, 1861, *The Writings of Sam Houston, 1813–1863,* ed. Amelia W. Williams and Eugene C. Barker (8 vols.; Austin, 1938–1943), VIII, 295–299. For later studies that also stress the role of heroes and anti-heroes see Edward R. Maher, "Secession in Texas" (Ph.D. diss., Fordham University, 1960); Leonard Bailey, "Unionist Editors in Texas during the Secession Crisis" (M.A. thesis, Texas Southern University, 1973); Oran Lonnie Sinclair, "Crossroads of Conviction: A Study of the Texas Political Mind, 1856–1861" (Ph.D. diss., Rice University, 1975).

3. Charles William Ramsdell, "The Frontier and Secession," *Studies in Southern History and Politics* (New York, 1914), 63–79. For a look at the particular features of East Texas and how they affected secession see Allan C. Ashcraft, "East Texas in the Election of 1860 and the Secession Crisis," *ETHJ,* I (July, 1963), 7–16. For the argument that the particular concerns of the commercial classes of Texas could motivate them to support secession see Earl Wesley Fornell, *The Galveston Era: The Texas Crescent on the Eve of Secession* (Austin, 1961), 267–301. For the argument that particular circumstances created unionism on the frontier see Floyd F. Ewing, Jr., "Origins of Unionist Sentiment of the West Texas Frontier," *West Texas Historical Association Year Book,* XXXII (Oct., 1956), 21–29.

political ideology.[4] After 1970, when Steven A. Channing's *Crisis of Fear: Secession in South Carolina* was published, a fourth interpretation of secession emerged. Channing called attention to the importance in South Carolina of people's perceptions "the forebodings of disaster based upon exaggerated racial and political fears." In a dissertation, "Slavery, Fear and Disunion in the Lone Star State: Texans' Attitudes toward Secession and the Union, 1846–1861," Billy D. Ledbetter drew upon Channing's example and refocused on slavery as the cause of secession. Ledbetter argued that not only did Texans desire to maintain the institution of slavery, but that they were powerfully motivated by a fear of slave insurrections resulting from Republican control of the North and the national government.[5]

Each of these interpretations of secession has merit, but none clearly explains either the persistent strength of unionism in Texas or the debate over secession. Well-organized leadership aided the secessionists' cause, but secession was not a conspiracy, nor was it the work of a small cadre of revolutionaries. In December, 1860, Franklin B. Sexton captured the spirit of the secession movement in Texas when he described a local secession meeting by writing, "The sober, reflecting, sterling men of the county were present [and] no division of feeling existed." Secession was both a spontaneous popular movement present in most counties of the state and a process openly led by the pillars of the community.[6]

While Ramsdell quite rightly pointed to the frontier and to local frontier concerns as a cause of secession, Texas in 1860, as he himself realized, was not simply a frontier state. Large portions of the eastern half of the state had a mature agrarian economy based upon slavery and cotton. If local considerations

---

4. Avery O. Craven, *The Growth of Southern Nationalism, 1848–1861* (Baton Rouge, 1953). For a Texas study which stresses the evolution of southernness see Nancy Ann Head, "State Rights in Texas: The Growth of an Idea, 1850–1860" (M.A. thesis, Rice Institute, 1960). For an early version of the argument that economic differences created a distinct South see Anna Irene Sandbo, "Beginnings of the Secession Movement in Texas," *SHQ,* XVIII (July, 1914), 41–73.

5. Steven A. Channing, *Crisis of Fear: Secession in South Carolina* (New York, 1970); Billy D. Ledbetter, "Slavery, Fear, and Disunion in the Lone Star State: Texans' Attitudes toward Secession and the Union, 1846–1861" (Ph.D. diss., North Texas State University, 1972); review of *Crisis of Fear* by Richard O. Curry in *Journal of American History,* LIX (Sept., 1972), 421 (quotation).

6. F. B. Sexton to Dear Judge, Dec. 2, 1860, Oran Milo Roberts Papers (Eugene C. Barker Texas History Center, University of Texas, Austin; cited hereafter as BTHC). Also see John Salmon Ford, "Memoirs of John Salmon Ford," V, 943–966, John S. Ford Papers, ibid.; Ernest William Winkler (ed.), *Journal of the Secession Convention of Texas, 1861* (Austin, 1912), 9–90; Sandbo, "Beginnings of the Secession Movement"; Anna Irene Sandbo, "The First Session of the Secession Convention of Texas," *SHQ,* XVIII (Oct., 1914), 162–194; Oran M. Roberts, "The Political, Legislative, and Judicial History of Texas for Its Fifty Years of Statehood, 1845–1895," Dudley G. Wooten (ed.), *A Comprehensive History of Texas, 1685 to 1897* (2 vols.; Dallas, 1898), II, 84–89.

were important, then slavery and the flow of cotton and other commodities out of the state might have been equally important in determining attitudes toward secession. Furthermore, within the frontier local considerations varied sharply from one county to the next.[7]

Although some Texans dreamed of a southern nation before 1861, they were few in number. Nor did the states' rights philosophy totally dominate state politics. Certainly Texans had a cultural heritage that tied them to the South. For that matter they also possessed a heritage that set them apart from the rest of the South. It was also true that the validity of secession as a legal and constitutional remedy for abuses to the rights of southerners went unchallenged except by the most militant of unionists. Nonetheless, their southern culture and their belief in the legality of secession did not prevent the majority of Texans from clinging tenaciously to the Union throughout the 1850s. Texans were still Americans, and for the most part American nationalists, prior to 1860. This was clearly illustrated in the state elections of 1859 when only moderates and unionists won high political office. Even in a man like John H. Reagan, later to be postmaster general of the Confederacy, American nationalism was evident. During his campaign for reelection to the U.S. House of Representatives, Reagan issued a circular in which he said in part, "These constant croakers of evil, these preachers of revolution, now think they have the Democracy of Texas in leading strings, and have set too, covertly at first, and now more boldly, to prescribe me, because I will not sympathize with their sectional, revolutionary, and wicked doctrines." Evidently the voters of the traditionally two-party First Congressional District did not radically oppose Reagan's unionist pronouncements, because he won a smashing seven-to-one victory at the polls.[8]

---

7. Randolph B. Campbell, "Planters and Plain Folk: Harrison County, Texas, as a Test Case, 1850–1860," *Journal of Southern History* (*JSH*), XL (Aug., 1974), 369–398; Walter L. Buenger, "Unionism on the Texas Frontier, 1859–1861," *Arizona and the West*, XXII (Autumn, 1980), 237–254.

8. "J. H. Reagan to the Voters Of the First Congressional District," Apr. 12, 1859, circular, John H. Reagan Papers (BTHC); *Texas Republican* (Marshall), Apr. 29, 1859. Election returns may be found in Walter L. Buenger, Jr., "Stilling the Voice of Reason: Texans and the Union, 1854–1861" (Ph.D. diss., Rice University, 1979), 266–391. For additional evidence of the attachment of Reagan and other Texans to the Union in 1859 see Billy D. Ledbetter, "The Election Of Louis T. Wigfall to the United States Senate, 1859: A Reevaluation," *SHQ*, LXXVII (Oct., 1973), 241–254; Reagan to A. H. Latimer, Aug. 26, 1859; Reagan to William Alexander, Oct. 3, 1859, Reagan Papers; *Standard* (Clarksville), June 4, Aug. 6, 13, 1869. For an in-depth discussion of the South's cultural nationalism see Emory M. Thomas, *The Confederate Nation, 1861–1865* (New York, 1979), 17–36; John McCardell, *The Idea of a Southern Nation: Southern Nationalists and Southern Nationalism, 1830–1860* (New York, 1979); Frank E. Vandiver, "The Confederacy and the American Tradition," *JSH*, XXVIII (Aug., 1962), 277–286.

Proponents of the Channing school might say that what changed Reagan's mind and the minds of his constituents about the Union was slavery and a fear of slave insurrection. Slavery undoubtedly played a central role in secession and its role needed to be emphasized in the 1970s. Still, to say that there was a steadily growing fear that slavery was threatened and that this alone made secession possible once the Republicans controlled the national government would be as misleading as to say that there was a steadily growing southern nationalism. Moreover, as Ramsdell pointed out long ago, slavery was virtually nonexistent in many portions of Texas. Fear of slave uprisings might unite all white Texans, but even at the height of the Texas Troubles, a near hysterical manifestation of Texans' fear of slave uprisings, many white Texans called the tales of abolitionists' plots exaggerations and the creation of partisan politics.[9] None of these four theories, then, fully explains the course and content of the debate over secession and the Union, or why Texans turned from unionists in 1859 to secessionists in 1861.

One problem with all previous studies of secession in Texas has been that they were narrowly focused. Slicing up society and individuals, scholars looked at just one facet, and consequently examined only one cause of secession. Conspirators caused secession. Pragmatic concerns encouraged secession. Southern nationalism made secession possible. Defense of slavery either as a constitutional prerogative or as a means of controlling a subordinate race drove southerners to secede. To some degree each of these was a cause of secession. Human beings

---

9. On the Texas Troubles see Donald E. Reynolds, *Editors Make War: Southern Newspapers in the Secession Crisis* (Nashville, 1970), 97–117; Ollinger Crenshaw, *The Slave States in the Presidential Election of 1860* (Baltimore, 1945), 92–108; *Weekly Alamo Express* (San Antonio), Sept. 17, 24, Oct. 1, 8, 1860; *State Gazette* (Austin), Sept. 29, Oct. 20, 1860; *Southern Intelligencer* (Austin), Oct. 10, 1860. Even Robert W. Loughery, the editor of the Marshall *Texas Republican,* one of the most radical of southerners, conceded that there was some exaggeration regarding the abolitionist plots. See *Texas Republican* (Marshall), Aug. 11, Sept. 8, 1860; Walter Prescott Webb, H. Bailey Carroll, and Eldon Stephen Branda (eds.), *The Handbook of Texas* (3 vols.; Austin, 1952, 1976), II, 84–85. On differences in the use of slaves among various regions of Texas see Ramsdell, "The Frontier and Secession," 63–67; Terry G. Jordan, "The Imprint of the Upper and Lower South on Mid-Nineteenth-Century Texas," *Annals of the Association of American Geographers,* LVII (Dec., 1967), 667–690. In regard to slavery and secession it is interesting to note that both Kentucky and Tennessee had more slaves and slaveholders than Texas, and Tennessee had nearly as high a percentage of its total population made up of slaves as did Texas. Yet Kentucky did not secede at all; and Tennessee seceded only after the firing on Ft. Sumter and Lincoln's call-up of troops to put down insurrection in the South. See Long, *The Civil War Day by Day,* 701–702; E. Merton Coulter, *The Civil War and Readjustment in Kentucky* (Chapel Hill, 1926), 1–144; Mary Emily Robertson Campbell, *The Attitude of Tennesseans toward the Union, 1847–1861* (New York, 1961), 211–212, 261. For a comparison of slaveholding patterns in the southern states see J[ames] G. Randall and David Donald, *The Civil War and Reconstruction* (Lexington, Mass., 1969), 68.

and their institutions provided leadership and direction for the secession movement. Pragmatic considerations must have played a role in many men's minds as they opted for secession. The existence of cultural diversity within the United States made secession easier. Slavery was at the heart of the secession crisis. The problem for modern students of secession is deciding what united these and other divergent causes and focused them clearly enough to prompt the lethargic mass of southerners to abandon their traditional government. What is needed is a new conceptual framework that moves beyond a monocausal approach and takes into consideration not only multiple causes but also the diversity and complexity of southern society.

Secession in Texas was part of the central conflict of the nineteenth century, a conflict between forces that encouraged the splintering of the United States into smaller social, political, and economic units and forces that bound the nation more tightly together. Secession, however, was not simply the triumph of localism over nationalism. Nor did it reflect some Hegelian dialectic in which the thesis of localism and the antithesis of nationalism were resolved in the synthesis of secession. Localism and nationalism were the reflex of each other. Factors that nourished localism could also stimulate nationalism. Moreover, a factor that encouraged localism or nationalism could often strengthen both a commitment to the Union and a belief in the necessity of secession. Slavery, for example, was the most prominent feature separating the South from the rest of the nation. Yet its slave/cotton economy tied the South to northern merchants and northern mills. The need to defend slavery was one argument for secession. As late as 1861, however, some Texans insisted that in the long run slavery was safer inside the Union than in a smaller, more vulnerable southern Confederacy. Thus slavery was both localistic and nationalistic in its implications and could create an impetus toward either secession or preservation of the Union. In a conceptual sense, the secession crisis in Texas involved a struggle among all those elements within Texas society that, like slavery, strengthened unionism or strengthened secession sentiment. What was curious about this struggle was that the two opposing concepts were surprisingly alike. In fact, it was the similarities between the forces behind unionism and secession as much as their differences that account for the success of the secession movement in Texas.[10]

---

10. For a definition of terms and an in-depth explanation of unionism, secession, and nationalism, see David M. Potter, *The Impending Crisis, 1848–1861* (New York, 1976); Paul C. Nagel, *One Nation Indivisible: The Union in American Thought, 1776–1861* (New York, 1964); Major L. Wilson, *Space, Time and Freedom: The Quest for Nationality and the Irrepressible Conflict, 1815–1861* (Westport, Conn., 1974).

If indeed the secession crisis in Texas had two interdependent dimensions, then understanding the cause of secession and the Civil War requires more than understanding the role of individuals, ideology, parochial interests, or instinctual fears. Understanding secession requires envisioning the nature of unionist and secessionist sentiment, and how in the end the imbalance between these two made secession possible.[11]

Though opposite in intent, sentiments for secession and unionism never existed without each other. This dualism grew out of the interlaced nature of localism and nationalism in antebellum Texas. Localism and nationalism coexisted in individual Texans as well as in the collective value system of the state. Texans accomplished this sleight of hand by either compartmentalizing nationalism and localism within nonconflicting spheres of thought and action, or by temporarily subordinating one set of values to the other. Local values related to slavery offer the clearest example of compartmentalization. Texans voted for a unionist ticket in 1859 and at the same time adamantly defended slavery. As long as local notions about slavery or any other divergent point of view were confined within a framework that did not impinge directly upon nationalism, both nationalism and localism existed together. This explains how the La Grange *True Issue* in the midst of the secession crisis ran on its masthead: "Our Country, Our State, the South and the Union."[12]

Texans, however, seldom achieved an exact equilibrium between localism and nationalism. From 1846 to 1848, spurred on by the euphoria of annexation and the Mexican War, Texans were more nationalistic. From 1849 through mid-1850, because of antipathy for President Zachary Taylor and the dispute over the Texas claim to eastern New Mexico, Texans were more localistic. From the closing months of 1850 up until 1854, encouraged by economic growth and stable borders, Texans elevated the Union above their sectional concerns. Then from

---

11. Assumptions about similarities between unionist and secessionist sentiments are largely based upon what secessionists and unionists were saying and writing in the fall and winter of 1860–1861. For secessionists' arguments see "A Declaration of the Causes Which Impel the State of Texas to Secede from the Federal Union," Winkler (ed.), *Journal of the Secession Convention,* 61–66; Reagan to Joseph Tyler, Dec. 23, 1860, *Texas Republican* (Marshall), Jan. 12, 1861; Peter W. Gray to the meeting of the citizens of Harris County, *State Gazette* (Austin), Nov. 24, 1860; "Speech of Judge Roberts," ibid., Dec. 8, 1860; Dallas *Herald,* Jan. 16, Feb. 20, 1861. For the unionists' reply see "Address to the People of Texas," in scrapbook, 31–34, John L. Haynes Papers (BTHC); *Southern Intelligencer* (Austin), Sept. 5, Oct. 10, 1860; *Union* (Galveston), Jan. 8, 12, 1861; Andrew J. Hamilton, *Speech of Hon. Andrew J. Hamilton of Texas on the State of the Union. Delivered in the House of Representatives of the United States, February 1, 1861* (Washington, D.C., 1861); *Harrison Flag* (Marshall), Jan. 12, 1861.

12. *True Issue* (La Grange), Jan. 24, 1861.

1854 through 1857, aroused by the controversy over slavery in Kansas and influenced by a steady influx of people from the plantation South, Texans became more localistic. Worried by the excesses of southern militants, from 1858 until mid-1860 the bulk of the Texas population moved once again toward the Union. About mid-1860 the move toward sectionalism began once more and continued until Texas seceded. In every case, except for the secession crisis, the development of either nationalism or localism was balanced by the resurgence of its countervailing force. This did not happen in the winter of 1860–1861 because of the conflicting and also surprisingly complementary appeal of the Union and secession.[13]

In Texas, unionism drew strength from cultural bias, ideology, party allegiance, the leadership of forceful personalities, and self-interest. Texas was a place of at least four distinct subcultures. These four groups were Lower South, Upper South, western European, and Mexican. Among the people who made up these groups those whose culture and point of origin derived from the Upper South or western Europe were by habit the staunchest advocates of the Union. This was all the more true when Tennesseans and Germans lived in cultural enclaves largely outside the day-to-day influence of other subcultures.[14] Ideological props of the Union fell into two categories. The first category derived from a set of internalized values. One reason that Texans from Tennessee, Kentucky, and Germany were unionists was that to a greater degree they accepted—indeed no longer even had to ponder the question—that the Union was of

---

13. A good overview of politics in the early statehood period may be found in Ledbetter, "Slavery, Fear, and Disunion in the Lone Star State," 36–224; Sinclair, "Crossroads of Conviction," 2–62. On the swings from nationalism to localism see Head, "State Rights in Texas"; William Campbell Binkley, *The Expansionist Movement in Texas, 1836–1850* (Berkeley, 1925).

14. Terry Jordan argues that Tennesseans and others from the Upper South preserved their distinct culture in Texas, and that one of the traits of this culture was a more persistent unionism. See "The Imprint of the Upper and Lower South," 685–688. On the high level of emotional commitment to the Union in Kentucky and Tennessee see Coulter, *Civil War and Readjustment in Kentucky,* 1–110; Campbell, *The Attitude of Tennesseans toward the Union,* 64–212. For further evidence that significant portions of Texas were geographically and culturally unlike the Lower South, and that one of the ways that the people of these regions differed from other Texans was a more persistent commitment to the Union, see Claude Elliott, *Leathercoat: The Life History of a Texas Patriot* (San Antonio, 1938), 41–67; J[acob] de Cordova, *Texas: Her Resources and Her Public Men: A Companion for J. de Cordova's New and Correct Map of the State of Texas* (Philadelphia, 1858), 189–190; J. W. Latimer, "The Wheat Region and Wheat Culture in Texas," *Texas Almanac for 1859* (Galveston, 1858), 65–69; E. L Dohoney, *An Average American* (Paris, Tex., [1911]), 71–88; Terry G. Jordan, *German Seed in Texas Soil: Immigrant Farmers in Nineteenth-Century Texas* (Austin, 1966), 60–117; Walter L. Buenger, "Secession and the Texas German Community: Editor Lindheimer vs. Editor Flake," *SHQ,* LXXXII (Apr., 1979), 379–402.

great value in and of itself. The Union and the Constitution were the mythic creations of the revered founding fathers. Nationalism grew from the blood and sacrifice of the Revolutionary War, the War of 1812, and the Mexican War. For romantic nationalists, the Union satisfied a longing for a strong nation of like people with common aims and goals—a nation undivided by petty jealousies and peculiar political structures.[15]

The second ideological category sprang from the functional purposes of the Union. One function of the Union was to fulfill the sense of mission many Americans shared: a mission to spread Anglo American civilization across the wilderness, to act as an example for the rest of the world, to preserve individual liberty, and, in the course of these virtuous deeds, to become increasingly prosperous. Another function of the Union was to provide stability and law. Stability was necessary to prevent the disintegration of the nation into a mass of violently competing individuals or anarchistic groups. In its roles as arbiter of internal disputes and as protector from foreign powers, the Union provided this stability. The Constitution, which unionists almost always linked with the Union, gave Texans and all Americans a rational and knowable legal framework that regulated the place of individuals and communities within the larger society. For a people with a sense of mission and conditioned to abhor social discord as the greatest of political evils, the Union, before 1860, seemed the best vehicle to achieve their goals and prevent their fears from being realized.[16]

Party affiliation reinforced this ideological unionism. Whigs, Know-Nothings, Democrats, and members of the Opposition all harbored shades of unionism, as did their particular philosophies. Whigs and Know-Nothings, however, emphasized the reverential nature of the Union, while Democrats stressed its ability to achieve other ideological goals. The Opposition, since it was composed of former Democrats, Whigs, and Know-Nothings, expressed unionism in all of its ideological forms. All of these parties gave legitimacy and reinforcement to individual points of view.[17]

---

15. *Standard* (Clarksville), June 28, 1859; James W. Throckmorton to Ben H. Epperson, Aug. 18, Sept. 13, 1859, Ben H. Epperson Papers (BTHC); *Weekly Alamo Express* (San Antonio), Nov. 5, 1860.

16. For a general statement of what the Union meant to Americans see Nagel, *One Nation Indivisible.* For Texas examples see the *Standard* (Clarksville), Aug. 13, 20, 1859, Mar. 10, Apr. 14, 18, June 23, Oct. 13, 20, 27, Dec. 22, 1860; Dallas *Herald*, Oct. 31, 1860; *Southern Intelligencer* (Austin), Oct. 10, 1860.

17. On the Opposition parties in the South see John V. Mering, "The Slave-State Constitutional Unionists and the Politics of Consensus," *JSH*, XLIII (Aug., 1977), 395–410. On Whig nationalism see Charles Grier Sellers, Jr., "Who Were the Southern Whigs?" *American Historical Review*, LIX (Jan., 1954), 335–346. For examples of Texas Whigs' unionism see *Weekly Journal* (Galveston), Jan. 7, 1853. On Know-Nothings' unionism see *Texas State Times* (Austin), Aug. 11, 1855; *Harrison Flag*

Individuals, though, not institutions, proved to be the most visible and important props of nationalism in Texas. Sam Houston, Andrew Jackson Hamilton, and other unionists reminded Texans of the worth of the nation. They spoke or wrote clearly of the often blurred feelings, sentiments, hopes, interests, and attitudes that caused people to identify with their nation. Because they were so highly individualistic, however, many of these personalities were not prone to united and concerted action with fellow unionists. Sam Houston, for example, was always uncomfortable with the notion of political parties, and his efforts to prevent secession often seemed erratic and out of step with those of other unionists. Still, before 1861 individual unionists helped to shift men's attention from ordinary pursuits to the nation.[18]

Ordinary pursuits, however, could also cause Texans to appreciate being a part of the United States. Perhaps more than any other Americans in the 1850s, Texans knew the real and practical value of membership in the United States. Not only could many remember what it was like to be citizens of a weak independent republic, but some had special interests which caused them to look beyond the borders of their state. Men of commerce still realized the advantages of access to large national markets. Men of means still considered desirable the financially sound government of the United States.[19]

This realization that the nation aided them directly was especially noticeable among Texas frontiersmen. Texas was not to be completely settled until the twentieth century, and in 1860 its frontier had reached scarcely more than 100 miles west of Austin. Up and down the frontier, from the Red River to the Rio Grande, frontiersmen depended upon the army for protection from the Comanches and other marauding tribes of Plains Indians. The army was notably

---

(Marshall), July 10, 1858. On the Democrats see *State Gazette* (Austin), May 14, 1859. On the Opposition, see *Harrison Flag* (Marshall), Sept. 22, 1860; *Union* (Galveston), Nov. 6, 1860; *Weekly Alamo Express* (San Antonio), Sept. 10, 17, 1860; *True Issue* (La Grange), Jan. 24, 1861.

18. For examples of unionist rhetoric see George W. Paschal to Ashbel Smith, May 27, 1859, Ashbel Smith Papers (BTHC); Throckmorton to Epperson, Aug. 18, Sept. 13, 1859, Epperson Papers; *Harrison Flag* (Marshall), Sept. 1, 1860; *Daily Herald* (San Antonio), July 15, 20, 1859; *Standard* (Clarksville), Mar. 9, 1861; Houston to H. M. Watkins and Others, Nov. 20, 1860, *Writings of Sam Houston*, ed. Williams and Barker, VIII, 192–197. On the individualism of unionists and the greater institutional strength of the Democrats see James Alex Baggett, "The Constitutional Union Party in Texas," *SHQ*, LXXXII (Jan., 1979), 233–264.

19. *Union* (Galveston), Jan. 24, 29, 1861; *Southern Intelligencer* (Austin), Sept. 5, Oct. 10, 1860, Jan. 20, 23, Feb. 6, 13, 1861; *Weekly Alamo Express* (San Antonio), Feb. 9, 16, 23, 1861. Thomas McKinney, who had been an important businessman in Texas since the 1830s, also opposed secession. See Webb, Carroll, and Branda (eds.), *Handbook of Texas*, II, 117; Thomas F. McKinney to Thomas Jack, William P. Ballinger, and Guy M. Bryan, Nov. 22, 1860, Guy M. Bryan Papers (BTHC).

inept in dealing with these Indians in the 1850s, but it was still an important means of defense—particularly in areas close to the scattered military posts. In these areas army purchases and salaries also supplied the cash that raised the frontier economy above the subsistence level. Because of the army's dual importance as defender from the Indian and economic stimulant, the Texas frontiersmen and the numerous citizens in the interior counties who identified with the frontiersmen keenly appreciated its presence. As long as the U.S. army stood in high repute, self-interest encouraged unionism.[20]

Self-interest, the influence of powerful personalities, ideological conceptions and beliefs, party politics, and certain cultural and regional biases within Texas all combined in 1858 and 1859 to produce a stunning revival of unionism. The force that tended to break the Union into smaller component parts, however, did not disappear from the body politic. Localism was instead only temporarily submerged. It, too, fed upon cultural biases, party politics, ideology, articulate spokesmen, and self-interest. Connecting and intertwining all of these facets of localism was slavery.[21]

Just as Texans from the Upper South seemed to have a cultural bias in favor of the Union, Texans from the Lower South more easily accepted secession. Until 1850, the largest percentage of Anglo immigrants came from the Upper South—primarily from Tennessee, Kentucky, and Missouri. Beginning in 1836, however, people from the Lower South—primarily from Georgia, Alabama, and Mississippi—came to Texas in increasing numbers. By 1860 Texans from the Lower South comprised the largest cultural group in the state. Moreover, these Texans were not equally dispersed among all regions of Texas but were concentrated in specific areas. Not only was the total number of people from the Lower South growing in Texas, but, because their numbers were relatively undiluted by peoples from other groups, their cultural voice remained clear. It would be a voice that would speak ardently for secession in 1860 and 1861.

Slavery and the plantation system were the most distinct features of the Lower South. Texans from the Upper South certainly owned slaves, as did a few Germans. Still, taken as a whole, farm size, crop selection, and lack of capital limited the impact of slavery on both these non-Lower South groups. Germans, while they might raise cotton, farmed less land more intensively, and they usually lacked the capital to buy slaves, or else preferred to invest their limited capi-

---

20. Latimer, "The Wheat Region," 69; *Zeitung* (New Braunfels), Oct. 10, 1856; *State Gazette* (Austin), Mar. 10, Nov. 17, 1860, Jan. 5, 1861; *White Man* (Weatherford), Sept. 13, 1860; Dallas *Herald*, May 18, 1859, Dec. 5, 1860; *Standard* (Clarksville), May 19, Oct. 20, 27, 1860.

21. Head, "State Rights in Texas," 1–100; Ledbetter, "Slavery, Fear and Disunion in the Lone Star State," 274–276; Sinclair, "Crossroads of Conviction," 124–204.

tal in other things considered more necessary for the efficient operation of their farms. Texans from the Upper South owned cotton plantations. This was especially true if they lived in East Texas, which was ideal for cotton and contained many former residents of the Lower South. If they lived in regions not dominated by lower southerners, however, they typically concentrated on corn, wheat, or livestock. They therefore needed fewer slaves and by habit, and perhaps by preference, were less inclined to acquire more slaves and expand heavily into the production of cotton. A Texas farmer from Alabama, on the other hand, grew cotton by habit and often aspired to the ownership of large numbers of slaves. It was not surprising that Texans from the Lower South who had the most to lose both at the time and in the future by any challenge from the North to slavery increasingly viewed the world from a local and not a national perspective.[22]

Significantly, this local perspective surfaced most clearly in lower southerners, the most dynamic of the four primary cultural groups in Texas. Texas in 1860 was not yet like Alabama, but the future seemed to hold promise that one day it would be so. Counties between Lower South-dominated East Texas, Upper South- or German-dominated North and West Texas, and Mexican-dominated South Texas—counties with a population drawn not only from the Lower South but the other primary source areas as well—seemed to be undergoing a process by which the fecund Lower South culture dominated the entire county. Over a period of years the agricultural and slaveholding habits that distinguished cultures in Texas began to merge into a culture much like that of the Lower South. Perceiving this ascendancy, visionaries talked of a better life tied to slavery, the plantation system, and Lower South culture. Not only the present reality of this culture but also its dynamic characteristic gave secession a strong cultural base.[23]

---

22. On the rate of population growth and its source in antebellum Texas see Barnes F. Lathrop, *Migration into East Texas, 1835–1860: A Study from the United States Census* (Austin, 1949), 34–65; Terry G. Jordan, "Population Origins in Texas, 1850," *Geographical Review,* LIX (Jan., 1969), 86–87; Jordan, "The Imprint of the Upper and Lower South," 667–672. On the habitual economic activity of cultural groups in Texas see ibid., 672–685; Jordan, *German Seed in Texas Soil,* 60–117.

23. For examples of those assimilated into a Lower South culture see John P. Osterhout to Brother Orlando, Feb. 1, 1860, John Patterson Osterhout Papers (Fondren Library, Rice University); Osterhout to Mother, Mar. 12, 1856, ibid.; C. Alwyn Barr, "The Making of a Secessionist: The Antebellum Career of Roger Q. Mills," *SHQ,* LXXIX (Oct., 1975), 129–144. For a look at one of the older Texas counties that matured over the course of the 1850s into a model Lower South plantation-dominated county see Campbell, "Planters and Plain Folk: Harrison County," 369–392. For examples of visionaries see *Texas Republican* (Marshall), Mar. 29, 1856; *State Gazette* (Austin), July 29, 1854, Nov. 17, 1860; *Weekly Telegraph* (Houston), Mar. 21, 1859. While the process of assimilation toward a

By 1857 the cultural transformation occurring in Texas society was reflected in the state Democratic party's increasing alliance with the Democratic parties of the Lower South. By 1858 ardent southerners who would be quick to resort to secession at any provocation controlled the apex of the state structure. By 1859 almost all moderate Democrats who had served as party functionaries and who had helped defeat and destroy the Know-Nothings from 1855 to 1858 had left the party and joined the newly formed Opposition party. As an institution the Democratic party was much stronger than the Opposition. Texans supported it out of loyalty and habit. Germans and Mexicans supported the party because it had defended them against the nativist Know-Nothings. Democrats like John H. Reagan still supported the party in 1859 because they hoped to reform its sectional character and revitalize its national heritage. Nor were the Democrats decimated by their losses in August of 1859. The party rapidly bounced back with the election of party war horse Louis T. Wigfall to the U.S. Senate by the Democratic-controlled legislature. Democratic editors continued to dominate the newspapers of the state and to place sectional writings into the hands of the public. All in all, the Democratic party was a powerful force—a force that was harnessed in 1860 and 1861 by its state and local leaders to the cause of secession.[24]

One reason that the Democratic party became an important force in the secession movement was that to a slight but noticeable degree its ideology always stressed the functional nature of the Union and emphasized that local customs and personal liberty must be defended. That is, the Union was a means to an end and not wholly a valuable thing in itself. For Democrats the Union was a means of fulfilling the American destiny. Thus it was that Democrats tended to be moderate secessionists and Whigs moderate unionists. Whigs certainly viewed the Union as necessary for social stability, law and order, and economic prosperity. Yet Whigs, in whatever group they later belonged, stressed more

---

Lower South model is difficult to gauge for the state as a whole, some indication of change over time in eastern Texas can be gained from studying the tables in Lathrop, *Migration into East Texas,* 84–100. One should remember that assimilation would not occur where other cultural role models were abundant or where the environment or economic conditions did not foster a Lower South culture. See Jordan, "Imprint of the Upper and Lower South," 667–685.

24. On the Democrats see Head, "State Rights in Texas," 1–100; Lubbock, *Six Decades,* 267–294; Ledbetter, "The Election of Louis T. Wigfall," 241–254; Paschal to Smith, May 27, 1859, Smith Papers; *Southern Intelligencer* (Austin), May 25, 1859. On the Know-Nothings and their effect on politics in Texas see Sister Paul of the Cross McGrath, *Political Nativism in Texas, 1825–1860* (Washington, D.C., 1930), 84–181; Waymon L. McClellan, "The Know-Nothing Party and the Growth of Sectionalism in East Texas," *ETHJ,* XIV (Fall, 1976), 26–36; Buenger, "Secession and the Texas German Community," 385–402.

heavily the sacred nature of the Union and spoke in reverential terms of their devotion to the nation. Such sentiments were not absent among Democrats, but they were not as dominant. Thus when Democrats became convinced that the Union threatened the very functions it was meant to achieve, they were more willing to leave behind the old church and seek a new vehicle to achieve salvation.[25]

Here, then, was a perfect example of goals that had once made men unionists converting them to secessionists. Secessionists wanted to change the form of their nation in 1860, but they did not want to change what they interpreted to be the meaning and purpose of a nation of Americans. Indeed, secessionist ideology gained power after November of 1860 because it stressed the dangers that remaining in the United States posed to the traditional purposes of that Union. For secessionists the Republican party symbolized the corruption and decay of their nation. As the presidential elections of 1856 and 1860 proved, it was purely sectional and not a national party. For Texans this sectionalism meant the poisoning of the governmental system whenever Republicans gained control of any branch of government. Texas secessionists had only to point to the chaos generated by the race for Speaker of the U.S. House of Representatives in 1859 or to the failure of the House to allocate money for the defense of the Texas frontier as proof of their arguments.[26] Republicans were also depicted as threats to the

---

25. On party affiliations and secession in Texas see Dohoney, *An Average American,* 71–88; Roberts, "The Political, Legislative, and Judicial History of Texas," 51–115; Lubbock, *Six Decades,* 267–294; Peyton McCrary, Clark Miller, and Dale Baum, "Class and Party in the Secession Crisis: Voting Behavior in the Deep South, 1856–1869," *Journal of Interdisciplinary History (JIH),* VIII (Winter, 1978), 446–447. For another point of view see Mering, "The Slave-State Constitutional Unionists," 395–410. For examples of the Whig heritage in action see *Harrison Flag* (Marshall), Sept. 15, 1860; *Alamo Express* (San Antonio), Nov. 5, 1860; Throckmorton to Epperson, Aug. 18, Sept. 13, 1859, Epperson Papers. For good examples of a Democrat's unionism see *Standard* (Clarksville), June 25, 1859, Dec. 22, 1860.

26. In 1859 the House of Representatives convened on December 5 and was unable to select a Speaker until February 1, 1860, because neither Democrats nor Republicans had a clear majority and both sides viewed the other party's candidates as dangerously sectional and biased. Finally, approximately twenty members of the American party, which held the balance of power in the Thirty-sixth Congress, cast their votes for the Republican, William Pennington. This controversy was closely tied to John Brown's raid into Virginia and the uproar over Republican endorsement of Hinton R. Helper's *Impending Crisis,* which southerners interpreted as incendiary propaganda. In Texas, Brown's raid, Helper's book, and the near breakdown of the governing process typified by the Speaker's controversy were used to demonstrate the malevolent effect of the Republicans on the nation. One result of the speakership controversy was that even after Pennington was elected it was difficult to pass legislation through the House that clearly favored either a Democratic or a Republican state. For Texans this meant that they were denied funds for frontier defense. Secessionists in Texas naturally cited this as another example of the evilness of Republicans. For more information

nation's role as preserver of law and order and guarantor of social stability. Time and time again secessionists shouted that Republican state governments broke statute law and the dictates of the Constitution when they passed personal-liberty laws that prevented the return of fugitive slaves. They argued persistently that the Republicans' reliance upon some higher moral or divine code was a threat to the very nature of law because it could be interpreted capriciously with no regard for minority rights. Secessionists insisted as well that Republican control of the federal government would eventually destroy slavery in the states where it already existed or would seriously impair the ability of white southerners to control their black slaves. The result of this would be anarchy and chaos. As John Reagan saw it, Texans faced a difficult choice: "The sad alternative is now submitted to us of the unconditional submission to Black Republican principles, and ultimately to free negro equality, and a government of mongrels or war of races on the one hand, or secession and the formation of a Southern Confederacy and a bloody war on the other."[27]

Conceptions of the meaning and purpose of an American nation, which shaped secessionist ideology, also shaped Texans' perceptions of self-interest. Leaders of Texas's legal and business communities often realized that secession, and with it the potential for war, would hurt their area's economy and create social instability. William Pitt Ballinger, a Galveston lawyer, recorded this gloomy note in his diary on December 30, 1860: "This [year] closes I fear most ominously—This Govt. will be overthrown & the Union destroyed. I hope for the best and it may be that public order & prosperity will not be weakened and that security will be given to the institution of slavery—But I have strong fears to the contrary, and my best judgement is that we are doing an unwise & may be a fatal thing."[28] In San Antonio and Austin, where the army greatly benefited the

---

on the Speakership controversy and the frontier see Ollinger Crenshaw, "The Speakership Contest of 1859–1860," *Mississippi Valley Historical Review,* XXIX (Dec., 1942), 323–338; Buenger, "Unionism on the Texas Frontier," 241–249; Ben H. Procter, *Not Without Honor: The Life of John H. Reagan* (Austin, 1962), 113–119.

27. Reagan to "a friend," Nacogdoches *Chronicle,* reprinted in *Texas Republican* (Marshall), Feb. 9, 1861 (quotation). Also see "Secession Broadsides," William H. Hamman Papers (Fondren Library, Rice University); Reynolds, *Editors Make War,* 76–117; *State Gazette* (Austin), Aug. 25, Sept. 22, Oct. 20, 1860; *Texas Republican* (Marshall), Sept. 29, 1860; *Countryman* (Bellville), Dec. 12, 19, 1860; Reagan to Roberts, Nov. 1, 20, Dec. 7, 1860, Roberts Papers.

28. William Pitt Ballinger, "Ballinger Diary," Dec. 30, 1860 (typescript, Rosenberg Library). For more information on Ballinger, whose social and business ties knit him into the commercial elite of Galveston, see Maxwell Bloomfield, "William Pitt Ballinger, Confederate Lawyer," American Lawyers in a Changing Society, 1776–1876 (Cambridge, Mass., 1976), 270–301. For further evidence that this commercial elite had good reason to oppose secession see *Union* (Galveston), Dec. 6, 1860;

local economy and where the Lower South culture was weak, the leaders of the anti-secessionist movement were usually also successful businessmen. In most cases, however, and this was certainly true of such East Texas commercial centers as Marshall, the culture and ideology of the commercial classes overrode their immediate self-interest. Moreover, secessionists seemed to convince businessmen, wealthy planters, and their lawyers—those people most involved in commerce—that the security of the slave system and the stable race relations and labor source that it provided were essential to their long-term prosperity and safety.[29]

Along the frontier, perceptions of what Republican control of the presidency would mean again aided the secessionists. Beginning about 1858 in the northern half of the frontier, the army and the federal government increasingly seemed more of a hindrance than a help. The army protected reservation Indians whom the Texans considered thieves and murderers, and it moved agonizingly slowly to counter the stepped-up raids of the Comanches and Kiowas in the three years prior to secession. Taking matters in its own hands, the Texas government organized Ranger companies and then sent the U.S. government a bill for their services. The U.S. House of Representatives, in which Republicans had a plurality, agreed to pay these bills at a snail's pace and was equally slow to allocate funds for badly needed cavalry units along the frontier. Since the army's prestige had been severely damaged along the northern frontier, and since past history gave proof that the army would be even more unresponsive to the needs of Texans if Republicans expanded their power within the federal government, many frontiersmen came to favor secession after the election of Abraham Lincoln to the presidency.[30]

Civilian (Galveston), Dec. 3, 1860; Fornell, *The Galveston Era*, 278–293. On other Texas businessmen or lawyers tied to commerce who viewed secession with reluctance, see McKinney to Jack, Ballinger, and Bryan, Nov. 22, 1860, Bryan Papers; Ralph A. Wooster, "Ben H. Epperson: East Texas Lawyer, Legislator, and Civic Leader," *ETHJ*, V (Mar., 1967), 29–42; Jane Lynn Scarborough, "George W. Paschal, Texas Unionist and Scalawag Jurisprudent" (Ph.D. diss., Rice University, 1972); Sinclair, "Crossroads of Conviction," 129–204; Ernest Wallace, *Charles DeMorse: Pioneer Editor and Statesman* (Lubbock, Tex., 1943), 1–142; Elliott, *Leathercoat*, 547.

29. McKinney to Jack, Ballinger, and Bryan, Nov. 22, 1860; Bryan Papers; *Texas Republican* (Marshall), Nov. 24, Dec. 1, 15, 1860; *Weekly Alamo Express* (San Antonio), Oct. 1, 8, 1860; *Southern Intelligencer* (Austin), Sept. 5, Oct. 10, 1860. For a typical example of secessionist rhetoric, see *State Gazette* (Austin), Nov. 17, 1860.

30. *White Man* (Weatherford), Sept. 13, 1860; Dallas *Herald*, May 18, 1859; *Standard* (Clarksville), May 19, Oct. 20, 27, 1860. On the frontier and its use by secessionists see Buenger, "Unionism on the Texas Frontier," 243–254; *State Gazette* (Austin), Aug. 11, Nov. 17, Dec. 1. 1860; Procter, *Not Without Honor*, 117–119; "An Ordinance to Dissolve the Union between the State of Texas and the

These inchoate factors that nourished secession among Texans as a whole in 1860 also drove certain gifted individuals to take a leading role in the public debate. Men of talent and position clarified the issues and organized the campaigns that made secession a reality. John Marshall, chairman of the state's Democratic party and editor of the influential *Texas State Gazette,* seemed to work toward secession throughout the 1850s. Most Texans, like John Reagan, however, were slower to accept disunion. Reagan, originally from Tennessee, shared an affection for the Union common to other Tennesseans like Sam Houston. Unlike Houston, however, Reagan seemed by late 1859 to be one of those Texans from the Upper South who was becoming assimilated into a Lower South culture. Perhaps it was his new experiences and new friends in Congress that caused the change. At any rate, avowedly frightened by the now ominous nature of the Union, Reagan realized by October, 1860, that the election of Lincoln could not be avoided and moved to join the secessionists. Like him, many talented and respected men accelerated the secession movement by lending it the force of their personalities, their reputations, their followings, and their abilities to articulate the issues.[31]

Unlike earlier times, this accelerating movement toward dissolution was not braked by a reawakened awareness of the pragmatic value of the Union, by the influence of Unionist leaders, by the resurgence of nationalist ideology, by the expression of this ideology in a political party, and by the inherent unionist tendencies of some Texas subcultures. Lincoln's election and the ascendancy of the Republican party made Texans question as nothing had before the ability of the United States to function as an American nation should function. After November of 1860 the Union seemed both unbeneficial and an unfit carrier of nationalist dreams. This perception was reinforced and the balance between attachment to the Union and to region was further endangered when a consensus in favor of secession virtually ended all debate on the matter in many parts of Texas. Still, even so powerful a force as consensus in a democracy could not submerge nationalism. Instead this nationalism caused Texans to focus on the Confederacy as the new hope for the fulfillment of old dreams and needs.

Other States . . . ," Winkler (ed.), *Journal of the Secession Convention,* 35–36; "A Declaration of the Causes Which Impel the State of Texas to Secede from the Federal Union," ibid., 61–66.

31. Procter, *Not Without Honor,* 97–126; Reagan to Roberts, Nov. 1, 1860, Roberts Papers; *Texas Republican* (Marshall), Jan. 12, 1861; Larry Jay Gage, "The Texas Road to Secession and War: John Marshall and the Texas State Gazette, 1860–1861," *SHQ,* LXII (Oct., 1958), 191–226. Charles R. Pryor, editor of the Dallas *Herald,* is another example of a moderate who threw his influence behind secession. See Dallas *Herald,* Jan. 9, 16, 1861; Webb, Carroll, and Branda (eds.), *Handbook of Texas,* II, 418.

By late 1860 many Texans had come to perceive Republican power in the national government and in the North as eroding both the ideological and pragmatic functions of the Union. Secessionists portrayed the Union as now incapable of providing stabilizing law, social harmony, military protection, and a guarantee of individual rights to its southern citizens. The question of secession became not simply a choice between defending slavery or defending the sanctity of the nation. The point of the secession debate in Texas was what Lincoln's election that November told and foretold about the nature of the Union. The argument that the Union had decayed, backed up by the specific examples of northern attitudes toward slavery, Republican neglect of the frontier, Republican disregard for the law, and Republican fomenting of social discord, weakened attachments to the nation based upon its role as a preserver of order, a promoter of future prosperity, and a keeper of such traditional values as a respect for the law. Thus the impact of parties and people moved by unionist ideology or a rational assessment of the Union's benefits was undercut.[32]

Unionism, however, did not cease to exist either within individuals or within groups, and habit, together with the emotional side of unionist ideology, would have created stronger opposition to secession in 1861 if it had not been for the force of consensus. Human societies, when threatened by an external enemy, have a tendency to require conformity of their members. In the winter of 1860–1861, in regions of Texas with substantial slave populations, a closing off of debate occurred. In that part of Texas most like the Lower South, which was roughly everything east of the Brazos River below a line running from Waco to Texarkana, secessionists, using the apparatus of the Democratic party and the Democratic press, spread their arguments into every hamlet. Meanwhile unionists were disorganized and silent. They lacked the strength of an institutional framework like the Democratic party. The unionists' silence sprang as well from a tactical decision to boycott all discussions of secession and hope that nearsighted visions of the Union would soon be replaced with a healthy nationalism. To an immeasurable degree, however, the silence of unionists arose from various forms of intimidation. Many times this intimidation was direct and overt. Newspaper editors who stridently opposed secession, like Ferdinand Flake of the German- and English-language *Union,* had their presses smashed. In other areas paramilitary groups, such as the minutemen of Harrison County or the Knights of the Golden Circle to which Newcomb took such exception, might have taken part in organized repression of unionist spokesmen and influenced voting. It is a fact, in any case, that secessionists used force to seize the

---

32. Ledbetter, "Slavery, Fear, and Disunion in the Lone Star State," 180–276.

federal government's property in Texas before the statewide referendum on secession, and that they occasionally tried to overtly intimidate or disrupt unionist spokesmen. Unionists also contended that fair election procedures in both the selection of Secession Convention delegates in January, 1861, and in the secession referendum of February 23, 1861, were not used. In such an atmosphere, physical intimidation might have forced some voters to favor secession despite reservations or to simply stay home.[33]

It seems probable, however, that more subtle forms of intimidation and persuasion were primarily responsible for the growing consensus in favor of secession in January and February of 1861. Since even most unionists agreed that secession was legal, the question before the public was whether it was justified. The answer came back a sure and emotion-packed "YES" from the secessionists and a rather timid "perhaps not" from the unionists. The secessionists were aided by their assured and direct approach, and the offering of a simple solution to a universally perceived problem. As the editor of the Bellville *Countryman* put it: "The so called cooperation men, most of whom among us seem to be equally as strongly opposed to any further aggression by the abolitionists, and who talk learnedly about maintaining our rights in the Union, have not presented a solitary plan of operation for doing so. The Secessionists do propose a remedy, and are striving to carry that into effect." Citizens were swayed by the force of such secessionist rhetoric and listened attentively to calls for unity in the face of northern aggression and declarations that the North would let the South leave the Union in peace. Men like William Pitt Ballinger expressed their concerns about secession in their private diaries, but seldom voiced them out loud where their friends would be offended and their business possibly damaged. In the

---

33. For an understanding of events in the winter and spring of 1860–1861 see *State Gazette* (Austin), Nov. 24, Dec. 8, 1860, Feb. 9, 23, 1861; Dallas *Herald*, Jan. 2, 9, 23, 1861, *Harrison Flag* (Marshall), Jan. 5, 12, 1861; *Union* (Galveston), Jan. 8, 12, 1861; *Texas Republican* (Marshall), Feb. 2, Mar. 2, 1861; Frank H. Smyrl, "Unionism in Texas, 1856–1861," *SHQ,* LXVIII (Oct., 1964), 187; C. A. Bridges, "The Knights of the Golden Circle: A Filibustering Fantasy," ibid., XLIV (Jan., 1941), 287–302; Dunn, "The KGC in Texas," 543–573. On the existence of paramilitary groups and the possible use of force during the secession crisis see *Texas Republican* (Marshall), Dec. 22, 1860, Jan. 5, Feb. 23, 1861; Newcomb, *Secession Times in Texas,* 6–12. On the tactics, actions, and opinions of unionists from December, 1860, to March, 1861, see Elliott, *Leathercoat,* 45–60; Dohoney, *An Average American,* 71–88; Friend, *Sam Houston,* 331–338; Sandbo, "The First Session of the Secession Convention," 181; *State Gazette* (Austin), Dec. 29, 1860. For a statement by unionists in February, 1861, see "Address to the People of Texas," scrapbook, 31–34, Haynes Papers. Timmons, "The Referendum in Texas," 14–22, makes several interesting observations about intimidation and voter manipulation by secessionists. On the use of force also see Maher, "Secession in Texas," 172–185; *Southern Intelligencer* (Austin), Mar. 6, 1861; Thomas North, *Five Years in Texas; or, What You Did Not Hear during the War . . .* (Cincinnati, 1871), 89–91.

end, either overtly or covertly, unionists were induced to stay home during public discussions and on election day, or they were convinced to quietly support secession.[34]

Each time the secessionists won a victory, either at the polls or in the propaganda campaign that accompanied the formation of consensus, the momentum of the secession movement increased. The silencing of one unionist or the decision of another simply not to speak out built a facade of unity that discouraged others from speaking out. The secession of six other states prior to the referendum in Texas made secession seem legitimate. Victories at the polls in the election of Secession Convention delegates in January of 1861, regardless of the margin of victory or whether unionists participated, produced an overwhelming majority in favor of the secessionists when the convention convened at the end of that month. The prompt and easy passage of a secession ordinance in turn encouraged Texans to endorse in the secession referendum of February 23, 1861, what was in many ways an accomplished fact. This was especially true because secessionists had secured the surrender of federal troops and property and begun moves to attach Texas to the Confederacy prior to that election. Through overt and covert intimidation, through control of the press and the speakers' platform, through better organization, through the advantages of a plan of action, and finally by taking advantage of momentum generated by a series of election victories, secessionists translated fears about the nature of the Union and the resultant decay of traditional props of the nation into a crushing consensus in favor of secession.[35]

Such a consensus was not predestined and there were some notable exceptions in Texas to its development. In Lamar County, on the fringe of the Lower South cultural region of Texas, E. L. Dohoney took part in a successful struggle to convince the county's voters to oppose secession. Looking back on these events later Dohoney declared: "This could have been done in nearly every

---

34. *Countryman* (Bellville), Jan. 16, 1861. Also see Ballinger, "Diary," Dec. 21, 31, 1860; *Texas Republican* (Marshall), Feb. 23, 1861.

35. *Texas Republican* (Marshall), Jan. 5, 12, 19, 26, 1861; *State Gazette* (Austin), Dec. 29, 1860, Jan. 5, 12, 19, Feb. 16, 23, 1861; "A Declaration of Causes Which Impel the State of Texas to Secede from the Federal Union," Winkler (ed.), *Journal of the Secession Convention*, 65; Lubbock, *Six Decades*, 305–306. O. M. Roberts is particularly revealing concerning the momentum of the secession movement. See Roberts, "Political, Legislative, and Judicial History," Wooten (ed.), *Comprehensive History of Texas*, 11, 88–114; "Memoirs of John Salmon Ford," V, 942–984. One unionist who did not regard secession as legal was George W. Paschal. On his long attempt to fight secession see Scarborough, "George W. Paschal," 39–136. Most other unionists resembled James Throckmorton. See Elliott, *Leathercoat*, 50–51.

county in Texas if the Union men had had leaders; but the leaders in the Democratic party, consisting of the principal planters and lawyers were all in the Secession movement, with a well organized revolution; which was precipitated on the people so suddenly that men naturally competent to lead, but untrained in politics, were so surprised, confused and morally bulldozed, that in only a few localities was any opposition attempted." In those numerous counties east of the Brazos River where a Lower South culture was either evolving or already present, secessionists "bulldozed" their way, superficially at least, to a near total acceptance of secession.[36]

Such acceptance was not universal, and unionism and nationalism persisted noticeably in the debates over secession that occurred in counties in the western and northern settled portions of the state. Here, as elsewhere, the component parts of unionism were undermined. Secessionist ideology and allegiance to the Democratic party swayed opinion in favor of secession. Powerful personalities and exponents of the cotton/slave culture argued persuasively that the Union was no longer a safe refuge. Self-interest, particularly on the northwestern frontier, convinced many that secession was advisable. In these areas of Texas, though, the force of consensus, while strong and following the same course as in other regions of Texas, was never as omnipotent as it was to the south or east. Here existed either great cultural diversity or else upper southern, western European, or Mexican cultural dominance. Here the Democratic party was either less institutionally sound or continued to face strong opposition from unionist groups. And here prominent citizens argued forcefully for the Union. Self-interest encouraged those whose wealth or safety depended upon the army or upon access to markets in the North to remain unionists. As a result, unionist ideology was undermined but never destroyed. Pioneer residents of slaveless Parker County, to the west of Ft. Worth, were just as concerned about the threat of the Republican party to law and social order as were the slaveholding citizens of plantation-dominated Harrison County, and they would express this concern by voting overwhelmingly for secession. Still, this fear of a Union corrupted by Republicans could not always overcome the mystical attachment to the nation found across Texas. In the winter of 1860–1861 Texans in the north and west echoed the words and sentiments penned by James Newcomb in November, when he was trying to drum up votes for a fusion ticket in opposition to John C. Breckinridge. In an editorial dated November 5, 1860, Newcomb wrote: "In the name of Washington, who exhorted us to cherish the Union, we call upon

---

36. Dohoney, *An Average American,* 74 (quotation). Also see *Texas Republican* (Marshall), Dec. 22, 29, 1860.

every American citizen to vote for the Union ticket. In the name of Jefferson, of Jackson, of Webster, of Clay, we call upon you to rebuke the fell spirit of disunion." Responding to such ecumenical calls in the names of men who were not only the patron saints of Democrats and Whigs, but above all heroes of the nation, many Texans in the north and west did indeed openly "rebuke the fell spirit of disunion."[37]

Lest the imagination run too wild, though, and invoke an image of a Texas split into two warring geographic and cultural regions by the issue of secession, a simple look at the facts reveals that a goodly number of Texans in the northern and western counties of the state voted in favor of secession, and that the vast majority of those who opposed secession eventually supported the Confederacy. As James W. Throckmorton, soon to be a Confederate general, put it in March of 1861: "While my judgment dictates to me that we are not justified by the surroundings or the occasion, a majority of the people of Texas have declared in favor of secession; the die is cast; the step has been taken, and regardless of consequences I expect and intend to share the fortunes of my friends and neighbors. . . . I have no doubt that the time will soon be upon us when the clash of arms will be heard and the blood of my countrymen will be shed in a great civil war. When it comes I will be in its midst. . . ." Once the war that Throckmorton had predicted began, Texans became all the more united and gathered together with their "friends and neighbors" to fight the enemy.[38]

In some sense the triumph of the secessionists and the existence of a bellicose Confederate States of America for five years was a victory for localism. Texans

---

37. *Weekly Alamo Express* (San Antonio), Nov. 5, 1860 (quotation). Political parties matured more slowly on the frontier because the population was sparse and the difficulty of survival great. Once competition began between political groups, however, competition itself forced greater party organization. This process had just begun on the frontier in 1860. See *Texas State Times* (Austin), June 30, 1855; Lubbock, *Six Decades,* 179–313; Sinclair, "Crossroads of Conviction." On the continued existence of a two-party system and a strong unionist voice see the *Standard* (Clarksville), Feb. 2, 9, 23, Mar. 2, 9, 1861; Dallas *Herald,* Jan. 16, 23, Feb. 13, 20, 27, 1861; New Braunfels *Zeitung,* Feb. 22, Mar. 1, 1861. For information on Parker County and the rest of the frontier see *White Man* (Weatherford), Sept. 13, 1860; Buenger, "Unionism on the Texas Frontier," 250–254. Voting returns and an analysis of their validity can be found in Timmons, "The Referendum in Texas," 15–19.

38. Elliott, *Leathercoat,* 59 (quotations). For a map showing the percentage vote against secession, see Jordan, "The Imprint of the Upper and Lower South," 687. On support of the Confederacy by former unionists see *Standard* (Clarksville), Mar. 2, 9, 16, 23, 1861; *State Gazette* (Austin), Mar. 16, 1861; *Southern Intelligencer* (Austin), May 8, 1861; Houston, "Speech at Independence," May 10, 1861; *Writings of Sam Houston,* ed. Williams and Barker, VIII, 301–305; Baggett, "The Constitutional Union Party in Texas," 263–264; Wooster, "Ben Epperson," 32–35. For additional information and a different point of view see Claude Elliott, "Union Sentiment in Texas, 1861–1865," *SHQ,* L (Apr., 1947), 449–477.

first began to accept the idea of secession because their local institution of slavery was challenged by the North and by the Republican party. When they came to believe that the Union's proper character would be subverted by the hegemony of the Republican party, Texans moved toward secession. Secessionist propagandizing by the regular Democratic party, the emergence of pragmatic local reasons for supporting secession, the identification of traditional local leaders with secession, the forced consensus in some cultural regions of the state, and the particular ideology of Texas secessionists all had a parochial nature. Even the decision made by many unionists to support the Confederacy was in large measure the result of their realization that their community, their county, their state, or their region was more their physical, emotional, and psychological home than the nation as a whole.

To describe the force of localism in creating secession and sustaining the Confederacy in its early days, however, does not negate the existence of nationalism at any time after 1860. Secessionists displayed a widely held assumption that it was only as part of a large and stable nation that Americans could achieve their individual and corporate goals. Almost from the beginning Texas secessionists were nation builders as well as destroyers of the Union. Texans toyed with the notion of restoring the Republic of Texas, but when they made their decision to secede it was clear that Texas would be part of the Confederacy. Six states had left the Union by February, 1861. While some of these states hesitated to leave the Union without a guarantee of cooperation from other southern states, Texans knew they would not be alone. As early as January, 1861, propagandists of secession in Texas began to argue that separate state secession, since it would be the fastest means of removing their state from the Union and uniting it with the other states of the cotton-growing South, was in effect the most efficient form of cooperating in the building of a new nation. In essence, the secession movement did not kill nationalism in Texas, but redirected it toward the Confederate States of America.[39]

---

39. On the possible restoration of Texas as an independent nation see Jimmie Hicks, "Texas and Separate Independence, 1860–1861," *ETHJ*, IV (Oct., 1966), 85–106. For examples of emerging Confederate nationalism and its similarity to unionism see Winkler (ed.), *Journal of the Secession Convention*, 64–65; *Texas Republican* (Marshall), Jan. 5, 12, 19, 26, 1861; Lubbock, *Six Decades*, 304–306. Also see Stephen B. Oates, "Texas under the Secessionists," *SHQ*, LXVII (Oct., 1963), 167–212. For a look at secession in some of the other six states of the original Confederacy see Channing, *Crisis of Fear*; William L. Barney, *The Secessionist Impulse: Alabama and Mississippi in 1860* (Princeton, 1974); Charles B. Dew, "Who Won the Election in Louisiana?" *JSH*, XXXVI (Feb., 1970), 18–32; McCrary, Miller, and Baum, "Class and Party in the Secession Crisis," 429–457; Ralph A. Wooster, "The Secession of the Lower South: An Examination of Changing Interpretations," *Civil War History*, VII (June, 1961), 117–127.

Texans hoped that they were entering a new nation that would become all the things the old Union had once been. Quickly most of the old props of the Union were marshaled to support the Confederacy. The homogeneous culture of the southern states received constant mention. The Confederacy was to be the inheritor of the American mission forfeited by the Union. It would prevent anarchy and protect its citizens from foreign powers. Significantly, beginning with early discussions of secession, Texans insisted that the constitution of their new nation be as much like that of the United States as possible. Secessionists argued that both Whigs and Democrats would be at home in a southern confederacy. The interests of frontiersmen and cotton growers, in their opinion, would be aided by entry into this new nation. Finally, it soon became clear that the personalities who would lead Texas and the Confederacy in the first years of nationhood would not be anarchists, but would, like John Reagan, be nation builders who had clung tenaciously to the Union throughout most of the 1850s. Secession and subsequent attachment to the Confederacy did not spring simply from localism, but came as well from the potent although at times weakly focused force of nationalism.[40]

Texans did not move toward secession in a straight and simple line. Perhaps only through imagery, then, can secession be reduced to the understandable. If so, the image of Texas and Texans that emerged in 1860–1861 was like the Roman god Janus. Two almost identical faces looking in opposite directions on the same head, secession and the Union, drew sustenance from the same body. Within their common brain secessionists and unionists were localists and nationalists at the same time. Janus, though, evokes an image of balance and inertia—an image that was untrue of Texas in 1861. Commitment to the United States began to evaporate when Abraham Lincoln and the Republican party achieved hegemony within the North and the national government. This event signaled to Texans, as none had done before, the irreparable decay of the Union. All the things that the nation had once done or Texans hoped the nation would do—preventing anarchy, protecting the frontier, insuring the protection of constitutional and legal rights—a Republican-dominated nation promised not to do. In fact, Republicans were perceived as anarchists, as attackers of the frontier as well as all other portions of Texas, and as law breakers. Even so, the pull of the Union was strong, and most Texans might have been willing to give the Republicans a chance to prove themselves worthy of their trust if the momentum

---

40. Lubbock, *Six Decades,* 304–313; *State Gazette* (Austin), Feb. 9, 16, Mar. 2, 16, 1861; *Standard* (Clarksville), Feb. 23, Mar. 9, 1861. McCardell, *Southern Nation,* 251, 271, 336–338, uses Reagan as an example of a typical southerner who did not become a southern nationalist until 1860. He also uses Reagan to prove his point that moderates with a tradition of nationalism led the Confederacy.

of the secession movement had not been constantly accelerated by a growing consensus in favor of secession which ended all debate over its wisdom in many parts of Texas. A greater attachment to one's state and region rather than the nation prompted even secession's critics to accept the dismembering of the Union. In a way that is difficult to measure, however, what made secession acceptable was the realization by most Texans that secessionists were nation builders as well as destroyers. Here again secession was intertwined with notions about the Union. Secession was a continuation of the past, not a radical departure from the past. Its purpose was not simply to tear apart the Union, but to dismantle it in order to construct a purer type of union which would achieve all the goals and purposes of a nation of Americans. Texans did not lose their nationalism in 1861, nor did they cease to define that nationalism in an American fashion. They refocused that nationalism on the Confederacy instead of the United States.

When Texas joined an earlier nation of Americans in 1845–1846 they acted with near unanimity and much joy. Far less joy and unanimity could be found in 1860–1861 when Texans left the United States for the Confederacy.[41] These two instances, however, were more alike than they seem. They were essentially two faces on the same head on the same body. For Texas the key to the riddle of secession lay in the interdependence of secession with all the ideas, values, interests, and habits connected with the Union.

---

41. From the notes O. M. Roberts made during the secession crisis to the present day the oddity of Texans crying for admission to the Union in 1845 and rejecting that same Union in 1861 has captured the imagination. See "Memoirs of John Salmon Ford," V, 949; Ledbetter, "Slavery, Fear, and Disunion," 1–3. A convenient comparison of the two events can be found in Friend, *Sam Houston*, 157–161, 330–341.

Photograph of Texas troops in San Antonio at the time of Major General David E. Twiggs's surrender of the Federal garrison to state authorities in February 1861. *Courtesy Daughters of the Republic of Texas.*

"Embarrassing Situation": David E. Twiggs and the Surrender of United States Forces in Texas, 1861

JEANNE T. HEIDLER*

Even before the people of Texas approved the secession ordinance, a Committee on Public Safety appointed by the state convention negotiated with Brigadier General David E. Twiggs, United States commander for the department of Texas, for the surrender of all Federal property in the state. Wishing to avoid unnecessary bloodshed and confronted by several hundred armed Texans commanded by Colonel Ben Mc-Culloch, Twiggs agreed to turn over Federal property on condition that he and his men be allowed to retain their sidearms and march to the coast for passage out of Texas.

Twiggs was denounced by northerners for the surrender and dismissed from military service. Many speculated that his actions were part of a southern plot in which Twiggs, a native Georgian with southern sympathies, willingly cooperated.

In the following article Jeanne T. Heidler, assistant professor of history at Salisbury State University in Maryland, examines Twiggs's role in the affair. She concludes that Twiggs, while not blameless, was a victim of circumstance. She believes

* Jeanne T. Heidler, "'Embarrassing Situation': David E. Twiggs and the Surrender of United States Forces in Texas, 1861," *Military History of the Southwest*, XXI (Fall, 1991), 157–172.

that the Federal government, which vacillated during the crisis, should share the blame.

For another view on this issue see, in addition to the article by Russell K. Brown and the book by J. J. Bowden referred to by Professor Heidler, Thomas W. Cutrer, Ben McCulloch and the Frontier Military Tradition *(Chapel Hill: University of North Carolina Press, 1993), esp. Chapter Ten.*

Following the presidential election of November 1860, the southern threat of secession became a reality. As one state after another followed South Carolina's lead, the government in Washington became increasingly concerned for the safety of Federal property in the southern states. Post offices, mints, arsenals, and, most important, fortifications were all threatened by increasingly belligerent Southerners. The largest concentration of Federal forts and soldiers in the South was located in Texas, a state that was slower than its southern neighbors in moving toward secession but which contained a significant secessionist element.

To complicate the situation further, the commander of the Department of Texas was a Southerner, Major General David E. Twiggs. A native Georgian, Twiggs had been in the United States Army for forty-eight years, was seventy years old, and suffered from poor health. He had been on sick leave for a year and returned to active duty in Texas after Lincoln's election. As he prepared to resume his duties, Twiggs's hope was that war could be averted and that he would play no part in it if war did come.

Two studies, J. J. Bowden's *The Exodus of Federal Forces from Texas, 1861* (1986) and Russell K. Brown's 1984 article in *Military Affairs,* examine the events surrounding Twiggs's return and his motivations for finally surrendering United States forces to Texas secessionists. Though the authors differ from each other (Brown implies that Twiggs returned to Texas to surrender the posts, and Bowden blames Twiggs's infirmities and cautious nature for the surrender), neither presents compelling evidence to explain the general's behavior. Caution alone would have prevented Twiggs from returning to active duty in 1860, and a conniving traitor would never have reached terms so favorable to United States forces as those Twiggs arranged with the Texas secessionists. Neither author examines the culpability of the United States government in the crisis. This article will outline Washington's neglect of the Texas crisis and explore the reasons for Twiggs's behavior.[1]

---

1. Bowden, *The Exodus of Federal Forces from Texas* (Austin, TX: Eakin Press, 1986), 3, 42, passim; and Brown, "An Old Woman with a Broomstick: General David E. Twiggs and the U.S. Surrender in Texas, 1861," *Military Affairs,* 48 (April 1984): 61.

When Twiggs ended his sick leave in the fall of 1860, he knew he would not be returning to the same army he had left months before. The campaign and election of 1860 had changed everything. The army in Texas was a microcosm of all the animosities and suspicions being experienced across the United States. Many of the southern soldiers in Texas looked to their general for guidance, while other officers and men viewed him with mistrust. In fact, one of Twiggs's subordinates, Lieutenant Colonel George Thomas, went so far as to warn the government about the danger of reinstating Twiggs in Texas. Thomas, while on leave in Washington, visited General Winfield Scott to warn him of Twiggs's disloyalty.[2]

Rather than being disloyal, Twiggs, like many Southerners, was torn between two conflicting loyalties—to the United States Army and to his native state—and for two months following his return to Texas he was constantly pulled back and forth by the forces representing each. On 13 November, Twiggs's son-in-law, Colonel Abram Myers, forwarded the general's reinstatement orders with the prediction that "we must have trouble." Myers, an ardent secessionist, hoped that any "trouble" between Federal authorities and secessionists would speed the process of separation.[3]

Twiggs resumed command of the department on 13 December believing that secession was inevitable. He had even delayed reporting to Texas in the hope that the secession of the South would eliminate his dilemma. But since he was no longer ill, too much delay would have brought about his forced retirement at a time before retirement pensions. Furthermore, there was still a glimmer of hope that one of the many compromise proposals being bandied about would produce a solution averting the crisis. When he did assume command from Colonel Robert E. Lee, Twiggs revealed his belief that the Union would soon be

----

2. Twiggs and Thomas had been feuding sporadically since the Mexican War, primarily over real and imagined slights inflicted on Thomas by Twiggs. Richard O'Connor, *Thomas: Rock of Chickamauga* (New York: Prentice-Hall, 1948), 90; Thomas B. Van Horne, *The Life of General George H. Thomas* (New York: Charles Scribner's Sons, 1882), 20; Robert G. Hartje, *Van Dorn: The Life and Times of a Confederate General* (Nashville, TN: Vanderbilt University Press, 1967), 76; Francis R. McKinney, *Education in Violence: The Life of George H. Thomas and the History of the Army of the Cumberland* (Detroit, MI: Wayne State University Press, 1961), 75–77, 85–86. Thomas began his leave in November 1860, relinquishing command of his regiment and temporary command of the department to Robert E. Lee. George F. Price, *Across the Continent with the Fifth Cavalry* (reprint of 1883 ed.: New York: Antiquarian Press, 1959), 199.

3. Myers to Twiggs, 13 November 1860, in United States War Department, *War of the Rebellion: A Compilation of the Official Records of the Union and Confederate Armies* (128 vols.; Washington: Govemment Printing Office, 1880–1901), series 1, 15:500, hereinafter cited as Official Records. Unless specified otherwise, any references are to series 1.

dissolved. He wrote to Scott on the same day, saying that he expected Texas to secede with other southern states and asking for Scott's advice should this occur. He would do his duty as commander, he assured Scott, by guarding all government ordnance and munitions in Texas as long as his position was "tenable"; but when that was no longer possible, he intended to go home.[4]

Scott responded on 28 December through his adjutant, Colonel George W. Lay, by reminding Twiggs of a conversation they had had in Augusta, Georgia, in 1832 when Twiggs had commanded the Augusta arsenal during the Nullification Crisis. Twiggs then had not wanted to use force against fellow Americans, but the situation in 1860 was even more volatile. Therefore, Scott remarked, since any instructions he could give would have political overtones, he first would have to consult President James Buchanan. He expected Twiggs to protect government property but not to take offensive measures against state forces. Scott sympathized with Twiggs's predicament, regretting that the War Department was not giving him instructions even on the South Carolina situation. He closed by advising Twiggs to use his best judgment.[5]

This was small comfort to Twiggs. Throughout the month of December he had been visibly anxious over the growing crisis and his role in it. He told Robert E. Lee to expect the dissolution of the Union within six weeks. When it happened, Twiggs informed Lee he would be going to New Orleans. In a letter of recommendation for one of his men, he wrote that separation was imminent and that the army might be disbanded. This attitude on the part of the commander undoubtedly influenced the already low morale of the soldiers in Texas.[6]

From the moment he resumed command, it was evident that Twiggs planned to avoid a fight at almost any cost. When Scott forwarded to Charles Anderson, the younger brother of Major Robert Anderson, a plan of his proposed strategy should war erupt, and asked him to show it around to people like Lee and Twiggs, Twiggs was visibly displeased. Even the suggestion that this crisis could turn into civil war disturbed him greatly. He must have felt very much alone. His immediate predecessor, Lee, made no secret of his antipathy for secession. Twiggs had always admired Lee, though he believed the colonel to be General Scott's pet. In fact, Twiggs was heard to remark in January 1861 that he knew

---

4. Twiggs to Scott, 13 December 1860, ibid., 1:579.

5. Col. George W. Lay to Twiggs, 28 December 1860, ibid.

6. Douglas Southall Freeman, *R. E. Lee: A Biography* (4 vols.; New York: Charles Scribner's Sons, 1934–1935), 1:416, 424; Twiggs's recommendation for soldier, 24 December 1860, in Compiled Service Records of Confederate Generals and Staff Officers, and Non-regimental Enlisted Men, National Archives, Washington, DC, hereinafter cited as Compiled Service Record of David E. Twiggs.

"General Scott fully believes that God Almighty had to spit on his hands to make Bob Lee. . . !"[7] Yet even Twiggs's sarcasm could not hide the fact that he felt the same way.

To insure that hostilities did not begin in Texas, Twiggs began importuning the War Department for instructions. On 27 December, before the arrival of Scott's reply to his first inquiry, Twiggs wrote to the Assistant Adjutant General, Lieutenant Colonel Lorenzo Thomas, asking for instructions regarding the disposition of Federal property should Texas secede. Twiggs assured Thomas that he would remain in Texas as long as he could, but he wanted plans made before the emergency was upon him.[8]

That this might be before any plans could be laid was Twiggs's worst nightmare. Even in December, long before the actual secession of Texas, talk that secessionists planned to seize the Federal arsenal in San Antonio caused him to reinforce the arsenal with militia. If the facility were attacked, there would be no Federal troops involved. This precaution proved to be unnecessary, but it did demonstrate the lengths to which Twiggs would go to prevent a clash between Federal and state officials.[9]

Early in the new year Twiggs continued pleading with the War Department for instructions. On 2 January he wrote to Washington that he expected Texas to secede by the end of the month. He needed instructions about the disposition of his troops so that some action could be taken immediately. Five days later he repeated his plea. Twiggs received no orders. He wrote to Scott on the fifteenth, reminding the general of his "embarrassing situation." If Texas seceded, he needed to know what to do with his men. He advised Scott that coercion would not preserve the Union and that whatever happened, he intended to follow Georgia should that state secede. He believed that as a Southerner he had no choice. In any event, because of his health he could be no more than a "looker on" in any conflict. He closed by requesting that he be relieved of command by 4 March, inauguration day.[10]

Twiggs certainly expected some response from the government, and he was bewildered, frustrated, and apprehensive when no orders arrived. By the middle

7. Freeman, *R. E. Lee,* 1:417–418; Twiggs's remark quoted in Alf J. Mapp, Jr., *Frock Coats and Epaulets* (New York: Thomas Yoseloff, 1963), 155.

8. Twiggs to L. Thomas, 27 December 1860, in *Official Records,* 1:579.

9. Caroline Baldwin Darrow, "Recollections of the Twiggs Surrender," in Robert Underwood Johnson and Clarence Clough Buel, *Battles and Leaders of the Civil War: Being for the Most Part Contributions by Union and Confederate Officers* (4 vols.; New York: Century Company, 1888), 1:33.

10. Twiggs to L. Thomas, 2, 7 January 1861, Twiggs to Scott, 15 January 1861, *Official Records,* 1:590, 581.

of January the secessionists had gained enough strength to call a convention for 28 January. Twiggs dutifully reported this latest development to the Adjutant General's office on 18 January, reiterating his pledge to "never fire on American citizens."[11] As much as he wanted some kind of instructions, what he obviously desired was permission to accede to any state demands.

Complicating matters was the growing disaffection between Texas secessionists and Governor Sam Houston. Whom was Twiggs to deal with—the governor or the secessionist-dominated legislature? Houston made the initial move by opening a secret correspondence on 20 January. He informed the general that he planned to send militia general J. M. Smith to Twiggs on a "confidential mission" to determine the latter's plans. The governor suggested that Twiggs turn over all public property to Houston's designated agent to prevent it from falling into the hands of a secessionist mob. Would Twiggs consider doing this? Houston insisted that it was just a suggestion, not a demand, and he pledged to abide by any agreement reached by Twiggs and Smith. Promising to keep Twiggs informed of all the legislature's deliberations, the governor told him to request any needed aid from the mayor of San Antonio or any other civilian authority.[12]

If Houston were testing Twiggs's loyalty or if this bizarre epistle was designed to secure an ally, he was disappointed on both counts. Twiggs responded that he simply had no instructions about what he should do after secession; therefore, he could not answer Houston's question until that situation arose. If Texas seceded and Houston demanded the surrender of public property, only then would he receive an answer. The rather curt, official letter offered little comfort to the besieged governor.[13]

Twiggs was much more concerned by Houston's warnings than he indicated to the governor. On 22 January he issued a special order to the San Antonio garrison, warning them of rumors that an armed mob was threatening to seize government stores. The men were to prevent that at all costs. To give substance to his resolution Twiggs ordered them to ready two six-pounder cannons, and he called into San Antonio three companies from outlying forts. Less than a week later, however, he must have thought his moves unduly provocative since he rescinded the order for two of the companies.[14]

---

11. Twiggs to Adjutant General, 18 January 1861, ibid., 1:581.

12. Houston to Twiggs, 20 January 1861, in Samuel Houston, *The Writings of Sam Houston, 1813–1863,* ed. Amelia W. Williams and Eugene C. Barker (8 vols.; Austin: University of Texas Press, 1938–1943), 8:234.

13. Twiggs to Houston, 22 January 1861, ibid., 8:285.

14. Special Orders, no. 10, 22 January 1861, and Special Orders, no. 13, 28 January 1861, *Official Records,* 1:581–582.

Twiggs quickly informed Adjutant General Samuel Cooper of his correspondence with Houston. Enclosing copies of Houston's letter and his own reply, he confided to Cooper that if Texas seceded and the governor asked him to surrender government property, he would give up everything but the men's arms. Again he begged for instructions, pointing out that the men were spread over 1,200 miles and that it would take some time to move them. Even before receiving this latest correspondence, the War Department had finally decided to act. On 28 January, Secretary of War Joseph Holt decided to relieve Twiggs of command of the Department of Texas and place in his stead New Yorker and staunch Unionist, Colonel Carlos A. Waite.[15]

Strangely, it took several weeks for these orders to reach the appropriate people so that Waite could make his way to San Antonio from Camp Verde, located about sixty-five miles northwest of the Alamo city. In those weeks all hell would break loose in Texas. In fact, Waite's orders to assume command were not issued until 4 February. These orders advised him to expect no instructions about the disposition of men and public property until Texas actually seceded. No explanation was given for the week's delay in the issuance of his orders.[16]

As if matters were not complicated enough, the War Department was discreetly acting on Twiggs's warnings. Either from fear of secessionist anger or more likely from a desire to deny the existence of a crisis, it was quietly trying to remove five light-artillery companies from posts on the Rio Grande. The orders were issued at the end of January, and Waite was informed of the move in his orders to assume command. In fact, a week later Lorenzo Thomas was writing to Waite as if he were already the commander of the department, giving him further instructions as to the disposition of those companies. There also seemed to be some question as to whether Twiggs was passing on these orders to the companies in question, prompting Thomas to correspond directly with Brevet Major W. H. French on the scene. There was no need for this concern; the day Twiggs received these instructions, 14 February, he issued the appropriate orders to the artillery companies and to the replacement troops.[17]

In the meantime, circumstances forced a conclusion in Texas. Although the Secession Convention voted to secede on 1 February, it also voted to send the matter to the people in a statewide referendum on 23 February; action would

---

15. Twiggs to Cooper, 23 January 1861, Special Orders, no. 22, 28 January 1861, ibid., 582.

16. L. Thomas to Waite, 4 February 1861, ibid., 586.

17. L. Thomas to Col. H. L. Scott, 30 January 1861, L. Thomas to Twiggs, 31 January 1861, L. Thomas to Waite, 4 February 1861, same to same, 7 February 1861, L. Thomas to French, 7 February 1861, and Special Orders, no. 25, by order of Twiggs, 14 February 1861, ibid., 585–589.

not be official until that vote was counted. Nevertheless, the convention wanted to move ahead by trying to negotiate the immediate surrender of Federal property in Texas.[18]

A Committee of Public Safety was appointed to supervise these negotiations and to direct the defense of the state. It appointed commissioners to meet with Twiggs in the hope that his southern sympathies would facilitate a quick, non-violent resolution of the crisis. In case Twiggs refused to cooperate and turn over the property, Benjamin McCulloch was appointed colonel of cavalry with authority to use force. As ominous as all of this sounded, the commissioners had secret instructions to allow Twiggs to wait until secession became official on 2 March if he would guarantee that all men and mobile Federal property would remain fixed at current positions. The commissioners were not to do anything to injure the pride of Twiggs or his officers, but at the same time they were to recruit as many of them as possible.[19]

Texan activity and the War Department's failure to provide him with any instructions compelled Twiggs to desperate action.[20] On 4 February he wrote Samuel Cooper that he was sending his aide-de-camp, Lieutenant T. A. Washington, to the War Department to obtain instructions. In his letter to Cooper, he warned the Adjutant General that he planned to negotiate with Texan authorities for the retention of his men's clothes, supplies, and transportation. In any event, it hardly seems likely that Twiggs would have sent Washington if he intended to surrender everything.[21]

Twiggs told his men to be ready to move with only light baggage at a moment's notice. He then informed his officers that he had requested instructions from Washington on five occasions with no response. Rather ominously, he assured them that he would remain with them to "attend to their comforts" until all of the arrangements for departure were made.[22]

---

18. Twiggs to Cooper, 4 February 1861, ibid., 586; E. W. Winkler (ed.), *Journal of the Secession Convention of Texas, 1861* (Austin: Austin Printing Company, 1912), 264.

19. Winkler, *Journal of the Secession Convention*, 264–267; John C. Robertson to O. M. Roberts, 6 March 1861, Robertson to McCulloch, 3 February 1861, Robertson to commissioners, 6 February 1861, in *Official Records*, 53:623, and series 2, 1:26–28.

20. The War Department did not acknowledge receipt of any of Twiggs's letters until 4 February, even though the earliest of his inquiries was received on 12 January. Cooper to Twiggs, 4 February 1861, Twiggs to L. Thomas, 27 December 1860, in *Official Records*, series 1, 1:579, 585.

21. Twiggs to Cooper, 4 February 1861, ibid., 586; Withers Diary, 16 February 1861, Papers of Lieut. Col. John Withers, Record Group 109, War Department Collection of Confederate Records, National Archives, Washington, DC.

22. "Surrender of United States Property by General Twiggs," *Harper's Weekly*, 9 March 1861, 151.

Formal negotiations between Twiggs and the Texas commissioners opened on 8 February. The general informed Thomas J. Devine, Samuel A. Maverick, and P. N. Luckett that he did not intend to surrender public property until 2 March. There is no indication that the commissioners had informed him of their secret instructions on this matter. Twiggs also made it clear that he would never surrender unless the men could keep their arms, a condition the commissioners were not willing to meet. Except for this disagreement, the meeting was quite amicable. Twiggs told the Texans of his southern sympathies and of having informed the War Department that he would not be responsible for starting a war. Yet the commissioners were troubled. They could not be sure if the old general's loyalty to the army would not outweigh his loyalty to the South. They were particularly disturbed by his obvious admiration for Winfield Scott and his praise for Scott's conduct during the current crisis. When Twiggs told them that Georgia had offered him a commission and that he had refused it because of ill health, they had to wonder if that was the only reason. Before they departed, Twiggs treated them to a brief lecture on the inadvisability of separation. They were in no mood to hear the general's advice—that the secession of Texas was unwise because the state, unlike other southern states, had a serious Indian problem and could not afford to defend itself.[23]

After musing over this interview, the commissioners later in the day sent a note to Twiggs's office, asking him to put in writing that he would surrender Federal property on 2 March. Twiggs replied, through his adjutant, that he would put nothing in writing. In fact, he was appointing his own commission to negotiate with the Texans, designating for this purpose Major H. Vinton, Major Sackfield Maclin, and Captain Robert H. K. Whitely.[24]

Twiggs's apparent reluctance to surrender and his belated refusal to talk with them directly now alarmed the commissioners. They immediately contacted John C. Robertson, chairman of the Committee of Public Safety, to inform him they believed that Twiggs was about to draw more men into San Antonio to resist Texas forces. They had therefore summoned Ben McCulloch to the field, instructing him to assemble his cavalry and come immediately to San Antonio. The next day Robertson wrote to McCulloch, instructing him to recruit to the Texas cause as many Federal soldiers as possible. The Texans were concerned that if Federal forces in the state united, they might march to New Mexico

---

23. Commissioners to Twiggs, 8 February 1861, Nichols to commissioners, 9 February 1861, Robertson to Roberts, 6 March 1861, commissioners to Robertson, 8 February 1861, in *Official Records*, 53:618, 626.

24. Special Orders, no. 20, by order of Twiggs, 9 February 1861; Nichols to commissioners, 9 February 1861; Robertson to Roberts, 6 March 1861, all in ibid., 1:505, 53:618, 624.

where they would be a threat to Texas should war come. State officials knew that the process of issuing such orders and moving the men into San Antonio would take a few weeks, so on 10 February the commissioners wrote to Robertson again, advising him to act quickly before Twiggs had time to call in men from outlying posts.[25]

In the meantime the commissioners tried to arrange a meeting with Twiggs's appointed representatives. A message to the officers, proposing a meeting at noon on the tenth, elicited only the officers' response that they could not meet with the commissioners until the morning of the eleventh. The latter immediately reported to Robertson that this was just another of Twiggs's attempts to stall.[26]

The sore point with the commissioners and Robertson was Twiggs's insistence on allowing his men to keep their arms. Texas authorities could not allow this valuable supply of weapons to leave the state. In the absence of any instructions, Twiggs apparently planned to surrender everything else, as indicated by his 9 February order to all post commanders to submit an inventory of all quartermaster supplies and munitions, except hand arms.[27]

At this point, if Twiggs truly intended to prevent the capture of Federal property, he should have issued orders for at least some of the men from outlying posts to come in to defend headquarters. Yet, he was still torn between loyalty and sentiment, and moreover he was determined not to be the one who started the war.[28]

In spite of rumors that state troops intended to seize some of the outlying forts and the supplies and munitions attached to them, Robertson and the commission were hesitant to use McCulloch until absolutely necessary. Texas had not yet officially seceded. On 15 February, however, Twiggs received notice that he was to be relieved of command by Waite. Whether he or some southern sympathizer on his staff leaked this information is unknown, but the commissioners knew about it by the end of the day.[29]

At the same time, it was an open secret that Ben McCulloch had two hun-

25. Commissioners to Robertson, 8 February 1861, Robertson to Roberts, 6 March 1861, commissioners to McCulloch, 8 February 1861, Robertson to McCulloch, 9 February 1861, commissioners to Robertson, 10 February 1861, ibid., 53:625–627, and series 2, 1:30–31.

26. Commissioners to Robertson, 10 February 1861, ibid., series 2, 1:31.

27. Robertson to Roberts, 6 March 1861, General Orders, no. 3, by order of Twiggs, 9 February 1861, ibid., series 1. 53:625, 1:589.

28. "The Secession of Texas," *Harper's Weekly,* 16 February 1861, p. 103.

29. Walter L. Buenger, *Secession and the Union in Texas* (Austin: University of Texas Press, 1981), 154–155; and Twiggs to L. Thomas, 18 February 1861, in *Official Records,* 1:590.

dred Texas Rangers right outside of town. More were on the way. In fact, by 14 February reliable reports in San Antonio indicated that McCulloch was approaching the town to seize public property. When asked by one of his officers under what circumstances Federal troops would be allowed to open fire, Twiggs insisted that "he would not be the first to shed blood." On reflection he changed his mind, instructing the men that they could fire only if state troops attempted to take their weapons.[30]

Before dawn on 16 February, McCulloch brought his Texans into town. Although all Federal soldiers were put on alert, they were also ordered to stay indoors. Seeing no sign of resistance, McCulloch's men began trying to get into the ordnance building; they demanded that the soldiers in the building turn over their arms. When approached by Brevet Major Larkin Smith, McCulloch warned that he could not control his men much longer and suggested that some kind of arrangement be made quickly. Twiggs arrived at his headquarters at the Alamo soon after and found it surrounded.[31]

Twiggs had only 160 men in San Antonio. By the end of the day, McCulloch commanded 500 state troops and 150 Knights of the Golden Circle. Still more Texas troops were on the way. McCulloch placed these men around the Plaza as well as the Alamo. When Twiggs arrived at headquarters, he and his adjutant, Nichols, approached McCulloch, who demanded that all Federal troops leave Texas without their arms. The men would rather be shot, observed Twiggs; further, he would rather die than damage their honor.[32]

The negotiations then moved from the street to the conference room in which Twiggs had met with the original commissioners, now returned. Everyone was concerned about hostilities accidentally erupting because of jittery men on both sides. Twiggs wanted to move his men to a camp outside of town away from the Texas soldiers. The commissioners were fearful of some sort of trick and would allow the move only if Twiggs gave his word that under no circumstances would the men leave the camp except to move to the coast. At about

---

30. Report of Lieut. Col. William Hoffman, 1 March 1861, in *Official Records*, 1:517.

31. "General Twiggs's Surrender to the Texans," *Harper's Weekly*, 23 March 1861, p. 182, quoted from *Galveston News*, 22 February 1861; Twiggs to Thomas, 19 February 1861, Brevet Maj. Larkin Smith to Col. William Hoffman, 23 February 1861, Capt. John H. King to Hoffman, 1 March 1861, *Official Records*, series 2, 1:2, 10–12.

32. Commissioners to Roberts, 2 March 1861, in Winkler, *Journal of the Secession Convention*, 282; "General Twiggs's Surrender to the Texans," *Harper's Weekly*, 23 March 1861, p. 182, quoted from *Galveston News*, 22 February 1861; Harold B . Simpson, *Frontier Forts of Texas* (Waco: Texian Press, 1966), 181; Rupert Norvall Richardson, *The Frontier of Northwest Texas, 1846–1876* (Glendale, CA: Arthur Clark Company, 1963), 227.

3:00 P.M. Twiggs agreed to these conditions. This point sealed, Twiggs also agreed to surrender Federal property in San Antonio. Then negotiations abruptly broke down. One witness later reported that the meeting became heated. Disagreement centered on what to do about light artillery batteries, the exit route Federal troops would take from the state, and whether all Federal troops would be allowed to retain their weapons. In principle, Twiggs viewed the light batteries as being to artillerists what small arms were to infantry. He was willing to compromise, however, by accepting the commissioners' demand that the men leave via the coast rather than march overland. But he stubbornly refused to surrender the light batteries or the small arms. Later in the day the commission sent a note to Twiggs, asking why it had not heard from him and advising him to surrender if he wanted to avoid a collision.[33]

The following day reports had undoubtedly reached the commissioners that Waite, almost at San Antonio, might arrive at any time. It was also apparent that Twiggs would not budge on the arms issue, since he reiterated in a note that it would be a disgrace to the United States Army, and therefore unthinkable, for him to agree to such a demand. The commissioners, aware that Waite would probably never surrender, agreed to Twiggs's terms. Not until the morning of the eighteenth did they reach final agreement on all of the remaining posts. The presence in town by that time of 1,100 Texas volunteers, facing Twiggs's 160 regulars, probably facilitated the negotiations.[34]

Once the agreement became official, both sides issued a flurry of instructions. The commissioners immediately announced in a circular that Federal troops were to leave Texas by the coast and were to take small arms, light artillery, camp equipment, and provisions. Everyone in Texas was to respect this agreement. For his part Twiggs immediately ordered his men to march to the coast to avoid any collision with Texas troops. The men were to evacuate all posts and would be allowed to take only specifically named items with them. He cautioned them to be on the alert for an attack from anyone, just in case some state troops decided that the commissioners' terms were too liberal.[35]

Some Federal officers, rather than surrender the posts to the Texas authorities, wanted to resist by joining together and marching north. Such officers and

---

33. Twiggs to L. Thomas, 19 February 1861, Report of Lieut. Col. William Hoffman, 1 March 1861, Report of Surgeon E. H. Abadie, n.d., in *Official Records,* series 2, 1:2, 10, and series 1, 1:517; commissioners to Twiggs, 17 February 1861, in Winkler, *Journal of the Secession Convention,* 294.

34. Twiggs to commissioners, 18 February 1861, commissioners to Twiggs, 18 February 1861, commissioners to Robertson, 18 February 1861, in *Official Records,* series 2, 1:5, 32–34.

35. Circular of commissioners, 18 February 1861; General Orders, no. 5, by order of Twiggs, 18 February 1861, both in ibid., series 2, 1:6, and series 1, 1:515–516.

men, however, were so small a minority that the plan was no more than a fantasy. A number of other officers and men immediately resigned from Federal service, joined the Texas forces, and helped to effect the transfer of Federal property to Texas authorities.[36]

Twiggs's main concern at this point was getting his official affairs in order. He began issuing reports and letters explaining why he had surrendered the posts. Twiggs also had to make provision for the men under his immediate supervision in San Antonio, and he had to prepare the men there, the first to surrender, for their march to the coast. All staff officers were ordered to report to their bureau chiefs in Washington, D.C.[37]

The following day, 19 February, Waite arrived in San Antonio, and Twiggs relinquished command. Waite wished to rescind the surrender but quickly realized that if he tried to bring the men together to resist, Texas forces would be able to isolate small groups before a rendezvous could be effected. Instead, he began protesting to the commissioners, complaining that state authorities had seized more than was covered by the agreement, particularly money that had arrived to pay the troops. Aside from these complaints, however, Waite cooperated with state authorities, issuing orders to the various posts to begin marching the men to the coast.[38]

Once these evacuations began, negotiations were conducted between local state commanders and Federal officers at the various posts. Colonel H. E. McCulloch of the state troops reported to the Committee of Public Safety that he was able to arrange much more satisfactory terms with the commander at Camp Colorado, future Confederate general Edmund Kirby Smith, than those reached in San Antonio with Twiggs. He lamented that he could do quite well for the state if he were not hindered by the San Antonio agreement.[39]

No matter how hard a bargain state officials believed Twiggs had driven, it was impossible to convince the nation that Twiggs had not intended to surrender Texas from the moment he had resumed command in December. The Federal government, through inaction and vacillation, had allowed a significant

---

36. Price, *Across the Continent,* 282; commissioners to Robertson, 18 February 1861, in *Official Records,* series 2, 1:32–34.

37. Special Orders, no. 27, by order of Twiggs, 18 February 1861, in *Official Records,* series 2, 1:6.

38. Report of Waite, 26 February 1861; General Orders, no. 6, by order of Twiggs, 19 February 1861; General Orders, no. 7, 19 February 1861; Waite to commissioners, 21 February 1861; Special Orders, no. 32, by order of Waite, 24 February 1861, all in ibid., series 1, 1:521, 591, 525–526, and series 2, 1:7; Carl Coke Rister, *Robert E. Lee in Texas* (Norman: University of Oklahoma Press, 1946), 160.

39. McCulloch to Roberts, 25 February 1861, in *Official Records,* 53:638.

amount of Federal property to fall into the hands of secessionists. Undoubtedly, the surrender of Federal property, amounting to nineteen posts and equipment valued at $1,300,000, was a blow, but it was hardly the first Federal property to fall into the hands of secessionists. Someone had to be blamed, however, and what better person to blame than an avowed southern sympathizer? For his action in Texas, Twiggs was dismissed from the service on 1 March.[40]

Given the situation in Texas and Twiggs's own determination to avoid hostilities, the question at the time should have been and still should be, did he have a choice? Moreover, did the administration of James Buchanan really want him to resist? Doubtless Twiggs intended to surrender; he certainly told enough people so, including the highest ranking people in the Army and War Department. But he was never instructed not to surrender, nor was he told to hold on to the bitter end. Waite was never given such instructions either. In fact, Waite was told that if Texas seceded he was immediately to march all Federal troops in Texas to Fort Leavenworth.[41] If the government had planned all along to abandon these posts in Texas, why was Twiggs not given these instructions?

Secretary of War Joseph Holt stated that Twiggs was dismissed because of "treachery to the flag of his country, in having surrendered, on the 18th of February, 1861, on the demand of the authorities of Texas, the military posts and other property of the United States in his department and under his charge."[42] The actual surrender had taken place less than two weeks before the issuance of this dismissal. Had these men gathered enough evidence in that time to prove treachery, or were they acting quickly to avoid criticism of the government's mishandling of the situation?

The evidence used to condemn Twiggs then and that used by historians since consists of a variety of speculations about his motives in surrendering the posts in Texas. He has been likened to Judas Iscariot and Benedict Arnold for doing openly what he had told everyone he would do. Some of his accusers even believed that he had come back to Texas with the sole purpose of surrendering, that he was part of a secessionist plot to take Federal property in Texas. He was accused of scattering his men at posts all over the state so that at the crucial moment they would be unable to come together to resist the rebellion, an accusation that overlooked the men's reason for being in Texas, which was to guard

---

40. "General Twiggs to His Troops," *Harper's Weekly*, 9 March 1861, p. 151; J. G. Randall and David Herbert Donald, *The Civil War and Reconstruction* (2nd rev. ed.; Lexington, MA: D. C. Heath and Company, 1969), 170; General Orders, no. 5, by order of Secretary of War Joseph Holt, 1 March 1861, in *Official Records*, 1:597.

41. L. Thomas to Waite, 15 February 1861, in *Official Records*, 1:589–590.

42. General Orders, no. 5, by order of Secretary of War Joseph Holt, 1 March 1861, ibid., 1:597.

the frontier against Indians. Even the most damning of Twiggs's statements, often used to prove his treachery, does nothing to contradict his oft-stated intention to surrender. He was quoted in early February by several people as saying that "if an old woman with a broomstick should come with full authority from the state of Texas to demand the public property, I would give it to her." The key phrase of course was "with full authority from the state of Texas."[43]

While Twiggs was roundly condemned in the North, he was generally perceived as a hero in the South. He was called "a true patriot" by a fellow Georgian even before he surrendered and was afterward praised by Braxton Bragg for having had the foresight to surrender before Waite assumed command. Later in the summer, after the first battle of Manassas (Bull Run), the *New Orleans Daily Picayune* hailed the surrender in Texas as one of the great events of the Confederacy. The legislature of the state of Georgia unanimously passed a resolution praising his conduct in Texas. The resolution went on to laud his bravery and patriotism throughout his career and to condemn what it called the fanatics of the North who were trying to besmirch his name.[44]

Not everyone in the South, however, considered his behavior patriotic. Ben McCulloch wrote to John H. Reagan, Confederate Postmaster General, that Twiggs was typical of the attitude of most soldiers in the Army in Texas because he would "do nothing to benefit the South." McCulloch, in fact, believed that Twiggs had betrayed the South by driving such a hard bargain with the state's commissioners; McCulloch thought Twiggs should have spent his time trying to recruit soldiers for the Confederacy before they left Texas.[45]

Once Twiggs had relinquished command to Waite, he began preparing to leave. The actions of Texas and of the Confederate government during and after his departure condemned Twiggs in all northern eyes. The state government was so grudging with transportation to the coast for the soldiers that not all officers and men had departed before the firing on Fort Sumter. When word of the war reached Texas, Confederate General Earl Van Dorn, a former Twiggs protégé,

43. Richard W. Johnson, *A Soldier's Reminiscences in Peace and War* (Philadelphia: J. B. Lippincott Company, 1886), 133–134; *New York Courier and Enquirer*, 29 May 1861, quoted in *Official Records*, series 2, 1:53–56; Albert G. Brackett, *History of the United States Cavalry, From the Formation of the Federal Government to the 1st of June, 1863* (reprint of 1865 ed.; New York: Greenwood Press, 1968), 208; "old woman" quote in Caroline Baldwin Darrow, "Recollections of the Twiggs Surrender," in Johnson and Buel, *Battles and Leaders*, 1:38.

44. John D. Stell to Joseph E. Brown, 11 February 1861, in Willard E. Wright (ed.), "A Letter n the Texas Secession Convention," *Southwestern Historical Quarterly*, 60 (October 1956): 291; Bragg to J. Davis, 25 February 1861, in *Official Records*, 1:608; *New Orleans Daily Picayune*, 10 August 1861; Georgia resolution, 9 March 1861, in *Official Records*, series 4, 1:135.

45. McCulloch to Reagan, 25 February 1861, *Official Records*, 1:609.

arrested the remaining Federal soldiers, including Colonel Waite, as prisoners of war. Although most of these men would eventually obtain paroles in exchange for promises not to fight for the duration of the war, to northern eyes it looked as if the original agreement had been violated. Before their release these prisoners were reputedly ill-clothed and ill-fed. To his credit, Twiggs pleaded with the Confederate War Department to allow him to feed and clothe them when a number of them passed through his new headquarters in New Orleans.[46]

It was entirely too late for him to win any friends or persuade anyone of his good intentions. Many in the North believed his name should "be stricken from the rolls of the army."[47] For the one remaining year of his life he would carry the appellation of "Traitor Twiggs" and ironically would live in fear of being captured by the United States Army. In fact, he would be remembered only for his actions of 18 February 1861 and not for his forty-nine years of service to the very army he now feared.

David Twiggs was in many ways a victim of circumstances. The same government that vacillated over the relief of Fort Sumter, wishing the problem would simply go away, allowed the situation to reach an explosive pitch before taking even the simplest action in Texas, and then after it was too late. Though the old, enfeebled Twiggs was certainly not blameless—there were other courses he could have chosen, from resignation to resistance—he should have shared the blame with a Federal government completely unprepared to meet the crisis.

---

46. *New York Courier and Enquirer,* 29 May 1861, quoted in ibid., 53–56; Twiggs to acting Confederate Secretary of War Judah P. Benjamin, 10 October 1861, ibid., series 2, 1:90.

47. "General Twiggs," *Harper's Weekly,* 9 March 1861, p. 158.

Sixth-plate ambrotype of Private Japhet Collins, Company D, "Bastrop County Rawhides," 12th Texas Cavalry, ca. 1861. *Courtesy Lawrence T. Jones III.*

"Rarin' for a Fight": Texans in the Confederate Army

RALPH A. WOOSTER AND ROBERT WOOSTER*

The outbreak of fighting at Fort Sumter in April 1861 caused great excitement in Texas. There was little difficulty in finding recruits for the Confederate army as men flocked to enlist. Within weeks military companies were formed in most Texas communities. Edward Clark, who had become governor after the secession convention declared the office vacant following Sam Houston's refusal to take an oath to support the Confederacy, worked with Brigadier General Earl Van Dorn, the newly appointed Confederate military commander for Texas, in enrolling, equipping, and training troops for the defense of the state. By the end of the year twenty-five thousand Texans were in the Confederate army.

Ralph A. Wooster, professor of history at Lamar University, Beaumont, and Robert Wooster, professor of history at Texas A&M University, Corpus Christi, trace the experiences of Texas Confederates from initial enlistment to final defeat in 1865. Using letters, journals, and diaries of common soldiers, the authors show that Texans went off to war with a wide-eyed innocence that was soon tempered by the violence and brutality of war.

* Ralph A. Wooster and Robert Wooster, "'Rarin' for a Fight': Texans in the Confederate Army," *Southwestern Historical Quarterly*, LXXXIV (Apr., 1981), 387–426.

In addition to the sources cited by the authors, including the pioneer study of Civil War soldiers by Bell I. Wiley, The Life of Johnny Reb: The Common Soldier of the Confederacy *(Indianapolis: Bobbs-Merrill Co., 1943), see Wiley,* The Life of Billy Yank: The Common Soldier of the Union *(Indianapolis: Bobbs-Merrill Co., 1951); James I. Robertson Jr.,* Soldiers Blue and Gray *(Columbia: University of South Carolina Press, 1988); Reid Mitchell,* Civil War Soldiers *(New York: Viking Press, 1988); and Larry J. Daniel,* Soldiering in the Army of Tennessee *(Chapel Hill: University of North Carolina Press, 1991).*

The firing on Ft. Sumter in April, 1861, released strong emotional feeling throughout the South. From the Potomac to the Rio Grande, thousands of young men volunteered for military service. In his study of the Confederate soldier in the Civil War, Bell I. Wiley notes that the man who was to become Johnny Reb was "rarin' for a fight." He cites a young volunteer from Arkansas who, feeling "like ten thousand pins were pricking me in every part of the body," left his community for the war front "a week in advance of his brothers."[1]

Many young Texans were also "rarin' for a fight" in the spring of 1861. William A. Fletcher, of Beaumont, was working on the roof of a two-story house when informed of the firing on Ft. Sumter. The news made Fletcher "very nervous thinking the delay of completing the roof might cause me to miss a chance to enlist. . . ." Finding no local military units being formed, he boarded a flatcar heading toward Houston to find a way of enlisting. Once in Houston he again found no companies being organized. So impatient was he to enlist he went to Galveston the following day, but found conditions there similar to Houston. He took a steamboat to Liberty, and finally persuaded the commander of a company being formed there to allow him to enlist.[2]

Most Texans experienced less difficulty than Fletcher in joining military units. By late spring companies were being formed in almost every community. Often these units were organized by local political leaders or by professional men with little military knowledge or background. The lack of weapons, ammunition, and other equipment often bewildered even those with previous military experience.[3]

---

1. Bell Irvin Wiley, *The Life of Johnny Reb: The Common Soldier of the Confederacy* (1943; reprint ed., New York, 1952), 15.

2. William A. Fletcher, *Rebel Private, Front and Rear* (1908; reprint ed., Austin, 1954), 6 (quotation), 7.

3. Allen C. Ashcraft, "Texas, 1860–1866: The Lone Star State in the Civil War" (Ph.D. diss., Columbia University, 1960), 74–77.

During the first few weeks, the companies drilled, received new members, and attended an endless round of public ceremonies featuring patriotic address-es by local dignitaries and veterans of the Texas Revolution and Mexican War. Ordinarily the speakers praised the South's determination to resist northern ag-gression and predicted quick victory for southern arms, but occasionally a more somber note was sounded. Ralph J. Smith, a private in Company K of the Sec-ond Texas Infantry, reported that deposed governor Sam Houston, a foe of se-cession, warned members of his company that they did not know what they were doing. Smith reported Houston's caution that "the resources of the north were almost exhaustless." He concluded, however, that the words of the old hero of San Jacinto had no effect: "He might as well had been giving advice to the inmates of a lunatic asylum. We knew no such words as fail."[4]

Many of the recruits received their military instruction, such as it was, in their local communities. Others were trained in one of the military camps creat-ed by Governor Edward Clark. Many of these, such as Camp Berlin, located near Brenham; Camp Honey Springs, on the west bank of Honey Creek near Dallas; and Camp Roberts, in Smith County, were primarily mustering or ren-dezvous stations. Others, such as Camp Bosque, seven miles from Waco; Camp

---

It should be noted that most Texans were initially recruited or enrolled in a company of infantry, a troop of cavalry, or a battery of artillery. These units, consisting of approximately one hundred men, and commanded by a captain, were later formed into regiments commanded by a colonel. The authorized strength of a Civil War regiment was ten companies, or approximately one thou-sand men, but some regiments, such as the First Texas, had twelve companies. A varying number of regiments formed a brigade, usually commanded by a brigadier general. Two to five brigades formed a division, normally commanded in Confederate service by a major general. Two or more divisions were combined to form an army corps, commanded by a lieutenant general. Two or more corps made up an army, usually commanded by a full general.

Some artillery batteries and cavalry troops were also organized into battalions. Composed of three or four batteries or troops, battalions were usually commanded by lieutenant colonels.

Most larger military units in Confederate service were known by the name of their commanding officer; e.g., Hood's Brigade was named for John Bell Hood, one of its early commanders. Most, but not all, regiments were designated by a number, e.g., Second Texas Infantry. In this paper, reference to such names as the Second Texas Infantry implies a regimental designation. For more on Civil War military organization, see Mark Mayo Boatner, III, *The Civil War Dictionary* (New York, 1959), 610–613.

For organizational histories of various Texas units, see Harry McCory Henderson, *Texas in the Confederacy* (San Antonio, 1955), and Lester N. Fitzhugh, *Texas Batteries, Battalions, Regiments, Commanders and Field Officers, Confederate States Army, 1861–1865* (Midlothian, Tex., 1959).

4. Ralph J. Smith, *Reminiscences of the Civil War and Other Sketches* (reprint ed., Waco, Tex., 1962), 2.

Clark, on the San Marcos River; and Camp Van Dorn, on Buffalo Bayou near Harrisburg, were larger camps where military instruction was received.[5]

One of the highlights of early military life for most Texas volunteers was the presentation of either the Confederate or the unit flag by local townspeople. This ceremony, which usually occurred when the company left for training camp or for the eastern theater of military operations, was "the last act of the farewell drama" and often was "a solemn affair." Albert B. Blocker, youthful bugler of the Third Texas Cavalry, recalled that his company, known as the Texas Hunters, received its flag at Jonesville on May 1, 1861. Miss Eudora Perry presented the handsome flag, made by the ladies of Harrison County, to the company before hundreds of citizens who had come to view the festivities. Patriotic speeches, parades, and a barbecue made the day one that young Blocker would not forget.[6]

An equally enthusiastic flag presentation and send-off was given the Henderson Guards of the Fourth Texas Infantry. Before leaving for Camp Van Dorn, the Guards assembled at the town of Fincastle, in southern Henderson County. Here, before hundreds of onlookers, the company commander, Captain William K. ("Howdy") Martin, received a beautiful homemade Confederate flag presented by Miss Ann Tindel. The flag was hoisted to the top of a 120-foot pine pole while Martin, a noted stump speaker, delivered a powerful oration with a "voice like thunder" and with a look like "he was mad enough to eat a Yankee raw."[7]

The Texas soldiers who marched off to war in 1861 wore a wide variety of uniforms. Val C. Giles, of the Fourth Texas Infantry, noted that no two companies had uniforms alike when his regiment was organized in the spring of that year. "We were a motley-looking set, but as a rule comfortably dressed," he later wrote. "In my company we had about four different shades of gray, but the trimmings were all of black braid." Jim Turner, of the Sixth Texas Infantry,

---

5. Bill Winsor, *Texas in the Confederacy: Military Installations, Economy and People* (Hillsboro, Tex., 1978), 8–38; Harold B. Simpson, *Hood's Texas Brigade: Lee's Grenadier Guard* (Waco, Tex., 1970), 20–21, 34–35.

6. Simpson, *Hood's Texas Brigade: Lee's Grenadier Guard*, 27 (quotations); Max S. Lale, "The Boy-Bugler of the Third Texas Cavalry: The A. B. Blocker Narrative," *Military History of Texas and the Southwest*, XIV (No. 2), 73.

7. J. J. Faulk, *History of Henderson County, Texas* (Athens, Tex., 1929), 129. For other descriptions of flag ceremonies see Charles Spurlin (ed.), *West of the Mississippi with Waller's 13th Texas Cavalry Battalion, CSA* (Hillsboro, 1971), 28; *Texas Republican* (Marshall), Apr. 27, June 1, 1861; O. T. Hanks, "History of B. F. Benton's Company, or Account of Civil War Experiences," 2–3, O. T. Hanks, Reminiscences, 1861–1862 (Archives, University of Texas Library, Austin); Jim Turner, "Jim Turner, Co. G, 6th Texas Infantry, C.S.A., From 1861 to 1865," *Texana*, Xll (No. 2, 1974), 150.

pointed out that in his regiment the uniforms were of "a dark pepper and salt grey color, and were trimmed with green." The First Texas Infantry wore dark uniforms with bright red stripes, while the men of Company E, Fourth Texas Infantry, sported uniforms of imported gray cloth trimmed in blue.[8]

A wide assortment of colors and materials was found among cavalry units recruited in Texas. Stephen B. Oates notes that trousers of the typical cavalryman were either gray woolen jeans or plaid woolen jeans, but that Captain Sam Richardson of the Walter P. Lane Rangers wore exotic leopard-skin pants. Coats were both single- and doublebreasted, with a variety of color and style. The hats of Texas soldiers, both infantry and cavalry, were generally wide-brimmed felt, or gray caps with visors. Many Texans, especially those from South Texas, preferred the Mexican sombrero.[9]

The weapons carried by Texas Confederates varied even more than their uniforms. Although regulations called for sabers and carbines, most cavalry units were equipped with shotguns, rifles, Bowie knives, and Colt revolvers. Theophilus Noel noted that when Henry H. Sibley's Brigade left San Antonio in 1861, the men were "armed with squirrel-guns, bear guns, sportman's-guns, shot-guns, both single and double barrels, in fact, guns of all sorts. . . ." The double-barreled shotgun was a weapon particularly favored by the Eighth Cavalry, a unit better known as Terry's Texas Rangers.[10]

Texas soldiers were given much freedom in choosing their weapons. O. T. Hanks, of the Fourth Infantry, recalled that:

evry fellow [was] equiped as he considered with the best Accounterments of war. There Arms Consisting of Almost evry Conceivable Kind of Gun that Could be Colected in the Country. . . . Our Bayonets were Butcher Knives Made by our Black Smiths out of Old files[.] Some were about 12 Inches long [and] $1\frac{1}{2}$ Inches wide[.] Others were 16 or 18 Inches long [and] abut 3 Inches wide. . . . Some Nice Jobs, others not, all owing to the taste of the person[.][11]

---

8. Mary Lasswell (comp. and ed.), *Rags and Hope: The Recollections of Val C. Giles, Four Years with Hood's Brigade, Fourth Texas Infantry* (New York, 1961), 23; Turner, "Co. G, 6th Texas Infantry," 150; Simpson, *Hood's Texas Brigade: Lee's Grenadier Guard,* 16–18.

9. Stephen B. Oates, *Confederate Cavalry West of the River* (Austin, 1961), 60–61; Bruce Marshall, "Night Sentinel: Texas Confederate Cavalry," *Military History of Texas and the Southwest,* X (No. 3, 1972), 157–158; Bruce Marshall, "Border Confederate," ibid., X (No. 4, 1972), 223–224.

10. Oates, *Confederate Cavalry,* 62–65; Marshall, "Confederate Cavalry," 157; Marshall, "Border Confederate," 223–224; Theo. Noel, *A Campaign from Santa Fe to the Mississippi* (Shreveport, 1865), 8; Leonidas B. Giles, *Terry's Texas Rangers* (Austin, 1911), 12–13; C. C. Jeffries, *Terry's Rangers* (New York, 1961), 19–20.

11. Hanks, "History of B. F. Benton's Company," 4–5.

When the Third Texas Cavalry was sent to Arkansas, one company was armed with rifles, two companies with shotguns, and one company with Minie carbines, while 110 men were supplied with Mississippi rifles and 150 with Sharps' rifles.[12]

Frequently Texans overburdened themselves with equipment and clothing as they rode or marched off to war. C. C. Cox took two saddle horses, two wagon horses, a wagon, side arms, medicines, bedding, camp utensils, and a black boy when he left his ranch near Indianola heading for the army.[13] William W. Heartsill, of the Lane Rangers, recalled that when he embarked for war in April, 1861, his horse "Pet" was carrying the following:

> myself, saddle, bridle, saddle-blanket, curry comb, horse brush, coffee pot, tin cup, 20 lbs ham, 200 biscuit, 5 lbs ground coffee, 5 lbs sugar, one large pound cake presented to me by Mrs C E Talley, 6 shirts, 6 prs socks, 3 prs drawers, 2 prs pants, 2 jackets, 1 pr heavy mud boots, one Colt's revolver, one small dirk, four blankets, sixty feet of rope, with a twelve inch iron pin attached; with all these, and divers and sundry little mementoes from friends.[14]

By the end of 1861 approximately 25,000 Texans were enrolled in the Confederate army. Fully two-thirds of these were in the cavalry, as Texans showed a decided preference for mounted service.[15] Sixteen regiments, three battalions, and three independent companies of cavalry were raised in Texas the first year of the war. Four of the regiments recruited that year, the Second Mounted Rifles, the Fourth Cavalry, the Fifth Cavalry, and the Seventh Cavalry, took part in Henry H. Sibley's ill-fated invasion of New Mexico Territory in late 1861 and early

---

12. Galveston *Weekly News*, Sept. 3, 1861. Julius Giesecke noted that his unit, Company G, Fourth Texas Cavalry, was originally equipped with spears, which they exchanged for guns in December, 1861. See Oscar Haas (trans.), "The Diary of Julius Giesecke, 1861–1862," *Texas Military History*, III (Winter, 1963), 233.

13. "Reminiscences of C. C. Cox, II," *Southwestern Historical Quarterly*, VI (Jan., 1903), 217.

14. William W. Heartsill, *Fourteen Hundred and 91 Days in the Confederate Army; or, Camp Life, Day by Day, of the W. P. Lane Rangers from April 19, 1861, to May 20, 1865*, ed. Bell I. Wiley (1876; reprint ed., Jackson, Tenn., 1954), 5.

15. The British traveler Lieutenant Colonel Arthur Fremantle of the Coldstream Guards noted this affinity of Texans for the cavalry. "At the outbreak of the war," he observed, "it was found very difficult to raise infantry in Texas, as no Texan walks a yard if he can help it." Arthur James L. Fremantle, *The Fremantle Diary,: Being the Journal of Lieutenant Colonel James Arthur Lyon Fremantle, Coldstream Guards, on His Three Months in the Southern States*, ed. Walter Lord (1863; reprint ed., Boston, 1954), 58. See also "Message of Edward Clark to the Texas Senate and House of Representatives," Nov. 1, 1861, *The War of the Rebellion: A Compilation of the Official Records of the Union and Confederate Armies* (Washington, D.C., 1880–1901), Series IV, Vol I, 716. (This work is cited hereafter as *Official Records*.)

1862. Wealthy sugar planter Benjamin F. Terry raised the most famous of all the mounted Texas units, the Eighth Cavalry, or Terry's Texas Rangers. The Rangers were originally scheduled for service in Virginia, but the need for additional troops in Kentucky resulted in the regiment being assigned to join Albert Sidney Johnston's command in that state.[16]

Even though Texans preferred cavalry service, seven regiments and four battalions of infantry were recruited in the Lone Star State in 1861. Three of these regiments, the First, Fourth, and Fifth, were ordered to Virginia in the fall of the year and there became part of the Texas Infantry Brigade, commanded first by Louis T. Wigfall and later by John Bell Hood. As Hood's Texas Brigade, the unit distinguished itself at Gaines' Mill, Second Manassas, Sharpsburg, and Gettysburg.[17]

The majority of Texans who enrolled in the Confederate army were in their early twenties. The median age of privates in Sibley's Brigade, for example, was 22 years at the time of enlistment. The three youngest privates of the brigade were J. D. Adams, B. F. Edens, and R. H. Horn, all age 16. R. J. Hill, age 59 years, was the oldest private in the brigade.[18]

---

16. Oates, *Confederate Cavalry,* 5–29; J. K. P. Blackburn, "Reminiscences of the Terry Rangers," *Southwestern Historical Quarterly,* XXII (July, 1918), 41–42; Oates, "Recruiting Confederate Cavalry in Texas," ibid., LXIV (Apr., 1961), 463–477. For the story of Sibley's Brigade, see the following works by Martin Hardwick Hall: "The Formation of Sibley's Brigade and the March to New Mexico," ibid., LXI (Jan., 1958), 383–405, *Sibley's New Mexico Campaign* (Austin, 1960); and *The Confederate Army of New Mexico* (Austin, 1978). An independent company was one that did not form part of an organized battalion.

17. The Eighteenth Georgia Infantry Regiment joined the three Texas regiments to form the brigade. J. B. Polley, *Hood's Texas Brigade: Its Marches, Its Battles, Its Achievements* (New York, 1910), 13. Polley, *Hood's Texas Brigade,* Mrs. A. V. Winkler, *The Confederate Capital and Hood's Texas Brigade* (Austin, 1894), and Donald E. Everett (ed.), *Chaplain Davis and Hood's Texas Brigade* (San Antonio, 1962), are the standard older accounts of the Texas brigade. The definitive modern work is the multivolume series by Colonel Harold B. Simpson: *Hood's Texas Brigade: Lee's Grenadier Guard; Hood's Texas Brigade in Poetry and Song* (Waco, Tex., 1968); *Hood's Texas Brigade in Reunion and Memory* (Waco, Tex., 1974); and *Hood's Texas Brigade: A Compendium* (Waco, Tex., 1977).

18. This information is based upon a study of ages in muster rolls of First, Fourth, and Fifth regiments as given in Hall, *Sibley's New Mexico Campaign,* 236–317.
The age breakdown for privates in the brigade was as follows:

Age	Number
Under 20	483
20–24	828
25–29	325
30–35	171
Over 35	77
	1,884

Noncommissioned and commissioned officers were slightly older. The median age for 240 noncommissioned officers in Sibley's Brigade was 26 years, while that for the commissioned officers was 27 years. The brigade's youngest noncommissioned officer was First Corporal Edward A. Leach, age 17, a member of K Company, Fifth Cavalry. Oldest noncommissioned officers were sergeants E. S. R. Patton and Charles Pate, both age 57. Joseph D. Sayers, age 19 years, staff officer in the Fifth Cavalry and future governor of Texas, was the youngest commissioned officer in the brigade. G. W. Eaton, second lieutenant, Seventh Texas Cavalry, age 56 years, was the oldest commissioned officer.[19]

Muster rolls indicate the majority of soldiers in other units were similar in age, if slightly older, to those in Sibley's Brigade. Median age for the 304 privates in Hood's Brigade whose ages were listed on muster rolls was 24 years. For 396 privates in Edward Waller's Thirteenth Texas Cavalry Battalion it was 25 years. Again, officers were generally older than privates.[20]

In the early days of the war the army discharged many soldiers for being under or over the regulation age limits of eighteen and thirty-five. A. B. Blocker, who enlisted as a bugler in the Third Cavalry at the age of sixteen, reported that the army discharged him and two others in 1862 for being too young. A fourth man was discharged at the same time for being over thirty-five. Harold B. Simpson notes that the First Texas Infantry released sixty–three men, including fifteen men in K Company alone, in the summer and fall of 1862 for being under or over age.[21]

Probably 80 percent of the Confederate soldiers from Texas were of English, Welsh, and Scottish stock, the majority being born in the southern United States. Even so, many other nationalities were represented in the ranks of Texas

---

19. Ibid.

20. These figures and conclusions are based upon muster rolls given in Simpson, *Hood's Texas Brigade: A Compendium,* 10–250; Spurlin (ed.), *West of the Mississippi,* 66–92. The median enlistment ages here are similar to the 23–year median enlistment age for the post-Civil War army. See Don Rickey, Jr., *Forty Miles a Day on Beans and Hay: The Enlisted Soldier Fighting the Indian Wars* (Norman, 1963), 17. Median ages of 23–25 years were found for Texas Confederates in Captain J. Duff Brown's Company of Thomas X. Waul's Legion, Captain Augustus C. Allen's Company of Richard Waterhouse's Regiment, Captain Edward M. Alexander's Company of Henry E. McCulloch's Regiment, Captain William H. Christian's Company of Oran M. Roberts' Regiment, and Captain Hiram S. Childress's Company of Nicholas H. Darnell's Regiment. See the muster rolls for these companies in the Archives Division, Texas State Library, Austin. Jerry Don Thompson, *Vaqueros in Blue & Gray* (Austin, 1976), 7, reports that the average age for Mexican American soldiers in the Civil War was 28 years.

21. Lale, "A. B. Blocker Narrative," Part III, *Military History of Texas and the Southwest,* XV (No. 1), 22; Simpson, *Hood's Texas Brigade: A Compendium,* 549. As the war continued, the age limits were expanded by Confederate conscription acts to cover men age seventeen through fifty.

regiments. Harold Simpson estimates that 5.0 percent of the troops in Hood's Brigade were Germans, 4.4 percent were Irish, and 1.6 percent were French. He also notes that Jews, Mexicans, Dutch, Indians, and one Indian, Ike Batisse, served in Hood's regiments. Company F, First Texas Heavy Artillery Regiment, the unit that successfully defended Sabine Pass in 1863, was made up of Irishmen recruited in Houston. The Third Texas Infantry, mustered in South Texas, contained many Mexicans and Germans; its executive officer, Lieutenant Colonel Augustus Buchel, was a native of the Rhineland. A career soldier, Buchel had also served in the Mexican and Crimean wars. He was commanding the First Texas Cavalry when killed at Pleasant Hill, Louisiana, in April, 1864.[22]

Although many Texas Germans opposed secession, large numbers of Germans served in Confederate units from Texas. Company G of the Fourth Texas Cavalry, Company B of the Seventh Texas Cavalry, and Company E of the First Texas Cavalry were almost entirely German. Waul's Legion, organized near Brenham in the summer of 1863 and commanded by Colonel Thomas N. Waul, had a sizeable number of Germans, as did also companies B and F of Terry's Rangers.[23]

Many of the Silesians who formed the tiny Polish colony in Texas preferred not to become involved in America's civil conflict. None of them owned slaves, and many had left Europe to avoid military conscription. Even so, a company commanded by Captain Joseph Kyrisk and known as the Panna Maria Grays was mustered for Confederate service in Karnes County. Other Silesians served with the Sixth Texas Infantry and the Twenty-fourth Texas Cavalry in the unsuccessful defense of Arkansas Post in 1863.[24]

Over 2,500 Mexican-Americans from Texas served in the Confederate army. Santos Benavides, former mayor of Laredo, was the best known of these Mexican Texans, or Tejanos, who wore the gray. Most of the men who served under Benavides, including his brothers Refugio and Christoval, were Tejanos

---

22. Simpson, *Hood's Texas Brigade: A Compendium*, 547; Ella Lonn, *Foreigners in the Confederacy* (Chapel Hill, 1940), 193–194, 500–501; Andrew Forest Muir, "Dick Dowling and the Battle of Sabine Pass," *Civil War History*, IV (Dec., 1958), 405–406, 417, 421–422.

23. Hall, *Sibley's New Mexico Campaign*, 240–243, 249–251, 285–287; Lonn, *Foreigners in the Confederacy*, 124–126, 500–501.

24. Lonn, *Foreigners in the Confederacy*, 128; T. Lindsay Baker, *The First Polish Americans: Silesian Settlements in Texas* (College Station, Tex., 1979), 64–77. Baker notes that information on the Silesian participation in the Civil War is limited and scattered. He points out that the muster rolls for the Panna Maria Grays list only four Silesians.

recruited along the Rio Grande. The Third and Eighth Texas Infantry had large numbers of Tejanos.[25]

As noted above, at least one Indian, Ike Battise, was in Hood's Texas Brigade. Chief John Scott and nineteen Alabama braves served with the Twenty-fourth Texas Cavalry in Arkansas during 1862. Later in the war over one hundred Alabama Indians were organized into an unattached cavalry company; they operated flat-bottom boats transporting farm products on the Trinity River to Confederate forces stationed along the Gulf Coast.[26]

Although most of the Texans who marched off to war were farmers or the sons of farmers, almost every occupation was represented in the ranks, which comprised laborers, planters, merchants, mechanics, students, clerks, carpenters, blacksmiths, teachers, brickmasons, painters, shoemakers, tailors, overseers, and shopkeepers. Numerous physicians enlisted, oftentimes as private soldiers.[27] One Civil War veteran was struck by the number of lawyers in his regiment, particularly by the number who were officers:

> Of the ten original captains who went to Virginia with the Fourth Texas Regiment in 1861, six of them were lawyers. . . . Of the thirty lieutenants, nearly one-third were lawyers. . . . Lawyers in war are like lawyers in peace, they go for all that's in sight. They held the best places in the army and they hold the best places in civil life. It's a mighty cold day when a lawyer gets left if chicken pie is on the bill of fare.[28]

With the passage of time, recruitment of soldiers became more difficult as the early enthusiasm for military service waned. Governor Edward Clark found meeting the repeated calls by Richmond authorities for additional troops to be a more serious problem each month. Passage of the first of several conscription laws by the Confederate Congress in April, 1862, momentarily gave impetus to volunteering, but, according to Bell Wiley, "it was of a spiritless sort, occasioned primarily by the desire of men subject to conscription to escape the odium attached to forced service." Clark's successors as governor, Francis R. Lubbock and Pendleton Murrah, found the task of enrolling soldiers even more difficult. Distaste for any form of military discipline and routine, the desire to remain at home with friends and loved ones, the possibility of obtaining occupational ex-

---

25. Thompson, *Vaqueros in Blue & Gray*, 5–6, 8, 17–23, 26–28, 45–49, 81; Thompson, "Mexican-Americans in the Civil War: The Battle of Valverde," *Texana*, X (No. 1, 1972), 1–19.

26. Howard N. Martin, "Texas Redskins in Confederate Gray," *Southwestern Historical Quarterly*, LXX (Apr., 1967), 586–592.

27. There were eleven physicians serving as privates in Hood's Brigade alone. Simpson, *Hood's Texas Brigade: A Compendium*, 552.

28. Lasswell (comp. and ed.), *Rags and Hope*, 48.

emption or hiring a substitute, and a growing dissatisfaction with policies of the Confederate government were all factors that contributed to the problem of enrolling troops.[29]

Governor Francis R. Lubbock reported to the legislature in November, 1863, that the number of Texans who had shouldered arms for the Confederacy then numbered about ninety thousand. Because of duplications and errors in reporting, the exact number of Texans who served in the Confederate army is not likely to be ascertained. The 1860 federal census lists 92,145 white males between the ages of eighteen and forty-five years living in the state. In view of the fact that many Texans both younger and older than these ages served, and assuming a normal population growth during the next four years, Texas had a potential force of between 100,000 and 110,000 men to send to war.[30]

Soldiers recruited early in the war anxiously awaited combat and became impatient with the delays in getting into action. Captain James P. Douglas, of the Third Cavalry, wrote to his girl friend in October, 1861, "we will in all probability have a fight soon. The boys are manifesting great joy at the prospect of an engagement, as I write (8 o'clock P.M.) they are talking and laughing merrily, and singing war songs around me." Another Texan, Ralph J. Smith of the Second Infantry, reported in March, 1862, that "after months of impatient waiting we were ordered to the front. At last a thousand hearts beat happily."[31]

Texans reacted to their first taste of battle in a variety of ways. George Lee Robertson, a corporal in Hood's Brigade, who participated in the Seven Days Battles around Richmond in the summer of 1862, was pleased that the fighting had not frightened him. "Well Ma," he wrote on July 12, "this is the third battle I have been in and have not yet been scared, which has surprised me very much." William A. Fletcher admitted that when he first went into battle he was suffering from diarrhea and "had quite a great fear that something disgraceful might happen . . . but to my surprise the excitement, or something else, had effected a cure." Ralph Smith remembered his first combat at Shiloh as being

---

29. Wiley, *Johnny Reb*, 124–125 (quotation); Fredericka Ann Meiners, "The Texas Governorship, 1861–1865: Biography of an Office" (Ph.D. diss., Rice University, 1975), 32–38, 45–47, 59–65, 104–105, 124–132, 135–138, 197–198, 226–230, 289–301.

30. Clement A. Evans (ed.), *Confederate Military History* (12 vols.; Atlanta, 1899), XI, 141; Stephen B. Oates, "Texas Under the Secessionists," *Southwestern Historical Quarterly*, LXVII (Oct., 1953), 187. Robert P. Felgar, "Texas in the War for Southern Independence, 1861–1865" (Ph.D. diss., University of Texas, 1935), 106, estimates that only fifty to sixty thousand Texans served in the Confederate army.

31. Lucia Rutherford Douglas (comp. and ed.), *Douglas's Texas Battery, CSA* (Tyler, Tex., 1966), 12 (first quotation); Smith, *Reminiscences of the Civil War*, 2 (second quotation).

very confusing. "In great battles with thousands on each side, especially privates, are like little screws in the wheel of a giant machine," he wrote. "All I remember for the first few minutes after was a terrible noise[,] great smoke, incessant rattling of small arms, infernal confusion and then I realized that the whole line of the enemy was in disorderly retreat."[32]

The brutalities of war drew comment from some Texans. After the battle of Wilson's Creek in Missouri in August, 1861, John J. Good wrote his wife, "men ride over the Battlefield and laugh at what would once shock them. . . ." W. W. Heartsill, of the Lane Rangers, remembered that during maneuvers on the night following the first day of fighting at Chickamauga, the Confederates "literally walked on dead men all night," and that, while the camp fires flickered rays over the battlefield, "the scene [looked] horrible, hundreds of ghastly corpse[s] mangled and torn. . . ."[33]

Val C. Giles of the Fourth Infantry confessed that he was frightened when called upon to perform picket duty following the battle of Gaines' Mill in 1862. The thought of the dead bodies of comrades who had fallen in the swamp that afternoon haunted Giles:

> As I stood in the gloomy solitude of the Chickahominy swamp that night I spied the biggest ghost I had ever seen before. I saw it rise up slowly out of the sluggish marsh not larger than a two-months-old calf at first, but the thing gradually grew broader, taller and whiter, until it looked to me as big as a box-car and high as a telegraph pole.[34]

Only later did he learn that the "ghost" that rose from the Chickahominy was the soft, pale light of phosphoric gases rising from the swamp.[35]

Troops from Texas played major roles in all of the great battles in Virginia and Maryland during 1862. The Fourth Texas Infantry of Hood's Texas Brigade led the assault at Gaines' Mill in the Seven Days fighting around Richmond in June and July; the Fifth Texas Infantry overran the enemy flank at Second Manassas and forced John Pope's army to retreat toward Washington in late August; and the First Texas Infantry drove Union forces back through the cornfield at

---

32. Robertson to mother, July 12, 1862, George Lee Robertson Papers (Archives, University of Texas Library, Austin); Fletcher, *Rebel Private, Front and Rear,* 16; Smith, *Reminiscences of the Civil War,* 3.

33. Lester Newton Fitzhugh (comp. and ed.), *Cannon Smoke: The Letters of Captain John J. Good, Good-Douglas Texas Battery, CSA* (Hillsboro, Tex., 1971), 58; Heartsill, *Fourteen Hundred and 91 Days,* 153.

34. Lasswell (comp. and ed.), *Rags and Hope,* 105–106 (quotation). For another Texan's description of the aftermath of Gaines' Mill see Andrew N. Erskine to his wife, June 26, 1862, Andrew Nelson Erskine Papers (Archives, University of Texas Library, Austin).

35. Lasswell (comp. and ed.), *Rags and Hope,* 106.

Sharpsburg on the morning of September 17, thus blunting the main Union assault. In the latter action, the First Texas sustained casualties of 82.3 percent, the highest of any regiment in a single day of the Civil War. The entire Texas Brigade suffered 516 casualties at Sharpsburg, a loss of over 60 percent.[36]

For some Texas soldiers taken as prisoners of war, grim conditions made the months of imprisonment a nightmare. Captured soldiers complained of disease, cold, poor food, malnutrition, inadequate clothing, and harsh prison guards. Decimus et Ultimus Barziza, a captain in the Fourth Texas Infantry captured at Gettysburg, was confined on Johnson's Island in Sandusky Bay of Lake Erie. In his account of his experiences, Barziza described bad food at the camp:

> Our rations were very scanty, and those who were so unfortunate as not to have friends and acquaintances in the North, often went to bed hungry. They pretended to issue us meat, sugar, coffee, rice, hominy, or peas, and candles; but this long array was only for appearance sake. . . . The hominy or rice they occasionally gave us was almost invariably musty and half-spoilt, while the apology for coffee was very unwholesome.[37]

Captain Samuel T. Foster of the Twenty-fourth Texas Cavalry, while admitting that "we get plenty to eat," complained that prisoners at Camp Chase, at Columbus, Ohio, were "treated just like so many beasts—we are never spoken to except when a guard hollows out after 8 Oclock 'Lights Out'." Val Giles, captured near the Tennessee River in October, 1863, spent twelve months confinement at Camp Morton, Indiana. Giles remembered that prisoners who tried to escape or bribe a guard were either "bucked and gagged" or swung up by the thumbs. Failure to obey prison rules resulted in a ride on "Morgan's Mule," a narrow piece of oak lumber placed on a twelve-foot-high pole, or a forced march up and down in front of the guard house while carrying forty pounds of wood on one's shoulders.[38]

---

36. Everett (ed.), *Chaplain Davis,* 82–83, 112 J[ohn] Bell Hood, *Advance and Retreat: Personal Experiences in the United States and Confederate Armies* (New Orleans, 1880), 25–26, 34–36, 40–44; J. M. Polk, "Memories of a Lost Cause," *Texas Military History,* II (Feb., 1962), 23–27 "Report of Brig. Gen. John B. Hood. . . ," *Official Records,* Series I, Vol, XI, Pt. 2, pp. 568–569; reports nos. 152–155, ibid., Vol. XII, Pt. 2, pp. 611–622; "Report of Brig. Gen. John B. Hood . . . ," ibid., Vol. XIX, Pt. 1, pp. 922–925; reports nos. 249–255, ibid., 925–937. The casualty figure of 516 is from the casualty report of the Army of Northern Virginia, ibid., 811.

37. Decimus et Ultimus Barziza, *The Adventures of a Prisoner of War, 1863–1864,* ed. R. Henderson Shuffler (Austin, 1964), 77. Newton Keen complained that prisoners at Camp Douglas "were hardly half fed." Billingsley (ed.), "Confederate Memoirs of Newton Asbury Keen," 180.

38. Norman D. Brown (ed.), *One of Cleburne's Command: The Civil War Reminiscences and Diary of Capt. Samuel T. Foster, Granbury's Texas Brigade, CSA* (Austin, 1980), 30. Lasswell (comp. and ed.), *Rags and Hope,* 224–229. For another description of prison conditions and "Morgan's Mule," see William Clyde Billingsley (ed.), "Such is War: The Confederate Memoirs of Newton Asbury Keen," *Military History of Texas and the Southwest,* VII (Fall, 1968), 176–186.

Not all the memories that Texans had of prison camp were bad. Barziza noted that prisoners at Johnson's Island had debating societies, a band, daily religious exercises, and a "good" hospital. Writing, card-playing, and gambling were all favorite pastimes for the Johnson's Island prisoners. Lieutenant Robert J. Brailsford and his prison messmates of the Twenty-seventh Texas Cavalry organized a club at Camp Chase in which they had some "enlivening debates." Julius Giesecke, a Texas German taken prisoner in Louisiana, "met a really nice Yankee Doctor who fed us almost all night with crackers, butter, whiskey and his political views." Benjamin M. Seaton, one of the men imprisoned at Camp Douglas, noted that members of his regiment suffered a good deal but "wer treated tolerable well[;] about as well as we cold exspect prisners of war to be treated." Henry C. Wright, taken during Sibley's retreat in New Mexico, was given almost total freedom and plentiful supplies, including coffee and sugar.[39]

Many regiments from Texas lacked discipline. Officers frequently could do little to control the fierce individualism of their troops, especially those in the cavalry. Leonidas B. Giles admitted that discipline in Terry's Rangers was lax: "if there was any serious attempt to discipline [the regiment,] the effort was soon abandoned." "Volunteers we began," he noted, "volunteers we remained to the end. If any wished to evade duty, they found a way, and the punishment for evasion was light." On one occasion, Colonel John A. Wharton, who became regimental commander after the deaths of Colonel Terry and Colonel Thomas S. Lubbock, ordered an enlisted man to drive a team of mules. Even though the soldier had been chosen for the assignment by drawing lots, he refused to do so and informed Wharton, "you may punish me as much as you want to, but I am not going to drive that wagon." To resolve the impasse a volunteer was hired to do the work for fifty dollars a month.[40] On another occasion, Private Isaac Dunbar Affleck, son of wealthy Washington County planter and agricultural reformer Thomas Affleck, was assigned by his captain to chop wood but refused to do so, allowing his slave, Alex, to perform the task in his stead.[41]

---

39. Barziza, *The Adventures of a Prisoner of War,* 82–83, 98 (first quotatiou); Edna White, "Mess at Camp Chase," *East Texas Historical Journal,* VI (Oct., 1968), 126 (second quotation); Oscar Haas (trans.), "Diary of Julius Giesecke, 1863–1865," *Texas Military History,* IV (Spring, 1964), 29; Harold B. Simpson (ed.), *The Bugle Softly Blows: The Confederate Diary of Benjamin M. Seaton* (Waco, Tex., 1965), 32; H. C. Wright Reminiscences, 22–23 (Archives, University of Texas, Austin).

40. Giles, *Terry's Texas Rangers,* 100; Jeffries, *Terry's Rangers,* 56–57.

41. Affleck to Mrs. Thomas Affleck, Oct. 18, 1864, I. D. Affleck Papers, in possession of Mr. Thomas D. Affleck, Jr., of Galveston. Like a number of southern aristocrats, Affleck had the services of a slave throughout the war. Alex, mentioned here, was the successor to a slave named Henry, who had replaced an older slave named Perry. For other examples of Texas soldiers who had slave servants see Robert W. Glover (ed.), *"Tyler to Sharpsburg": The War Letters of Robert H. and William*

Commanders could, however, mete out punishment if they believed the occasion demanded it. For striking an officer, a private in Sibley's Brigade was forced to walk behind the baggage train tied with heavy irons for a month. A soldier in the Third Texas Cavalry was punished by having his head shaved, the word "thief" posted on his back, and being marched through camp to the tune of the "Rogue's March."[42]

Deserters received the most severe form of punishment, death by a firing squad. Although enthusiasm for the war had been high among Texans in the early part of the war, various factors, including dissatisfaction with military discipline, inadequate pay and rations, concern for families at home, increasing disillusionment over military failures, and sometimes cowardice, led to a steady increase in the number of soldiers who left the army. By the end of the war, 4,664 Texans were listed as deserters, many of them living in the woods and brush of North Texas.[43]

Military authorities believed the execution of captured deserters before their comrades in arms served as a warning to soldiers who might be inclined to leave their units. The soldiers themselves had mixed feelings, some believing the executions necessary, others considering them cruel and unjust. Benjamin Seaton, of the Tenth Infantry, described such a "sad occurance [sic]" in August, 1862, when four men were executed before the entire brigade near Little Rock. Seaton believed that "it has to be done," but lamented that "it is hard fer a man to be marched out in an old field and [be] shot." Private Jim Turner, of the Sixth Infantry, found such an execution of a deserter near Dalton, Georgia, to be "a horrible sight and seemed to us like a terrible butchery." Newton A. Keen of the Sixth Cavalry refused to watch the execution of three deserters from his regiment and argued that there would be fewer desertions if the officers performed their duties better.[44]

H. Gaston (Waco, Tex., 1960), 5; Simpson, Hood's Texas Brigade: A Compendium, 548; David B. Gracy, II, "With Danger and Honor," Texana, I (Spring, 1963), 124; and Bob Hill to sister, Dec. 8, 1862, John W. Hill Papers (Archives, University of Texas Library, Austin).

42. W. Randolph Howell diary, Nov. 18, 1861, W. Randolph Howell Papers (Archives, University of Texas, Austin); William A. Faulkner, "With Sibley in New Mexico: The Journal of William Henry Smith," West Texas Historical Association Year Book, XXVII (Oct., 1951), 116; Douglas (comp. and ed.), Douglas's Texas Battery, 10; Fitzhugh (ed.), Cannon Smoke, 84.

43. Ella Lonn, Desertion During the Civil War (1928; reprint ed., Gloucester, Mass., 1966), 71, 89, 231; Robert S. Weddle, Plow-Horse Cavalry: The Caney Creek Boys of the Thirty-fourth Texas (Austin, 1974), 97–100; Sam Farrow to wife Josephine, July 30, 1863, Sam W. Farrow Papers (Archives, University of Texas, Austin).

44. Simpson (ed.), Bugle Softly Blows, 18–19 (second, third, and fourth quotations); Turner, "Co. C, 6th Texas Infantry," 169; Billingsley (ed.), "Confederate Memoirs of Newton Asbury Keen," 50.

Ninth-plate ambrotype of Private William Burgess, Company D, 27th Texas Cavalry (Whitfield's Legion), ca. 1861. *Courtesy Lawrence T. Jones III.*

Ninth-plate tintype of unidentified Confederate soldier. *Courtesy Lawrence T. Jones III.*

The desertions, however, embarrassed some Texans. George L. Griscom, adjutant in the Ninth Texas Cavalry, wrote in his diary on September 5, 1863, that there was "a general depression of feeling in the reg't in regard to the late disgraceful doings of the boys that left us." In writing to his father, James Monroe Watson declared, "I never want you to feed a deserter nor a playout. . . . I think the citizens ought to drive all of the sulkers and playouts to the front."[45]

Many of the soldiers criticized their officers. Robert H. Gaston, a member of the First Texas Infantry, wrote to his sister early in the war to report that the brigade commander, Louis T. Wigfall, "has one great fault. He loves whiskey too well. He has been drunk several times since we came here." Similarly, William Henry Smith, a private in Sibley's Brigade, complained that the field officers of the brigade were "drunk all the time, unfit for duty—incompetent to attend to their duty." Another member of the brigade, James Franklin Starr, noted that "among the soldiers I hear ridicule and curses heaped upon the head of our genl. They call him a coward, which appears very plausible too."[46]

Newton Keen was critical of most of the officers in the Sixth Texas Cavalry. Of Captain J. S. Porter, Keen wrote, "He was an ignorant old goose not having sense enough to command pigs, much less soldiers." Robert Hodges, Jr., a sergeant in the Eighth Texas Cavalry, criticized his officers: "I think that Col. Terry is pursuing a very unwise course," Hodges reported, "in fact I think he has acted the saphead ever since he left home." When Terry was killed two weeks later at Woodsonville, Kentucky, however, Hodges referred to him as "our gallant and beloved leader Col. Terry."[47]

Some officers were popular with their men. John Bell Hood, who commanded the Texas Brigade in its early days, was generally well regarded by the Texans who served with him in Virginia, although they often chided him. When Hood

---

45. Homer L. Kerr (ed.), *Fighting with Ross' Texas Cavalry Brigade, C.S.A.: The Diary of George L. Griscom, Adjutant, 9th Texas Cavalry Regiment* (Hillsboro, Tex., 1976), 81; Judy Watson McClure, *Confederate from East Texas: The Civil War Letters of James Monroe Watson* (Quanah, Tex., 1976), 31. Similarly, A. Lafayette Orr of the Twelfth Texas Cavalry complained in a letter to his brothers about girls at home showing favors to cowards and deserters. John Q. Anderson (ed.), *Campaigning with Parsons' Texas Cavalry Brigade, CSA: The War Journals and Letters of the Four Orr Brothers, 12th Texas Cavalry Regiment* (Hillsboro, Tex., 1967), 136.

46. Glover (ed.), *"Tyler to Sharpsburg,"* 6 (first quotation); Faulkner, "With Sibley in New Mexico," 137 (second quotation); David B. Gracy, II (ed.), "New Mexico Campaign Letters of Frank Starr, 1861–1862," *Military History of Texas and the Southwest,* IV (Fall, 1964), 182.

47. Billingsley (ed.), "Confederate Memoirs of Newton Asbury Keen," 112; Maury Darst, "Robert Hodges, Jr., Confederate Soldier," *East Texas Historical Journal,* IX (Mar., 1971), 26 (second and third quotations), 28 (fourth quotation).

ordered one soldier, Bill Calhoun, to leave a warm fire and rejoin his unit, he told Calhoun, "I don't know why you are loitering here, so far behind your command." Calhoun replied: "Yes, and what you don't know, General Hood, would make a mighty damned big book."[48]

Hood was not so well liked by Texans serving in the western armies. When he was appointed to replace the popular Joseph E. Johnston as commander of the Army of Tennessee, most Texans in that army were highly critical. Samuel Alonza Cooke declared that the appointment of Hood "threw a damper on our army and most of us felt it was a death stroke to our entire army." Another Texan, Newton Keen, believed that as long as Johnston was in command things went well, but "when the army was put under hood [sic] all things went wrong." Samuel T. Foster, of Hiram B. Granbury's Brigade, argued that "Genl Joe Johnson [sic] has more military sense in one day than Hood ever did or ever will have."[49]

All Texas soldiers seemed to dislike Braxton Bragg. W. W. Heartsill believed, "if Genl [Joseph E.] Johnston (as reported) is in command; then we have no fears, if however Bragg is maneuvering; then we will not be surprised to wake up one of these September mornings and find the entire Army at or near Atlanta instead of Nashville as we all so much desired." Another Texan, Robert F. Bunting, claimed that Bragg was "universally cursed" and "out-generaled in every sense of the word."[50]

Soldiers who spent the war in Texas had mixed reactions to their officers. Earl Van Dorn, who commanded the district of Texas in the early months of the war, was first viewed with suspicion but soon won his men's support. Texans regarded his replacement as district commander, Paul Octave Hébert, "as a man of no military force or practical genius. . . ." The loss of Galveston to a Union naval force in early October, 1862, assured his unpopularity with Confederate Texans, who demanded that he be replaced with a more aggressive commander. Hébert's successor, John Bankhead Magruder, was a Virginian with a better reputation. Most soldiers agreed with Colonel John S. ("Rip") Ford, himself a

---

48. Lasswell (comp. and ed.), *Rags and Hope,* 119, 120 (quotations).

49. Bill O'Neal (ed.), "The Civil War Memoirs of Samuel Alonza Cooke," *Southwestern Historical Quarterly,* LXXIV (Apr., 1971), 543; Billingsley (ed.), "Confederate Memoirs of Newton Asbury Keen," 104, 105 (second quotation), 112; Brown (ed.), *One of Cleburne's Command,* 159 (third quotation).

50. Heartsill, *Fourteen Hundred and 91 Days,* 147; Bunting to "Editor Telegraph," July 7, 1863, Robert Franklin Bunting Papers (typed transcript; Archives, University of Texas Library, Austin. This letter was published in the Houston *Tri-Weekly Telegraph* on Aug. 19, 1863.).

highly respected officer, that "the advent of General Magruder was equal to the addition of 50,000 men to the forces of Texas."[51]

On occasion Texans admitted that their first impression of an officer was incorrect. When Camille Armand Jules Marie, Prince de Polignac, a French aristocrat, was appointed commander of a consolidated brigade of Texas infantry and dismounted cavalry in Louisiana, the Texans were furious. They protested to the district commander, General Richard Taylor, and threatened not to serve under Polignac. Taylor reminded the officers and men of their duty and promised that he would remove the Frenchman if the Texans remained dissatisfied after their first military action under his command. The troops were skeptical but agreed to give Polignac a try. In subsequent battles at Mansfield and Pleasant Hill he won their respect and admiration as a courageous soldier, whom they came to regard affectionately as their "Polecat."[52]

While Texans might be divided in their attitudes toward commanding officers, their diaries and letters reflect close agreement in their contempt for the enemy. Decimus et Ultimus Barziza, who spent many months in a federal prison camp, characterized northerners as "a peculiar people," who "are extremely bigoted, and actually bloated with self-love." He considered them to be "agitators and schemers, braggarts and deceivers, swindlers and extortioners," who yet pretended to "godliness, truth, purity, and humanity." Nicholas A. Davis, a chaplain in Hood's Brigade, believed northerners to be "meddlesome, impudent, insolent, pompous, boastful, unkind, ungrateful, unjust, knavish, false, deceitful, cowardly, swindling, thieving, robbing, brutal and murderous." John Truss, a young soldier from Bastrop who served with the Twelfth Texas Cavalry, complained that Union soldiers in Arkansas "cannot stand up and fight us with even numbers like men of honor," but preferred to "lay in the bushes five times our number," and "if they by accident get the upperhand of one of our men . . . will then shoot him, murder him in cold blood." Truss concluded that enemy soldiers were "the lowest down men in the world. There is nothing to [*sic*] mean for them to do."[53]

51. Thomas North, *Five Years in Texas; or, What You Did Not Hear during the War from January, 1861, to January, 1866* (Cincinnati, 1871), 105 (first quotation), 106; Oates, "Texas Under the Secessionists," 194–195; John Salmon Ford, *Rip Ford's Texas,* ed. Stephen B. Oates (Austin, 1963), 343 (third quotation).

52. Richard Taylor, *Destruction and Reconstruction: Personal Experiences of the Late War,* ed. Richard B. Harwell (1879; reprint ed., New York, 1955), 150–151; Alwyn Barr, *Polignac's Texas Brigade* (Houston, 1964), 29 (quotation), 30–54; "Incidents of Banks's Campaign: Mansfield and Pleasant Hill (April, 1864)," Augustus M. Hill Papers (Archives, University of Texas Library, Austin).

53. Barziza, *The Adventures of a Prisoner of War,* 59 (first and second quotations), 60 (third and fourth quotations); Everett (ed.), *Chaplain Davis,* 147; Johnette Highsmith Ray (ed.), "Civil War

Some men were convinced that the enemy would go to any length to defeat the South. Samuel A. Cooke, captured at Arkansas Post, believed that Union authorities deliberately put together on the same transport boats captured Confederates and northern troops who had smallpox, in order to infect as many southerners as possible. Captain James Douglas, of the Third Cavalry, reported that three patients died in the Van Buren, Arkansas, hospital from poison quinine, which "was brought from Memphis, and I understand, smuggled in there from the North, which shows the cannibal spirit of our enemies who are willing to resort to savage means of destroying us with poison."[54]

Texans resented the use of black troops by the Union government. Sergeant D. H. Hamilton, of the First Texas Infantry, reported that an attack by a black regiment determined the Texans to hold their position. In repulsing the enemy assault, the Texans, according to Hamilton, "killed in [their] front about a million dollars worth of niggers, at current prices." Many Texas soldiers believed that blacks should not be taken as prisoners of war. Dunbar Affleck declared that if Terry's Rangers came into contact with such troops, they intended "to hoist the black flag and give no quarter."[55] George W. Littlefield, also with the Rangers, stated that when he and his comrades learned they might be fighting black soldiers, "all of our command determined if we were put to a fight there to kill all we captured."[56]

Texans who served in New Mexico or along the Rio Grande were often critical of the Mexican and Indian populations. James Franklin Starr, a member of the Fourth Texas Cavalry, believed the inhabitants of New Mexico were "universally a low, ignorant, degraded race." James H. Kuykendall, who served along

Letters from Parsons' Texas Cavalry Brigade," *Southwestern Historical Quarterly,* LXIX (Oct., 1965), 218 (sixth, seventh, eighth, and ninth quotations).

54. O'Neal (ed.), "Civil War Memoirs of Samuel Alonza Cooke," 538; Douglas (comp. and ed.), *Douglas's Texas Battery,* 30. Northern soldiers apparently had a more ambivalent view of their southern foe. While some expressed hatred for the enemy, others admired the character of Confederate soldiers. See Bell Irvin Wiley, *The Life of Billy Yank: The Common Soldier of the Union* (Indianapolis, 1952), 346–353.

55. D. H. Hamilton, *History of Company M, First Texas Volunteer Infantry, Hood's Brigade, Longstreet's Corps, Army of the Confederate States of America* (Waco, Tex., 1952), 61, 62 (quotation); Affleck to Mr. and Mrs. Thomas Affleck, Mar. 25, 1863, Affleck Letters.

56. Gracy, "With Danger and Honor," 139–140. Tacitus T. Clay, on the other hand, pitied the blacks who were serving in the Union army. Judy Winfield and Nath Winfield, *War Letters of Captain Tacitus T. Clay, C.S.A.* (Chappell Hill, Tex., 1968), 8. Another Texan, Major Maurice K. Simons, captured at Vicksburg, was shocked at the sight of white Union soldiers saluting black guards at Vicksburg. Walter H. Mays, "The Vicksburg Diary of M. K. Simons, 1863," *Texas Military History,* V (Spring, 1965), 36.

the Rio Grande, considered the Indians "simple, yet, barbarious, children of nature," but regarded the Mexican Texans as lazy, stupid, and ignorant. A classic
example of nineteenth-century Texas racial prejudice was penned by George L.
Robertson. Stationed in South Texas, Robertson complained to his sister that of
"all the contemptable, despicable people on earth the greasers in my estimation
are the lowest, meaner even than the Commanche [*sic*]." The Mexican Texans,
he believed, "are ugly, thieving, rascally, in every way and to be educated only
makes a greaser the grander rascal."[57]

Food, clothing, and shelter were subjects of concern to all Civil War soldiers.
Here again, Texan recollections and comments varied greatly. Andrew J. Fogle, a
member of the Ninth Texas Infantry, complained bitterly about the lack of variety in his diet. "[W]e hafto live li[k]e dogs," he wrote in the fall of 1863. "[W]e
get nothing but a litle beefe and corn [m]eal and that is [a] very unp[l]esent
dish to me[.] I have [h]erd it sed that a man can get usto any thing but I never
will get usto living on beef and corn bred." Another Texan, Private William M.
Oden, expressed the age-old grievance of enlisted men that the officers were fed
well while the troops received nothing. "I wish to god that evry officer in all the
confederate states had to starve about five or six days then they would know
how to fed the soldiers and I think they would know how we feal on the subject," Oden wrote his wife. James Melville Foster, a trooper in the Thirty-sec-
ond Texas Cavalry, reported that his regiment was frequently near starvation
while on patrol in Louisiana.[58]

Other soldiers found food more plentiful. Harvey C. Medford, a private in
Lane's Rangers, serving in Texas and Louisiana in 1864, listed beefsteak, bacon,
pork, bread, molasses, coffee, cornbread, biscuits, corn fritters, and oysters as
part of his camp fare, which he supplemented by eating in restaurants, hotels,
and private homes. Dunbar Affleck, stationed in East Texas late in the war, reported that "we live high here, we are feasting all the time."[59]

---

57. Gracy (ed.), "New Mexico Campaign Letters of Frank Starr," 184; James Kuykendall journal,
1862 (Book XII), 12–16, 92 (quotation), James H. Kuykendall Collection (Archives, University of
Texas Library, Austin); Robertson to sister, Mar. 26, 1864, Robertson Papers.

58. Andrew J. Fogle to Miss Lou Harris, Oct. 18, 1863, Andrew J. Fogle Papers (Archives, University of Texas Library, Austin. The quotation is taken from the original letter rather than from the
typed transcript, which contains some errors.); William M. Oden to wife, Oct. 6, 1862, William M.
Oden Papers (Archives, University of Texas Library, Austin); Carl Duaine, *The Dead Men Wore
Boots: An Account of the 32nd Texas Volunteer Cavalry, CSA, 1862–1865* (Austin, 1966), 90.

59. Rebecca W. Smith and Marion Mullins (eds.), "Diary of H. C. Medford, Confederate Soldier,
1864," *Southwestern Historical Quarterly,* XXXIV (Oct., 1930), 114–117, 119, 121–122, 129, 136–137;
Affleck to Mrs. Thomas Affleck, Feb. 5, 1865, Affleck Letters. For other examples of the abundance
of food see W. B. Hunter to sister Mary, Oct. 11, 1863, Mary J. Minor Letters (Archives, University

Many Texas soldiers supplemented their camp fare by dining with citizens who were willing to open their homes to boys in gray. During his two years' duty in Louisiana, H. C. Wright, a young soldier from Polk County, always found a welcome even though local residents frequently had little to spare. George W. O'Brien, of Beaumont, apparently intended to take half-a-dozen chickens from residents of Ville Platte, Louisiana, but, "having had paraded before our eyes the ghosts of poverty and dead husbands," settled for a dinner of eggs and yams, followed by a smoke, rum, and a game of billiards.[60]

Most Texas Confederates proved better foragers than Captain O'Brien. Hogs and chickens were items particularly vulnerable to theft. Virgil S. Rabb explained the feeling of the soldiers: "the government tries to feed us Texians on Poor Beef, but there is too Dam many hogs here for that, these Arkansaw hoosiers ask from 25 to 30 cents a pound for there Pork, but the Boys generally get it a little cheaper than that[.] I reckon you understand how they get it."[61]

Members of Hood's Brigade had a special reputation as foragers. Even General Robert E Lee recognized these talents, remarking to the brigade commander that "when you Texans come about the chickens have to roost mighty high." Chicken houses, pigpens, corncribs, and beehives were all targets. In the Pennsylvania campaign of 1863 these were supplemented by loaves of bread, chunks of corned beef, hams, bacon, jellies, pickles, jams, fresh butter, and milk "appropriated" from local farms.[62]

In their letters home, men frequently asked that some item of clothing be sent to them by whatever means available. Wiley F. Donathan wrote in October, 1863, that he needed socks, overshirts, pants, and a vest. Henry G. Orr, a member of the Twelfth Cavalry, wrote to his mother requesting heavy jeans, a

Texas Library, Austin); John Thomas Duncan (ed.), "Some Civil War Letters of D. Port Smythe," *West Texas Historical Association Year Book*, XXXVII (Oct., 1961), 157; and Elvis E. Fleming (ed.), "A Young Confederate Stationed in Texas: The Letters of Joseph David Wilson, 1864–1865," *Texana*, VIII (No. 4, 1970), 353–354.

60. H. C. Wright Reminiscences, 55–56; Cooper K. Ragan (ed.), "The Diary of Captain George W. O'Brien, 1863," *Southwestern Historical Quarterly*, LXVII (Jan., 1964), 414. Other examples of local hospitality are found in Duncan C. Carothers diary, May 30, 1863, pp. 23–24, Carothers Family Papers (Archives Division, Texas State Library, Austin); [Ephraim Shelby Dodd], *Diary of Ephraim Shelby Dodd, Member of Company D, Terry's Texas Rangers, December 4, 1862–January 1, 1864* (Austin, 1914), 6.

61. Rabb to brother, Jan. 4, 1863, Mary Rabb Family Papers (Archives, University of Texas Library, Austin).

62. Hood, *Advance and Retreat*, 51 (first quotation); Simpson, *Hood's Texas Brigade: Lee's Grenadier Guard*, 209, 210, 253–256, 259–261; Polley, *Hood's Texas Brigade*, 148; Hamilton, *History of Company M*, 45, 47–48, 51–52.

well-lined overcoat, linsey or cotton overshirt, pants, slippers, and a pair of socks. The following year he requested the following items, to be divided between himself and his brother: two coats, two pairs of pants, four cotton shirts, two pairs of drawers, two woolen overcoats, and four pairs of socks.[63]

As the war continued, lack of suitable footwear became an increasingly serious concern for Texans, especially those serving in Tennessee and Virginia, where heavy snows and ice made conditions for men without adequate footwear nearly intolerable. The problem became especially acute for Texans in Hood's Brigade during the 1863–1864 winter campaign in East Tennessee. Many of the men, with no shoes at all, left bloody prints in the snow wherever they marched. Others were shod in "Longstreet moccasins," named for James Longstreet, the corps commander. Longstreet encouraged the men to make footwear by cutting green rawhide into the shape of a shoe and then tying it to the foot with a rawhide string. The moccasins were not comfortable because the rawhide shrunk when it dried, thus pinching the foot.[64]

Some Texans took shoes and other items from dead Union soldiers. John Good reported that the troops in his command deliberately aimed at an enemy with the thought of securing his shoes or other clothes. William A. Fletcher frequently took needed supplies from dead Union soldiers. On one occasion he found several letters to the dead man from a sweetheart. Fletcher did not feel "one pang of regret for being a party to breaking up that match." "She wanted me whipped," he noted, "she got that; I wanted dead Yankees—I got that."[65]

Soldiers stripping the dead of shoes and clothing sometimes received rude shocks. Jim Ferris, a soldier in the Fifth Texas Infantry, was attempting to remove the leggings from a fallen Union foe he assumed was dead. Suddenly the "dead man" said, "Great God alive, man! Don't rob me before I am dead, if you please!" Ferris stammered an apology, gave the wounded Yankee his canteen of water to keep, and proceeded to find another body—this time dead—from which he removed the desired leggings.[66]

---

63. Donathan to "My Dear Sir," Oct. 30, 1863, Wiley F. Donathan Family Correspondence (Archives Division, Texas State Library, Austin); Anderson (ed.), *Campaigning with Parsons' Texas Cavalry Brigade*, 71, 118.

64. All Confederates were affected by shortages of boots and shoes, but, as the Confederate troops most distant from their homes, Texans received fewer shoes and less clothing from their own state than did other Confederates. Simpson, *Hood's Texas Brigade: Lee's Grenadier Guard*, 184–185, 371–377; "Reports of Col. John C. Moore, Second Texas Infantry," Apr. 19, 1862, *Official Records*, Ser. 1, Vol. X, Part 1, 560–563; Muster Roll, Capt. C. N. Alexander, Co. A, 7th Texas Infantry (Archives Division, Texas State Library, Austin); Hamilton, *History of Company M*, 40–41.

65. Fitzhugh (ed.), *Cannon Smoke*, 58; Fletcher, *Rebel Private, Front and Rear*, 75.

66. J. B. Polley, *A Soldier's Letters to Charming Nellie* (New York, 1908), 78 (quotation), 79.

Texans registered fewer complaints about their living quarters than about food and clothing. In the field, soldiers slept under their blankets out in the open, or, if the weather was severe, in ditches or low places to avoid the cold winds. In more permanent camps, squad tents and wooden huts provided shelter. One Texas soldier described his winter abode in Virginia to his mother:

> It is made [of] pickets chinked and dubbed with a tent fly for a roof. We have the best fire place and chimney in the company. The fire place is made of brick to above the Jam[b] and from there up mud and sticks. Our house is about 12 feet square . . . our guns are in racks on the walls; our utensils consist of one skillet[,] a stew kettle[,] a bread pan[,] a frying pan & a large kettle[.][67]

Many soldiers found the long hours of camp life quite dull. Robert Hodges believed camp life in Kentucky to be most unsatisfactory. "I myself am tired of lazing in camps and doing nothing," he wrote to a friend. "I'll tell you what's a fact. This soldiring [sic] is a poor business." A fellow Texan stationed near Galveston agreed. Noting the boredom, endless drills, and sickness in camp, he concluded he was "tired of the dull monotony of camp life."[68]

In an effort to overcome their burden, the troops turned to various forms of entertainment. Men from Hood's Brigade built a log theater in which they could see plays and listen to concerts. Some of the performers were amateurs recruited for Hood's Minstrels, others were professional entertainers. Similar theatrical performances were staged in other areas where large groups of soldiers were encamped.[69]

Sports flourished among the Texas troops. Townball (a form of baseball played with two rather than four bases), horse racing, footracing, wrestling, and jumping were all popular diversions. Snowball fighting was a new experience for many Texans. The first large encounter of this type for them occurred in Virginia shortly after the battle of Fredericksburg. A snowball battle began between two companies, then spread to the regimental, brigade, and division level. Soon, nearly ten thousand troops, including the Texans in Hood's Brigade, were in-

---

67. G. L. Robertson to his mother, Jan. 4, 1862, quoted by Wiley, *Johnny Reb,* 60–61. See also John Wesley Rabb to his mother, Jan. 11, 1865, Rabb Family Papers.

68. Darst, "Robert Hodges, Jr.," 23; Letter from "Amicus," Bellville *Countryman,* Dec. 18, 1861 (third quotation). A similar view was expressed by J. D. Garland, a courier with the Second Texas Brigade, who wrote "I am perfectly disgusted with army life. It is so monotonous, nothing animating about it at all." Garland to sister, Feb. 25, 1864, J. D. Garland Letters (Archives, University of Texas Library, Austin).

69. Lasswell (comp. and ed.), *Rags and Hope,* 53: Polley, *Hood's Texas Brigade,* 139–140; Virgil S. Rabb to sister, Mar. 18, 1863, Rabb Family Papers.

volved. Similar snowball engagements occurred in the Army of Tennessee in the winter of 1863–1864.[70]

Reading was a source of relaxation for some Texas Confederates, although reading matter was sometimes difficult to obtain. James P. Douglas, an artillery captain in the Third Texas Cavalry, expressed a keen literary interest in his letters. While serving in the trenches around Atlanta during 1864, Douglas read works of Shakespeare and Sir Walter Scott. Douglas particularly enjoyed Scott's poetry, and, in a letter written to his wife while Sherman battered at the gates of Atlanta, suggested that she would "fall in love with Ellen Douglas of 'The Lady of the Lake' and Lucy of 'The Bridal of Triermain'."[71]

While some men like Douglas dabbled in Shakespeare, most Texans found newspapers more suitable. Early in the war the W. P. Lane Rangers even printed their own newspaper, first the *Camp Hudson Times* and later, when they moved to Fort Lancaster, *The Western Pioneer*.[72] The vicissitudes of war and the lack of adequate facilities prevented most Texas units from duplicating this journalistic feat, however.

Many soldiers succumbed to the twin evils of gambling and excessive drinking. Diaries and letters of Civil War participants give numerous illustrations of Texas soldiers submitting to both temptations. Card playing was the most common form of gambling, but dice throwing and horse racing also proved popular. One Texas soldier, William ("Buck") Walton, related that Confederates even bet money on fights between lice which they had taken from their clothes and bodies.[73]

A notorious gambler's den flourished near Fredericksburg, Virginia, during the winter of 1862–1863, where thousands of dollars changed hands. A similar

70. Desmond Pulaski Hopkins diary, Mar. 15, Apr. 1, 1862, Desmond Pulaski Hopkins Papers (Archives, University of Texas Library, Austin); Anderson (ed.), *Campaigning with Parsons' Cavalry Brigade*, 15; Fletcher, *Rebel Private, Front and Rear*, 52, 53; Polk, "Memories of a Lost Cause," 20; Lasswell (comp. and ed.), *Rags and Hope*, 167–172; Turner, "Co. G, 6th Texas Infantry," 170.

71. Douglas (comp. and ed.), *Douglas's Texas Battery*, 101. For other comments on reading habits see William H. Neblett to Lizzie, Apr. 9, 1863, and Jan. 17, 1864, Lizzie Scott Neblett Papers (Archives, University of Texas Library, Austin).

72. Heartsill, *Fourteen Hundred and 91 Days*, 56–74. Camp Hudson was located near Del Rio, Texas, on San Pedro Creek, near Devils River. Fort Lancaster, built by the United States government in the 1850s, was located on the Pecos River. Winsor, *Texas in the Confederacy*, 21, 23.

73. Buck Walton, *An Epitome of My Life: Civil War Reminiscences* (Austin, 1965), 73–74. For a description of "louse fighting," see Wiley, *Johnny Reb*, 38–39. Wiley also describes races between lice, but we have found no mention of this in diaries and letters of Texas soldiers. Texas Confederates did have many comments on the lice themselves, or "gray backs" as they called them. See Fletcher, *Rebel Private, Front and Rear*, 9–10, 12–18; Hamilton, *History of Company M*, 39–40, 75.

gambler's "paradise" was located at the foot of Missionary Ridge at Chattanooga in the fall of 1863. Here, in an area covering several acres, stood dozens of tents and brush arbors where soldiers congregated to engage in every imaginable form of chance.

Texans assigned to Bragg's army enjoyed the pleasures of this gamblers' haven until Grant's army overran the area in November of that year.[74]

Excessive consumption of alcohol was often a more serious problem than gambling. In gambling the individual soldier was the victim, but the consequences of heavy drinking could sometimes be far-reaching. Some of Terry's Rangers were involved in an altercation in Nashville in 1861 when, under the influence of alcohol, they fired off their pistols, causing a riot. Two policemen were killed and another wounded before the disturbance could be brought under control.[75]

Other Texans refused to be tempted by vice. Indeed, some men found the war a time of finding or renewing their spiritual faith. Religious revivals swept through the western Confederate armies in 1863 and 1864. R. F. Bunting, a minister in Terry's Rangers, noted that the revival movement was very strong in the camps of northern Georgia in 1863. Thirty-six men publicly professed their faith in Jesus, he reported, while many others renewed their religious vows. George W. Littlefield, serving in the western armies, at first remained skeptical of the revival movement, but by the end of summer, 1863, was himself involved and informed his wife that he intended to become a "changed man." Wiley Donathan, another Texan, reported that a great revival swept Joe Johnston's army in the spring of 1864. "I then solemnly resolved to seek the pardon of my sins and be a Christian," Donathan wrote.[76]

74. Lasswell (comp. and ed.), *Rags and Hope,* 156–163; William Carothers to Mrs. S. Carothers, Mar. 6, 1863, Duncan C. Carothers Papers (Archives Division, Texas State Library, Austin); A. E. Rentfrow to sister, Feb. 11, 1862, A. Henry Moss Papers (Archives, University of Texas Library, Austin).

75. J[ames] K. P. Blackburn, *Reminiscences of the Terry Rangers* ([Austin], 1919), 10–11; Wiley, *Johnny Reb,* 50, notes that the "evil of illicit sexual indulgence, though admittedly common to every large army that history has known, is scantily treated in Confederate records." Although prostitution flourished in the larger cities of the Confederacy, especially Richmond, the authors have found no mention of the subject in diaries and letters of Texas Confederates.

76. Bunting to "Editor Telegraph," June 3, Aug. 23, 1863, Bunting Papers. (These letters were published in the Houston *Tri-Weekly Telegraph* on July 15 and Sept. 30, 1863, respectively.) Gracy, "With Danger and Honor," 134; Kerr (ed.), *Ross' Texas Cavalry Brigade,* 80; W. F. Donathan to brother and sister, Apr. 2, June 4, 1864, Donathan Family Correspondence. For another expression of faith see Colonel William P. Rogers to wife, June 5, 1862, William P. Rogers Papers (Archives, University of Texas Library, Austin).

For many Texans the war provided the first opportunity to see something of the world outside of their own localities. Many were overwhelmed by what they saw. Robert Gaston from Tyler found that the city of New Orleans "presents many strange and curious sights to me. . . . The fine buildings, hundreds of drays, carriages etc. continually running the streets & the eternal hum of busy hundreds strike the stranger with astonishment."[77]

The beautiful mountains of Virginia and Tennessee deeply impressed most Texans who saw them. O. T. Hanks believed the view of the Blue Ridge and Cumberland mountains was "worth a good part of a Mans Life." Benjamin Seaton found the view from Lookout Mountain in Tennessee to surpass "in sublimity and grandeur anything we ever beheld."[78]

Not all Texas Confederates were impressed with the areas they saw, however. Lieutenant Flavius W. Perry, serving with the Seventeenth Cavalry near Arkansas Post, believed "this country was never made . . . for white people to live in, nothing but frogs and craw fish can live here long. . . ." Perry concluded, "I don't think the Yankeys would have it if they could get it."[79]

Many Texas soldiers were more interested in the local girls and women than in the scenery. Private Henry Smith of Sibley's Brigade was quite taken with the daughters of a local resident. "I have got to loving one of them, she is so pretty," he wrote. "I believe I will marry her & take her back home with me and show her to the homefolks."[80] While recovering from an injury, Stephen A. Bryan, member of a pioneer Texas family, was so impressed with the "beautiful & rich, accomplished & refined" young ladies of Rapides Parish, Louisiana, that he thought he might "return to this Parish to look for a fortune."[81] George W. Littlefield, in Tennessee, wrote to his fiancee back in Texas that he had found "the prettyest little woman here that is anywhere I know." While promising his fiancee that he would not forget her, Littlefield admitted that if she were to

---

77. Glover (ed.), *"Tyler to Sharpsburg,"* 4.

78. Hanks, "History of B. F. Benton's Company," 12; Simpson (ed), *Bugle Softly Blows,* 43 (second quotation).

79. Joe R. Wise (ed.), "Letters of Lt. Flavius W. Perry, 17th Texas Cavalry, 1862–1863," *Military History of Texas and the Southwest,* XIII (No. 2), 27.

80. Faulkner, "With Sibley in New Mexico," 140. Smith was not totally honest with his sweetheart back home, to whom he wrote at almost the same time: "Sweet girl I often think of you in these wild woods of New Mexico, where no friend is near, no kind female is near our camps to watch over us so tenderly as our girls did at Home." Ibid., 141.

81. Bryan to James P. Bryan, Mar. 5, 1863, James Perry Bryan Papers (Archives, University of Texas Library, Austin).

marry someone else, the Tennessee belle would be his next choice, for "I am all-most tempted to love her."[82]

Confederate soldiers from Texas frequently complained that they were not re-ceiving letters from loved ones at home. William T. Gibbons, serving with the Fourteenth Cavalry, wrote to his wife that "sometimes I almost conclude that you have forgotten that there is such a being on earth as myself[,] having writen [sic] & received no answers." In another letter to her he declared that he would pay fifty dollars for a letter from her at any time. Similarly, James M. Watson wrote to his father in August, 1863, that "it is disheartening to me to write for I haven't received but one letter from home since I left and it was dated May 2." "You don't know how bad I want to hear from home and to hear from the neighbors," he wrote.[83]

A letter from home meant more to Texas Confederates than almost anything else. Bluford Alexander Cameron thanked his family for sending him a packet of clothes but lamented that no letter accompanied the clothing. "I opened the Sack and commenced Searching the Pockets of evry article and expected in evry pocket I Searched to find a Letter," he wrote, "but I Searched through and through but alas found no letter."[84]

The mail service itself was often the reason soldiers did not hear from home as regularly as they wished. Colonel George W. Guess, with the Thirty-first Cavalry Regiment, expressed the soldier's view of the post office when he wrote, "I wish the cursed post office at Dallas with all the infernal meddlers with other peoples' business were sunk into the lowest depths of the bottomless pit, & you could get one that could be carried on properly & honestly."[85]

The unreliability of government mail service caused many soldiers to depend upon couriers riding from army camps back to Texas. These couriers consisted of soldiers on leave, haulers of military supplies, tradesmen, ministers, and those

---

82. Gracy, "With Danger and Honor," 14. In January, 1863, while home on leave, Littlefield mar-ried his Texas fiancee, Alice P. Tiller. For other examples of Texans' interest in the opposite sex, see Smith and Mullins (eds.), "Diary of H. C. Medford," 140; Samuel B. Barron, Lone Star Defenders: A Chronicle of the Third Texas Cavalry, Ross' Brigade (New York, 1908), 31; and E. J. Oden to sister, May 29, 1863, Oden Papers.

83. William T. Gibbons to Mrs. A. A. Gibbons, Oct. 23 (first quotation), 30, 1863, W. T. Gibbons Letters (photostatic copies, Archives Division, Texas State Library, Austin); Watson, Confederate from East Texas, 17–18.

84. J. S. Duncan (ed.), "Alexander Cameron in the Louisiana Campaign, 1863–1865," Military History of Texas and the Southwest, XIII (No. 1), 46.

85. Guess to Sarah Horton Cockrell, Dec. 16, 1862, George W. Guess Letters (Archives, Universi-ty of Texas Library, Austin).

traveling on government business. From the army posts they carried letters to friends and relatives at home, souvenirs of various kinds, and items that were difficult to secure at home such as writing paper and envelopes. From home they brought letters, food, clothing, and items that relatives and friends believed would be helpful to the men in gray.[86]

The thought of going home was seldom out of the soldier's mind, but furloughs became increasingly difficult to obtain. "I thought I would get to come home before now," one Texas soldier wrote, "but a man has to be sick or a mighty good hand at possum to get furloughs." John E. Brown believed that he "had just as well try to fly to Virginia as to apply for a furlough. . . ."[87]

Sick and wounded soldiers especially thought of home. "It is natural for all of [us] to want to be at Home Sweet Home," wrote one Texan. "A Soldier can put up with many hard things when health[y and] not murmer [*sic*] but let him get sick & then Home [Sweet] Home."[88]

Disease swept through Confederate armies early in the war. A variety of illnesses, including measles, mumps, malaria, diarrhea, colds, pneumonia, and bronchitis, affected the troops from Texas. At one time only 25 of 800 men in the Fifth Texas Infantry, camped near Richmond, were fully fit for duty. About half of the Fourth Texas was also on sick call at the same time. The rate of disease, especially measles and mumps, also ran high among Texas cavalry units stationed in Arkansas. Texas units serving in Louisiana suffered from a high incidence of malaria. Some cases of yellow fever were reported in Texas units stationed on the Gulf Coast.[89]

Medical care was poor in the early days of the Civil War. Most of the officers and men knew little of personal hygiene; camps were located in low, insect-in-

---

86. Weddle, *Plow-Horse Cavalry,* 129–137, provides an excellent description of the courier riders in Northeast Texas during this period.

87. Ray (ed.), "Civil War Letters from Parsons' Texas Cavalry Brigade," 219–220 (first and second quotations); John E. Brown to father and mother, Feb. 16, 1863, John E. Brown Letters (Archives, University of Texas Library, Austin). The men of the Fifth Texas Infantry even petitioned President Davis on the matter of additional furloughs, but to no avail. Elvis E. Fleming, "Some Hard Fighting: Letters of Private Robert T. Wilson, 5th Texas Infantry, Hood's Brigade, 1862–1864," *Texas Military History,* IX (No. 4, 1971), 297–298.

88. Carothers diary, 42.

89. Polley, *Hood's Texas Brigade,* 17; Barron, *Lone Star Defenders,* 59–60; John H. Harrison, "Texas' Tenth Cavalry, C.S.A." *Military History of Texas and the Southwest,* XII (No. 2, 1975), 96; William E. Sawyer and Neal Baker, Jr., "A Texan in the Civil War," *Texas Military History,* II (Nov., 1962), 275–278; Charleen Plumly Pollard (ed.), "Civil War Letters of George W. Allen," *Southwestern Historical Quarterly,* LXXXIII (July, 1979), 49; "Report of Lieut. Col. A. W. Spaight," *Official Records,* Ser. 1, Vol. XV, 145.

fested areas; food was not properly prepared or handled; and doctors and surgeons were inadequate in numbers and training. "There are about five [doctors]
in our regiment," wrote one Texan, "& I am, this day, a better physician than
either [*sic*] of them."[90]

Even though the number of Confederate casualties increased markedly in
1863 and 1864, Texans continued to believe that the South would ultimately be
victorious. The fall of Vicksburg and Lee's failure at Gettysburg dampened but
did not destroy the confidence of Texas Confederates. The defeat of Nathaniel
P. Banks's Red River expedition in the spring of 1864 was a source of great encouragement, particularly to those Texans on duty in the Trans-Mississippi
West. These same western Confederates predicted that Lee would defeat Ulysses
S. Grant in the campaigns in Virginia.[91]

Most Texas Confederates believed that William T. Sherman could not capture Atlanta. Captain James P. Douglas, whose battery was in the thick of the
fighting around Atlanta, wrote to his wife in mid-August that "affairs are bright-
ening here. People and army seem to be more sanguine of success." Even when
Sherman forced the Confederates to evacuate the city, Douglas remained confident. In a letter he informed his wife that we "had to give up Atlanta," but
predicted that "the nomination of McClellan and Pendleton will secure the defeat of Lincoln and possibly close the war." Another Texan in the Army of Tennessee, Wiley Donathan, was pleased when Hood withdrew from Georgia and
took the offensive by heading for Tennessee. "Our prospects were never
brighter," wrote Donathan, "for a great Change has been wrought within the
last two weeks."[92]

Hood's Tennessee campaign proved to be disastrous. After sustaining heavy
casualties at Franklin in late November, Hood drove on to Nashville, where in
mid-December superior Union forces destroyed most of his army. For the first
time, many Texas Confederates expressed despair. Captain Douglas, in a letter
he cautioned not to be shown "out of our own family," stated, "our country is

---

90. George W. Guess to Sarah Horton Cockrell, July 29, 1862, Guess Letters. John A. Templeton
had an equally strong aversion to hospitals. "There is more danger in a hospital than in the field of
battle," he wrote. "I never have been in a hospital, but If I ever do have to go to one on account of
sickness I will make my will before starting." John A. Templeton to father, May 16, 1862, John A.
Templeton Letters (Archives, University of Texas Library, Austin).

91. Anderson (ed.), *Campaigning with Parsons' Texas Cavalry Brigade,* 142–143; Fleming, "Letters
of Private Robert T. Wilson," 295–296.

92. Douglas (comp. and ed.), *Douglas's Texas Battery,* 123 (first quotation), 127 (second quotation),
128 (third quotation); Donathan to sister, Oct. 18, 1864, Donathan Family Correspondence.

in much the worse condition it has ever been. If a great deed is not done this winter, the Yanks will close the war in the spring."[93]

Other Texans remained defiant. Even after Lee's army surrendered in April, 1865, some Texas Confederates wanted to carry on the struggle. Captain Samuel T. Foster, with Granbury's brigade in North Carolina, admitted that Lee's surrender had had "a very demoralizing affect on the army," but still believed "we will whip this fight yet." George Lee Robertson, serving in South Texas, vowed to fight on. "If I can't have a confederacy I don't want anything else," he wrote. Even after he learned of Lee's surrender, W. W. Heartsill believed that if the southern people would unite as one, "the Trans-Mississippi could defy the combined powers of all Yankeedom."[94]

Edmund Kirby Smith, commander of the Trans-Mississippi department, also believed the war should continue and urged his soldiers to remain at their posts. Most Texans in the department, however, agreed with Americus L. ("Lee") Nelms that "it would be folly in us to fight on this side of the river now." Thus, regiments and companies melted away in May as men headed home. There was little that Smith could do but sign the terms of surrender at Galveston on June 2.[95]

Texas Confederates made their way to their homes as best as they could. The homeward journey posed few obstacles to Texans in the Trans-Mississippi, but for those Texans in Virginia and the Carolinas the trip sometimes took months. Most of them returned with little more than the clothes on their backs. Many found conditions at home quite changed. Relatives and loved ones had died or been killed in war, slaves were now free, money was scarce, and a Union army of occupation was moving into the state. Most Confederate Texans, however, felt no bitterness at their sacrifice, but pride that they had fought gallantly for a cause in which they deeply believed.[96]

---

93. Douglas (comp. and ed.), *Douglas's Texas Battery,* 153.

94. Brown (ed.), *One of Cleburne's Command,* 163 (first and second quotations); Robertson to Julia, May 8, 1865, Robertson Papers; Heartsill, *Fourteen Hundred and 91 Days,* 239.

95. Weddle, *Plow-Horse Cavalry,* 158; Oates, "Texas Under the Secessionists," 212.

96. For accounts of the trip home see Hamilton, *History of Company M,* 69–71; Lasswell (comp. and ed.), *Rags and Hope,* 278–280; Fletcher, *Rebel Private, Front and Rear,* 145–158; Walton, *An Epitome of My Life,* 93–94; Brown (ed.), *One of Cleburne's Command,* 173–187; Weddle, *Plow-Horse Cavalry,* 162–163.

Stereograph of monument in Comfort, Texas, ca. 1866. This monument stands over the graves of the Texas German Unionists killed on August 10, 1862, in the Battle of the Nueces. Nineteen died in the early-morning attack by mounted Confederate soldiers, and nine more who were wounded in the attack were executed shortly thereafter. *Courtesy Lawrence T. Jones III.*

Union Sentiment in Texas, 1861–1865

CLAUDE ELLIOTT[*]

Not all Texans supported the Confederate cause. The late Claude Elliott, professor of history and dean of graduate studies at Southwest Texas State College (now University), believed that no more than one-third of the people of Texas actively supported the Confederacy. Another one-third remained neutral and one-third supported the Union, either actively or passively.

In this article Elliott describes the main areas where unionist strength prevailed and discusses the reaction, often violent, by Confederate sympathizers to these dissenters. In northeast Texas dozens of unionists were hanged. In Central Texas Confederate authorities took steps to prevent suspected unionists from leaving the state. In one instance thirty-two Texans were killed and others wounded by Confederate cavalry while trying to flee from Texas. Martial law was declared in several South Texas counties because of suspected unionist activity.

A recent book by Richard B. McCaslin, Tainted Breeze: The Great Hanging at Gainesville, Texas, 1862 *(Baton Rouge: Louisiana State University Press, 1994), fully describes the hangings that occurred in North Texas. Another work, James Marten's* Texas Divided: Loyalty and Dissent in the Lone Star State, 1856–1874 *(Lexington: University Press of Kentucky, 1990), discusses the role played by Texas*

---

[*] Claude Elliott, "Union Sentiment in Texas, 1861–1865," *Southwestern Historical Quarterly,* L (Apr., 1947), 449–477.

unionists before, during, and after the Civil War. For more on the death of the thir-
ty-two Texans trying to leave the state see Robert W. Shook, "The Battle of the Nue-
ces, August 10, 1862," Southwestern Historical Quarterly, *LXVI (July, 1962),*
31–42.

The election of Lincoln, "the Black Republican," was the signal for South Carolina to secede. In less than a week after the election the South Carolina Legislature, then in session, called for a convention to meet at Charleston on
December 17, 1860. The convention met and, on December 20, adopted a secession ordinance. From Charleston the virus spread rapidly, and soon the entire South was drawn into the maelstrom.

Pressure groups which favored following the example of South Carolina almost instantly gained the ascendancy in government circles throughout the
South. These secessionist leaders in Texas urged that the legislature be convened
in order that secession machinery might be set into motion, but Sam Houston,
the governor, assumed the role of obstructionist and steadfastly refused to make
the call. He hoped in this manner to prevent the calling of a convention. Houston and his unionist followers were foiled in this purpose by determined secessionists who, on December 3, issued an "Address to the People of Texas" calling
for a convention to consider secession, fixing January 28 as the date, and nam-
ing Austin as the place.[1] On December 17, 1860, Houston called the legislature
to meet in a special session, on January 21, 1861, one week in advance of the
meeting of the Texas convention. He hoped, with the support of his Union
friends, to get the state Senate to refuse to recognize the legality of the convention which was to begin its sessions on January 28. The attempt was made under the leadership of James W. Throckmorton, Houston's most able and loyal
Union supporter, but the effort failed.[2] The House of Representatives recognized the convention on January 28, and the Senate concurred on the same day.

Excitement ran high as the convention came into session on January 28, but
the outcome was never in doubt. When the vote was taken on February 1, the
Unionists were able to muster only seven votes against the secession ordinance.
The only opportunity left then for the Unionists was to defeat secession in the
election which the convention had set for February 23. The Unionists were unsuccessful in doing this except in a few scattered counties, and Houston, as a
last resort, considered an appeal to force to keep Texas in the Union. He called
in four of his Unionist friends and presented the proposition to them, but they

---

1. *Southern Intelligencer,* February 18, 1861.

2. *Senate Journal,* January 22, 1861, Eighth Legislature, Special Session, 37.

advised against it. Houston followed their advice[3] and on March 29 addressed a note to Colonel C. A. Waite, of the United States Army at San Antonio, in which he declared:

> I have received intelligence that you have, or will soon receive orders to concentrate United States troops under your command at Indianola to sustain me in my official functions. Allow me most respectfully to decline any such assistance of the United States government.[4]

Throckmorton went into the Confederate service; Houston retired to his home in Huntsville; and official opposition to the disruption of the Union was at an end.

Texas was not ripe for revolution in 1861. There were few persons who felt that they were going into the war because of oppression, wrong, or outrage, or that the situation was of sufficient gravity to demand of them the supreme sacrifice. They had voted for secession supinely hoping that the step they took did not mean war, blindly trusting such leaders as Louis T. Wigfall, W. S. Old-ham, T. N. Waul, and O. M. Roberts to steer them away from bloodshed and conflict. When, in April, 1861, all hopes of avoiding war were dashed to earth by the Sumter incident, the people of Texas were dazed and stood bewildered as they faced the storm. The public mind had not been made to realize that war was a distinct possibility as a consequence of secession. It is extremely doubtful, therefore, whether more than one-third of the people of Texas actively support-ed the Confederacy. It is believed that one-third remained neutral and that one-third, actively or passively, gave support to the Federal cause.[5]

The wavering mind was kept alert and Union sentiment was kept alive in Texas through a strong Union leadership, partly passive. The actions of these Union leaders, whether silent or articulate, gave substance to thoughts in doubtful minds. These Unionists, as far as their activities in the war were con-cerned, fall roughly into three classes: those who actively and openly supported the Federal cause; those who remained outwardly neutral; and those who sub-mitted.

Chief among those who gave active support to the Union were E. J. Davis, John Hancock, A. J. Hamilton, John L. Haynes, James P. Newcomb, and Sam

---

3. A. W. Terrell Papers, MSS., University of Texas Archives.

4. Houston to Waite, March 29, 1861, in *The War of the Rebellion: A Compilation of the Official Records of the Union and Confederate Armies* (Washington, 1880–1901), Series I, Vol. I, p. 551. Here-inafter referred to as the *Official Records*.

5. Robert P. Felgar, Texas in the War for Southern Independence, 1861–1865 (Ph.D. Thesis, Uni-versity of Texas, 1935), 324.

Houston. Davis recruited and organized a regiment of Texas Unionists in Mexico and was captured while recruiting near Matamoras on March 15, 1863. Governor Albino Lopez of the state of Tamaulipas intervened in his behalf, and General Hamilton P. Bee released him because he did not wish to prejudice the Confederate cause in Mexico.[6] In March, 1864, Davis led a force of two hundred Texans against Laredo, but he was defeated. He was then transferred to Louisiana, where he remained until the end of the war. John Hancock, a Union Democrat during the 1850's, gave full support to Houston in his efforts to keep Texas in the Union, but he did not have so spectacular a record as Davis. He went into Federal territory but returned to Texas at intervals during the war.[7]

A. J. Hamilton was among the most militant Unionists and was regarded as a traitor. He was not safe in Austin and consequently fled to the hills, along the Colorado above Austin, where he remained until 1862, when he left for the United States by way of Mexico. At Washington he was made brigadier general and military governor of Texas. In the late summer of 1863 he went to New Orleans, where he remained to seek an opportunity to assume the military governorship of Texas. On January 1, 1864, he issued an "Address to the People of Texas," pointing out that the people had been deceived from the beginning by Southern leaders. On June 17, 1865, President Andrew Johnson appointed Hamilton provisional governor of Texas.[8]

John L. Haynes and James P. Newcomb had widely different records, yet each gave undivided allegiance to the United States. Haynes became colonel of the Second Texas Regiment, organized at Matamoras, before he was transferred to Louisiana. James P. Newcomb, the fiery editor of the *Alamo Express,* left San Antonio for Mexico in a hurry after a mob of members of the Knights of the Golden Circle raided his office, destroyed the press, and set fire to the building. He spent the war years in Mexico and California.[9]

Sam Houston gave "lip service" to the Confederacy but never conceded that secession was either right or legal, and his influence was felt throughout Texas. He refused to take the oath of allegiance to the Confederacy, and Edward Clark was sworn in as governor. Retiring to his home in Huntsville, Houston waited

6. *Official Records,* Series I, Vol. XV, p. 1010.

7. Dudley G. Wooten, *A Comprehensive History of Texas, 1685–1897* (2 vols.; Dallas, 1898), II, 333, 338, 345; see also John Henry Brown, *History of Texas, 1686–1692* (2 vols.; St. Louis, 1892–1893), II, 428.

8. C. W. Ramsdell, *Reconstruction in Texas* ("Columbia University Studies in History, Economics, and Public Law," XXXVI [New York, 1910]), 55.

9. J. P. Newcomb, *Sketch of Secession Times in Texas and Journal of Travel from Texas . . .* (San Francisco, 1863), 12.

and plotted to overthrow the Texas regime, separate it from the Confederacy, and re-establish the Texas Republic. He gave aid and comfort to the enemy by opposing martial law and conscription, and by casting reflections upon Jefferson Davis. The enemies of the Confederacy rejoiced and took courage when they heard "Old Sam" disparagingly refer to Davis as "Little Jeffy."

E. M. Pease, former governor, and George W. Paschal were among the outstanding Unionists who remained, for the most part, neutral. Pease refused to recognize the Confederacy as legitimate but withdrew from his law practice and lived quietly in Austin, respected by both factions. Paschal, a noted lawyer, had an extremely lucrative law practice in Austin. He abandoned this practice and spent most of the war years in writing. Most unpopular, he was constantly in danger. He moved to New York after the war and did not again take up his residence in Texas.[10]

J. W. Throckmorton, E. W. Cave, and B. H. Epperson were strong Unionists who embraced the Southern cause out of love for their state. Throckmorton rendered valuable service as brigadier general and as state senator; Cave recruited state troops; and Epperson gave generously of his money to the Confederate cause, not being physically qualified for service in the field.[11]

Each of these men, whether militant or passive, contributed largely to disaffection in Texas. They gave encouragement to thousands of men who began in 1861 with mental reservations, moved on to open hostility and draft dodging, and ended in forced service, desertion, and final disaster. Though not on the scene of action, they played their part well.

The hideous spectre, disaffection, prompted partly by the unyielding attitude of many prominent men of Texas, began to show itself even before secession had been accomplished. The northern counties, particularly Denton, Cooke, Wise, and Collin, had been settled largely by migrants from the northern states, who had few slaves, who had little interest in the states' rights theory, and who had, therefore, a lively contempt for the Confederate cause. It was in this seething hotbed of Union sentiment that the first plot was hatched: a plot to dismember Texas in case of secession. A written document which set forth such a plan, purported to have issued from the Unionist ring at Austin, was extensively circulated in Collin and Denton counties. This strange document, dated January 15, 1861, read as follows:

Whereas the political movements in the state of Texas indicate that the obligations which bind us to the Federal Government by the Constitution of the United States are

---

10. J. T. Vanee, "George Washington Paschal," *Dictionary of American Biography* (New York, 1934), XIV, 288.

11. Felgar, Texas in the War for Southern Independence, 324 ff.

about to be abrogated by a State Convention; and whereas should such state Convention so far disregard the wishes of the Conservative Union men of the State of Texas, and especially the northern portion of the state, as to declare the State of Texas out of the Union without submitting their action to the people of Texas for ratification at the ballot box; and whereas should the state Convention act so as to disregard the anticipated action of the southern Convention, therefore we resolve, as a *Dernier Resort,* to make an effort to unite a sufficient number of the northern counties of Texas into a state, and make application at the proper time for admission into the Union.[12]

Soon after this article appeared in the *Southern Intelligencer,* a night call was made on the editor by a group of secessionists who warned him against printing incendiary articles in his paper. Nothing more was heard of the dismemberment plan.

In late 1862 a dangerous plot known as the "Conspiracy of the Peace Party" was discovered in the northern counties, particularly in Cooke, Wise, Grayson, Collin, and Denton. This Peace party was made up of Union sympathizers and those who were loyal to neither side but who were dissatisfied with the war. The organization was secret, with signs, grips, and passwords. The members were first sworn to secrecy, and those who were found worthy were entrusted with three degrees. The first degree bound the member to secrecy and obligated him to avenge an attack on a fellow member. The second degree supposedly tested the candidate on robbery and jayhawking, while the third pledged him to support a movement to re-establish the old Union.[13] The two prime objectives were to resist the draft and keep up a spy system for the army of the North. In case of a draft of the militia to meet an invasion by the Federal army, the members were instructed to enlist and desert to the enemy when the battle was on. Their plans embraced a plot to cooperate with two Union armies which were to invade Texas concurrently, one from Kansas, and one by way of Galveston. With the coöperation of the Unionists the two armies would meet triumphantly at Austin.[14]

The time and place of organization of the Peace party is not known, but most of the enlistments came after September 1, 1861. The party extended to all classes of the community: clergymen, professional men, and farmers. Some of the members of the secret order were unscrupulous men who deserved no quarter, while some were misguided Union men who were neighbors, and even friends, of such staunch Unionists as Throckmorton and Epperson, and who had been cheered, sustained, and confirmed by their speeches before the day of

12. Editorial correspondence, *Southern Intelligencer,* January 31, 1861.
13. *Texas Republican,* November 1, 1862.
14. *Tri-Weekly Telegraph,* October 27, 1862.

secession.[15] Others, respectable citizens, were inveigled into the organization under false pretenses, being told that the purpose was to promote the interest of peace. They did not comprehend the implication of their actions.

This Peace party or Loyal League was strongest in Cooke County. In the Cross Timbers a few miles from Gainesville, the county seat, was a settlement made up almost entirely of Union sympathizers who were termed abolitionists or "Black Republicans." The plot was uncovered there when Newton Chance, a Confederate soldier of Wise County, was approached by a drunken officer (Childs) of the league in a Gainesville hotel and asked to become a member of the secret order. Chance reported this immediately to Brigadier General William J. Hudson, of the Confederate army, in command at Gainesville. On the following night Newton Chance and his brother Joe attended the secret sessions and were initiated. They got much information about the purpose of the league, its officers, its members, and its future plans.

Excitement ran high, and a reign of terror began as the news about the organization spread like a prairie fire through the county. General Hudson declared martial law and issued orders requiring every able-bodied man in the county to report for duty. Rumors spread thick and fast. Unionists were reported to be fleeing from place to place in the night; armies of Unionists were said to be planning to fight their way northward to burn homes and kill men, women, and children.[16]

In the excitement the populace rose en masse and hanged about twenty-five Unionists without benefit of trial. The militia searched the county and arrested about one hundred and fifty. A jury was formed, and the trial began. Some confessed; others were convicted; forty were hanged. It was said that the trees in North Texas indeed bore strange fruit.[17]

In Wise, Grayson, and Denton counties a more sane course was followed. General Hudson ordered Captain John Hale, commandant at Decatur, county seat of Wise County, to arrest Peace party members. A trial commission of fifty, presided over by Reverend William Bellamy, a Methodist preacher, was formed. Five were convicted and hanged. The others were sentenced to serve the Confederacy.[18] In Grayson County forty men were arrested, but through the influence of James W. Throckmorton, then in the Confederate service, all except

---

15. San Antonio *Express,* May 8, 1861.

16. C. N. Jones, *Early Days in Cooke County, 1848–1873* (Gainesville, 1936), 67–70.

17. Thomas Barrett, *The Great Hanging at Gainesville, Cooke County, Texas, October, A. D. 1862* (Gainesville, 1885); C. D. Cates, *Pioneer History of Wise County,* 131. One report put the number of executions, legal and otherwise, at 171 in Cooke County alone; 32 were hanged on one tree.

18. *Ibid.,* 131–132.

one were declared innocent.[19] In Denton County several arrests were made, but all were set free except one who was shot to death while in prison.

After these executions matters appeared quiet in the Northern Sub-District of Texas, composed of these and adjoining counties. Beneath the surface, however, the current of dissension and disaffection ran swifter and swifter. As late as 1864, H. E. McCulloch, in command at Bonham, wrote to Lieutenant General E. Kirby Smith, in command of the Trans-Mississippi Department, that the situation was almost out of hand. He said that disloyalty was widespread, that his "brush men" were deeply involved, and that his troops were not free from it. He warned that his section would be lost to the Confederate cause unless some good troops were sent to his support, and that speedily. He proposed to send his "brush men" down into Bowie County in order to get them close to the loyal troops of General Sam Bell Maxey and to place new and dependable troops between them and the Federals. He urged Smith to "establish a court here, try and execute some of these fellows for desertion, and send some of these disloyal men who harbor deserters and spout treason to some safe place in heavy irons."[20] Disloyalty, disaffection, and impending disaster were written between the lines. The Galveston *Tri-Weekly News* gave further evidence of the state of affairs in North Texas when it reported that Colonel G. A. Jackson left Bonham with a force of one hundred men on an expedition west and returned four weeks later with sixteen men. About forty miles west of Lampasas Springs the. company mutinied, and fifty-six of the men took charge and left for California.[21]

Union feeling was rampant from the beginning in Bexar County and the surrounding area. Even before the Sumter incident a Federal officer, stationed in San Antonio, observed widespread Union feeling in his vicinity. He wrote that the plan of Unionists was to effect a peaceable change in the views of the people through the agency of the press and the ballot box. He was impressed with the tremendous strength of the loyalists and professed to believe that "a few thousand dollars expended on the press would revolutionize sentiment in Texas."[22] One Union agent of the press in San Antonio was the *Weekly Alamo Express,* edited by James P. Newcomb. This was the bitterest sheet in Texas, the San Antonio *Express* not having yet made its appearance. Sentiment must have been

---

19. McKinney *Courier-Gazette,* August 24, 1906.

20. McCulloch to Smith, February 6, 1864, *Official Records,* Series I, vol. XXXIV, p. 945.

21. Galveston *Tri-Weekly News,* May 29, June 3, 1864.

22. Colonel C. A. Waite to Assistant Adjutant General, San Antonio, April 1, 1861, in *Official Records,* Series I, Vol. I, p. 550.

widespread, as Newcomb, in the columns of the *Express,* made no effort to make Unionist activities a secret. For instance in April, 1861, a notice which had been posted widely over San Antonio, appeared in the columns of his paper to the effect that a public meeting would be held on the Main Plaza on Tuesday night, April 9. The notice invited all those to be present who were in favor of preserving the government from total destruction, and "restoring harmony and prosperity to our distracted country." At this meeting General Robert Taylor spoke on the "Reconstruction of the Union," but the crowd refused to hear Judge Paschal. The Unionists retired to Paschal's home, where the address was given. In describing this meeting editor Newcomb exclaimed: "So ended a glorious night. We have given the Reconstruction ball a roll. Let it be kept rolling over the state until all opposition is crushed out."[23]

In the same issue Newcomb paid his respects to the Confederacy and to Jefferson Davis. He said that the so-called Southern Confederacy was "conceived in sin, shapen in iniquity, and born out of due time, because it was rushed into the world with indecent haste expressly to prevent the people from beholding its deformities." He had little to say against Davis except that he was vain, proud, weak, imprudent, ambitious, unprincipled, a vile traitor, a trained rebel, and an inflated bigot. It was soon after this outburst that the Knights of the Golden Circle visited Newcomb's office with the dire consequences previously noted.

Loyal San Antonians awoke early one spring morning in 1862 to find treasonable placards written in German, posted at prominent places in their city, the work—evidence seemed to show—of the German element. The note was addressed to "German Brothers" and pointed out that the Confederate paper was worthless. "We are always ready," the notice said. "Inform everyone that the revolution has broken out."[24] This was most distressing news to San Antonians, especially since it had just been discovered that the Germans in San Antonio had organized militia composed of seventy-three men, well armed with shotguns, rifles, and pistols.[25]

H. E. McCulloch, Confederate commander of the Sub-Military District of the Rio Grande, stationed at San Antonio, gave further proof that the vicinity of San Antonio was a hotbed of distloyalty when he wrote to Major Davis that there was "a considerable undercurrent of sentiment" against the Confederate cause in his district. He reported that Unionists everywhere celebrated the defeat of the Confederate forces, shouted "we have gained a victory," sent up

23. *Weekly Alamo Express,* April 11, 1861.

24. McCulloch to Boyer, San Antonio, March 31, 1862, *Official Records,* Series I, Vol. IX, p. 705.

25. McCulloch to Lubbock, March 27, 1862, MSS., Governor's Letters, Texas State Archives.

small balloons to show their jubilation, and fired small guns by way of rejoicing. Their principal scheme was to discredit the state and the Confederacy by breaking down the currency. This they attempted to do by demanding several times as much in Confederate currency for supplies as they required in silver or gold.[26]

McCulloch had not overestimated the plans to depreciate Confederate money. This scheming went on at such pace that loyal Confederates were soon forced to take cognizance of it. In April, 1862, a mass meeting in San Antonio proposed to take strenuous action against any person who should attempt to depreciate state treasury warrants or Confederate notes or bonds by either "shaving the paper" or by charging exorbitant prices. It was agreed that any persons found guilty of such an offense would be treated as disloyal and that their names would be published throughout the state in newspapers, pamphlets, and handbills. Regardless of wealth, social, or official position, death would be the penalty for those who persisted.[27]

An attitude of coolness and indifference toward the cause of the Confederacy remained evident in San Antonio throughout the war. As late as October, 1863, Confederate leaders found it necessary to call mass meetings to devise ways and means of forcing men into an open expression of their attitudes and to get able-bodied men to enlist. Precinct committees were created with power to enroll men and to publish their names if they refused service, either active duty or home defense. It was nesessary to take this action against slackers.[28]

These fruitless efforts went on through all the war years only to have it reported two months before the breakup came that, in San Antonio, there was no evidence that a war was in progress. A newsman insisted that there was at least a brigade of able-bodied men in San Antonio engaged in the mad scramble for war profits. He thought it strange that men could carry sacks of coin but could not carry a musket. "What a difference there is between firearms and specie!" he exclaimed.[29] Never, he believed, had there been a more disgraceful scramble for the "almighty dollar" since the money changers were driven from the temple.

No doubt many of the so-called "slackers" in San Antonio were men who had drifted there from other sections, some on their way out of the States. The roads leading out of San Antonio, particularly those to Monterrey and Mata-

---

26. McCulloch to Davis, San Antonio, March 3, 1862, in *Official Records*, Series I, Vol. IX, pp. 701, 702.

27. *Semi-Weekly News* (San Antonio), April 28, 1862.

28. *Texas State Gazette* (Austin), October 7, 1863. One of these meetings was held at San Pedro Springs and was presided over by Samuel A. Maverick. T. J. Devine participated.

29. Galveston *Tri-Weekly News*, February 22, 1866.

moras, were clogged with notorious Unionists almost before the noise of battle was heard. They made their exodus to avoid the draft, to cooperate with others of like sentiment in prejudicing the Confederate cause in Mexico, and to act in concert with men from Austin, Fredericksburg, and from other points in Texas.[30]

So numerous were those making their exodus from Texas that Confederate authorities were forced to take drastic steps to prevent anyone from leaving the state except those known to be friendly to the Confederacy. Only a few weeks after machinery had been set up to apprehend these disloyal men, a United States consul, stationed at Matamoras, wrote that

the crowds of refugees from Texas do not diminish in the least, although it is very difficult, owing to the strict watch kept upon their movements, for them to get out. Many are arrested, some are hung; others are taken and pressed into service.[31]

Another United States consular official stationed at Monterrey urged the secretary of state to send a recruiting force to the border of Texas and assured him that three thousand men could be enlisted for the Union cause. He said that he had been informed that there were more than three hundred Union men at Monterrey being fed by charity. Charles Hunter, writing from the steamer *Montgomery* off the Rio Grande in July, 1862, reported that he had forty Unionists on board and that seventy or eighty were on the *Kensington*. He said that they had on board three Unionists of influence from Texas, one a judge, another a celebrated lawyer, and the third an influential politician. They were on their way to Washington, according to Hunter, to propose the immediate occupation of Texas. Hunter insisted that Unionists were so numerous that they could drive the secessionists out of Texas if they could only be armed.[32]

Acting in accordance with these reports, United States authorities notified the consul at Matamoras (October, 1862) that a boat would be sent within thirty days to pick up such Union refugees as would like to enlist in a Texas regiment then being formed at New Orleans and asked him to notify all loyal Texans. No expidition could be sent, however, as all satisfactory ports were under control of the Confederacy.[33]

At the outset, even before the unhappy days of conscription, an exceedingly troublesome situation arose among the Mexican population along the Rio

---

30. McCulloch to Davis, March 29, 1862, *Official Records,* Series I, Vol. IX, pp. 704–706.

31. Pierce to Seward (Matamoras), May 5, 1862, *ibid.,* 684, 686.

32. Hunter to Seward, July 18, 1862, *ibid.,* XV, 622.

33. Benjamin F. Butler (New Orleans) to Consul at Matamoras, October 30, 1862, and A. J. Hamilton to N. P. Banks, *ibid.,* 688, 618.

Grande from Zapata County to Fort Brown near the mouth of the river, inspired, no doubt, by the presence of the Unionists from the Confederate States. In November, 1861, the commanding officer at Ringgold Barracks (Rio Grande, Starr County) reported that the majority of Mexicans of Zapata County had not taken the oath of allegiance to the Confederacy; that, in reply to his order, only twenty responded; and that some had declared openly and definitely their intention to support no government except the government of the United States. Armed resistance followed attempts to force them to take the oath, whereupon Captain Nolan, attached to Fort Ringgold, attacked and killed several. Most of the remaining inhabitants fled across the river opposite Carrizo, deserting their homes entirely or leaving workmen to care for their stock. The presence of this disloyal element made it a military necessity that a part of the armed forces of Ringgold be stationed at Carrizo to protect loyal Confederate citizens.[34] Unfortunately these Mexicans in Zapata who refused to take the oath of allegiance had the support and encouragement of a strong element in the state of Guerrero, Mexico. The members of this group had declared their intention of going into the service of the United States if such force appeared on the Rio Grande.[35]

At Fort Brown, farther down the river, the situation was likewise perplexing. The best arrangement Confederate authorities could make with the Mexicans was that of neutrality, and as late as October, 1861, Hamilton P. Bee reported that the Mexican inhabitants on the American side of the river were quiet but warned that they could not be relied upon in case of invasion. He predicted that, if Fort Brown should be reoccupied by Federal troops, two or three thousand mounted guerrilla troops would be enlisted immediately and neutrality would be transformed into hostility.[36] He urged, therefore, that the Confederacy make every effort to hold Brownsville in order to keep quiet and neutral "a large and efficient force of a race embittered against us by real or imaginary wrongs."

The situation in the Southwest grew worse and worse during 1861 until, at the year's end, complete chaos and disorganization existed. At Brownsville there were only two companies of infantry, one of which was composed entirely of Mexicans who were wholly susceptible to bribery and corruption. Lieutenant Colonel August C. Buchel, commanding at Fort Brown, reported that fourteen of this Mexican company had deserted and had crossed the river into Mexico

---

34. Brewin (Ringgold) to Ford, November 7, 1861, *ibid.*, IV, 132.

35. Ford to Stith, November 11, 1861, *ibid.*, 137.

36. H. P. Bee to Secretary of War (Richmond), October 12, 1861, *ibid.*, 119.

and that the remaining ones could be enticed very easily with a few dollars and "a little whiskey."[37]

The situation along the Rio Grande was considerably complicated by a revolution across the river in the state of Tamaulipas. The Mexican population of Texas found that service in the revolutionary army of Tamaulipas offered more satisfaction in pay and conditions of service, and that it opened an avenue of escape from giving aid and comfort to a cause which they detested. The Mexicans knew, too, that the Confederate force in the region was wholly inadequate, that the Rio Grande service was exceedingly unpopular among soldiers everywhere, and that it would likely remain so. The inside of this trouble, however, was given by a Fort Brown officer when he wrote that

the condition of the troops is such that I must candidly confess I am not greatly surprised at their yielding to inducements offered by parties on the other side of the river. The most of them are but scantily clothed, and they have received no pay; and they know the state of the government credit quite as well as I do myself.[38]

Conditions grew from bad to worse along the river and in May, 1862, martial law was declared in Cameron, Hidalgo, and Starr counties with A. N. Mills as provost marshal. Many arrests were made, and in May, 1862, Colonel Luckett, stationed at Brownsville, reported emphatically that "we are in a fair way to get rid of the reprobates who have lived under a government they secretly detested."[39]

The unsettled condition along the lower Rio Grande was further remedied in 1863 when a friendly arrangement was made with Don Albino López, governor of Tamaulipas. By this agreement passports for crossing the river were to be required. To make the requirements effective, the state of Tamaulipas would station troops at Reynosa, Camargo, Mier, and Guerrero, while the Confederates would set up watching posts at Edinburg, Rio Grande City, and Carrizo. This in no way settled the question of desertions, but authorities preferred to proceed with an inadequate settlement rather than risk disturbing the good relations between Mexico and the Confederacy.[40]

The situation on the lower Rio Grande, in spite of martial law, and all the efforts of loyal Confederates, was never satisfactory. In November, 1863, a Confederate company of Mexicans under command of the Mexican, Vidal, staged a

---

37. Buchel to Davis, December 5, 1861, *ibid.*, 152, 153.

38. Luckett to Davis, December 31, 1861, *ibid.*, 165.

39. *Semi-Weekly News*, May 22, 1862, quoting the Fort Brown *Flag*.

40. H. P. Bee to López, February 18, 1863, *Official Records*, Series I, Vol. XV, p. 993.

daring mutiny some miles above Brownsville. Vidal had been in communication with Federal blockaders off the mouth of the river and had plotted to aid in the capture of the city. Expressmen were dispatched to order Vidal to report to Captain Taylor at Fort Brown. One of the men sent out was killed; the other, though wounded, was able to return and report. Citizens turned out en masse, and they soon had a force of three hundred armed from the Fort Brown arsenal. General Hamilton Bee appealed for aid to the governor of Tamaulipas, as he expected Vidal to coöperate with the Federals in the capture of Brownsville. The governor responded, and the mutiny was broken up. As to the loyalty of the three hundred citizens to the Confederacy, it should be noted that when the Federal troops appeared under General N. P. Banks "not a dozen stood by General Bee." Dye, mayor of Brownsville, and Judge Bigelow Palmer, loud in their proclamations of loyalty to the Confederacy, were among the first to take the the Federal oath.[41]

One of the most determined groups of Union sympathizers dwelt in the Central Texas area around Gillespie County. The Union activity center was at Fredericksburg, but the leaders there drew support from the surrounding counties of Llano, Blanco, Kendall, Kerr, as well as Travis, which adjoined Blanco. This element in Gillespie County soundly defeated secession in the election of February 23, 1861, by the overwhelming vote of 398 to 16.[42] Blanco and Travis likewise defeated it.

When the war started and the question of the choice of an enrolling officer for Gillespie and the surrounding counties was raised, J. W. Sansom, a moderate Unionist, applied for the position. J. M. Patton and others from Fredericksburg immediately wrote to the adjutant general at Austin and warned against the choice of Sansom on the ground of his unionism. Patton said that Sansom had declared that "I will be __ __ if I ever fight against the Federal Government," and had described him (Patton) as an old fool who was willing to fight for the Southern men's negroes.[43]

Jacob Kuechler, the man chosen as enrolling officer, proved to be not only a Unionist, but a traitor. Kuechler proposed to enroll in frontier companies only those loyal to the United States, and those who wished to get into a company for service in the Confederacy could not even get an audience with him. On two occasions citizens from Kerr County met with about thirty citizens of

41. Galveston *Tri-Weekly News,* November 20, 23, 1863.

42. Ernest William Winkler (ed.), *Journal of the Secession Convention* (Austin, 1912), 88–90. Most of these counties had a large number of Germans. The percentage was as follows: Kendall, 81; Gillespie, 75; Kerr, 55; Llano, 10; Travis, 8.

43. J. M. Patton to Adjutant General, January 7, 1862. Adjutant General's Correspondence, State Library, Austin, Texas.

Gillespie at Live Oak Mill, about five miles from Fredericksburg for the purpose of enlisting, but Kuechler refused to meet with them.[44] The men of Kerr and Gillespie petitioned Governor Lubbock to remove Kuechler, complaining that he gave no notice of his appointment; that he established no office for the enrollment of the men; that he enrolled only Germans who were Unionists and who could vote for him for commanding officer; and that he enlisted Germans from Blanco County, which was not included in his district.[45]

This deep-rooted opposition, however, gave no further evidence of its strength prior to March, 1862, when P. O. Hebert declared martial law in Texas. Hebert's declaration required all alien males over sixteen years of age to take an oath of allegiance to the state of Texas and to the Confederacy. Almost immediately this powerful but dormant Unionist sentiment was aroused, and the Union Loyal League, which had been organized in June, 1861, held a meeting. Five hundred male Unionists met on Bear Creek in Gillespie County and organized three companies from Kendall, Kerr, and Gillespie counties. Fritz Tegner was chosen major, and an "advisory board" was appointed. The advisory board and the officers held a joint meeting and then dispersed to await further developments, only after declaring their intentions of preventing the conscription of "Union sympathizers."[46]

Few men from these counties went into the Confederate army but entered service for home and frontier protection instead, hoping, it was charged, to escape conscription by this ruse.[47]

When Governor Lubbock was reasonably certain that a military force would be required to quell the disturbances, he gave orders for Captain Kuechler's Company to disband and, at the same time, dispatched Captain James Duff with two companies of partisan rangers to Fredericksburg. Duff left San Antonio on May 28, arrived on the scene May 30, and immediately declared martial law in Gillespie County and precinct number five in Kerr. He declared himself to be provost marshal and gave the citizens six days in which to report to him

44. D. H. Farr to Lubbock, January 28, February 13, 1862, MSS., Governor's Letters, Texas State Archives.

45. Quinlan, Jackson, and thirty-six others of Kerr County to Lubbock, February 14, 1862. See also Nelson, Hunter, and seventy-four others of Gillespie County to Governor Lubbock, February 13, 1862, MSS., Governor's Letters, Texas State Archives.

46. Texas Historical Records Survey Division of Community Service Program, Works Progress Administration, *Inventory of the County Archives of Texas No. 86, Gillespie County* ([Fredericksburg], 1941).

47. Several such companies were recruited as follows: The Minute Company, forty men, Braubach, commander; The Gillespie Rifles, forty-six men, Charles Nimitz, commander; Krauskopf's Company, fifty-seven men; Frontier Defense company, sixty-two men, W. J. Locke, commander; Wahrmund's Company; and Jacob Kuechler's company.

and take the oath of allegiance. Duff and his men encountered difficulties from the first in getting forage for their horses because their friends had little and others would not sell for paper money. Duff likewise found that the people were reserved and reluctant to give testimony which would lead to the arrest of the offenders. Of this reluctance Duff wrote:

> I found beyond doubt that the few citizens of the place who were friendly to this government did not possess the moral courage to give information to the Provost Marshal of the sayings and doings of those who were unfriendly.[48]

Duff, therefore, called a meeting and took affidavits concerning the attitude of Sheriff Braubach, Captain Kuechler (state troops), F. W. Dobbler (grocery-man), and F. Lochte (merchant). Jacob Kuechler escaped, but the other three finally were arrested and sent to the guardhouse in San Antonio.[49] Duff returned to San Antonio June 21, 1862.

Duff's expedition, however, did not end the trouble. After his visit the advisory board of the Loyal Union League held a meeting and disbanded its three companies but at the same time invited and advised the Union men who would not submit to meet Major Fritz Tegner, August 1, on the headwaters of Turtle Creek in Kerr County prepared to leave for Mexico. Sixty-one men volunteered to go, and they left their rendezvous on Turtle Creek on the afternoon of August 1. The company, as it was finally organized, was composed of sixty-three Germans, one Mexican, and five Americans under the command of Fritz Tegner. Lieutenant C. D. McRae, at San Antonio, was ordered to pursue the group and break up the organization.[50] With ninety-four men he overtook the Unionists on the western fork of the Nueces, near Fort Clark in Kinney County. The men were not on the alert, as they believed they had eluded the Confederates, but they had been betrayed by one of their own members, Charles Bergmann.[51] They were completely surprised when McRae attacked in the early dawn of Au-

---

48. Duff to Major E. F. Gray, June 23, 1862, *Official Records,* Series II, Vol. IV, p. 786.

49. While on this excursion, Duff went into Medina, Blanco, and Kendall counties, where he made several arrests.

50. His company consisted of detachments from Captain Donalson's Company, Captain Duff's Partisan Rangers, Captain Davis's Company, and Taylor's Battalion. Duff, who was one of McRae's key men in this massacre, was a Scotch adventurer. He had served in the United States army, but he had been dishonorably discharged prior to his arrival in Texas. Some time after the war he went to Paris, France, where he remained for the rest of his life. How the people of Gillespie County still feel about this massacre on the Nueces is well expressed by Don H. Biggers, who said in commenting on Duff's death in Paris: "Thus the land his savage crime had stigmatized was saved the further shame of having its soil polluted with his decaying carcass." See Don H. Biggers, *German Pioneers in Texas* (Fredericksburg, 1925), 59.

51. Charles Bergmann, who led Duff's men to the camp of the sleeping Germans, went to Mexico

gust 10, 1862. Thirty-two were killed and many wounded, while two of McRae's men were killed and eighteen wounded. On October 18, 1862, seven more of Tegner's men were killed while attempting to cross the Rio Grande.

McRae did not report any prisoners. As a matter of fact, his official report stated that the Germans fought with desperation and asked no quarter. This part of his report lends credence to accounts which claim that at least nine of the wounded men were brutally murdered.[52] In connection with the Nueces affair, J. Weinheimer, Sr., writing thirty-four years later, said that McRae shot most of the wounded immediately and that the others were taken to White Oak Creek in Gillespie, where they were either hanged or shot.[53]

Following the battle on the Nueces, Duff returned to Gillespie, captured and hanged about fifty men, and killed many "bushwhackers," as those who fled to the hills were called. To the friends of these men, whose only crime was that they had the courage to refuse to support a cause to which they could not subscribe, these acts of Duff's men constituted a crime which could not be justified even by the rules of savage warfare. That Duff had the right to pursue the men no one may doubt, but the killing of prisoners and leaving their bodies unburied may well be questioned. Three years after the Nueces affair, friends and relatives gathered the bleached bones of the victims and buried them at Comfort, Kendall County, where a monument was erected in their memory.

Gillespie County furnished few soldiers for the Confederacy, but it suffered acutely because of persecution and because of a lack of vital necessities. The families of soldiers in the state service were cared for partially by the county and partially by the Fredericksburg Southern Aid Society. For the comfort of soldiers and their families the society subscribed more than $5,000 worth of clothing and produce in one year.[54] Of a county tax of thirty-seven and one-half cents on the hundred dollars assessed valuation in 1864, twelve and one-half cents was diverted to support the indigent families of soldiers. Later in 1864 the tax was increased to fifty cents, a portion of which could be paid in wheat, bacon, or fruit.[55]

---

after the war, where, it was reported, he was killed by a "Seminole Indian Negro." At the time of his death Bergmann was the leader of a band of outlaws. *Ibid.*

52. C. D. McRae to Gray, August 18, 1862, *Official Records,* Series I, Vol. IX, p. 615. See also J. W. Sansom, *Battle of Nueces in Kinney County, Texas* (San Antonio. 1905).

53. J. Weinheimer, Sr., "Memories about Times of War," in *Festausgabe der Deutschen Kolonie Friedrichsburg* (Fredericksburg, 1896), 120–122.

54. Ada Maria Hall, The Texas Germans in State and National Politics, 1860–1865 (M.A. Thesis, University of Texas, 1938), 81.

55. Record of Commissioners Court (1850–1866), Volume A, p. 296 ff. Courthouse Records, Fredericksburg, Texas. Because of their German extraction, and because of their civil war record, the

The Union leaders in most of the active centers of Texas looked for advice and encouragement to Austin, where sentiment was intense even prior to secession. Amelia Barr said of these exciting days in Austin that Union sentiment had caused bitterness between her friends of many years standing. To a friend she confided that:

> I am ashamed to say that Austin is a scandalously Yankefied Union loving town which means that the majority of the citizens want Peace and Picayunes at any price. There are you know a lot of Yankee families here and it is their nature *to pollute everything they come in contact with*—There are very few who would not "trade" their very souls for a good "consideration."

Her viewpoint was perhaps prejudiced, as is illustrated by the story that, when an Austin Unionist described to her the newly elected Lincoln as such a good man who read his Bible and prayed three times a day, she replied that she thought him "much too good" and that he should "go to Heaven rather than to Washington."[56]

Travis County Unionists held their first public meeting after secession at Buass Hall in Austin on the night of February 9, 1861. The resolutions adopted that evening condemned the states for seceding, endorsed the Crittenden Compromise, and laid plans to defeat secession in the February 23 election. They achieved their goal in Travis County by a vote of almost four to one.[57]

Another good evidence of the strength of Unionism in Travis may be found in a petition circulated in protest against the Travis County delegates' taking their seats in the convention. This petition boasted 250 signers.[58]

Some of the Travis Unionists volunteered for Confederate service, some were drafted, some sought jobs which entitled them to exemption, and others procured substitutes. Many of them went into the hills above Austin and hid for days, weeks, and even months, in caves and thickets or along the Colorado, awaiting an opportunity to escape from the country. Some escaped and entered

---

people of Gillespie were persecuted during the first World War. Gillespie County, however, furnished more than its quota of men (360) and bought more than its share of Liberty bonds.

56. Amelia Barr to Jennie, Austin, February 15, 1861. Barr Papers, University of Texas Library, Austin.

57. *Southern Intelligencer,* February 13, 1861. Outstanding Unionists at this meeting were James W. Throckmorton (Collin), B. H. Epperson (Red River), S. M. Swenson, Thomas Stanley, J. D. McGary, G. H. Burdett, Alfred Smith, J. E. Henry (Grayson), R. N. Lane, A. P. Blocker, George H. Gray, George W. Davis, Judge Josiah Fisk, Bob Taylor (Fannin), and George W. Paschal.

58. Frank Brown, Annals of Travis County (MS., University of Texas Archives), Chapter XXI, 6–12. Delegates from Travis were John A. Green, H. N. Burdett, and George M. Flournoy.

the Union service. They went to Mexico, usually taking a course above and away from the settlements. Most of these men in Austin were unmolested for the first year of the war, but Confederate tolerance ebbed with misfortune. Judge Paschal was arrested; Swenson hid his gold under his fireplace and escaped to Mexico; and Jack Hamilton was expelled from the city, and his house burned.[59] Many able-bodied young men who were not well known found refuge in the various state offices as employees and remained throughout the war.[60]

In 1862 public opinion closed in on the Austin Unionists. Caught in the net was Reverend Charles Gillette of St. David's Episcopal Church. Gillette's lot had not been easy. Most of his parishioners were Unionists, while his bishop, Alexander Gregg, was an ardent Confederate. The bishop issued a prayer which was to be used in Episcopal churches throughout the diocese of Texas. This prayer petitioned for the success of the Confederate cause, and in it were the words "grant that the unnatural war which has been *forced* upon us, may speedily be brought to a close." Gillette would read all the prayer except the objectionable portion. The annual convention (1862) established the Episcopal Church of the Confederacy and adopted Bishop Gregg's prayer and required that it be read in full in all the churches of the diocese. Bishop Gregg read the prayer in full when he was in Austin. It was said that those who subscribed to "the doctrines according to Abe Lincoln" attended when Rector Gillette preached; those who believed in the "gospel according to Jeff Davis" appeared when Bishop Gregg had charge. Ultimately Gillette was forced to resign as rector, and he left Texas never to return. When the Confederate cause was lost, Bishop Gregg moved to San Antonio. It is interesting to note that Gregg was the first Austin man to take the required oath of allegiance to the government after the breakup.[61]

Many of these Unionists who left Austin during the war were separated from their families; all suffered physical inconveniences; and some suffered the pangs of conscience. Typical of these was Thomas H. Duval, who retired to his acres outside of Austin and remained until October 10, 1863. At his home there he

---

59. Many others made their exodus. Among them were Josiah Fisk, Amos Morrill, George H. Gray, William D. Price, W. C. Smith, Edward Swisher, Thomas H. Duval, Mrs. T. H. Duval, James Reed, J. B. McFarland, and E. B. Turner.

60. Galveston *Tri-Weekly News*, February 27, March 10, 1865.

61. Writers Program of the Works Projects Administration (comp.), *St. David's Through the Years* (Austin, 1942), 32–41. Judge George W. Paschal, John H. Robinson, E. M. Pease, A. J. Hamilton, W. L. Robards, J. H. Herndon, Robert Barr, Swante Palm, John M. Swisher, John Hancock, George Hancock, D. W. C. Baker, James H. Raymond, and S. M. Swenson were members of St. David's.

was bombarded by Confederates from the town which he had purposely left. On April 16, 1863, he recorded in his diary that "while I was working in the garden out comes Bishop Gregg (rabid Confederate) and his wife—Aunt Polly bore the whole weight—Laura took to her scrapers and I stayed in the garden."[62] To add to his embarrassment the Confederate draft officials began to close in on him. He was determined that he would not shoulder a gun to break up the "government of our fathers," that, before he would do so, he would sacrifice his own life. A draft took place on August 1, 1863, and on that day he recorded in his diary: "My name not drawn today—I'm in good luck."[63] Pressure increased, however, and he left Austin for Brownsville on October 10, 1863.

The life the refugee Unionists lived was one of hardships: their sacrifices were tremendous but futile. Reflecting this are the entries in Duval's diary for 1864. The entry for January 2, 1864, said: "Dreamed about home and wife—my enemies were after me and I was hiding about for my life—existence very wearying." On February 27, he recorded: "I am suffering mentally the torments of the damned and feel that death would be welcome in spite of all the darkness and mystery beyond it." March 5, he wrote: "I am sick at heart and weary of life. A sense of approaching ruin and misery is crushing me with the weight of a mountain."[64] Could it be that these Unionists regretted having cast their lot against their own people?

Disturbing conditions in North Texas, in San Antonio and vicinity, along the Rio Grande, in Gillespie and the surrounding area, and in Austin were matched by similar conditions elsewhere. In certain counties in the south central portion of the state, particularly Austin, Washington, Fayette, Lavaca, and Colorado counties, Union sentiment was at a high pitch many months prior to February 1, 1861. As a matter of fact, Unionist meetings were frequent, enthusiastic, and well attended in these counties throughout 1860. Speeches were vehement, and the press was caustic in branding as traitors those who would divide the Union. The editor of a Fayette County paper, early in 1860, adopted as a slogan "Our Country, Our State, The South, The Union" and constantly urged that the Union must be preserved. Secession, however, was approved by the voters of all these counties except Fayette.[65]

What appeared to be an extremely unpatriotic scheme was devised in these

---

62. Entry of April 16, 1863, Diary of Thomas Howard Duval (MS., University of Texas Library), p. 30.

63. *Ibid.,* August 1, p. 47

64. *Ibid.,* January, February, March, 1864.

65. La Grange *True Issue,* October 4, 1860. The vote was as follows: Austin, 825 for, 212 against; Washington, 1131 for, 43 against; Fayette, 580 for, 626 against; Lavaca, 592 for, 36 against; Colorado,

counties, particularly Fayette, to keep the men out of the Confederate army. As soon as the first gun was fired, the men of these counties rushed to enroll in the service of the state troops or in the state militia, and to organize stay-at-home companies. A casual visitor to Fayette in 1861 would have been impressed with the war-like appearance of things, and an uninformed Unionist would have prayed that all counties were not like Fayette. A little investigation would have shown, however, that the oratory, martial music, and military preparation were not for participation in the war, but rather to avoid it. Loyal Confederates, and even moderate Unionists, became disgusted with this sham and freely gave vent to their feelings. The editor of the La Grange *True Issue,* a Unionist who had fought secession with all his power, vehemently condemned these stay-at-home activities. Of these unpatriotic maneuvers he wrote:

> We are tired of seeing the "Dixie Greys," the "Silver Greys," the "Iron Greys," the "Dapple Greys," the "Mounted Greys," the "Amerrican Greys," the "Spanish Greys," and all the other Greys parading around town with stripes running down their backs (presumably yellow), and carrying double-barreled shotguns and six-shooters.[66]

Twenty-four companies had been organized in Fayette by October, 1861, yet only approximately one hundred fifty men were in the Confederate service. Patriots of this area became sensitive and began comparing their counties with others of the state. For instance, they pointed out that the voting population of Milam County was about seven hundred and that Milam had four hundred men in Confederate service. Fayette County with a voting population of thirteen hundred had only one hundred fifty in the Confederate army, and some of these were under age. The indifference or evasion was shown in other ways, too. A call was made for citizens to assemble at the courthouse in La Grange on September 23, 1861, to organize a Soldiers Aid Society. It was reported that "a large assemblage of about one dozen" was present on the occasion. It should be said, however, that before the year closed, Fayette had six companies in the Confederate States army, two of them out of Texas, one in Kentucky and one in Arizona.[67] Loyal Confederates believed such evasion was disgraceful in war times, but the men in these companies professed to believe that the governor would

---

584 for, 330 against. See E. W. Winkler (ed.), *Journal of Secession Convention of Texas,* 88–90.

66. La Grange *True Issue,* October 11, 1861. There had been fifteen flag presentations and many musters, drills, and camp drills in Fayette during the summer of 1861 with accompanying "blood and thunder" speeches. The *Issue* complained, however, that not "a Black Republican had been seen, let alone killed, by an active company of Fayette."

67. La Grange *True Issue,* September 27 and October 31, 1861.

call them into the service en masse. The *True Issue* insisted that if they were expecting such call, they would "wait until Gabriel blows his trumpet."[68]

From the military correspondence of the time it does not appear that the attacks by the editor of the *Issue* were in any way too severe. A few months after this editorial was published, William G. Webb wrote to Governor Lubbock to report the treasonable acts of two postmasters in Fayette County, Robert Zapp at Long Prairie and William Lewis at Cedar, and to ask for their removal. He enclosed a letter which had fallen into his hands, written by James Smith, a Fayette County man, to his brother, who was planning to go to Missouri to evade the draft. This letter painted a grim picture of the desperate situation in that county and ran, in part, as follows:

I am sorry to hear that you are going to Missouri. You need not go there to get clear of a draft. You can do better closer home. If you will come down here all will be right and you will be safe. You may rest assured that what I tell you, you can depend on. Be sure and come and bring your loose stock. Also all the arms you can. *We have the power and are going to use it—The Union men are uniting from Austin to the Coast* and I am satisfied they are in the majority. Bring as much powder and lead as you can.[69]

Union sentiment was rampant in these counties in 1860 and 1861, but the Conscription Act of 1862 was required to intensify it and cause it to flare up in what threatened to be a full-fledged rebellion. On November 28, 1862, A. J. Bell, the enrolling officer for Austin County, reported that in certain German settlements in Austin and adjoining counties opposition to conscription was being seriously contemplated, that meetings were being held to concert measures of resistance, that previous meetings had been well attended; and he urged that Captains R. W. Hargrove and J. B. McCown, both stationed at Hempstead in Austin County, be detailed to enforce conscription. Bell could not depend on the militia, as most of the militiamen sympathized with the disaffected element.[70]

Only a few weeks later Bell reported that Austin and adjoining counties were

---

68. The following companies of Texas state troops or Texas militia were organized in Fayette alone in 1861: Lone Prairie German Company; Dixie Rangers; Milton Guards; Beat No. 10; Dixie Greys; Round Top Guerrillas; Gates Company; Mounted Infantry; Rutersville German Company; High Hill Light Infantry; Oso Guards; Round Top Guards; Ross Prairie Company; Plum Grove Rifles; Lyons Mounted Riflemen; Silver Greys; Reserve Company; Shropshire Company; Fayetteville Home Guards; Bachelor Rifles; Wigfall Mounted Infantry; Company, Beat 12. See Muster Rolls, Archives, Texas State Library, Austin, Texas.

69. Webb to Lubbock, April 2, 1862, MS., Governor's Letters, Texas Archives.

70. A. J. Bell to J. P. Flewellen (superintendent of conscription), November 28, 1862, *Official Records,* Series I, Vol. XV, p. 887.

in a state of open rebellion against the Confederate government and that incendiary meetings were being held daily in open defiance of military authorities. At Shelby Prairie (upper Austin County) a meeting was held on December 31, 1862, attended by six hundred Unionists. This meeting had representatives from Austin, Washington, Fayette, Lavaca, and Colorado counties, each of which had been organized into "beats." The resolutions adopted by the representatives required that "the Chairman appoint one man from each 'beat' to return home and call his men together," and organize them into companies of infantry and cavalry. By January 3 these organizations had been completed, drilling had been started, and a picket guard (mounted and armed) had been established to communicate information to the commanding officers. Treason was in the air.[71]

Bell further pointed out that the men drafted on December 23, 1862, had refused to be sworn in and that the conscript captain whom he had assigned to Industry, Austin County, had been driven from his office. He again called for help and insisted that anything less than one full regiment of cavalry would be defeated.

At a meeting at Biegel's settlement (Fayette County) on January 4, 1863, the one hundred twenty participants openly declared their intentions in a communication to Brigadier General W. G. Webb at La Grange. They declared that they would not take the oath prescribed by the Confederacy and declared further that

the past has already taught us how regardlessly the Government and the County authorities have treated the families of those who have taken the field. We have been told that they would be cared for, and what, up to this time, has been done? They were furnished with small sums of paper money which is almost worthless and which has been refused by men for whose sake this war and its calamities were organized.[72]

They refused, therefore, to answer the Confederate call unless guarantees of the safety and welfare of their families were forthcoming.

Many accounts of similar activities were made to army officials. Eyewitnesses described a meeting of more than five hundred at Roeder's Mill (Austin County) in January, 1863. "The Germans are concentrating at Frelsburg [Colorado County] with the avowed purpose of resisting conscription," ran another account. "The negroes are to be free, and Jack Hamilton [Unionist] is in the Country," they declared triumphantly. According to reports their combined strength ranged from one thousand to fifteen hundred.[73]

---

71. Bell to Flewellen, January 3, 1863, *ibid.*, 925.

72. C. Amberg *et al.* to W. G. Webb, January 4, 1863, *ibid.*, 929.

73. W. G. Webb to A. G. Dickinson, January 4, 1863, *ibid.*, 926–928. See also McCown to Green, *ibid.*, 921.

Confederate authorities, though slow in recognizing conditions in these counties, finally dispatched army detachments to the vicinity. By special orders, January 8, 1863, martial law was declared in Colorado, Austin, and Fayette counties. Colonel Peter Hardeman was ordered with his entire regiment to Fayette. Major George T. Madison was sent to La Grange with twenty-five men. Lieutenant R. H. Stone with the same number was detailed to restore order in the Bellville community; while Hardeman himself took fifty men to assist in the arrest of the ringleaders.[74] The leaders were apprehended and turned over to the civil authorities, since their acts had been committed prior to a declaration of martial law. John B. Magruder wrote Lubbock that he was encouraged over the situation and that a better state of feeling existed. The assistant adjutant general urged that martial law be declared in De Witt and Lavaca counties also, but Magruder did not see fit to do so.[75] A visit from Governor Lubbock and the news of the Confederate victory at Galveston, combined with the declaration of martial law, had a salutary effect on the Germans, and late in January the adjutant general was able to report that the rebellion had been broken up.[76]

That the difficulties cleared up, even a little, is remarkable in view of the reports of the outrages perpetrated by the Confederate military forces in these counties. Adjutant General Webb said that Colonel Hardeman's command constituted the most disorderly set of men he had ever seen and that they committed all kinds of excesses. The planters and inhabitants complained that they took everything in sight.

That the Confederate cause in Fayette was not so bright as the adjutant general painted it became apparent as disturbing reports continued to circulate. The *True Issue* pointed out that although Fayette was "a very healthy county," there were approximately three times as many applications to the conscript surgeons for certificates of disability as in any other county in the district. The Galveston *News* in commenting on this said, "If Fayette County is physically healthy, it is politically very sickly." To this the *Issue* replied: "True, O, King! I must not be deterred from saying that there are not many good and true southern men here."[77]

A much later issue of the same paper made an appeal to all soldiers to come forward and "show their hands." A Confederate, Leslie Savage, who had lost an arm in the service, had just arrived in the county as enrolling officer. On the arrival of Savage the editor of the *True Issue* again lambasted the populace of

74. Henry L. Webb to Major B. Bloomfield, January 11, 1863, *ibid.,* 936, 942.

75. Magruder to Lubbock, February 11, 1863, *ibid.,* 974, 975. See also Webb to Turner, *ibid.,* 1021.

76 .Webb to Turner, January 21, 1863, *ibid.,* 955, 956.

77. *True Issue,* May 16, 1863.

Fayette; this was as late as the fall of 1864.

I trust before six weeks shall roll over our heads *our only trump* which has turned up in Fayette since the war commenced will put our *bluffers* at defiance,—Our trump, the Enrolling Officer, I will designate not only as a trump of hearts, but a trumpet that blows aliens and all other croakers to the battlefield to strike one *faint* blow in defense of their wives and children whom they would rather see polluted than strike one blow against that *Glorious Old Union* as they call it.[78]

Less than a month prior to the breakup in 1865, a Fayette County citizen wrote to Willard Richardson, editor of a Galveston paper, and asked why the conscript authorities could not enforce the laws and send the men to the front. This correspondent insisted that; if the conscript bureau could not do better throughout the state than it had done in Fayette, it should dismiss its enrolling officers and send them to the front. As a matter of fact, he said, the county had never been conscripted and the enrolling officer and his two clerks were less than forty years of age. Too many people had the "conscript limps."[79]

Fayette County citizens, in spite of the great number of disloyal men, from the first took cognizance of the needs of the soldiers. On June 22, 1861, the county commissioners appropriated $250 each to the Fayette Guards and the "Rough and Ready Rebels." In October of the same year the commissioners authorized the issuance of $9,000 in county bonds, appropriating the entire amount for the equipment of soldiers, with the stipulation that no company of one hundred was to receive more than $3,000 and that this money was not to be used to buy horses.

In May, 1862, the commissioners levied a twenty-cent tax on the one hundred dollar valuation "to relieve the necessities of the families of soldiers who are in indigent circumstances." They followed this with the adoption of a policy of issuing fifteen dollars to each new county soldier. To provide further for the families, the court authorized the chief justice to procure cloth and cotton cards from the penitentiary.[80]

The correspondence of Governors Lubbock and Murrah, 1861 to 1865, is literally filled with petitions and requests for exemption from the service. Most of these petitions were dated at post offices in the various centers above described as Unionist areas. A brief examination of the reasons which prompted requests for exemption is revealing. Some of the reasons were as follows:

---

78. *Ibid.,* September 24, 1864. Italics mine.

79. Galveston *Tri-Weekly News,* March 22, 1865.

80. Minutes County Court, Vol. B, pp. 282–361, in Commissioners Court Minutes, Courthouse, La Grange, Texas.

I cannot respond without personal sacrifice; I'm a wagoner; I'm a very useful man; I make spinning jennies; I'm a wheelwright; I own a corn mill; I'm a poor man; our wives can't take corn to the mill; I'm the only druggist and the community is "tolerably sick"; I'm a saltmaker; need another policeman; shortsighted; our young men are accustomed to riding horsebaek and therefore dread the infantry.

What threatened to be bold revolution in various sections of Texas in 1861 had simmered to passive resistance by the close of 1864. What was much more alarming, however, than Union activities was the fact that by year's end the whole state of Texas was fast becoming indifferent to the war, a disturbing symptom of the chaos which was about to engulf the whole South. The fortunes of the entire Confederacy were ebbing fast, and realists dared to whisper about restoring the Union, treason in 1861. Confederate army defeats and the influence of those who had never loved the Confederate cause had begun to bear fruit. Gloom and uncertainty, soon to pass into despair, settled quickly over Texas.

The Tenth Legislature met in extraordinary session on October 29, 1864. Rumors of an invasion from the North were flying thick and fast. Brigadier General H. E. McCulloch had just reported that it was the plan of the enemy to press into northern Texas, effect a lodgement somewhere on Red River, stir up and combine the disloyal element, hold that part of Texas, and use it as a base of operations into other parts of the South. Fear reigned supreme in the legislative halls.[81] In the cloakrooms and in other secluded places around the Senate chamber and the hall of the House of Representatives, whispered opinions about the reconstruction of the Union became more audible. As the rising tide of discussion came out into the open, determined men set themselves sternly against it. The first resolutions on the subject of reconstruction were introduced into the Senate by Senator Edward R. Hord. These resolutions were bitter and denunciatory and declared in vehement terms the determination of Texas to fight to the "last ditch" and never to reconstruct the Union.[82]

Senator Throckmorton of Collin County, who had served in the Confederate army despite his Union sentiments, was now the most influential Unionist in Texas, Sam Houston having reached the journey's end in 1863. Throckmorton tried to block the Hord resolutions, fearing that the discussion might extend to the masses to the detriment of the cause already nearly lost. Failing in this, he countered with a substitute which briefly declared that it was not within the

---

81. McCulloch to Turner, April 6, 1864, *Official Records,* Series I, Vol. XXXIV, Part III, pp. 742, 743.

82. E. D. Wooten to B. H. Epperson, October 30, 1864, in Epperson Papers, MS., Library, University of Texas.

power of a state to make either peace or war, and that the power to reconstruct the Union belonged to the Confederate government. This substitute, by inference, recognized the right of the Confederacy to subscribe to the re-establishment of the Union, a mild Unionism which only the exigencies of the hour would have tolerated.[83] The tide of the Confederacy was fast running out. There was yet a little time left, however, for men to hide their heads beneath the sand; and so they did, by endorsing the Hord resolutions, twelve to ten. Texan leaders were not realists in 1861; they were no more so in 1864.

As the year 1865 was inauspiciously ushered in, the telegraphic wires were daily burdened with messages of Confederate defeat, desertions, death, and destruction. As the people crowded around news centers to get the story as it came from the wires, Unionists smiled, while loyal Confederates turned away with sadness in their hearts. Then came the news of Lee's surrender. The most useless war in the history of mankind had come to an end.

---

83. Houston *Tri-Weekly Telegraph,* November 9, 1864.

Carte de visite of unidentified member of Company A, 1st Texas Cavalry. *Courtesy Lawrence T. Jones III.*

Texans in the Union Army, 1861–1865

FRANK H. SMYRL*

Slightly more than two thousand Texans served in the Union army. Best known of these was Edmund Jackson Davis, former district judge in South Texas, who left the state to form the First Texas Cavalry (Union). Under Davis's command the First Texas saw action in southern Louisiana in 1863 as part of a Federal effort to occupy the bayou country. Later that year troops of the First Texas were among the Union forces that captured Brownsville and moved up the Rio Grande toward Eagle Pass.

A second regiment of Texas Union cavalry, commanded by John L. Haynes, a former state legislator from Rio Grande City, was organized in December 1863. This regiment was made up primarily of Mexican Texans, many of whom were born in Mexico. Along with the First Cavalry, the Second Cavalry campaigned in South Texas in early 1864. In the summer of 1864 most of the two regiments were transferred to Louisiana, where they remained for the rest of the war.

In this article the late Frank H. Smyrl, professor of history at the University of Texas at Tyler, describes the role played by those Texans who served in the Union army. Smyrl states that 2,132 of these Union soldiers from Texas were white and 47 were black. Jerry Don Thompson, Vaqueros in Blue and Gray *(Austin: Presidial Press, 1976), 81, points out that over one-third (958) of these Texans in blue were*

* Frank H. Smyrl, "Texans in the Union Army, 1861–1865," *Southwestern Historical Quarterly,* LXV (Oct., 1961), 234–250.

Mexican Texans. See also Thompson's Mexican Americans in the Union Army *(El Paso: Texas Western Press, 1986) and Richard Current,* Lincoln's Loyalists: Union Soldiers from the Confederacy *(Boston: Northeastern University Press, 1992).*

By February 1, 1861, it was clear that the secessionists were in control of Texas,[1] despite an anti-secessionist governor and other public figures known to have Unionist sympathies. Throughout the war, Confederate Texas would be unable to ignore the strong feeling within the state in favor of an undivided nation, but secession ended the opposition of several influential Unionists: Governor Sam Houston retired peacefully to his Huntsville, Texas, home where he gave lip-service to the Confederacy but hoped somehow to separate Texas from the Confederacy and re-establish the Republic of Texas;[2] James Webb Throckmorton supported the Confederacy for the same noble reason that animated Robert E. Lee; former Governor Elisha Marshall Pease, never recognizing the Confederacy, simply kept quiet. But for some Texans, secession was a call to arms on the side of the United States, and it is to these men and their subsequent service in the Union army that this article is devoted.

By Texans of the Confederacy and die-hard Confederate sympathizers of the century following the Civil War, these men have been considered vile and despicable traitors, worthy of nothing more pleasant than a military firing squad—preferably a Confederate one. From a more detached point of view, it appears that a Texan who voluntarily gave his services to the Union in support of an undivided nation must have been a brave man either seeking adventure or willing to die for his beliefs. Unionists made of weaker stuff stayed at home or on the run. No one forced these Texans to choose the Union side, and each must have been aware that whether the Federal forces were victorious or not and whatever his gain, his loss would inevitably be great. He could have remained in Texas, as many did, quietly going about his business, in some danger perhaps, but not so much as that he faced in front of Confederate guns. Whatever the motive, it is estimated that 2,132 whites and 47 Negroes from Texas sought and found service in the Union armies.[3]

---

1. The vote on the Ordinance of Secession was 166-8. E. W. Winkler (ed.), *Journal of the Secession Convention of Texas, 1861* (Austin, 1912), 48–49. Elsewhere (p. 408n) Winkler states that the vote was 167-7.

2. Claude Elliott, "Union Sentiment in Texas, 1861–1865," *Southwestern Historical Quarterly,* L, 452.

3. Frank Klingberg, *Southern Claims Commission* (Berkeley and Los Angeles, 1955; University of California Publications in History, Volume L), 43; *Congressional Globe,* 41st Congress, 2nd Session, 3018 (April 27, 1867). These figures are based on a report by the Adjutant-General.

By far the most important Texan who became a Union soldier was Edmund Jackson Davis, and it is fitting that he organized and led by far the most important official unit of Texas troops to fight under the Stars and Stripes. Davis was a tall, slender, graceful sort of man, measuring six feet two and a half inches, of fair complexion and possessing a rather fine face and delicate blue eyes suggesting a generous character. Born in St. Augustine, Florida, of wealthy parents in 1827, he became a cadet at West Point and volunteered for service in the Mexican War. He moved to Texas in 1848 and occupied himself as a postal clerk, deputy customs officer, lawyer, and district attorney. He was a district judge when the war began. After running unsuccessfully for a seat in the secession convention, he decided to leave Texas. His escape was made good when in May, 1862, he boarded a Federal blockader at the mouth of the Rio Grande. In the fall of that year he began organizing what was to become the First Texas Cavalry (Union).[4]

By November 12, 1862, Major General Benjamin F. Butler was making plans for the use of E. J. Davis's troops.[5] Davis had arrived at Butler's headquarters with his refugees and "renegades" six days before, and it was already obvious that they desired service nearer home.[6] Butler proposed to send them and other troops to Galveston, which was temporarily under Federal control. He hoped to hold that important Texas port and possibly to take Houston.

Still there existed a great need for troops in Davis' regiment. Butler proposed to Leonard Pierce, Jr., Union consul at Matamoros, that all Texas refugees in that Mexican city who were willing be sent by military transport to Galveston, hoping that many of them would then volunteer for service under Davis. "Of course [wrote Butler] it will be improper to enlist even Americans as soldiers on Mexican soil, but there can be no impropriety in sending Americans to do their duty to their country."[7]

After Major General Nathaniel P. Banks had replaced Butler in command at New Orleans, the troops of Davis embarked from New Orleans on the night of December 31, 1862. Their immediate goal was still Galveston, where one of the ships, the *Cambria*, carrying two companies of the First Texas, arrived about 7:00 P.M., January 2, 1863. The weather was bad, and fear of sticking on the bar

---

4. Clipping frorn *Weekly Free Man's Press* (Galveston), July 25, 1865, in E. J. Davis File (Biographical Files, Texas History Center, University of Texas Library).

5. Butler to Pierce, November 12, 1862, *War of the Rebellion: A Compilation of the Official Records of the Union and Confederate Armies* (70 vols. in 128; Washington, 1880–1901), Ser. I, Vol. XV, 591.

6. Frederick H. Dyer, *A Compendium of the War of the Rebellion* (New York, 1959), 1647; Quintero to Benjamin, March 21, 1863, *Official Records*, Ser. I, Vol. XXVI, Pt. II, 68.

7. Butler to Pierce, November 12, 1862, *ibid.*, Ser. I, Vol. XV, 592.

off the island caused the naval commander to anchor for the night. The following day brought no relief in the weather, and six men were sent ashore in search
of a pilot and assistance. The next day, January 4, broke clear, and the bark *Cavallo,* flying Union colors, was seen approaching. Unwillingly the pilot of the
Cavallo boarded the *Cambria,* where he was immediately recognized as a Confederate named T. W. Payne. Galveston had fallen back into the hands of the
Confederacy, and two companies of the First Texas almost did. Keeping Payne
aboard, the *Cambria* turned away, leaving the six men it had sent ashore to look
out for themselves as well as the *Cavallo,* which became the ship without a pilot.[8]

The Federals were extremely lucky in making their escape, for at Galveston,
on board the *Harriet Lane,* was Major General John Bankhead Magruder. Magruder was aware that the vessel *Cambria* carried not only the larger part of the
First Texas and 2,500 saddles, but Davis as well. Just as Payne was recognized as
a Confederate, one of the six men sent ashore had been recognized as a deserter.
Magruder had planned carefully the attempt to trick the *Cambria* into coming
into port, only to have it fail when Payne was recognized. Magruder had the
captured deserter shot publicly; the other captives, on both sides, were treated
as prisoners of war.[9]

Davis escaped the Confederates at Galveston, but at Brownsville he did not
fare so well. By March 6, 1863, part of the Federal fleet carrying the First Texas
reached the Rio Grande, among them the *Honduras,* on which Davis was then
sailing.[10] Weather again prohibited communication with the shore, and it was
not until March 10 that Davis reached Matamoros. He and five other men went
ashore in a small craft, the *Honduras* remaining in Mexican waters at a safe distance from Confederate defenses at Point Isabel. The Confederates were ready
for any attempt that the Federals might make an invasion, but Brigadier General Hamilton P. Bee, commanding at Brownsville, did not expect one. He
thought at that time that Davis would simply pick up his family and any deserters or refugees he could in Matamoros, and return to New Orleans.[11] At least
Bee could hope.

At three o'clock in the morning of March 15, a group of Confederates, sometimes called Texas Rangers, crossed the Rio Grande without orders and captured
Davis, a man named William Montgomery, and three or four others, and car-

---

8. Bach to Banks, January 7, 1863, *ibid.,* 205.

9. Magruder to Cooper, February 16, 1863, *ibid.,* 219–220.

10. The *Cambria* returned to New Orleans before Davis and his Texans went on to Brownsville,
ibid., 200.

11. Bee to Dickinson, March 11, 1863, *ibid.,* 1013–1014.

ried them back into Texas. News of this breach of Mexican neutrality reached Bee unofficially at noon that day. He had little choice but to surrender the prisoners when it was demanded of him by Governor Albino Lopez of Tamaulipas, but it was too late for Montgomery. He had already been hanged. Feeling ran high in Matamoros against the Confederacy, but the quick return of the living prisoners quieted the city. Montgomery's death seemed to bother no one. Though it must have been difficult for a Confederate commander to give up such a prisoner as Davis, no matter what the circumstances of his capture, Bee's action was fully supported by his superiors. Mexican neutrality could not be traded for E. J Davis.[12]

General Bee was fairly accurate in his guess as to what Davis' business at Brownsville was. He had come for his wife, and he had come for his potential recruits. But at least part of the troops Davis brought back to Texas with him were left to serve in their native state under Major General Napoleon J. T. Dana while Davis returned to New Orleans by water to continue building his regiment. By the end of April he had organized enough new recruits to be considered a part of the Defenses of New Orleans, as the army was organized at that time, under Brigadier General Thomas West Sherman.[13]

The initial action that the First Texas saw in Louisiana was on the Amite River. This operation, begun on May 18, 1863, in conjunction with the Sixth Michigan and the One Hundred Twenty-eighth New York, had as its purpose to gain control of the Jackson Railroad. Fighting was limited to light skirmishing, but the five Texas companies did their part in making the operation a success. All the railroad depots were destroyed, a railroad-car factory was demolished, as well as a Confederate shoe factory and tannery.[14] Before the Texans saw their next action, a reorganization of troops took place, and the five Texas companies serving in Louisiana were re-formed into three.[15] Thus they entered the field of battle as a part of the aggressive Banks' further attempt to push west from New Orleans by land in the summer of 1863. In the operations around Brashear City (Morgan City) in mid-June, only a minor role fell to the Texans. They were told to hold a flank position and do reconnoitering and they engaged in no heavy combat.[16]

12. Quinterro to Benjamin, April 20, 1863, *ibid.*, Ser. I, Vol. XXVI, Pt. II, 49: Bee to Dickinson, March 15, 1863, *ibid.*, Ser. I, Vol. XV, 1016–1017; Lopez to Bee, March 23, 1863, *ibid.*, 1025; Magruder to Cooper, March 31, 1863, *ibid.*, 1031.

13. *Ibid.*, 713.

14. Sherman to Headquarters, Department of the Gulf, *ibid.*, 406.

15. *Ibid.*, Ser. I, Vol. XXVI, Pt. I, 531.

16. Smith to Cahil, June 21, 1863, *ibid.*, 584.

At this point, Colonel Davis was called away from his cavalry unit, leaving it in the hands of Lieutenant Colonel Jesse Stancel, to go on a rather special mission. He was sent to New York with a group of 500 Confederate prisoners who were more or less in the way in Louisiana.[17] Upon his return he was given a more routine assignment. In early September, as a part of the Nineteenth Army Corps under General William B. Franklin,[18] he and his troops sailed from New Orleans for the Texas coast. Their goal was to take and hold Beaumont and the Houston-Beaumont Railroad, which was considered militarily strategic by the Federals.[19] The Confederates under Lieutenant Dick Dowling effectively took care to block those plans. The campaign, called the Sabine Pass Expedition, lasted until September 11. No fighting on the part of the First Texas was reported. The unit returned to New Orleans in time for the Teche Campaign of October, 1863, west of New Orleans. In this campaign they saw perhaps their hardest service to date.

The Nineteenth Corps to which the First Texas belonged reached the fighting front on the morning of October 9. Immediately the First Texas was thrown across Vermillion Bayou, leaving the infantry behind to construct bridges. It ran into a determined Confederate force but succeeded in pushing it back. This was but one of the times when Texan would battle Texan in the course of the Civil War.[20]

The First Texas saw limited service at New Iberia and at Carrion Crow Bayou before being called back to New Orleans on October 17.[21] Five days later they were aboard transports on the Mississippi headed for Texas to take part in the Rio Grande Campaign. Eight days on the water found the Texans at home once again, though stormy weather at the mouth of the Rio Grande prevented their landing for another two days.[22]

One of the best known Texans in the Union Army did no actual fighting. He was Andrew Jackson Hamilton, who had been Attorney General of Texas, a member of the Texas Legislature, and a member of the Thirty-sixth Congress of the United States. Hamilton was born in Huntsville, Alabama, on January 28, 1815. He was admitted to the bar in Alabama in 1841 and moved to LaGrange, Texas, in 1846, where he continued his law practice until he entered public

---

17. Emory to Dix, June 30, 1863, *ibid.,* 608–609.

18. Special Orders, No. 216, August 31, 1863, *ibid.,* Ser. I, Vol. LIII, 569.

19. Banks to Franklin, August 31, 1863, *ibid.,* Ser. I, Vol. XXVI, Pt. I, 287–288.

20. Banks to Beckwith, October 9, 1863, *ibid.,* 758.

21. Stone to Ord, October 17, 1863, *ibid.,* 770–771.

22. *Ibid.,* 429.

office. Hamilton refused to leave his seat in congress when other Southerners walked out. When he did return to Texas, he was elected to the Texas Legislature on a Union ticket.[23] Instead of taking the oath of allegiance to the Confederacy, Hamilton decided to leave Texas. He found his life in danger and was forced to hide in the hills west of Austin for some time before making his way to Mexico. When he did leave however, he was not alone. A traveler from Rio Grande City reported having seen and talked with Hamilton and a party of seventeen refugees at Mier. Hamilton's party told him that they had ridden night and day from Austin until they had reached "safety" on the Rio Grande. Claiming that their only purpose in leaving Texas was to evade the conscript law, the party told the traveler of other persons near Austin awaiting an opportunity to join them in flight.[24]

By August 16, 1862, Hamilton's group of refugees had grown in number to sixty and had made its way to Matamoros. A man who saw him at the Montezuma House in that city reported that "Hamilton seemed to keep remarkably quiet, and was generally so much occupied with reading that he could hardly find time to speak to his former secession friends." Lack of money was his towering problem. The general opinion was that he sought to get his men to New York.[25]

Washington, not New York, was his ultimate goal. Horses and guns had to be sold to raise the money necessary for expenses, but Hamilton found himself in Washington by October, 1862. In the company of New York politicians he had an interview with Secretary of War Edwin M. Stanton, urging immediate occupation of Texas by Federal troops.[26]

Abraham Lincoln became interested in the tall Texas Unionist and offered him an interview on November 8. He wrote to Seward the following: "Will be glad to see Col. Hamilton & his friends whenever it may be convenient for them."[27] From his activity in Washington at this time stemmed Hamilton's appointment as military Governor of Texas. The appointment took effect some time between November 8 and 14, 1862.

News of this appointment reached Texas and caused, among others, the following reaction by the *Texas State Gazette*: "Would that he should determine to

---

23. New Orleans *Daily Picayune,* April 3, 1861 (Afternoon Edition).

24. *Texas State Gazette* (Austin), August 20, 1862.

25. *Tri-Weekly News* (Galveston), August 30, 1862.

26. Ludwell H. Johnson, *Red River Campaign: Politics and Cotton in the Civil War* (Baltimore, 1958), 15.

27. Roy P. Basler (ed.), *The Collected Works of Abraham Lincoln* (9 vols.; New Brunswick, 1953–55), V, 492.

attempt the part of his great prototype Cataline [Catiline], and head the troops who are to march against us."[28]

Banks, not Hamilton, was to lead the troops against Texas. Hamilton sailed with Banks' troops from New York on December 4, 1862, with New Orleans the immediate (though secret) goal.

Hamilton and his supporters had strongly advocated the invasion which resulted in the short occupation of Galveston in 1862. With the loss of that port in early 1863, it was no longer part of the plans of Banks and his superiors in Washington to invade Texas. In fact, on January 19, 1863, Banks told the "Governor" that he possibly might never invade Texas again. Hamilton and his followers again left for Washington—this time hoping to secure for Hamilton a military department in Texas.[29] Speaking to a New York audience, he said that a Federal army would be hailed with shouts in Texas, and would meet with little or no effective resistance. To this the Bellville *Countryman* retorted, "Jack is right about the shouts. But they will be of a kind that have made federals and traitors tremble on many a field since the secession ball opened."[30]

The ultimate result of Hamilton's efforts during his second Washington campaign was an expression of confidence in him by Lincoln. Lincoln wrote to Banks, "I really believe him [Hamilton] to be a man of worth and ability; and one who, by his acquaintances there [Texas], can scarcely fail to be efficient in re-inaugurating the National authority."[31]

Hamilton reported to Major General Banks at New Orleans on October 13, 1863, where by order of the War Department, he was supplied with a cavalry guard known as Hamilton's Body Guard.[32] As military governor he had been charged to "re-establish the authority of the Federal Government in the State of Texas and to provide the means of maintaining the peace and security to the loyal inhabitants of that State until they shall be able to establish a civil government." Much discretion was left to Hamilton in carrying out these instructions,

---

28. *Texas State Gazette* (Austin), November 5, 1862.

29. Johnson, *Red River Campaign*, 29.

30. Bellville *Countryman*, October 25, 1863.

31. Lincoln to Banks, September 19, 1863, Basler, *The Collected Works of Abraham Lincoln*, IV, 465–466. In this letter Lincoln left a blank for Hamilton's first name or initials, indicating that the Texan had not made such an overwhelming impression on him.

32. There is little evidence that the men who made up Hamilton's Body Guard were actually Texans. They are, however, listed in the index of the *Official Records* as "Texas Troops (U.)." The Second Texas Cavalry, a much larger group than the original guard, was sometimes also called Hamilton's Body Guard.

and he was promised the support of the Lincoln government in whatever he did.[33]

Banks agreed to make another attempt on Texas in spite of his failure at Sabine Pass and the loss of Galveston, but he insisted that Hamilton remain in New Orleans until he heard of the success of the invading force, which included Davis and the First Texas Cavalry. Success came. Hamilton proceeded to Brownsville to set up his headquarters, extremely satisfied with the progress he had made in the past few months.[34]

Hamilton arrived in Brownsville on December 1, 1863. He appeared much more concerned about his family's safety (members of which had been in Texas since his departure a year earlier) than about the raising of troops or the planning of campaigns. He seemed content to leave that to Banks and Dana. Next to his family, he was interested in the establishment of a Federal court at Brownsville. Writing to Secretary Stanton on the subject, he said:

"There will certainly be much need of a court here, if for no other purpose, to settle questions arising under the act of Congress providing for the confiscation of property of persons engaged in the rebellion."[35]

Over the proposed court, Hamilton found opposition. Dana felt that such a court had no place in a territory under martial law. Dana complained that Hamilton was meddling in his affairs and obstructing investigations that Dana was carrying on by withholding information.[36] This clash of authority came to an end, however, late that month when Major General Francis Jay Herron arrived to replace Dana.[37]

The aggregate strength of the Federals when they began the Rio Grande expedition was 6,988 men, with about half present for duty, and sixteen pieces of field artillery. A look at the First Texas shows its strength to be 16 officers, 205 men present for duty, and a claimed aggregate total of 310 men present and absent.[38]

Davis continued to build his forces after he reached Texas, promising prospective recruits that they would be required to serve only "during the campaign in Texas."[39] By December 2, he had mustered in an additional 115 volunteers.[40]

---

33. Stanton to Hamilton, November 14, 1862, *Official Records,* Ser. III, Vol. II, 782.

34. Banks to Lincoln, December 4, 1863, *ibid.,* Ser. I, Vol. XXVI, Pt. I, 832.

35. Hamilton to Stanton, December 19, 1863, *ibid.,* 866.

36. Dana to Stone, December 11, 1863, *ibid.,* 842.

37. Banks to Stanton, December 26, 1863, *ibid.,* 902.

38. *Ibid.,* 398.

39. Dana to Banks, November 15, 1863, *ibid.,* 412–413.

40. Dana to Stone, December 2, 1863, *ibid.,* 831.

Carte de visite of Colonel and Mrs. John L. Haynes, 1st and 2nd Texas Cavalry. *Courtesy Lawrence T. Jones III.*

Carte de visite of First Sergeant Patricio Perez, Company A, 2nd Texas Cavalry, and Company I, 1st Texas Cavalry. *Courtesy Delia Alaniz.*

On November 20, the First Texas, along with the Thirty-seventh Illinois and a field battery, marched on Ringgold Barracks, near Rio Grande City.[41] The purpose of taking that remote spot was to hinder, if not stop, Confederate trade with Mexico. The move did succeed in stopping all trade of importance between Rio Grande City and Brownsville, and it threatened trade as far up as Eagle Pass. There was even some hope of connecting with the Federals under Brigadier General James H. Carleton in New Mexico and controlling the whole river.[42] Davis had little trouble while at Rio Grande City. Neither he nor his detachment at Roma, Texas, also on the Rio Grande, met any opposition. Davis had not been able to carry out the ambitious plan of occupying the whole river, however, when he returned to Brownsville. There simply was not enough Federal strength in the area.

Back at Brownsville, the First Texas Cavalry found a new regiment being formed. On December 15, 1863, the Second Texas Cavalry was officially organized,[43] with John L. Haynes as colonel. Haynes had received his commission on November 5, and had busied himself since that date recruiting men in the Rio Grande area. Dana reported that on December 26 Haynes had about three hundred men in his regiment. That brought the strength of Texans in the Union arrny on the Rio Grande to 29 officers, 719 men present for duty, and 1,037 in the aggregate total of men present and absent.[44] These figures include only those properly enlisted.[45]

Haynes's background was much the same as that of Davis. Born in Virginia in 1821, he had grown up in Mississippi and had been a lieutenant in the Mexican War. When that war was over he made his home in Rio Grande City. He was elected to the Texas Legislature from Starr County in 1857 and 1859.[46]

The winter of 1863–1864 found the Texans in poor fighting condition. Anxiously Dana wrote to New Orleans explaining the situation and begging for

---

41. *Ibid.*, 429–430.

42. *Ibid.*, 880.

43. Dyer, *A Compendium of the War of the Rebellion*, 1647.

44. *Official Records*, Ser. I, Vol. XXVI, Pt. I, 893.

45. The *Official Records* indexes Braubach's Company with "Texas Troops (U.)," but there is no record of their ever being mustered into service. From Brownsville Dana wrote the following about the group: "Braubach is here with about 50 men." Dana to Stone, December 27, 1863, ibid., 885–886.

46. William De Ryee and R. E. Moore, *The Texas Album of the Eighth Legislature* (Austin, 1860), 107; signed statement of Daisy B. Tanner, in John L. Haynes File (Biographical Files, Texas History Center, University of Texas Library).

supplies for the cavalry.

Owing to the destitute condition of the First Texas Cavalry when they reached here, and the number of cavalry recruits who have been enlisted since our arrival, the supply of clothing which I brought down has been entirely exhausted, and the new recruits and many of the old men are now suffering from want of it. I ordered requisitions for 500 new suits, which went forward some time ago, but no supplies have yet been received. I have to-day approved requisition for 1,000 suits more, and hope they will, by some peremptory means, be hurried forward.[47]

Davis, commanding all cavalry on the Rio Grande, also expressed concern for the condition of his troops in letters to his superiors. For the use of his 875 effectives in February, 1864, he considered only 500 of his horses "tolerably serviceable," and hardly 200 of these "capable of doing immediately a serious job of work." It is in this same letter that some indication is given as to the nationality of the men serving under him as Texans. He writes of "443 Mexicans and 500 Americans (including in this designation Germans, Irish, &c), the whole (including the part brought from New Orleans) being recruited here [Brownsville] . . ." Presumably many of his "Mexicans" were really legal citizens or residents of Texas.[48]

Once again Davis and his cavalry regiments were called on to move up the Rio Grande, again with the purpose of stopping trade between the Confederacy and Mexico. The attempt failed for Davis was stoutly contested by the Confederates at Laredo and again fell back to his base at Brownsville.[49]

Leaving the Texas cavalry units in Texas for further service, Davis was sent to Louisiana to command the Fourth Brigade of the Nineteenth Army Corps in the humiliating retreat of Banks' Red River Campaign.[50] While Davis was gone, desertion threatened the Texan organizations, particularly the Second Texas, which was doing service up the Texas coast from Brownsville. Had Davis been on the scene, some of the trouble might have been averted, but the proximity of the Texans to their homes and families was a large temptation to give up the unpleasant military life and desert.[51] This fact, and the fact that Davis needed his troops, were enough to cause the Texans to be sent back to Louisiana.

---

47. Dana to Stone, December 27, 1863, *Official Records,* Ser. I, Vol. XXVI, Pt. I, 885.

48. Davis to Ord, February 20, 1864, *ibid.,* Ser. I, Vol. XXVI, Pt. II, 187.

49. Herron to Stone, January 26, 1864, *ibid.,* 218; Elliott, "Union Sentiment in Texas, 1861–1865," *Southwestern Historical Quarterly,* L, 451.

50. McClernand to Banks, April 8, 1864, *Official Records,* Ser. I, Vol. XXXIV, Pt. III, 88.

51. McClernand to Irwin, April 9, 1864, *ibid.,* 102.

Around June 16, with the exception of two companies and a few officers who needed to remain in Texas, the First and Second Texas Cavalry embarked for Louisiana.[52] They were soon followed by Vidal's Partisan Rangers.[53]

Adrian J. Vidal,[54] a man of Spanish descent, commanded a unique company which had served first under H. P. Bee in the Confederate Army. On the night of Monday, October 26, 1863, Vidal's company mutinied, shooting at least two of their former comrades, and left the Confederate service. Attempts to trace them down were made on both sides of the Rio Grande, with some success. Only a few days later some twenty-two of Vidal's party were captured, but the remaining forty-odd escaped.[55] Confederate commanders were unable to explain the whole episode.[56]

Vidal and his band hid for a while, but on November 10, Vidal's Partisan Rangers were organized in Brownsville and mustered into the service of the Union.[57] They were a part of no regiment, but served often with the cavalry units under Davis after his return from the second expedition up the Rio Grande. Vidal's command in the Union army included at first 89 men armed and equipped, who were to serve at least one year.[58] In early July, 1864, only a month after the larger part of the First and Second Texas Cavalry were sent to Louisiana, Vidal's Partisan Rangers embarked for New Orleans, only to be mustered out of service at the end of the month.[59]

TEXAS TROOPS (U.) AT BROWNSVILLE, SPRING, 1864[60]

Regiment of Organization	No. of Companies	Estimated Aggregate Strength	Condition
1st Texas	9	621	Armed, with few horses
2d Texas	5	413	Armed, with few horses

---

52. Herron to Drake, June 16, 1864, *ibid.*, Ser. I, Vol. XXXIV, Pt. IV, 408–409; Herron to Dwight, June 26, 1864, *ibid.*, 559–560.

53. *Ibid.*, 614.

54. Sometimes incorrectly called Adrian I. Vidal.

55. Bee to Headquarters, October 28, 1863, *Official Records*, Ser. I, Vol. XXVI, Pt. I, 448–449; Tarver to Ringgold Barracks, October 28, 1863, *ibid.*, 447–448.

56. Bee to Ruiz, October 28, 1863, *ibid.*, 450.

57. Dyer, *A Compendium of the War of the Rebellion*, 1647.

58. Dana to Stone, December 2, 1863, *Official Records*, Ser. I, Vol. XXVI, Pt. I, 830–831.

59. Dyer, *A Compendium of the War of the Rebellion*, 1647.

60. Babcock to Drake, May 25, 1864, *Official Records*, Ser. I, Vol. XXXIX, Pt. IV, 30.

Vidal's Partisan Rangers	1	77	Armed, with few horses

In Louisiana, Davis's troops were kept busy. At daylight on July 5, 1864, Davis moved out of Morganza toward the Atchafalaya River with 400 cavalry and two regiments of infantry to stop reported movements of Confederate artillery near Simsport (Simmesport). Arriving in the vicinity, he learned that the Confederates were not there, but had gone on toward Alexandria and were headed for Shreveport. Davis' men encountered a picket from the Twenty-Third Texas Cavalry (Confederate) under Colonel Nicholas C. Gould and captured three of his men. At Simsport they captured two more Confederates who had been detailed as ferrymen. Davis concluded that his large force had marched to Simsport uselessly, and he returned to Morganza.[61]

A reorganization among the Texas troops under Davis took place on July 14, becoming effective November 1, 1864. Upon the recommendation of Davis, the First and Second Texas Cavalry consolidated, and the new organization was called the First Texas Volunteer Cavalry.[62] It occupied the next few weeks doing reconnaissance duty west of Morganza.

Desertion continued to plague the Texans who had remained at Brazos Santiago. The commander under whom they were serving complained in a letter to Herron's headquarters:

It is my painful duty to inform you that no dependence can be placed upon the detachment of the First Texas Cavalry left with my command. They desert at every opportunity. No less than nine deserted yesterday, taking with them their horses, arms and accouterments. Three more deserted last night from a picket-post. Major Noyes informs me that among these men were some whom he considered the most reliable of the detachment, and that he was unable to send after and arrest them as he dare not trust the First Texas, and the New York cavalry were unacquainted with the roads.[63]

Two weeks later, however, he was able to report an improvement; since the above letter had been sent, no desertions occurred. On the health of the troops, he reported that it was fair, although a shortage of fresh vegetables was felt to no small degree. Two-thirds of his men in the hospital were there because of scurvy.[64] Upon receipt of an order dated August 19, 1864, the detachment of the

61. Davis to Speed, July 7, 1864, *ibid.*, Ser. I, Vol. XLI, Pt. I, 43; Wilson to Lee, July 4, 1864, *ibid.*, Ser. I, Vol. XLI, Pt. II, 41; Speed to Davis, July 4, 1864, *ibid.*

62. Special Orders, No. 67, July 14, 1864, *ibid.*, 180; Dyer, *A Compendium of the War of the Rebellion*, 1647.

63. Day to Clark, August 3, 1864, *Official Records*, Ser. I, Vol. XLI, Pt. II, 532.

64. *Ibid.*, Ser, I, Vol. XLI, Pt. I, 212.

First Texas serving in Texas was relieved of duty there and ordered to report to Davis at Morganza.[65] By the time they reached Davis, the First Texas Volunteer Cavalry had been brigaded and attached to the Nineteenth Arrny Corps along with a Louisiana, a New York, and an Illinois unit.[66]

There was little rest for the weary "Texas Travelers," as the detachment of the First Texas under Major Edward J. Noyes might have been called. Hardly had they arrived in Morganza than they were ordered back to New Orleans and back to Brazos Santiago.[67]

West of Morganza, Davis still labored to keep the Confederates on the far side of the Atchafalaya from Morganza, Baton Rouge, and New Orleans. Besides being confronted with the regular Confederate army, Davis was also faced with the threat of Quantrill's band of raiders which was reported operating in the region. Davis was ordered to treat those outlaws, if caught, with little respect, and not to bother the commissaries with them.[68]

A most unusual report of the First Texas Volunteer Cavalry was submitted on November 26, 1864. Instead of the usual kind which lamented the sad condition of troops, this one described them as in "excellent serviceable condition." One report on Davis' brigade reads in part as follows:

> The entire mount of his [Davis'] men is good; their horses are conditioned for active and hard service. In fact, there were not among 1,200 ten that could be exchanged for any better among the horses in the country. Having inspected about 1,200 carbines I found but one that was not clean and in excellent service condition. His horses are well and thoroughly groomed, and all their mounts well kept.[69]

Mid-December saw the First Texas Volunteers ordered to Lakeport, Louisiana, where they were to remain ready for service anywhere they might be called. A reorganization of troops at that time gave Davis command of a new brigade of cavalry which consisted of the Texas troops, the Second Illinois, and the Fourth Wisconsin cavalry regiments.[70] This order, however, was superseded in less than two weeks by another, which placed Davis at the head of a reserve corps of cavalry stationed at the mouth of the White River. Besides the First Texas, then commanded by Philip G. Temple, the Eighty-Seventh Illinois, First

---

65. Special Orders, No. 222, August 19, 1864, *ibid.,* 769.

66. Special Orders, No. 107, August 24, 1864, *ibid.,* Ser. I, Vol. XLI, Pt. II, 831–832.

67. Special Orders, No. 248, September 12, 1864, *ibid.,* Ser. I, Vol. XLI, Pt. III, 183–184.

68. Lawler to Christensen, October 21, 1864, *ibid.,* Ser. I, Vol. XLI, Pt. IV, 154.

69. Roberts to Drake, November 26, 1864, *ibid.,* 684–686.

70. Special Orders, No. 14, December 14, 1864, *ibid.,* 874–875.

Louisiana, and Second New York were under Davis.[71]

Shortly thereafter Davis was once again taken away from all Texas troops, and once again the detachment of Texans at Brazos Santiago was brought back to Louisiana, joining the larger group at Baton Rouge, then under Haynes. Davis was promoted to the rank of Brigadier General, the highest rank achieved by a Texan in the Union armies,[72] and on February 27, went from Baton Rouge to assume temporary command of Union forces in the District of Morganza.[73] In less than a month he was serving in a similar capacity in the District of Baton Rouge, but at the request of Major General Lew Wallace, who had succeeded to the command of troops in Texas, he was soon ordered to Brazos Santiago.[74] Wallace was about to begin negotiations with Confederate commanders Ford, Walker, Slaughter, and Kirby Smith for a surrender of Texas troops, and he felt that Davis could be of considerable assistance to him in the talks he expected to carry on. Both Davis and Wallace went to Galveston and began communicating with the Confederates on March 30. The Confederacy was known to be crumbling, and indeed, Robert E. Lee was on the run in Virginia. Davis began communicating with Edmund Kirby Smith at Galveston in mid-May, and on May 31 sent Kirby Smith the following note:

> I am here in conformity with instructions from Maj. Gen. E. R. S. Canby, U. S. Army, for the "purpose of conferring with you in relation to the details of the terms of surrender of the military convention" held in New Orleans between Lieutenant-General Buckner, of the C. S. Army, on the part of yourself, and Major General Osterhaus, U. S. Army, on the part of Major-General Canby. The inclosed letter from General Canby explains this more fully. I have here also the copy of the terms agreed upon by Generals Buckner and Osterhaus and approved by General Canby, which awaits your approval and signiture [sic]. I will meet you at the time and place you may choose to appoint.[75]

On June 2, E. Kirby Smith joined E. J. Davis at Galveston to sign the surrender terms which had already been signed by Major-General E. R. S. Canby on May 26. Kirby Smith reported to Davis that a complete disorganization of Confederate forces west of the Mississippi had commenced about May 20, and on June 5 the Union flag was raised at Galveston.[76]

With Kirby Smith's signature on the surrender terms, Davis proceeded back to New Orleans according to his orders. Having done light service around Fort

---

71. *Ibid.,* 973.

72. Hamilton was the only other Texan to hold this rank.

73. Special Orders, No. 26, January 27, 1865, *Official Records,* Ser. I, Vol. XLVIII, Pt. I, 654.

74. Dyer to Davis, March 17, 1865, *ibid.,* 1201.

75. Davis to Smith, May 31, 1865, *ibid.,* Ser. I, Vol. XLVIII, Pt. II, 693.

76. Davis to Christensen [no date], *ibid.,* 775; Stanton to Seward, June 23, 1865, *ibid.,* 976.

Hudson and Vidalia, the First Texas Volunteer Cavalry was given its final assignment. It was ordered on June 29 to the Military District of the Southwest for duty under Major-General Philip H. Sheridan in Texas, where it was mustered out of service on November 4, 1865.[77]

Texan had fought Texan, and the following years were to prove that Kirby Smith's surrender to Canby did not end all ill feeling brought on by that fact. Texans today generally consider themselves a part of the South and are proud that Texas was a part of the Confederacy. But in the interest of history it should be recognized that not all Texans of 1861–1865 wanted the Confederacy, and that many did their utmost to bring about its end.

---

77. Special Orders, No. 173, June 29, 1865, *ibid.,* 1025; Dyer, *A Compendium of the War of the Rebellion,* 1647. Dyer actually says the First Texas was mustered out on November 9, 1864, but this is undoubtedly an error, and 1865 is intended.

Quarter-plate tintype of Private Wady T. Williams, Company C, "Grimes County Rangers," 5th Texas Cavalry, ca. 1861. *Courtesy Lawrence T. Jones III.*

The Formation of Sibley's Brigade and the March to New Mexico

Martin Hardwick Hall[*]

From the days of the Republic, Texans had a special interest in New Mexico. When the Civil War began many Texans were determined to add the area to the Confederacy. Some viewed the region as a prospect for slave expansion; others saw New Mexico as the gateway to California and the Pacific. In July 1861, veteran frontiersman John R. Baylor and several companies of the Second Texas Mounted Rifles occupied the Mesilla valley of southern New Mexico. Soon thereafter Baylor issued a proclamation creating the Confederate Territory of Arizona with himself as military governor.

While Baylor was occupying southern New Mexico, Henry Hopkins Sibley, an experienced military officer formerly stationed in New Mexico, was in Richmond, Virginia, discussing plans with President Jefferson Davis for the conquest of all of New Mexico Territory. Davis appointed Sibley brigadier general with orders to proceed to Texas where he was to organize forces necessary for an expedition into New Mexico.

In Texas Sibley raised three regiments of cavalry which were organized into a brigade under his command. As the late Martin Hall, professor of history at the

* Martin Hardwick Hall, "The Formation of Sibley's Brigade and the March to New Mexico," *Southwestern Historical Quarterly*, LXI (Jan., 1958), 383–405.

University of Texas at Arlington, points out in this essay, Sibley and his men were confident of success. They left San Antonio in November and arrived at Fort Bliss near El Paso in late December. In the ensuing New Mexico campaign Sibley's Brigade defeated the Federals in two major battles but was forced to abandon the operation because of the loss of eighty supply wagons and the inability to take other supplies from the enemy. "What had begun as a glorious invasion," writes Hall, "came to an end in a near disastrous route."

For additional information on the New Mexico campaign see Hall's two books, Sibley's New Mexico Campaign *(Austin: University of Texas Press, 1960), and* The Confederate Army of New Mexico *(Austin: Presidial Press, 1978); Jerry Don Thompson,* Henry Hopkins Sibley, Confederate General of the West *(Natchitoches: Northwestern University Press, 1978); and Donald S. Frazier,* Blood and Treasure: Confederate Empire in the Southwest *(College Station: Texas A&M University Press, 1995).*

On February 1, 1861, the Texas Secession Convention voted to take the state out of the Union. Fifteen days later, General David E. Twiggs, the Federal commander in Texas, surrendered his department to state officials. By terms of the capitulation, the nineteen Federal posts were evacuated and the troops withdrawn. This left the western frontier undefended against Indians, as well as open to a possible invasion by Union forces from New Mexico. The Texas authorities took steps to regarrison the forts, and Lieutenant Colonel John R. Baylor, commanding a portion of the 2nd Regiment Texas Mounted Rifles, marched to Fort Bliss, the westernmost post in the state.[1]

Baylor reached his destination during the first week of July, 1861.[2] Soon after occupying Fort Bliss with his force of 375 men, he became aware of the danger of offensive action from the Union forces stationed forty miles to the north at Fort Fillmore, New Mexico. Instead of complacently waiting for the Federals to attack, Baylor determined to strike first. By the end of July, the Texan's "lightning" campaign had resulted in the surrender of most Union troops located in the southern part of New Mexico, bringing practically the whole of the southern section of that territory under Confederate control.[3] With the danger from enemy troops temporarily removed, Baylor created a "Provisional Government

---

1. Robert Underwood Johnson and Clarence Clough Buel (eds.), *Battles and Leaders of the Civil War* (4 vols.; New York, 1884–1888), I, 33–39.

2. Ibid., II, 103.

3. Baylor to Washington, September 21, 1861, *War of the Rebellion: A Compilation of the Official Records of the Union and Confederate Armies* (130 vols.; Washington, 1880–1901), Series I, Vol. IV, 17–20.

for the Territory of Arizona," and made himself military governor. But his force was small and Baylor realized that it would be only a matter of time before the remaining superior Federal forces to the north would rally and attempt to eradicate what he had accomplished. In Baylor's opinion the "vast mineral resources of Arizona, in addition to its affording an outlet to the Pacific," made its acquisition by the Confederate government of considerable importance. Now that he had taken possession of the territory, the colonel expressed the hope that a "force sufficient to occupy it . . . [would] be sent by the Government, under some competent man."[4]

The Confederacy had already found a "competent" man, for while Baylor was engaged in his campaign in the Mesilla Valley of New Mexico, Henry Hopkins Sibley, a veteran cavalryman, distinguished in appearance with long sideburns and bushy mustache, was commissioned a brigadier general in the army of the Confederacy with instructions to raise a brigade and invade the territory of New Mexico.[5]

Sibley was originally from Louisiana. From 1838, the date of his graduation from the United State Military Academy, until his resignation, Sibley had served with distinction in the regular army. As a young lieutenant of the 2nd Dragoons, he had taken part in the Seminole wars in Florida. Later he fought in the Mexican War, attaining the rank of captain in 1847. Sibley was present at the siege of Vera Cruz, the skirmish of Medelin, the battles of Cerro Gordo, Contreras, Churubusco, Molino del Rey, and the capture of Mexico City. Because of his "gallant and meritorious conduct" at Medelin, Sibley received the rank of brevet major. He was stationed in Kansas during the antislavery conflict, and he later took part in two Utah expeditions to quell the Mormon disturbances. He then marched to New Mexico in 1860 to engage in a campaign against the Navajo Indians.[6] While stationed in New Mexico in 1852, Sibley superintended the building of Fort Union, the post which came to be the most important military base in New Mexico when the war broke out.[7] Aside from his military exploits, Sibley also achieved success as an inventor, for he designed the "Sibley tent," patterned after the plains Indians' tipis, which was adopted by the United States Army.[8]

---

4. Baylor to Van Dorn, August 14, 1861, ibid., 23.

5. Hubert H. Bancroft, *History of Arizona and New Mexico, 1530–1888* (San Francisco, 1889), 688.

6. Theophilus F. Rodenbough (comp.), *From Everglade to Cañon with the Second Dragoons* (New York, 1875), 453.

7. William C. Whitford, *Colorado Volunteers in the Civil War: The New Mexico Campaign in 1862* (Denver, 1906), 32.

8. *Appleton's Cyclopaedia of American Biography* (7 vols.; New York, 1888–1901), V, 521.

When the Civil War began, Sibley was stationed in New Mexico. He was promoted to the rank of major on May 13, 1861, but he resigned the day he received his promotion in order to join the Confederate Army.[9] After tendering his resignation, Sibley left the territory for the capital of the Confederacy. The stage from El Paso to San Antonio ran semiweekly, making the journey in six days. While awaiting transportation at Hart's Mill (near present-day El Paso, Texas), Sibley wrote to his former commander, Colonel William W. Loring, who was soon also to cast his lot with the Confederacy. Jubilantly Sibley wrote that at last he was under the "glorious banner of the Confederate States of America" which "was indeed a glorious sensation of protection, hope, and pride." When the Federal troops at Fort Bliss withdrew to San Antonio, they left behind much public property. Sibley suggested that Loring, as commander of the Ninth Military District, remain at his command a little longer in order to allow the Texas forces, which were already on their way, to take charge of the materiel. Should Loring be relieved of his command too soon to prevent an attempt on the part of his successor to recapture the stores, Sibley advised his former commander to send a notice by extraordinary express to Judge Simeon Hart, a leading citizen of the area. In this same letter Sibley regretted more than ever "the sickly sentimentality" which had overruled him in his desire to bring his whole command with him. Sibley felt certain that the best of the rank and file of the soldiers in New Mexico were pro-Southern. By leaving without bringing his troops with him, he believed he had "betrayed and deserted" his men.[10]

From Hart's Mill, Sibley proceeded to Richmond, Virginia, where on July 5, 1861, he was commissioned a brigadier general.[11] With such an active and distinctive background in the regular army, the Confederacy had every reason to expect great things of this newly commissioned general.

During his tour of duty in the territory of New Mexico, Sibley had acquired a great deal of information concerning the resources of the country, the condition of the Federal forces, and the amount of government stores and supplies there. Upon his arrival in Richmond, Sibley informed Jefferson Davis of these matters and submitted to him a plan of campaign.[12] The President approved of Sibley's bold scheme. On July 8, 1861, Samuel Cooper, the adjutant and inspector general of the Confederacy, instructed Sibley that "in view of . . . [his] recent service in New Mexico and knowledge of that country and the people,

---

9. Rodenbough, *From Everglade to Cañon,* 453.

10. Sibley to Loring, June 12, 1861, *Official Records,* Series I, Vol. IV, 55–56.

11. *Appleton's Cyclopaedia,* V, 520.

12. Johnson and Buel (eds.), *Battles and Leaders of the Civil War,* II, 700.

the President . . . intrusted . . [him] with the important duty of driving the Federal troops from that department, at the same time securing all the arms, supplies, and materials of war." Sibley was further "authorized to take into the Confederate service all disaffected officers and soldiers on the original commissions of the former and enlistments of the latter." Without delay Sibley was ordered to Texas where, in concert with Brigadier General Earl Van Dorn, he was to organize "in the speediest manner possible, from the Texas troops, two full regiments of cavalry and one battery of howitzers, and such other forces" as he deemed necessary.[13] Later Sibley realized that two regiments would not be sufficient, and he asked the secretary of war for more. Subsequently Sibley was authorized to accept any additional armed regiments which the governor of Texas might tender to him.[14] As far as possible Van Dorn was to supply from the depots under his command the materiel for the armament and equipment of the "Sibley brigade."[15] If he was successful in his efforts to drive the Federal forces from New Mexico, President Davis directed Sibley to organize a military government within the territory, the details of which were to be submitted to Davis at the earliest possible time. Sibley's orders were of a general nature, for it was not considered necessary to confine him to minor matters which might arise from time to time. In this respect he was to be guided by circumstances and his own good judgment.[16] In other words, the general was allowed practically a free hand in the conduct of the New Mexico campaign.

The distant and relatively unimportant territory of New Mexico was not the main objective of this campaign—far from it. It was merely a means to attaining the real aim, the conquest of California.[17] Not only would the gold supply from the West be diverted to the Confederacy, but the South would also gain two good seaports on the Pacific. The remoteness of this coast would have made it impossible for the Union Navy to have blockaded it,[18] thus the South would have been assured of a steady flow of supplies from the West.[19] The prestige factor of conquering the West might also have been an aid in the recognition of the Confederacy by a foreign power.

Although the Department of Texas was to supply the men and some of the necessary equipment and materiel, Sibley's campaign, in the main, was to be

---

13. Cooper to Sibley, July 8, 1861, *Official Records,* Series I, Vol. IV, 93.

14. Chilton to Sibley, September 25, 1861, ibid., 111.

15. Cooper to Van Dorn, July 9, 1861, ibid., 93.

16. Cooper to Sibley, July 8, 1861, ibid.

17. Johnson and Buel (eds.), *Battles and Leaders of the Civil War,* II, 700.

18. Ibid., 697–698.

19. Ibid., 700.

self-sustaining. Upon arrival in Arizona the brigade was to be furnished with arms and equipment out of the supplies already captured by Baylor and by any additional supplies which might be taken in the course of the campaign.[20] Indeed, Sibley counted on a rapid conquest of New Mexico's forts and depots so that his army could subsist "on the enemy's country."[21] Foodstuffs were to be procured from the Mesilla Valley and the Rio Grande Valley in and around El Paso. Negotiations for further supplies, particularly commissary items, were to be opened with the governors of the states of Chihuahua and Sonora.[22]

Many factors made Sibley confident of victory. Baylor's short campaign in the Mesilla Valley had cleared the way for an invasion to the north. Sibley, viewing the Federal Army in New Mexico as insufficient and inefficient, consequently thought that it would fall easily before the might of his brigade.[23] There seems to have been a belief among the Texans that the Mexican population might come to their aid, or at least not hinder their efforts. Friends of the cause reported that the Mexicans could be depended upon for supplies[24] because they were completely controlled by Anglo-Americans, most of whom in the area around present-day El Paso were Southern sympathizers.[25] It was also assumed that since New Mexico was commercially dependent upon states of Southern sympathies, especially Missouri and Texas, the people would support the Confederate cause.[26] In addition, the territory of New Mexico had a slave code, Congressional Delegate Miguel Otero was a secession advocate, and three newspapers in the territory (the Santa Fe *Gazette,* the Tucson *Arizonian,* and the Mesilla *Times*) were pro-Southern. These facts assured Sibley and the Texans that New Mexico was pro-Confederate in its outlook and would aid the entrance of a liberating army.[27]

Sibley assumed that once the territory of New Mexico was brought under Confederate control, many men from the West would flock to his banner.[28] A large number of the people of the territory of Colorado possessed Southern

---

20. Ibid.

21. Theo. Noel, *A Campaign from Santa Fe to the Mississippi* (Shreveport, 1865), 14.

22. Johnson and Buel (eds.), *Battles and Leaders of the Civil War,* II, 700.

23. Noel, *Campaign from Santa Fe to the Mississippi,* 14.

24. A. A. Hayes Jr., *New Colorado and the Santa Fe Trail* (New York, 1880), 162.

25. William W. Mills, *Forty Years at El Paso, 1858–1898* (Chicago, 1901), 38–39.

26. Canby to Assistant Adjutant-General, June 11, 1861, *Official Records,* Series I, Vol. I, 606.

27. Charles S. Walker, "Causes of the Confederate Invasion of New Mexico," *New Mexico Historical Review,* VIII, 88.

28. Johnson and Buel (eds.), *Battles and Leaders of the Civil War,* II, 700.

sympathies[29] and the Mormons of Utah were known to have no love for the Union, particularly after the two military campaigns waged against them.[30] General Edwin V. Sumner, the Union commander in California, estimated that there were 20,000 Southern sympathizers in his state and that if the Confederacy "should ever get an organized force into this State, as a rallying point for all the secession element, it would inevitably inaugurate a civil war here immediately."[31] With such favorable developments on the horizon, Sibley confidently planned that as soon as New Mexico was occupied "an army of advance would be organized, and 'On to San Francisco' would be the watchword."[32]

Happily Sibley left Richmond, arriving in San Antonio, Texas, in the middle of August, 1861. Setting up his headquarters in San Antonio, he was fully confident that he would be able to raise and organize his brigade within a short time. Many unexpected difficulties arose, however, which shattered Sibley's dream of rapidly marching his command into the field. The new general was disappointed in not receiving as much cooperation from Governor Edward Clark as he desired. This was not because of any lack of zeal on the part of the chief executive of the state, for it was but a "consequence simply of the very inefficient system of the State military organization to which the governor had recourse to supply the troops." Clark ordered enough companies, which had reported to him as organized, to join Sibley for active duty. Most of these units which were called to the colors, however, proved to be either entirely disbanded or so reduced in numbers that they did not meet the minimum set for the Confederate service. Reliance on this method of raising troops caused the first serious delay. A further cause of retardation was the idea, prevalent throughout the state, that the "Sibley brigade" would be filled only with the companies ordered out by the governor. Consequently, other companies not so organized did not offer their services to the general. As a result, Sibley was forced to appeal directly to the public,[33] particularly through the medium of the patriotic press, for recruits.[34] Even so, "it required some time to counteract the effects of the misplaced reliance under the State system." Competition for men which grew out of the calls for the several regiments required for service east of the

29. Whitford, *Colorado Volunteers in the Civil War*, 36.

30. Hubert H. Bancroft, *History of Utah, 1540–1886* (San Francisco, 1889), 538.

31. Sumner to Townsend, September 7, 1861, *Official Records*, Series I, Vol. L, i, 610.

32. Johnson and Buel (eds.), *Battles and Leaders of the Civil War*, II, 700.

33. Sibley to Cooper, November 16, 1861, *Official Records*, Series I, Vol. IV, 141–142.

34. Noel, *Campaign from Santa Fe to the Mississippi*, 5–6.

Mississippi was another determent in the filling of the ranks.[35] Apparently a good many men of Texas preferred glory in the East rather than in the desolate and barren wastelands of Arizona and New Mexico.

Recruiting was but one problem which Sibley faced. Because the people of Texas expected an attack on the Gulf Coast, officials were exceedingly reluctant to allow war materiel to be removed from the state.[36] Although many in the "Sibley brigade" brought their own weapons,[37] every company reported itself short of arms. "In virtue of the authority delegated to . . . [him] in the written instructions of his excellency the President," Sibley found it necessary to attempt to buy serviceable firearms and to construct lances. Since there was not a dollar in the hands of his disbursing officers, the general was forced to resort to the credit of the Confederate government for these purchases.[38]

According to orders, General Earl Van Dorn, commander of the Department of Texas, was to have supplied Sibley with as much materiel of war as possible. Soon after Sibley's arrival, Van Dorn was relieved from duty and Colonel Henry E. McCulloch temporarily assumed his office. General P. O. Hebert was appointed the new departmental commander, but he did not immediately come to headquarters to assume command. Shortly McCulloch and Major Sackfield Maclin, the assistant quartermaster and acting ordnance officer of the department, left to meet Hebert at Galveston. For several weeks there was not an officer within Sibley's reach to whom he could apply for the issuance of ordnance supplies. Faced with this new frustration, Sibley assumed the responsibility of ordering the remaining subordinates to issue supplies which were indispensable to the brigade and which could be spared from the service of the department itself. Although the general had obviously overstepped his authority, he justified his action on the assumption that to have awaited the return of a responsible officer would have incurred another indefinite delay which would have "probably paralyzed" his command for the winter. Sibley's anxiety to get his army on the march was greatly increased by the arrival of a dispatch from Colonel John R. Baylor[39] which stated that the enemy, with a force of 2,500 men, was on the march to the Mesilla Valley.[40] Earlier Sibley had advised Baylor to make a demonstration against Fort Craig in order to draw the

---

35. Sibley to Cooper, November 16, 1861, *Official Records*, Series I, Vol. IV, 141–142.

36. Ibid., 142.

37. William A. Keleher, *Turmoil in New Mexico, 1846–1868* (Santa Fe, 1952), 161.

38. Sibley to Cooper, November 16, 1861, *Official Records*, Series I, Vol. IV, 142.

39. Ibid., 143.

40. Baylor to Sibley, October 25, 1861, ibid., 132.

Federals out to attack his smaller force. With the Federals lured from the security of their strong point and with the expected timely arrival of his troops, Sibley hoped to destroy or capture the enemy.[41] The delays which Sibley had encountered, however, threatened to make his plan backfire and might mean the destruction of Baylor's small army, as well as the loss of territory which Baylor had already gained for the Confederacy.

The first company to join Sibley was raised in Guadalupe and Caldwell counties and was commanded by William P. "Gotch" Hardeman. On August 27, 1861, this unit, along with all others in the brigade, was sworn into service "for during the war." It was designated Company A of the 4th Regiment Texas Cavalry. By September 20, the full complement of companies had been mustered into service. The 4th Texas Regiment was organized without the privilege of allowing the men to elect their field officers. Shortly after its organization, which was effected at the camp first established by Hardeman on the Leon Creek, the regiment was moved to Camp Sibley on the Salado Creek, five miles from San Antonio on the Austin road.[42] Colonel James Reily, originally from Ohio,[43] who was the "beau ideal of a gentleman and officer" and the "very counterpart in looks and actions of Robert E. Lee,"[44] commanded the regiment. Other officers included Lieutenant Colonel William R. Scurry and Major Henry W. Raguet.[45]

Colonel Thomas Green began organizing the 5th Regiment Texas Cavalry at Camp Manassas on the Salado Creek two miles above the camp of the 4th Regiment.[46] "Daddy" Green, as the colonel was commonly called, "was a very fine specimen of the Southern planter. Never was a commander . . . more beloved than he by 'his boys.'"[47] Green was born in Virginia in 1814, but his family later moved to Tennessee. In January, 1836, at the age of twenty-one, Green entered the ranks of the revolutionary army in Texas and fought his first battle at San Jacinto. In 1841 he was engaged in skirmishes and expeditions against the Indians and he served with great distinction in the forces of the

---

41. Sibley to Cooper, November 8, 1861, ibid.

42. Noel, *Campaign from Santa Fe to the Mississippi,* 6–7.

43. Denison to Chase, May, 1862, in S. H. Dodson (comp.), "Diary and Correspondence of Salmon P. Chase," *Annual Report of the American Historical Association for the Year 1902* (2 vols.; Washington, 1903), II, 301.

44. Theophilus Noel, *Autobiography and Reminiscences of Theophilus Noel* (Chicago, 1904). 69.

45. Noel, *Campaign from Santa Fe to the Mississippi,* 147–148.

46. Ibid., 6.

47. R. H. Williams, *With the Border Ruffians, Memories of the Far West, 1852–1868* (Toronto, 1919), 179.

Republic of Texas during the Mexican invasion of the frontier in 1842. During the Mexican War he fought gallantly in the battle of Monterrey and his daring aggressiveness won for him commendation as a soldier and a leader. After the war, until 1861, he was employed in the office of clerk of the Supreme Court of Texas.[48] Other important personnel of the 5th Regiment were Lieutenant Colonel Henry C. McNeill, Major S. A. Lockridge,[49] and Lieutenant Joseph D. Sayers,[50] who eventually became governor of Texas.

On October 4, 1861, Captain Powhatan Jordan's company was mustered in as Company A of the 7th Texas Cavalry under Colonel Wllliam Steele.[51] Steele was born in Albany, New York, and had graduated from the United States Military Academy in 1840. Like Sibley, he had served with the 2nd Dragoons in Florida. During the Mexican War he earned the brevet of captain for his bravery in the battles of Contreras and Churubusco. Later he was stationed in New Mexico, Kansas, Dakota, and Nebraska, where he took part in various expeditions against the Indians. He resigned his commission in the United States Army in May, 1861, to join the Confederacy.[52] Steele set up Camp Pickett, several miles above the 5th Regiment on the Salado, for the training of his 7th Regiment.[53] Lieutenant Colonel J. S. Sutton[54] and Major A. P. Bagby were his most important subordinates.[55]

With the organization of the three cavalry regiments, the "Sibley brigade" formally came into being. The following officers composed the staff:

Brigadier General Henry H. Sibley, commander.

Major A. M. Jackson, assistant adjutant general.

Major R. T. Brownrigg, chief commissary.

Captain W. H. Harrison, paymaster and quartermaster.

Major W. L. Robards, chief of ordnance.

---

48. Clement A. Evans (ed.), *Confederate Military History* (12 vols.; Atlanta, 1899), XI, 231–232; Robert F. Kroh, Tom Green: Shield and Buckler (Master's thesis, University of Texas, 1951).

49. Major Lockridge left Cincinnati five or six years before, soon after the burning of the steamer *Martha Washington,* in which affair he was implicated. His real name was William Kissane. He had also been a colonel with William Walker in Nicaragua. Ovando J. Hollister, *A History of the First Colorado Regiment of Volunteers* (Denver, 1863), reprinted as *Boldly They Rode* (Lakewood, Colorado, 1949), 114; Noel, *Campaign from Santa Fe to the Mississippi,* 121.

50. Ibid., 148.

51. Ibid., 7.

52. Evans (ed.), *Confederate Military History,* XI, 257–258.

53. Noel, *Campaign from Santa Fe to the Mississippi,* 11.

54. Ibid., 122. Sutton had been on the ill-fated Texan Santa Fe Expedition.

55. Ibid., 147.

Captain J. E. Dwyer, inspector general.

Lieutenant T. P. Ochiltree, aide-de-camp.

E. N. Covey, chief surgeon and medical director.[56]

The rolling hills about San Antonio echoed with shouts and commands as the eager recruits were drilled and instructed. The troops "had roll calls by morning and by night, as also tattoo and reveille according to the forms prescribed on page 2299 of the revised edition of the military statutes." To make certain that each regiment was thoroughly drilled on the most improved tactics, Winfield Scott's *Infantry-Tactics* and W. J. Hardee's *Rifle and Light Infantry Tactics* were consulted on all occasions.[57] The articles of war were read to the men[58] and the strictest guard and discipline were maintained.[59] Within a short time, Sibley's troopers were being whipped into fighting form.

The brigade was armed with practically every type of small arms in existence. There were "squirrel-guns, bear guns, sportsman's-guns, shotguns, both single and double barrels,"[60] navy revolvers, Minié muskets, and common rifles.[61] Few armies probably have ever had a more motley collection of weapons. In addition to the small arms, one battery of mountain howitzers was attached to the 4th Regiment and another to the 5th Regiment. Green's regiment had two companies, commanded by Captains Willis L. Lang and Jerome B. McCown, which were armed with lances and six shooters.[62] The picturesque lancers, who were Sibley's pride and joy, bore weapons that consisted of three-by-twelve-inch blades mounted on nine-foot shafts[63] that also boasted eight-by-seventeen inch red pennants.[64]

Recruited largely from frontier areas, Sibley's men were the flower of Texas youth—"the best that ever threw a leg over a horse or that had ever sworn

---

56. Ibid.

57. Ibid., 7–8; Winfield Scott, *Infantry-Tactics; or Rules for the Exercise and Manoeuvres of the United States' Infantry* (New York, 1854); W. J. Hardee, *Rifle and Light Infantry Tactics, for the Exercise and Manoeuvres of Troops When Acting as Light Infantry or Riflemen* (Philadelphia, 1855).

58. Walter A. Faulkner, "With Sibley in New Mexico: The Journal of William Henry Smith," West Texas Historical Association *Year Book,* XXVII (1951), 115.

59. Noel, *Campaign from Santa Fe to the Mississippi,* 7–8.

60. Ibid., 8.

61. Denison to Chase, May, 1862, in Dodson (comp.), "Diary and Correspondence of Salmon P. Chase," *Annual Report of the American Historical Association, 1902,* II, 301.

62. Noel, *Campaign from Santa Fe to the Mississippi,* 11; Evans (ed.), *Confederate Military History,* XI, 150.

63. Hollister, *Boldly They Rode,* 110.

64. Noel, *Campaign from Santa Fe to the Mississippi,* 11.

allegiance to any cause. All-around men, natural-born soldiers they were under twenty-five, with a liberal sprinkling of older ones who had seen more or less service on the frontier."[65] As the Mesilla *Times* later expressed it:

The Confederate 'Army of New Mexico' is composed of what is probably the best material for an army that the world affords. That distinct type of mankind, the south-western frontiersman, inured to all hardships, of indomi[ta]ble energy, familiar with the use of firearms, at home on horse-back, and fired with the love of country and for the redress of wrongs. There is no conflict which they would not undertake, and none can occur on these lines in which they will not be perfectly successful.[66]

On October 21, 1861, a brigade review was held, with Sibley's daughter presenting a battle flag to a company of lancers.[67] By the end of October Sibley had completed the recruiting and training of his brigade and felt that he was ready to begin the campaign in New Mexico.[68] Shortly the men were issued a full military uniform which included a haversack, pants, drawers, pantaloon boots, and a broadcloth coat with brass buttons.[69] The time had come to take up the seven-hundred-mile march to Fort Bliss.

On November 7, 1861, "at the usual hour in the morning, 'boots and saddles' was sounded." The baggage had been weighed the day before (fifteen pounds per man), and the wagons had been loaded. All was in readiness. Fifteen minutes later "assembly" was heard, and in a short time the soldiers of Reily's 4th Regiment were in their saddles and ready to take up the line of march. After forming the regiment in a solid square so all could hear, Reily eloquently addressed the assemblage. He told his men that they were on the eve of leaving a land that many might never see again. On this day they would "bid adieu to all friends, home, and happy firesides, to try . . . [their] fortunes in the field in the defense of . . . [their] country's honor." He declared that they were soldiers together, and that a people, who in after years would prove grateful to them for their acts, expected much from them. On closing his remarks, he removed his hat and requested all to do likewise. Then in a "solemn, pious, and fervent tone,

---

65. Noel, *Autobiography,* 57.

66. Mesilla *Times,* January 15, 1862. Microfilm courtesy of the New-York Historical Society, New York City.

67. Faulkner, "With Sibley in New Mexico," West Texas Historical Association *Year Book,* XXVII (1951), 114.

68. Sibley to Cooper, November 16, 1861, *Official Records,* Series I, Vol. IV, 143.

69. Faulkner, "With Sibley in New Mexico," West Texas Historical Association *Year Book,* XXVII (1951), 114.

he offered up to the High God, in behalf of the cause, of those under him, of those around him, and for himself," a most stirring prayer. "Everyone was moved to tears and solemn thoughts."[70]

In a few moments came the command, "By fours from the right, march!" And the 4th Texas Cavalry proudly marched from Camp Sibley into San Antonio to the strains of "The Texas Ranger." The men were again formed into a solid column in the main plaza of the city. At this time a flag was presented to the regiment "in the name and in behalf of the ladies of Nacogdoches." Reily again addressed his men, and then General Sibley, astride his horse, stepped forward to say a few words. "In a few 'unguarded remarks'" the old general "convinced all that he was no orator; yet in his speech, which was short, he displayed a great deal of originality and much determination." He informed the men of the regiment that they were still "green, green saplings; bending to discipline," but that they would make the best soldiers in the world and he was proud of them. He told them that they would precede him but a few days and that he did not fear the result of the campaign with such men to follow him as were those whom he had the honor to address and to command. After bidding the regiment "adieu," three rousing cheers were given for Sibley,[71] and the troopers started on the road to Fort Bliss. "With drums beating and flags flying," the gallant force marched away. "Every man, from the General downwards, [was] confident of victory."[72]

The main road to Fort Bliss, consisting of about seven hundred miles of wagon ruts, passed through vast, rolling plains, bleak and inhospitable deserts, and rugged mountains. Most of this route lay within the realm of hostile Indian tribes. Since water was too scarce at many places for a whole regiment to travel together, the 4th Regiment was divided into three sections.[73] Aside from the wagons which carried materiel of war, two wagons were allotted to each company to carry the men's baggage. An additional wagon was given to each company for the use of the officers. Daily travel would be limited by the miles the beeves could be driven and by the distance between water holes.[74]

On November 9, Captain William J. Hardeman led the first division of the 4th Regiment on the line of march. The next day Lieutenant Colonel William R. Scurry started out with his section, and on the eleventh Colonel Reily

---

70. Noel, *Campaign from Santa Fe to the Mississippi*, 8–10.

71. Ibid., 9–10.

72. Williams, *With the Border Ruffians*, 201.

73. Noel, *Campaign from Santa Fe to the Mississippi*, 10.

74. Reminiscences of H. C. Wright (MS., Archives, University of Texas Library).

himself brought up the rear detachment. The regiment traveled in this manner until San Felipe Springs were reached. At that point Major Henry W. Raguet arrived and took command of Hardeman's division.[75] As the regiment passed by Fort Clark, an express from Colonel Baylor to brigade headquarters in San Antonio was received. The governor of Arizona urgently requested reinforcements. When Reily learned of the contents of the dispatch, he ordered the divisions of his regiment to set off on "double quick time."[76]

Green's 5th Regiment left Camp Manassas on November 7. As the troops passed through San Antonio, the ladies of the city waved their white handkerchiefs "the same as to say brave boys victory awaits you." Baylor's urgent express arrived in San Antonio, and these soldiers were also ordered on a forced march to Fort Bliss. As the regiment proceeded from San Antonio, General Sibley reviewed the men from his carriage on a hill a short distance away. "The whole regiment shouldered arms and marched by in regular order," whereupon "the old General pulled off his hat and gave them a general salute."[77]

That night the command camped on the prairie near Castroville. The following day as the regiment passed through the town of D'Hanis, the old Mexican women ran to the road with their butter, eggs, chickens, and watermelons, but none of the soldiers bought anything. As the command advanced into Uvalde County the men of Captain I. G. Killough's company were detailed as ammunition guards. They were ordered to load their guns and be on a constant lookout. This was Indian country and would continue to be, almost to the very limits of Fort Bliss. On November 17 a private struck Captain Killough. The soldier was immediately court-martialed and condemned to be "chained hard and fast" to the baggage wagon for the duration of a month.[78] As the regiment passed by Fort Clark, a large number of sick men were left in the hospital there.[79] Fort Clark was situated near the source of Las Moras Creek about thirty miles north of the Rio Grande.[80]

Green's men had been marching in a body until they reached San Felipe

---

75. Noel, *Campaign from Santa Fe to the Mississippi*, 10.

76. William W. Heartsill, *Fourteen Hundred and 91 Days in the Confederate Army* (Marshall, 1876), 47.

77. Faulkner, "With Sibley in New Mexico," West Texas Historical Association *Year Book*, XXVII (1951), 115–116.

78. Ibid.

79. Heartsill, *Fourteen Hundred and 91 Days*, 47.

80. The post was established in 1852 to protect the southwestern frontier, particularly the road to California, from the depredations of Mexicans and Indians. Federal troops abandoned the fort on March 19, 1861. T. H. S. Hamersly (comp.), *Complete Regular Army Register of the United States: For*

Springs. From that point on to Fort Bliss, the regiment was divided into three divisions.[81] At San Felipe Springs a general court-martial was held for three men who had been found sleeping while on sentry duty. Each man was condemned to close confinement on bread and water for ten days, but the sentences were later remitted.[82]

On November 24, while encamped on Yellowstone Creek in Maverick County, Major S. A. Lockridge, commanding the first squadron, had the misfortune of losing all of his beef cattle and work steers. The following day, the squadron arrived at Fort Hudson, and on December 1, it reached Fort Lancaster, a distance of about 333 miles from San Antonio.[83] Fort Lancaster, another in the line of frontier posts, was situated about a half mile above the junction of Live Oak Creek with the Pecos River.[84] Six days later the squadron marched by Fort Stockton, a post established in 1859 on Comanche Creek and Comanche Trail[85] on the main route across a vast dry and barren prairie. Since the springs and creek had been a favorite haunt of the Comanche Indians, the fort was founded to guard the mail route from San Antonio to El Paso and to form a link in the chain of forts needed to protect emigrants and goods going to Chihuahua and California.[86] Passing through the rugged Limpia Mountains, a squadron of the 5th Regiment on December 16 reached Fort Davis[87] which was at the mouth of a three-quarter mile long canyon. Fort Davis, named in honor of Secretary of War Jefferson Davis,[88] was established in 1854 on Limpia Creek, 446 miles from San Antonio[89] and about 72 miles southwest of Fort

---

One Hundred Years, 1779 to 1870 (Washington, 1881), Part II, 128; *Circular No. 4,* A Report on Barracks and Hospitals with Descriptions of Military Posts, War Department, Surgeon General's Office (Washington, 1870), 203; Summary of Principal Events, *Official Records,* Series I, Vol. I, 502.

81. Noel, *Campaign from Santa Fe to the Mississippi,* 11.

82. Faulkner, "With Sibley in New Mexico," West Texas Historical Association *Year Book,* XXVII (1951), 117.

83. Ibid., 117–119.

84. First garrisoned in 1855, Fort Lancaster was evacuated by Federal forces on March 19, 1861. Hamersly (comp.), *Complete Regular Army Register,* Part II, 140; Summary of Principal Events, Official Records, Series I, Vol. I, 502.

85. Faulkner, "With Sibley in New Mexico," West Texas Historical Association *Year Book,* XXVII (1951), 120; Hamersly (comp.), *Complete Regular Army Register,* Part II, 155.

86. *Circular No. 4,* p. 223; Summary of Principal Events, *Official Records,* Series I, Vol. I, 502. In April, 1861, the Federal garrison abandoned Fort Stockton.

87. Faulkner, "With Sibley in New Mexico," West Texas Historical Association *Year Book,* XXVII (1951), 120–121.

88. *Circular No. 4,* pp. 227–228.

89. Hamersly (comp.), *Complete Regular Army Register,* Part II, 152.

Stockton.[90] The site was chosen because of its location on the road between San Antonio and El Paso, its fine climate, its defensibility, its position relative to marauding Indians, and its proximity to Presidio del Norte which it also served to protect.[91] Since Fort Davis was situated in a mountain fastness, a guide was obtained to help lead the divisions of the regiment through the mountain passes. The command traveled over "nature's beautiful valleys," and many saw their first mustangs.[92]

On Christmas Day the troops of the squadron ate a breakfast consisting of biscuits, coffee, and poor beef—hardly a banquet worthy of the yuletide season. The same day the men marched a distance of fifteen miles. Arriving at Fort Quitman, about eighty miles southeast of Fort Bliss, the troops stood "upon the Rio Grande and look[ed] upon the dividing line between the Confederate States of America and the United States of Mexico."[93] The post lay on a gradual slope to the Rio Grande which was about four hundred yards west of the fort.[94] At this place hay was obtained for the regiment's horses. While there the men of the squadron were read the articles of war. Since Mexico was so near, a strong guard was maintained constantly. "All along the Rio Grande Valley, the water from the river . . . [was] very unhealthy for horses [and gave] them the scours." On New Year's Day the breakfast was not much better than that of Christmas: beef, biscuits, curshaw, and coffee without sugar. On this same morning, Colonel Green's Negro stole his horse, apparently fleeing across the Rio Grande into Mexico. The adjutant and several troops, after obtaining a pass from the local alcalde, went into that country to look for the thief, but the Negro was not to be found.[95]

At last the three divisions of the 5th Regiment arrived at Fort Bliss where they were reunited. Making from fifteen to twenty miles a day, the arduous forced march from San Antonio to Fort Bliss had taken a little less than two months. The 4th Regiment, having preceded the others, reassembled and then moved up

90. Faulkner, "With Sibley in New Mexico," *West Texas Historical Association Year Book,* XXVII (1951), 120.

91. *Circular No. 4,* pp. 227–228; Summary of Principal Events, *Official Records,* Series I, Vol. I, 502. Troops of the United States 8th Infantry abandoned the post on April 13, 1861.

92. Faulkner, "With Sibley in New Mexico," *West Texas Historical Association Year Book,* XXVII (1951), 121.

93. Ibid., 122; Summary of Principal Events, *Official Records,* Series I, Vol. I, 502; Hamersly (comp.), *Complete Regular Army Register,* Part II, 150. Fort Quitman was established in 1858. The federal garrison left the post on April 5, 1861.

94. *Circular No. 4,* pp. 230–231.

95. Faulkner, "With Sibley in New Mexico," *West Texas Historical Association Year Book,* XXVII (1951), 122–123.

the valley into the territory of Arizona.[96]

While the brigade had been in the process of being trained at the camps near San Antonio, Sibley had engaged the services of two merchants and traders near Fort Bliss who were to supply the troops with foodstuffs.[97] When he had assurances of adequate provisions and had sent two regiments on the march, Sibley decided that the time had come to "move with . . . [his] headquarters to assume in person the command of . . . [his] forces in the Territory of Arizona, and to conduct the military operations there and in New Mexico." On November 18, Sibley left San Antonio[98] traveling by coach. He could make the journey to Fort Bliss in a fraction of the time that his regiments could, encumbered as they were by large numbers and slow-moving baggage wagons. At Fort Lancaster the lieutenant commanding that post ordered his company to appear in uniform, armed and mounted, to escort Sibley and to pay him full general's honors. When Sibley arrived, he took charge of the company to see how well it was drilled. The sergeant was on the right, marking by two's. "The command was given by the Gen'l, 'file left,' which was of course unheard, and on they went at a brisk trot," ascending a near-by mountain. "As they disappeared the General turned around muttering 'gone to hell.' In the evening the Company returned and found that the General had gone on his way rejoicing to New Mexico."[99]

Five companies of Steele's 7th Texas Cavalry took leave of San Antonio on November 30. Four left on December 15 and Company H remained in San Antonio to escort Captain W. H. Harrison, the brigade paymaster. On January 6, Company E was detained at Fort Clark because measles had broken out in that company after it had begun its march. Fortunately the disease did not spread, only fifteen men being lost.[100]

On December 14, 1861, General Sibley assumed "command of all the forces of the Confederate States on the Rio Grande at and above Fort Quitman and all in the Territory of New Mexico and Arizona."[101] The troops under Sibley were designated as the "Army of New Mexico" with headquarters temporarily fixed at Fort Bliss.[102] The "Arrny of New Mexico" included not only the original

96. Noel, *Campaign from Santa Fe to the Mississippi*, 11–12.

97. Sibley to Cooper, November 8, 1861, *Official Records*, Series I, Vol. IV, 132.

98. Sibley to Cooper, November 16, 1861, ibid., 141.

99. Heartsill, *Fourteen Hundred and 91 Days*, 49.

100. Noel, *Campaign from Santa Fe to the Mississippi*, 11.

101. Benton to McCulloch, December 31, 1861, *Official Records,* Series I, Vol. IV, 164. Sibley's assumption of command of that part of Texas "at and above Fort Quitman" conflicted with the jurisdiction of Ben McCulloch, commander of the Western Military District of Texas.

102. General Orders, No. 10, December 14, 1861, ibid., 157–158.

brigade but also Colonel Baylor's portion of the 2nd Regiment Mounted Rifles, and Hunter's and Phillips' battalions of Arizona and New Mexico volunteers.[103] Although the general declared martial law throughout the area under his command, he did not intend to "abrogate or supersede the powers of Colonel John R. Baylor." To be sure, Sibley had taken charge of all troops, but Baylor was still to continue to exercise the functions of the office of civil and military governor of the Territory of Arizona.[104]

After the bulk of his brigade had arrived from San Antonio, Sibley issued the following:

GENERAL ORDER—No. 2.
Head-quarters Army of N. M.,
Ft. Bliss, Tex., Jan. 9th, 1862.

The General Commanding expresses to the Troops under his command, his high appreciation of the patience, fortitude, and good conduct, with which, in spite of great deficiencies in their supplies, they have made a successful and rapid march of seven hundred miles, in mid winter, and through a country entirely devoid of resources.

The General congratulates his troops upon the prospect of early and important services, for the successful accomplishment of which, their past conduct is an ample guarantee; and he is assured that he will never be disappointed in his early boast, that 'We could go any where, and do any thing.'

  By order of
   Brig. Gen. H. H. Sibley.
   Tom P. Ochiltree, A. de C. & A. A. At. Gen., A. N. M.[105]

Sibley's lack of foresight and adequate planning began henceforth to manifest itself. True, the general had hoped to reach New Mexico early in September, but when he found that was impossible, he should have taken measures for a winter campaign. The middle of January found him still at Fort Bliss with only two and a half regiments.[106] These were not only poorly armed and lacking in sufficient ammunition,[107] but also badly clothed and ill fed.[108] "Forage there was none; commissary supplies were getting scarce; the cold season was coming; clothing was being needed; all of which the country afforded none."[109] There

103. Noel, *Campaign from Santa Fe to the Mississippi*, 12.

104. General Orders, No. 12, December 20, 1861, *Official Records*, Series I, Vol. IV, 159.

105. Mesilla *Times*, January 15, 1862.

106. Sibley to Cooper, May 4, 1862, *Official Records*, Series I, Vol. IX, 507.

107. Denison to Chase, May, 1862, in Dodson (comp.), "Diary and Correspondence of Salmon P. Chase," *Annual Report of the American Historical Association, 1902*, II, 301.

108. Mesilla *Times*, January 15, 1862.

109. Noel, *Campaign from Santa Fe to the Mississippi*, 12.

were no quartermaster's funds on hand to supply the daily and pressing needs of the brigade, and what the Mesilla and Rio Grande valleys could produce had long been consumed by Baylor's force.[110]

Apparently the commissary supplies which Sibley's two agents were to procure were insufficient, and expected foodstuffs from Mexico were not forthcoming. The general's biggest blunder had been in banking too heavily upon capturing from the Federal forces everything that he would need. As a result, he did not think it necessary to start from San Antonio with more provisions than would actually be needed to subsist the command en route. Sibley was confident that he would be able to move into the Territory of New Mexico without resistance and take possession of all its garrisons, forts, and depots of supply.[111] This was truly a gambler's dream, for the general failed to realize that perhaps during his absence from the territory, a vigorous Union commander might have reinforced the fortifications and called up additional troops, and thus challenge an invader every foot of the way. A more able and cautious general would have taken cognizance of possible changes in the military set-up of the enemy. In addition he would have better equipped and supplied his army before undertaking such an arduous campaign. Sibley had tried to get more arms and materiel for his brigade, but had failed. Since one of the reasons for this venture in the first place was to seize the supply depots of the enemy, perhaps Sibley should not be blamed too harshly. But in any perspective, the New Mexican campaign was a gamble—victory or disaster lay uneasily in the hands of fate.

While the brigade was awaiting the order to march northward into New Mexico, the ranks were daily being thinned by "those two terrible scourges to an army smallpox and pneumonia."[112] Smallpox had broken out among Baylor's men several weeks before Sibley's arrival and by the middle of January the 2nd Regiment reported 104 cases with six deaths. Hasty efforts were made to vaccinate all men who had not yet contracted the disease.[113] Winter weather and inadequate clothing and blankets accounted for the great number of pneumonia victims.

With the establishment of a general hospital at the little town of Dona Ana, Sibley "determined to move forward with the force at hand."[114] The brigade

---

110. Sibley to Cooper, May 4, 1862, *Official Records,* Series I, Vol. IX, 507.

111. Noel, *Campaign from Santa Fe to the Mississippi,* 12–14.

112. Sibley to Cooper, May 4, 1862, *Official Records,* Series I, Vol. IX, 507.

113. Mesilla *Times,* January 15, 1862.

114. Sibley to Cooper, May 4, 1862, *Official Records,* Series I, Vol. IX, 507.

advanced northward along the Rio Grande to the abandoned post of Fort Thorn where it momentarily halted to regroup and to await the arrival of five companies of the 7th Regiment.[115] When all was at last in readiness, the Army of New Mexico set out from Fort Thorn. The long awaited invasion of New Mexico had begun.

After Baylor had cleared the Mesilla Valley of Union troops and had established the Territory of Arizona, his attention was divided between the continuing Federal danger to the north and the incursions of hostile Indians. Through spies and scouts, the colonel was able to keep abreast of Union activities. Though several times his patrols clashed with those of the enemy, none of the encounters was of a serious nature. The Apache Indians, quick to take advantage of the withdrawal of the Federal troops from Arizona, began to terrorize the whole western section of the country. Baylor's force was too small to regarrison the abandoned posts or to cope adequately with this menace. To help solve the manpower shortage, Baylor created the Arizona Guards. These were militia units whose membership was made up of the citizenry of a locality. When danger appeared, the guardsmen temporarily left their homes to take up arms against the Indians. The Arizona Guards worked in cooperation with the regular Confederate troops and were under the direction of Colonel Baylor.

Confederate tenure in Arizona was extremely frail during the period before the coming of the "Sibley brigade." The Federals had been busily concentrating an army at Fort Craig and were just on the verge of launching an offensive when Sibley's timely arrival thwarted the movement.

In the ensuing New Mexican campaign, the Army of New Mexico would win the only two major battles, but the Confederates would lose in the end. They would lose because they could not overcome the barren and inhospitable nature of the land and the dogged resistance of Colonel Edward R. S. Canby, the Federal commander. Other factors contributing to defeat were lack of supplies and the inability to seize them from the Federals, the arrival of Union reinforcements from Colorado, and the destruction by a Federal detachment of some eighty wagons loaded with irreplaceable supplies. The Texans found themselves deep within a hostile country hundreds of miles from any possible base of supply. What had begun as a glorious invasion came to an end in a near disastrous rout.

The Confederate retreat resulted not only in the firm retention of New Mexico by the Union, but also the abandonment of the Territory of Arizona. While Sibley had been away to the north, Baylor had inaugurated a campaign

---

115. Noel, *Campaign from Santa Fe to the Mississippi,* 15.

of extermination against the hostile Indians. This policy was repugnant to Jefferson Davis, so the colonel was subsequently removed from the governorship. In 1863 Baylor became a member of the Confederate Congress from Texas, and he continued to serve in that capacity for the duration of the war.

Sibley made no effort to retain Arizona for several reasons. Of primary importance was the fact that his campaign had as its goal the seizure of California. Since the failure to take New Mexico had rendered that objective impossible, it was purposeless to keep an army in relatively unimportant Arizona. In addition the area was stripped of supplies and another Federal force was on its way from California to contest the Confederate occupation. Completely demoralized and disgusted with the country, Sibley's troops were anxious to return East. The general had no recourse but to march the thinned ranks of his army back to San Antonio. This action left the frontier of West Texas undefended and allowed Federal occupation as far east as Fort Davis.

Sibley's star had risen rapidly only to descend with equal facility. From the end of this campaign to the conclusion of the war, he was relegated to a subordinate position under Generals Richard Taylor and E. Kirby Smith. Henry Hopkins Sibley had gambled and lost.

Sixth-plate ambrotype of Captain James Bell Stevenson, Company I, "Grimes County Greys," 20th Texas Infantry. *Courtesy Georgia Lee Whatley.*

Texas Coastal Defense, 1861–1865

ALWYN BARR[*]

While Sibley and his Texas cavalry were fighting for control of New Mexico Territory, other Texans were defending the four-hundred-mile Texas coastline from enemy attack. When the war began the Texas coast was virtually undefended. As Alwyn Barr of Texas Tech University, the author of numerous studies of Texas participation in the Civil War, points out in this essay, Texans moved quickly to fortify the coastline once the war began. Equipped with cannon from captured Federal forts, artillery companies were soon stationed at Sabine Pass, Galveston, San Luis Pass, Matagorda Island, and Aransas Pass.

Although a blockade of the Texas coast was instituted in 1861 it was the following year before Union forces attempted landings on the coast. Federal forces were driven off at Corpus Christi in August 1862 but were more successful at Galveston in October, capturing the state's largest seaport. Texas Confederates, including members of the Sibley Brigade now back from New Mexico, recaptured Galveston on New Year's Day 1863. A major Union assault against Sabine Pass was repulsed in September of that year, but Federal troops successfully occupied Brownsville in November. Most of these enemy troops were removed in early summer 1864 to support Nathaniel P. Banks's army in Louisiana. As Barr notes in his article, Galveston was the only major seaport still in Confederate hands at the end of the war.

* Alwyn Barr, "Texas Coastal Defense, 1861–1865," *Southwestern Historical Quarterly,* LXV (July, 1961), 1–31.

For more on the defense of the Texas coast see Charles C. Cumberland, "The Con-
federate Loss and Recapture of Galveston, 1862–1863," Southwestern Historical
Quarterly, LI (Oct., 1947), 109–130; Norman Delaney, "Corpus Christi—The
Vicksburg of Texas," Civil War Times Illustrated, XVI (July, 1970), 4–9, 44–48;
Lester N. Fitzhugh, "Saluria, Fort Esperanza, and Military Operations on the Texas
Coast, 1861–1864," Southwestern Historical Quarterly, LXI (July, 1957), 66–100;
and Ralph A. Wooster, "The Texas Gulf Coast in the Civil War," Texas Gulf His-
torical and Biographical Record, I (Nov., 1965), 7–16.

When Abraham Lincoln established a naval blockade of the Southern coast on
April 19, 1861, Texas' four hundred mile stretch of beaches and harbors rated
second only to Florida in length. Although somewhat distant from the fighting
fronts, it was of immediate importance to the civilian population of the state, as
well as a source of military supplies for the Trans-Mississippi region of the Confederacy. Retention of the Texas coast to keep open trade through nothern Mexico also became of increasing necessity as the Federal blockade tightened on
Southern ports. The need to hold open all routes for the influx of goods was
compounded by Union conquest of the Mississippi River, cutting off the Trans-
Mississippi area from the Southern heartland. Blockade running into Texas
ports received a further stimulus from the Federal capture of most other Southern harbors as the war progressed. Thus the coast of Texas was the scene of constant activity throughout the Civil War, as its regional importance steadily
increased.

Realization of the need for defense did not create the means. Texans in 1861
found themselves utterly helpless before a sea assault, and could breathe only an
uneasy sigh of relief because the original Federal fleet numbered but forty-two
ships for the entire Southern blockade.[1] Texas ports were guarded by no such
brick fortifications as protected New Orleans, Mobile, Savannah and
Charleston. Few heavy cannon were to be found in Texas, none mounted for
defense for her coastline, yet the essence of coastal attack and defense in the
1860s still lay in the artillery duel between warships and heavy artillery batteries.
With batteries protected by fortifications, opposing the mobility of warships,
many factors might effect the outcome. Morale and training of the men on each
side, channel obstructions, the range and number of guns engaged on each side,
and supporting troops in large operations all weighed to some extent in such a
struggle.

During the American Civil War brick forts, such at Fort Sumter, were found

---

1. Charles B. Boynton, *The History of the Navy During the Rebellion* (New York, 1867), 97.

to be out-of-date, and were replaced wherever possible by earthworks. Even then a Confederate engineer admitted, "No forts now built can keep out a large fleet unless the channel is obstructed."[2] For such purposes dams, sunken vessels, rocks, piles, chains, rafts, ropes, and torpedoes were employed.

Ordnance in use for warships and coastal defenses during the 1860s ranged from eighteen-pounders to twelve-inch Columbiad smoothbores, and included rifled cannon up to two-hundred-pounders. Extreme ranges for the more common pieces were:

Eighteen-pounder	1592 yards at	5°	elevation
Twenty-four-pounder	834 yards at	5°	elevation
Thirty-two-pounder	1922 yards at	5°	elevation
Eight-inch Columbiad	4817 yards at	27.30°	elevation
Ten-inch Columbiad	5654 yards at	39.15°	elevation
Thirty-pounder Parrott rifle	4874 yards at	15°	elevation
One-hundred-pounder Parrott rifle	8428 yards at	35°	elevation[3]

In February of 1861, at the direction of the Secession Convention in Texas, Colonel John S. Ford led an expedition which captured Brazos Santiago and Fort Brown on the Rio Grande. There, from United States forces, were taken the first heavy cannon later used in defense of Texas harbors. Ford reported thirty-two guns captured, all smoothbores, including eight eight-inch howitzers, four twenty-four-pounder howitzers, twelve twenty-four-pounder siege guns, four ten-inch mortars, four twelve-pounder field guns, and 7293 rounds of ammunition. Some of the pieces, however, were without proper carriages.[4]

Twelve of the newly acquired guns were immediately forwarded to Galveston, where Sidney Sherman, a San Jacinto veteran, had been placed in charge of the city's fortification. The Secession Convention also voted during March, 1861, to entrench Sabine Pass, Matagorda Island, Aransas Pass, and Port Isabel. In April, Sherman was replaced by Captain John C. Moore, a former West Pointer and college professor from Tennessee, who later rose to brigadier general. He soon received additional cannon, taken during March at Fort Clark in West Texas. The entire confiscation of heavy ordnance there had included four twenty-four-pounders and two eight-inch howitzers.[5]

2. [Victor] Von Scheliha, *A Treatise on Coast-Defense: based on the Experience Gained by Officers of the Corps of Engineers of the Army of the Confederate States . . .* (London, 1868), 47.

3. U.S. War Department, *Instruction for Heavy Artillery* (New York, 1863), 236–239, 242.

4. Ernest William Winkler (ed.), *Journal of the Secession Convention of Texas, 1861* (Austin, 1912), 352.

5. *Ibid.*, 99, 133, 394; Francis R. Lubbock (C. W. Raines, ed.), *Six Decades In Texas or Memoirs of Francis Richard Lubbock, Governor of Texas in War-Time, 1861–63, a Personal Experience in Business,*

In June, 1861, Captain Walter H. Stevens, assisting in the fortification of Galveston, submitted to President Jefferson Davis the first comprehensive plan for Texas coastal defense. He suggested two twenty-four-pounders at Sabine Pass, four or five eight-inch Columbiads at Galveston, a twenty-four-pounder covering the mouth of the Brazos River, three thirty-two-pounders on Pass Cavallo, and two twenty-four-pounders at Aransas. Eight to ten companies of artillery would be normally sufficient, he felt, though reinforcements would be necessary in the event of a full scale invasion.[6]

July, 1861, brought the conflict closer to home for most Texans with the appearance of the Federal warship *South Carolina* under Commander James Alden to enforce the blockade at Galveston. Alden, an ingenious officer, armed the schooners *Dart, Shark,* and *Sam Houston* from among his first ten captures along the Texas coast. By their use he extended the blockade to Sabine Pass with only the original crew and guns from his single warship.[7]

With the blockade a reality enlistments in Texas coastal artillery units increased, each company being rushed to its position immediately upon mustering into the service. In Galveston the Third Battalion Texas Artillery, composed of seven companies, was organized under Major Joseph J. Cook. A graduate of the United States Naval Academy, Cook had personally raised Company A in Fayette County as the Active Company of Dixie Grays during June, 1861. When Cook was promoted to major, Captain Sidney T. Fontaine succeeded to his command.[8] Company B, raised in Galveston by Augustine S. Labuzan, came under the leadership of Captain A. R. Wier when Labuzan became major of the

---

War, and Politics (Austin, 1900), 317; Ordnance Stores seized at U.S.A. posts in Texas, 1861 (Texas Adjutant General's Papers, Archives, Texas State Library) Fort Clark; George W. Cullum, *Biographical Register of the Officers and Graduates of the U. S. Military Academy at West Point, N.Y., . . .* (2 vols.; New York, 1868), II, 239.

6. W. H. Stevens to Jefferson Davis, June 12, 1861, *The War of the Rebellion: A Compilation of the Official Records of the Union and Confederate Armies* (130 vols.; Washington, 1880–1901), Series I, Vol. IV, 92; cited hereafter as *Official Records.*

7. Commander James Alden to Lieutenant Samuel R. Knox, July 26, 1861, *Official Records of the Union and Confederate Navies in the War of Rebellion* (31 vols.; Washington, 1894–1927), Series I, Vol. XVI, 595; cited hereafter as *Official Records, Navies.*

8. Confederate Muster Roll (73) (MS., Archives, Texas State Library); Dudley G. Wooten (ed.), *A Comprehensive History of Texas 1685–1897* (2 vols.; Dallas, 1898), II, 572; *List of Artillery Officers C.S.A.* (University of Texas Library binder's title; no title page, Marcus J. Wright lettered on spine), 134. The book is certainly the work described as U.S. War Department, Records Office, *Artillery Organization, etc. of the Confederate Army* (Washington, ?) in John Page Nicholson, *Catalogue of library of Brevet Lieutenant-Colonel John Page Nicholson Relating to the War of the Rebellion 1861–1866* (Philadelphia, 1914), 45.

battalion after Cook's promotion to lieutenant colonel in December, 1861.[9] Captain E. B. H. Schneider headed Company C, while Samuel Boyer Davis, original commander of Company D, turned his battery over to Captain Charles M. Mason in late October to accept a staff appointment. Company E was raised by Captain Edward Von Harten. Captain Frederick H. Odlum commanded Company F, also known as the Davis Guards, which had been enlisted in time to accompany Ford's Rio Grande Valley expedition of February, 1861. Odlum's men were principally Irish dock workers, recruited like most of the battalion in Galveston and Houston.[10] Company G, led by Captain John H. Manly, had been a pre-war social organization known as the Houston Artillery.[11]

In September, 1861, Colonel Joseph Bates was appointed commander of the Fourth Texas Volunteer Regiment on coastal duty between San Luis Pass and Caney Creek. His unit, accepted for Confederate service as the Thirteenth Texas Infantry, actually included two artillery companies from the time of its organization. The artillery contingent was later increased to four batteries, of which Companies D and H, under Captains William G. Moseley and William E. Gibson were equipped with field guns. Companies B and F, led by Captains James S. Perry and William R. Jones, served the heavy guns at the mouth of the Brazos River near Velasco.[12]

Further south in the Matagorda Bay-Corpus Christi area three additional companies of artillery were raised for coastal service. Daniel D. Shea raised a battery known as the Van Dorn Guards, while Dr. Joseph M. Reuss recruited the Indianola Artillery Guards from Calhoun County. These units had elected officers and forwarded their rolls to the governor, even before he issued a call for three batteries to serve in their area.[13] His appeal, stemming from a requisition of three companies in August by Brigadier General Earl Van Dorn, commander of the District of Texas, was fulfilled by Captain Benjamin F. Neal's battery from the Corpus Christi area. Neal, who as a private citizen had written

9. *Ibid.*, 135; Confederate Muster Roll (1702) (MS., Archives, Texas State Library).

10. *List of Artillery Officers C.S.A.*, 135; Winkler, *Journal of the Secession Convention of Texas, 1861*, p. 324; Galveston *News*, March 16, 1861; Francis Robertson Sackett, *Dick Dowling* (Houston, 1937), 16.

11. Confederate Muster Roll (298) (MS., Archives, Texas State Library); List of Artillery Officers C.S.A., 135; Houston *Tri-Weekly Telegraph*, May 6, 1859.

12. Brigadier General P. O. Hébert to Colonel J. Bates, September 26, 1861, *Official Records*, Series I, Vol. IV, 111–112; *List of Artillery Officers C.S.A.*, 48, 55, 81, 99.

13. *Ibid.*, 52, 110, 138; Confederate Muster Roll (115) (MS., Archives, Texas State Library).

President Davis in April, 1861, about the need for artillery on the Texas coast, recruited his company in September and October.[14]

To complete Van Dorn's requisition of artillery, which included a request for one company at Sabine Pass, Captain J. R. Burch's Company B of Major James B. Likens' Sixth Texas Infantry Battalion was designated heavy artillery after its organization in November, 1861.[15]

While men were being recruited to serve coastal batteries a citizens' committee from Galveston left on July 25, 1861, for Richmond, armed with a requisition from General Van Dorn for heavy ordnance. Spurred on by the presence of blockaders off their city and a personal knowledge of its short ranged, inadequate batteries, William Pitt Ballinger, John S. Sydnor, and M. M. Potter arrived in Richmond on August 4.[16] On the same day Cook's men exchanged their first shots with the Federal ships, which shelled the port to test its defenses. Under a storm of protest from foreign consuls in the city Commander Alden ceased his bombardment and the blockade continued as before.[17]

In Richmond, Ballinger and his friends, unaware of events at home, were referred by the Secretary of War to Major Josiah Gorgas, Chief of the Ordnance Bureau. He offered them four ten-inch Columbiads, two eight-inch Columbiads, and two soon to be completed eight-inch rifled pieces, adding that carriages for the guns and some thirty-two-pounders could be had in New Orleans. The return trip, begun on August 15, proved to be a series of repeated delays, caused by railroad tie ups and the slush of fall roads in western Louisiana under incessant rains. On October 24, 1861, when Ballinger reached Galveston to assume an appointment as Receiver of Property of Alien Enemies, the cannon were still mired deep in mud east of the Sabine River. It appears probable that the guns did not reach Galveston until the early months of 1862.[18]

Despite a lack of powerful defenses as a deterrent, the Federal fleet remained relatively inactive off the Texas coast during the remainder of 1861. At Galveston a few blockade runners were taken, and on November 12 a boat attack success-

---

14. Texas Adjutant General's *Report*, 1861, p. 4; B. F. Neal to Jefferson Davis, April 28, 1861, *Official Records*, Series I, Vol. I, 629–630; Confederate Muster Roll (518) (MS., Archives, Texas State Library).

15. *List of Artillery Officers C.S.A.*, 16.

16. William Pitt Ballinger Diary, August 4, 1861 (MS., Archives, University of Texas Library).

17. Commander Alden to consular officers in Galveston, August 6, 1861, *Official Records, Navies*, Series I, Vol. XVI, 606–607; Oran M. Roberts, "Texas" in Vol. XI, *Confederate Military History* (Clement A. Evans, ed., 12 vols.; Atlanta, 1899), 71.

18. Ballinger Diary, August 6, 1861–October 24, 1861 (MS., Archives, University of Texas Library); Houston *Tri-Weekly Telegraph*, November 10, 1862.

fully surprised and partially burned the Confederate patrol schooner *Royal Yacht*.[19]

Ashore, Commander William W. Hunter of the Confederate Navy and Brigadier General Paul O. Hébert, newly appointed Confederate commander in Texas, pushed efforts to fortify Galveston and Houston. An attempt was also made to improvise a harbor defense fleet by the purchase of river steamers and the renovation of captured government vessels.[20] Lacking heavy ordnance, however, Hébert felt that because of the

superior naval armament of the enemy and his entire possession of the sea, it will be almost impossible to prevent a landing at some point upon this extensive and unprotected coast, I have settled upon it as a military necessity that he must be fought on shore or in the interior.[21]

After the *Royal Yacht* affair Hébert's apprehensions increased to the point of removing part of the artillery in Galveston to Virginia Point, mainland end of the island's railroad bridge. In January, 1862, however, the city's batteries were increased from eight to thirteen heavy guns, probably the pieces acquired originally by Ballinger's party in Richmond. With such an addition to the island's defenses Hébert continued to garrison both Fort Point and Pelican Spit, key positions covering the harbor mouth.[22]

At Pass Cavallo, the main entrance to Matagorda Bay, Captain Shea's battery stood guard with four twenty-four-pounders by early October. His isolated position on Matagorda Island near the lighthouse remained exposed, however, because of orders not to entrench until the proper point for works could be chosen by engineers.[23] Darwin M. Stapp, brigadier general of Texas militia, after inspecting Shea's position reported to General Hébert in late October that Reuss' battery, with two twelve-pounders and a six-pounder, was also present and temporary works had been thrown up to shield the guns. He also suggested the removal of both batteries to the mainland unless they were supported by other troops to protect against boat landings.[24]

19. Galveston *Tri-Weekly Civilian*, November 9, 1861; Captain Henry Eagle to Flag Officer W. W. McKean, November 12, 1861, *Official Records, Navies*, Series I, Vol. XVI, 755–756.

20. *Ibid.*, 835, 840–841, 844, 847–849; *Official Records*, Series I, Vol. IV, 112, 117, 122, 126–127.

21. General Hébert to Secretary of War Judah P. Benjamin, October 24, 1861, *ibid.*, 127.

22. *Ibid.*, 166; Ballinger Diary, November 29, 1861 (MS., Archives, University of Texas Library); Log of the *Bayou City*, *Official Records, Navies*, Series I, Vol. XVI, 869.

23. Report of Colonel August C. Buchel, *Official Records*, Series I, Vol. IV, 116–117. Activity in the Matagorda Bay-Corpus Christi area has been well presented by Lester N. Fitzhugh, "Saluria, Fort Esperanza, and Military Operations on the Texas Coast, 1861–1864," *Southwestern Historical Quarterly*, LXI, 66–100.

24. D. M. Stapp to General Hébert, October 17, 1861, *Official Records*, Series I, Vol. IV, 123–124.

Another inspection in December by Colonel Robert R. Garland found the artillery properly positioned to engage Federal warships but short of ammunition and still unsupported in an incomplete earthwork styled Fort Washington by its garrison. On December 7 and 8, during Garland's visit, Shea's men engaged a Union blockader at extreme range, firing sixteen rounds with little effect.[25]

In December, Governor Francis R. Lubbock responded to appeals from the Aransas area by requesting three or four heavy cannon from Fort Brown in Colonel Henry E. McCulloch's Western Sub-District of Texas. Such a battery, he believed, would protect intracoastal trade carried on behind the island chain with Matamoros, as well as the mail and private property in the Aransas-Corpus Christi region.[26]

Blockaders off the Texas coast in early 1862 numbered only five, thinly spread in an attempt to cover its numerous harbors while the main gulf squadron under Admiral David G. Farragut attacked New Orleans. During January the ships *Midnight, Arthur,* and *Rachel Seaman* engaged the shore batteries at Velasco and Pass Cavallo, testing their strength and range.[27] Shea, still unsupported on Matagorda Island in February, hired a patrol boat to inform him of any landing to his rear. At the same time he began earthworks to cover the land approach to his guns. Bates' defenses at Velasco were also reportedly stronger, improved by cannon originally intended for Aransas Pass.[28]

Because of an almost complete lack of artillery in the Aransas vicinity, Union warships were able to shell repeatedly the off shore islands. Captain Neal, commanding the defenses there, reported his battery as equipped with two light six-pounders, and almost completely lacking in powder. Federal boat raids were also effective in destroying some property, although Shea and Neal were able to deal with most of them quickly. It was during this rather trying period that Shea received a promotion to major in command of an artillery battalion, composed of his own company under Captain John A. Vernon, and that of Captain Reuss.[29]

----

25. Colonel R. R. Garland to Major S. B. Davis, December 6, 14, 1861, *ibid.,* 153–154, 156–157; Captain D. D. Shea to Major S. B. Davis, December 9, 1861, *ibid.,* 156; Lieutenant James Trathen to Flag Officer W. W. McKean, December 18, 1861, *Official Records, Navies,* Series I, Vol. XVII, 6.

26. Governor Francis R. Lubbock to Colonel H. E. McCulloch, December 23, 1861 (Executive Record Book 1861–1863, Archives, Texas State Library).

27. *Official Records, Navies,* Series I, Vol. XVII, 71; Vol. XVIII, 690–691; Lieutenant James Trathen to Captain Henry Eagle, January 24, 1862, *ibid.,* Vol. XVII, 79–80.

28. Captain D. D. Shea to Commodore W. W. Hunter, February 3, 1862, *ibid.,* 167; Major C. G. Forshey to Major S. B. Davis, February 19, 24, 1862, *Official Records,* Series I, Vol. LIII, 787–789.

29. Major D. D. Shea to Colonel R. R. Garland, February 18, 1862, *ibid.,* Series I, Vol. IX,

Activity in the Galveston area during early 1862 was limited to the burning of a beached blockade runner in San Luis Pass by a Federal boat party in April.[30] Hébert's fear of attack from the sea was heightened, however, because his district had been stripped of its supporting units to build up General Van Dorn's army in Arkansas for the Pea Ridge campaign.[31]

With the exit of most units from the Galveston garrison Lieutenant Colonel Joseph J. Cook was promoted to colonel and his battalion was increased to a full regiment, known as the First Texas Heavy Artillery. To this end Companies H, I, K, and L, under Captains Thomas J. Catching, D. M. Jackson, David G. Adams, and N. J. King, were raised and added to the command between April and June, 1862. John H. Manly, former commander of Company G, was promoted to lieutenant colonel of the new regiment, while Edward Von Harten, captain of Company E rose to the rank of major in the enlarged unit.[32]

All Hébert's nightmares seemed about to come true on May 17, 1862, when Captain Henry Eagle of the Federal frigate *Santee* demanded the surrender of Galveston. Having engaged the city's batteries two days before with the schooner *Sam Houston,* Eagle's threat of attack appeared quite real. Many guns had already been removed from the city. Those remaining on Pelican Spit were spiked by Colonel Cook, who prepared to evacuate his troops rather than fight should a landing be made. Totally without army support, Eagle ran out his bluff and the blockade again settled into normalcy.[33]

Skirmishing continued along the entire coast in July with clashes at San Luis Pass, Matagorda, and Aransas Pass between small boat crews and shore patrols. Lieutenant John W. Kittredge with the bark *Arthur* was especially troublesome in the Aransas region, entering the pass to obstruct intracoastal trade and shell Neal's camp.[34] A similar bombardment was beaten off at Velasco by Bates' men

483–486; Captain B. F. Neal to Colonel H. E. McCulloch, February 22 1862, *ibid.,* 562; Major W. O. Yager to Lieutenant B. E. Benton, April 25, 1862.

30. Colonel J. Bates to Major S. B. Davis, April 6, 1862, *ibid.,* 545.

31. Judah P. Benjamin to General Hébert, February 24, 1862, *ibid.,* 700.

32. *List of Artillery Officers C.S.A.,* 134–136; Houston *Weekly Telegraph,* April 7, 1862.

33. Captain H. Eagle to Admiral Farragut, June 4, 1862, *Official Records, Navies,* Series I, Vol. XVIII, 536; Ballinger Diary, May 16, 17, 1862 (MS., Archives, University of Texas Library); X. B. DeBray, *A Sketch of the History of DeBray's 26th Regiment of Texas Cavalry* (Austin, 1884), 6; Colonel J. J. Cook to General Hébert, General Hébert to Colonel J. J. Cook, May 7, 1862, *Official Records,* Series I, Vol. IX, 710–711.

34. Colonel C. Livenskiold to Brigadier General H. P. Bee, July 17, 1862, *ibid.,* 610–613; Captain B. F. Neal to Colonel C. Livenskiold, July 16, 1862, *ibid.,* 613–614.

with an eighteen pounder on August 11, but caused their commander to request heavier ordnance for his important post.[35]

Kittredge again captured the spotlight later in August when he took the steam gunboat *Sachem* into Corpus Christi Bay, followed by the *Bella Italia, Corypheus, Reindeer,* and *Arthur,* all sailing vessels. In the following week he captured or ran aground two Confederate patrol boats and demanded the right to inspect former government buildings in Corpus Christi. When refused by Major Alfred M. Hobby on August 14, he served forty-eight hour notice on the town.[36]

True to his word Kittredge brought his tiny fleet into the bay north of town at dawn on the 16th and opened fire with six or seven heavy guns. Protected by an old earthwork, erected by General Zachary Taylor in 1845, Hobby drove off the first attack at 6:00 a.m., and the second by 3:00 p.m. with a twelve and an eighteen-pounder. Under a rain of nearly three hundred shot and shell Hobby's men had maintained their position at a cost of one wounded.

Following a lull on Sunday the Union warships renewed their assault during the 18th. Hobby had added another cannon to his battery, and continued to hold the shore side earthworks. In a further effort to dislodge the Confederates, Kittredge sent some of his seamen ashore with a field gun. Hobby countered with a stirring southern charge, which drove the Federals back to their ships. Defeated in every effort to capture the port, Kittredge shelled the empty town, but total Southern casualties in victory were only two wounded and one killed.[37]

Once the town had been successfully defended its position was rapidly improved by subsequent events, beginning with the arrival of Captain Herman Willke's battery of two twenty-four-pounder howitzers and four twelve-pounders on August 27.[38] Hobby's local popularity increased even more when Captain John Ireland's company of his battalion captured Lieutenant Kittredge, surprised while ashore south of Corpus Christi in early September.[39] To insure against heavier assaults on the community, Felix A. Blucher rebuilt the north battery, adding a bombproof, and constructed two new batteries on the south

---

35. Colonel J. Bates' report, August 16, 1862, *ibid.,* 616.

36. Captain John Harding's report, August 27, 1862, *ibid.,* 617; Captain John Sands' report, August 27, 1862, *ibid.,* 618; Lubbock, *Six Decades in Texas,* 410.

37. Major A. M. Hobby's reports, August 16, 18, 1862, *Official Records,* Series I, Vol. IX, 621–623; *Ranchero Extra* (Corpus Christi), August 19, 1862.

38. Brigadier General H. P. Bee's report, August 26, 1862, *Official Records,* Series I, Vol. IX, 619–621.

39. Brigadier General H. P. Bee's report, September 24, 1862, *ibid.,* 624.

side of town. The new water battery housed two twenty-four-pounder howitzers, while a sunken position on the bluff held an eighteen-pounder.[40]

As early as July 30, 1862, Major Getulius Kellersberger reported the works at
Sabine Pass to be inadequate and the battery of two thirty-two-pounders and
two eighteen-pounders poorly equipped.[41] Before the engineer's suggested im-
provements had been made, however, three Federal vessels entered the pass and
engaged the fort on September 24, 1862. Captain K. D. Keith commanding the
local artillery company, a part of Ashley W. Spaight's Battalion, held the position until after dark under a continuous bombardment from beyond extreme
range for his cannon. Major Josephus S. Irvine, a San Jacinto veteran commanding in Spaight's absence, ordered the pieces spiked and all stores removed
from the works which were abandoned by 8:00 a.m. the next morning. Yellow
fever had cut into the battalion's strength but reinforcements arrived quickly
and the Union sailors limited their efforts to burning the railroad depot at
Beaumont, and destroying the fort, two schooners, and later the railroad bridge
over Taylor Bayou.[42]

Having struck at both ends of Texas' coastal defenses the Federal blockading
fleet in early October aimed its main blow at Galveston, the commercial, military, and diplomatic center of Texas affairs. General Hébert, aware of the increased Union activity, assumed the ultimate goal to be Galveston and decided
its defense was impossible. Work continued only on Fort Hébert at Virginia
Point, while the heavy guns finally available in Galveston were all removed except one on Fort Point. Citizens of the island community were bitterly opposed
to any retreat, accusing Hébert of greater love for his cannon than for their
city.[43]

Other batteries were filled with Quaker guns made of wood on October 4,
1862, when the Union gunboat *Harriet Lane* steamed into the harbor with a
surrender demand for Colonel Cook. Because of a delay in replying, caused by

40. Felix A. Blucher to Major E. F. Gray, October 15, 1862, *ibid.*, Series I, Vol. XV, 827–828.

41. Major J. Kellersberg [G. Kellersberger] to Colonel X. B. DeBray, July 30, 1862, *ibid.*, Series I,
Vol. IX, 729. Kellersberger, born in Switzerland in 1821, came to America in 1849, where he married
and worked as an engineer in California and Mexico prior to the war.

42. Lieutenant Colonel A. W. Spaight's reports, September 26, October 2, 1862, *ibid.*, Series I,
Vol. XV, 144–145, 146–147; Acting Master Frederick Crocker to Admiral Farragut, October 24, 1862,
Official Records, Navies, Series I, Vol. XIX, 227–229: Houston *Tri-Weekly Telegraph*, September 29,
October 3, 1862.

43. Ballinger Diary, October 4, 1862 (MS., Archives, University of Texas Library); Galveston
Weekly News, October 15, 1862; P. W. Gray to Jefferson Davis, November 20, 1862, *Official Records*,
Series I, Vol. XV, 868–869; Colonel X. B. DeBray's report, October 19, 1862, *ibid.*, 836.

a lack of small boats to communicate with the ship, Commander William B. Renshaw brought his remaining seven warships up the channel. The garrison of Fort Point opened on the advancing Union fleet with their ten-inch gun, only to see it dismounted by an eleven-inch shot from the gunboat *Owasco*. After fire from two twenty-four-pounders fell short, resistance ceased, for Galveston lay under the guns of Renshaw's gunboats. A four day truce was agreed to, allowing the Confederates under Colonel Cook to evacuate, since the Union fleet had no troops with which to occupy the island. Activity continued at both Virginia Point and Eagle Grove, island end of the railroad bridge, where parts of Cook's regiment improved their entrenched positions.[44]

Lavaca became the next focal point of action when Renshaw took two of his ships into Matagorda Bay later that month. On October 31 he appeared off the town, demanding its capitulation at 1:00 p.m. When refused by Major Shea, the Union commander allowed only ninety minutes for the residents to be removed, despite a yellow fever epidemic then in progress. Having thus made himself duly infamous for such harshness, Renshaw opened a close range bombardment of the town that afternoon. Shea's guns under Vernon and Reuss returned an effective crossfire on the warships, however, forcing their withdrawal beyond range of the shore batteries. Lavaca was again shelled at long range on November 1, but no further attempts to seize the town were made.[45]

Major General John Bankhead Magruder brought a fresh breath of fighting spirit to Texas in the fall of 1862, when he replaced Hébert as district commander. Magruder began immediately upon his arrival to plan an attack aimed at the recapture of Galveston, pressed onward perhaps by the hint of failures in the Seven Days' fighting near Richmond during the past summer.

For the amphibious part of his assault force "Prince John" Magruder placed two river steamers, protected by cotton bales, under Captain Leon Smith. A thirty-two-pounder rifle was placed aboard the *Bayou City* to be served by Captain A. R. Wier with volunteers from Cook's artillery. Lieutenant L. C. Harby led the men from Lieutenant Colonel William H. Griffin's Battalion who were to fire two twenty-four-pounders on the *Neptune*. Sharpshooters from the cavalry regiments of Colonels Tom Green and Arthur P. Bagby, formerly participants

44. Commander W. B. Renshaw to Admiral Farragut, October 8, 1862, *Official Records, Navies,* Series I, Vol. XIX, 254–260; Houston *Telegraph Supplement,* December 8, 1862; Colonel J. J. Cook's report, October 9, 1862, *Official Records,* Series I, Vol. XV, 151–153; Colonel X. B. DeBray's report, October 12, 1862, *ibid.,* 148–149.

45. Lieutenant George E. Conklin to Major E. F. Gray, November 1, 1862, *ibid.,* 181–183; Houston *Tri-Weekly Telegraph,* November 3, 10, 1862; Lubbock, *Six Decades in Texas,* 413–414.

in Brigadier General Henry Hopkins Sibley's New Mexico Expedition, also volunteered for service aboard both boats.[46]

Ashore Magruder left Lieutenant Colonel John H. Manly in charge of the Virginia Point batteries, and placed Major Edward Von Harten in command of the artillery to be moved into Galveston under cover of darkness. Fourteen field guns, including the batteries of Captains George R. Wilson and William G. Moseley, were to fan out along the city's entire waterfront prior to opening on Renshaw's fleet. An eight-inch Dahlgren gun was mounted on a railroad flat car which would be wheeled over the bridge and brought into action at short range. Captain Sidney T. Fontaine with his battery received orders to recapture Fort Point and set up three siege guns there to assist in shelling the Union warships. For support of his twenty shore pieces Magruder had an assortment of cavalry and infantry units commanded by Brigadier General William R. Scurry.[47]

The object of such a military concentration, six Federal gunboats, lay in Galveston harbor, almost completely unaware of their danger until the last minute. At anchor in the bay were the *Westfield,* flagship with six guns, another converted ferry boat, the *Clifton,* with eight heavy cannon, an altered merchant ship, *Sachem,* mounting five guns, the *Owasco,* only regular warship of the fleet, armed with four cannon, a small schooner with one gun, the *Corypheus,* and a former United States revenue cutter mounting five heavy guns, the *Harriet Lane.*[48]

Ashore on Kuhn's Wharf at the end of Eighteenth Street were 264 men and officers of the Forty-second Massachusetts Infantry, who arrived from New Orleans on December 25 as a garrison for Galveston. Because of their numerical weakness no attempt had been made to entrench the town or burn the railroad bridge connecting it with the mainland. Most of the fleet lay near the wharf, with the *Harriet Lane* in the shallow channel above it off Twenty-ninth Street.[49]

After a false start in late December, New Year's night was chosen for the surprise assault, with the hope that celebrations of the occasion would help lower

---

46. Robert N. Franklin, *Battle of Galveston, January 1st 1863* (Galveston, 1911), 5; Major C. G. Forshey to Colonel X. B. DeBray, December 23, 1862, *Official Records,* Series I, Vol. XV, 908; General Magruder's report, February 26, 1863, *ibid.,* 211–220.

47. *Ibid.;* Wooten, *A Comprehensive History of Texas 1685–1897,* II, 532; Houston *Tri-Weekly Telegraph,* January 19, 1863.

48. Frank Moore, (ed.), *The Rebellion Record: A Diary of American Events . . .* (12 vols.; New York, 1862–1868), VI, 339; Franklin, *Battle of Galveston, January 1st 1863,* p. 6; Statistical Data of U.S. Ships, *Official Records, Navies,* Series II, Vol. I, 59, 67, 99, 168–169, 195, 238.

49. Charles P. Bosson, *History of the Forty-Second Regiment Infantry, Massachusetts Volunteers 1862, 1863, 1864* (Boston, 1886), 61–77; Lieutenant Charles A. Davis' report, January 10, 1863, *Official Records,* Series I, Vol. XV, 206–207.

the efficiency of Union guards in Galveston. Artillery wheels were hard to muffle, however, and Massachusetts' pickets reported Confederate cannon in the market place by 1:00 A.M. After the moon set between 3:00 and 4:00 A.M., Southern guns opened on Federal ships from an arc of positions two and a half miles long. Colonel Cook led a predawn charge through shallow water against the Union held wharf, only to be repulsed because his troops' ladders were too short.[50]

Wasting shot and shell at first, the *Sachem, Owasco,* and *Corypheus* later depressed their cannon to fire along Galveston's shadowy thoroughfares, and drove Southern gunners to cover in an unequal duel between field artillery and nine to eleven-inch naval guns. The Union flagship, *Westfield,* trying to move up channel just after midnight, went aground on Pelican Spit near the harbor's mouth. Repeated efforts by the *Clifton* were of no avail in dislodging it as action began. Commander Renshaw then sent the *Clifton* to aid the other warships in silencing the Confederate guns.[51] Confederate land forces were still in action but nearing defeat at the moment when a Northern reporter penned this vivid description of the battle:

Overhead and around night was slowly retiring before day; the dim light prevalent being rent by the frequent flashes of cannon, the soaring aloft of shell, and the omnipresent short-lived blaze of musketry, while the hellish discord beggars all description.[52]

Action was far from ending, however, for with excellent timing the *Neptune* and *Bayou City* began their rush toward the isolated *Harriet Lane* at dawn. Aided by surprise, with Federal attention centered on the shore batteries, their swift approach was hindered only by the untimely explosion of Captain Wier's heavy piece aboard the *Bayou City.* Although Wier and two of his men were killed, both river boats closed quickly to rifle range and the Texas sharpshooters swept the *Harriet Lane's* decks with fire. Attempts to ram the Union vessel failed at first and a shot from her pivot gun sank the *Neptune* in shallow water near by. Despite stiff resistance, continued heavy fire by Tom Green's sharpshooters settled the issue, forcing the Yankee seamen below decks. There they were captured when the *Bayou City* rammed and boarded her helpless adversary only moments later. Both officers of the captured vessel were found mortally wounded on her deck, their loss a key factor, no doubt, in the ship's defeat.

---

50. W. S. Long's report, January 10, 1863, *ibid.,* 208–210; Bosson, *History of the Forty-Second Massachusetts Infantry,* 87–95.

51. A. J. H. Duganne, *Camps and Prisons, Twenty Months in the Department of the Gulf* (New York, 1865), 236; Major General N. P. Banks' report, January 3, 1863, *Official Records,* Series I, Vol. XV, 199–206; General Magruder's report, February 26, 1863, *ibid.,* 211–220.

52. Moore, *The Rebellion Record,* VI, 341.

Fearful of injuring Federal prisoners, the *Owasco* retired after a tardy attempt to aid the *Harriet Lane*. White flags were raised by both sides and a surrender demand was presented to the nearest Union gunboat. Unable to enforce their ultimatum, the Confederates could only watch as the Federal fleet sailed out to sea. Without any central leadership each ship captain had fought his own separate fight, ending in a withdrawal by mass consent. Commander Renshaw, unable to free the *Westfield,* removed his crew and set a fuse to the ship's magazine. A premature explosion caught the commander aboard, however, killing him and his small boat crew in the concussion and wreckage. Besides the *Harriet Lane,* Magruder had captured the Massachusetts infantry who were forced to surrender when left unsupported, and inflicted over 150 casualties on the Union Navy while retaking Galveston. Even twenty-six killed, including Captain Wier and Lieutenant Sidney Sherman, Jr. of the artillery, plus 117 wounded must have seemed small price for such a success.[53]

Following up his Galveston victory, Magruder transferred Company F of Cook's regiment to Sabine Pass with an eight-inch rifled Columbiad for service on the cottonclad ram fleet there. The Davis Guards under Captain Frederick Odlum were placed aboard the *Josiah H. Bell* with their heavy piece, called "Annie" in honor of their commander's niece, the wife of Lieutenant Richard W. Dowling. Two twelve-pounders were mounted on the *Uncle Ben,* another river steamer, to be served by Captain K. D. Keith's artillerymen from Spaight's Battalion. Reinforced with riflemen of Spaight's command, the assault force moved from Beaumont down to Sabine Pass on January 20, led by Major Oscar M. Watkins. Outside the pass lay two Federal blockaders, a sloop, *Morning Light,* armed with nine heavy guns, and the schooner, *Velocity,* mounting two light howitzers. Both vessels were commanded by Captain John Dillingham.

Having removed the channel obstructions, Watkins' steamers sailed as the sun rose on January 21, 1863, heading for the blockaders. Both Union vessels ran before the attackers but were steadily overhauled on a nearly calm sea because they were strictly sailing ships. Opening at a range of over two miles, the *Bell's* gun crew exhibited uncanny accuracy in dismounting one of the *Morning Light's* cannon. Their fire was then momentarily silenced by a crudely cast shot which refused to be rammed home. Pressing on to within rifle range the *Bell's* sharpshooters cleared her opponent's decks, forcing surrender. Not to be outdone, the *Uncle Ben* brought the *Velocity* around with three solid shot and both

---

53. Commander Henry Wilson to Admiral Farragut, January 8, 1863, *Official Records, Navies,* Series I, Vol. XIX, 439; General Banks' report, January 3, 1863, *Official Records,* Series I, Vol. XV, 199–206; General Magruder's report, February 26, 1863, *ibid.,* 211–220; Bosson, *History of the Forty-Second Massachusetts Infantry,* 100–115.

Federal ships were towed back to Sabine Pass. Without loss Watkins had taken 109 prisoners, after inflicting thirteen casualties, while further destroying the Northern blockade of Texas' coast. After attempts to float the *Morning Light* over the bar failed, the sloop was scuttled and burned off the pass upon the appearance of other Union warships.[54]

News of the Sabine Pass affair was an almost anticlimactic blow for Commodore Henry H. Bell, who had been sent to Galveston by Admiral Farragut to renew the blockade and if possible recapture the city. Upon his arrival on January 10, 1863, Bell bombarded the city only to be rebuked by foreign consuls, again in residence there. Entering the harbor, he found beyond his means, for Magruder had removed all channel buoys, and most of his vessels were of too deep draft to navigate the shallow bars without a pilot. Nothing was left for him, except to stand off the island watching its defenses grow, counting new guns as they were mounted.[55]

On the night of January 11, 1863, the dull boom of naval guns drifted in from the Gulf of Mexico to questioning ears ashore at Galveston. It was later found that Captain Raphael Semmes had brought the Confederate sea raider *Alabama* into the Gulf to attack the transports of a rumored invasion fleet headed for Texas. Sighting the *Alabama* off Galveston, the Federal gunboat *Hatteras* under Lieutenant Commander H. C. Blake had given chase on the eleventh, hailing after dark. Receiving the name of a British vessel in reply, Blake sent a boat party to check the stranger's papers, only to be surprised and sunk by a ripping broadside after the boat pulled away. Semmes picked up the Yankee crew and outran Bell's fleet, which arrived too late to effect the course of action.[56]

Commodore Bell would have been rudely shocked could he have seen the excellent staging which produced the vivid picture of massive defense before him at Galveston. Magruder, who believed the city untenable, nevertheless called for 2000 slaves to fortify it as part of a grand game of bluff. Works sprung up almost overnight under the skilled direction of Colonel Valery Sulakowski and Major Getulius Kellersberger.

To fill their awesome fortifications until real ordnance could arrive, the foreign born engineers improvised Quaker guns of wood, which frowned impres-

54. Duganne, *Camps and Prisons*, 243–246; Galveston *Tri-Weekly News*, February 2, 1863; Surgeon J. W. Sherfy to Secretary of Navy Gideon Welles, April 12, 1864, *Official Records, Navies*, Series I, Vol. XIX, 558–562; Major O. M. Watkins to Captain E. P. Turner, January 23, March 14, 1863, *ibid.*, 564–566, 567–570.

55. Admiral Farragut to Commodore H. H. Bell, January 3, 1863, *ibid.*, 479; Commodore H. H. Bell to Admiral Farragut, January 24, 1863, *ibid.*, 554.

56. Semmes to Mallory, May 12, 1863, *ibid.*, Series I, Vol. II, 683; Bell to Farragut January 12, 1863, *ibid.*, Series I, Vol. XIX, 506.

sively on the Union blockaders. Two heavy cannon were mounted aboard rail-road cars and run into the entrenchments on extended side tracks. Changing positions at night, they furthered the deception by lobbing shells at the fleet from different batteries each day.[57] Masquerade time continued until a few days after one of the year's most intense storms, which blew over one or two of the fake cannon. Then at a truce meeting, in a burst of gleeful satire, Federal offic-ers informed the Confederates that "they had seen two . . . artillerymen carry a large cannon, which ordinarily weighed some 5400 pounds, into position all alone, and they did not think it advisable to tie into such strong men as that."[58]

To improve the efficiency of defense between Matagorda Bay and Corpus Christi, Magruder combined Major Alfred M. Hobby's infantry battalion with Major Daniel D. Shea's artillery in February to form the Eighth Texas Infantry. Hobby was promoted to colonel, Shea to lieutenant colonel.[59]

May, 1863, brought a unique request to Governor Francis R. Lubbock from a citizens' committee in Houston. The group asked that Captain Henry S. Lub-bock, the governor's brother, be furloughed to superintend the construction of a "Sub Marine Propeller" for attaching torpedoes to blockaders. Although no fur-ther mention was made of the project, it provided proof of Texan determination to defend their coasts, as well as ingenuity exceeded only by the partially suc-cessful use of such a vessel at Charleston in 1864.[60]

Bell's constant reports on Southern entrenching at Galveston continued into May, when he outlined the system of fortifications for his commander, Admiral Farragut. South Battery contained two rifled guns in bombproof casemates. Continuing northward along the beach were a middle battery, and the largest work of all, Fort Magruder, near the Old Hospital. Fort Point mounted eight casemate guns, while Pelican Spit held six more. Three new works covered the inner harbor and piles blocked the channel between Pelican Island and Virginia Point. He estimated that 5000 men would be necessary to conquer and garrison the island fortress.[61]

---

57. Ballinger Diary, January 5, 16, 1863 (MS., Archives, University of Texas Library); DeBray, *History of DeBray's 26th Regiment of Texas Cavalry,* 11; Getulius Kellersberger (Helen S. Sundstrom, trans.), *Memoirs of an Engineer in the Confederate Army in Texas* (Austin, 1957), 27–29.

58. *Ibid.,* 29.

59. Confederate Muster Roll (95) (MS., Archives, Texas State Library).

60. W. B. Baker and others to Governor F. R. Lubbock, May 15, 1863 (Texas State Military Board Papers, Archives, Texas State Library).

61. Commodore H. H. Bell to Admiral Farragut, May 12, 1863, *Official Records, Navies,* Series I, Vol. XX, 183–184.

The formidable works described by Bell were inspected from within by Magruder, Governor Lubbock, and their combined staffs in June, 1863, and appeared much as Colonel Arthur Fremantle of the British Army had viewed them while passing through Texas in May. All agreed to their strength, especially since real cannon had been added. Some guns had been returned from Houston, and although the *Harriet Lane's* armament had been ordered to Louisiana, six cannon were reclaimed from the *Westfield's* hulk.[62] By July, Commodore Bell pronounced the fortifications too strong for an assault by the normal blockading fleet without powerful army support.[63]

In August occurred a short lived mutiny by part of Galveston's garrison, surprising in view of their otherwise steady service. The refusal to drill by men of the Third Texas Infantry on August 10, 1863, followed the next day by parts of Cook's artillery, focused attention on the morale problems in coastal defense. While poor provisions and lack of pay were given as major reasons, constant exposure to disease in an unhealthy area, worry over Indian raids on their families near the frontier, and the general monotony of garrison duty with its inactivity must also be weighed in assessing the causes. The dissidents were brought quickly into line by firm yet understanding officers, well acquainted with the unmilitary quirks of volunteers.[64]

During the final four months of 1863, Confederate troops in Texas were left little time for personal problems. Once Vicksburg and Port Hudson fell, opening the Mississippi to the North, Federal efforts turned toward conquest of Texas, to forestall such a move by Maximilian's French armies in Mexico.

Sabine Pass was chosen for the first Union attack, as a weakly held point protected, supposedly, by only two thirty-two-pounders. Once in Federal hands the pass would provide access to Beaumont, a perfect base for operations in Texas because of its rail connection with Houston over flat country. To carry out his planned invasion of Texas, Major General Nathaniel P. Banks in New Orleans brought together four light draft gunboats, the *Clifton, Sachem, Arizona,* and *Granite City,* under Lieutenant Frederick Crocker. The ships were to escort and support 4000 troops of the Nineteenth Army Corps, commanded by Major

---

62. Lubbock, *Six Decades in Texas,* 486; Arthur James Lyon Fremantle (Walter Lord, ed.), *The Fremantle Diary* (Boston, 1954), 55–56; Houston *Tri-Weekly Telegraph,* June 4, 1863; Galveston *Tri-Weekly News,* June 10, 1863; Brigadier General W. R. Boggs to General Magruder, June 30, 1863, *Official Records,* Series I, Vol. XXVI, Part 2, 97–98.

63. Commodore H. H. Bell to Admiral Farragut, July 3, 1863, *Official Records, Navies,* Series I, Vol. XX, 372.

64. Lieutenant Colonel E. F. Gray's report, August 4, 1863, *Official Records,* Series I, Vol. XXVI, Part 1, 241; Colonel X. B. DeBray's reports, August 11, 12, 1863, *ibid.,* 242–245.

General William B. Franklin. After delays caused by the imagined presence of the Confederate sea raider *Alabama* off Sabine Pass, the Federal fleet gathered late on September 7 in sight of its objective.[65]

With all hope of surprise lost it was decided to force the defenses rather than attempt a landing on the marshy coast. Crocker chose to lead the way up the Texas channel of Sabine Pass in the *Clifton,* followed by the *Granite City,* while the *Sachem* and *Arizona* were to pass up the Louisiana channel and take the Southern battery in reverse from Sabine Lake. Franklin agreed and ordered a transport to land troops below the works once action had begun. The infantry in turn would charge the fort when its garrison had been driven to cover by Crocker's warships.

A far different reception awaited the Union advance than was anticipated. Fort Griffin, the new Confederate battery position, lay near the head of Sabine Pass on the Texas side, above the old works abandoned in 1862. Built only that summer after word leaked out about new attempts on Texas, the fortification was a hundred yards wide and surrounded by swamps. Its armament included two thirty-two-pounders dug up and repaired under the direction of Major Kellersberger, engineer in charge of constructing the new position. To those pieces were added two twenty-four-pounders and two thirty-two-pounder howitzers, mounted only hours prior to the engagement. Captain Frederick Odlum's highly skilled Davis Guards, Company F of Cook's artillery, had been returned to the scene of their earlier success in anticipation of an invasion attempt. Daily practice on stakes driven in both channels of the pass had helped each gun crew zero in every inch of the area they would be called on to defend.[66]

Crocker opened the action on September 8, 1863, at 6:30 A.M., by lobbing twenty-six shells at the fort with a thirty-pounder Parrott rifle from a position near the Louisiana shore lighthouse. Lieutenant Richard W. Dowling, commanding in Odlum's absence, kept his men under cover, however, refusing to disclose the strength of his battery by firing on a target beyond its range. Firing ceased at 7:30 A.M., to be renewed at 11:00 A.M. when the Confederate steamer *Uncle Ben* dropped down Sabine Lake to Fort Griffin. Three shells from the

65. Commodore H. H. Bell to Secretary of Navy Gideon Welles, September 4, 1863, *Official Records, Navies,* Series I, Vol. XX, 515; General N. P. Banks' report, September, 1863, *Official Records,* Series I, Vol. XXVI, Part I, 287–292.

66. J. Thomas Scharf, *History of the Confederate States Navy: From Its Organization to the Surrender of Its Last Vessel* (New York, 1894), 524; Moore, *The Rebellion Record,* VII, 427; Lubbock, *Six Decades in Texas,* 507; Kellersberger, *Memoirs of an Engineer in the Confederate Army in Texas,* 29–31; Sackett, *Dick Dowling,* 38–40.

Sachem's Parrott rifle passed over both fort and steamer, again resulting in no casualties.[67]

During the morning Colonel Leon Smith, commanding the Marine Department of Texas, had been forwarding troops from Beaumont. Hurrying to the fort that afternoon, he arrived with Captain Odlum and Captain W. Spalding Good of the ordnance department soon after all four Union gunboats got under way for their assault at 3:40 P.M. Waiting until the Federal ships were only 1200 yards away, Dick Dowling called his gunners from their bombproofs to answer the rain of shot and shell falling around them. Lieutenant Niles H. Smith, actually an engineer, commanded one section, Dr. George H. Bailey another, and Dowling the third. One of the howitzers ran backward off its platform on the second or third shot, cutting Confederate fire power at a crucial moment.[68]

Offsetting results came quickly, however, for Dowling's men used their practice stakes well in sighting on the *Sachem* as she steamed up the far channel. On the third or fourth round a thirty-two-pound shot found her steam drum, leaving the gunboat a helpless wreck, piled high with dead and wounded from the explosion. Having blocked the Louisiana channel to further advance, the Southern gun crews hurriedly shifted to meet the rush of Crocker's *Clifton*, rapidly approaching their works loaded with sharpshooters. When only 500 yards separated warship and battery a cannon ball carried away the gunboat's tiller rope, throwing her out of control and soon aground. From that position Crocker continued to fight until two of his three guns bearing on the Confederate works were partially disabled and the ship's boiler exploded from another direct hit. The five Southern cannon in action had fired 107 times in thirty-five minutes, or better than once every two minutes; an almost unheard of speed for heavy artillery.[69]

Rather than brave the uncanny accuracy of Dowling's gunners, the *Arizona* and *Granite City* withdrew from the pass, leaving both *Sachem* and *Clifton* in Confederate hands. Immediate results of the action were 350 prisoners and two

---

67. Lieutenant Commander W. H. Dana to Commodore H. H. Bell, September 9, 1863, *Official Records, Navies,* Series I, Vol. XX, 522; Captain F. H. Odlum's reports, September 8, 9, 1863, *Official Records,* Series I, Vol. XXVI, Part 1, 309–310.

68. Lieutenant R. W. Dowling's report, September 9, 1863, *ibid.,* 311–312; Dallas *Morning News,* April 23, 1902. Herein is an account written from articles by W. P. Doran, a reporter for the Galveston *News* and Houston *Telegraph* during the war, who talked to participants on September 9, 1863.

69. Duganne, *Camps and Prisons,* 261–266; Henry Hall and James Hall, *Cayuga in the Field. A Record of the 75th New York Volunteers,* . . . (New York, 1873), 142–143; Lieutenant F. Crocker to Secretary of Navy Gideon Welles, April 21, 1865, *Official Records, Navies,* Series I, Vol. XX, 544–548; Lieutenant Amos Johnson to Acting Rear Admiral H. K. Thatcher, March 4, 1865, *ibid.,* 552–553; Houston *Tri-Weekly Telegraph,* October 27, 1863.

gunboats, mounting thirteen heavy guns, all at no cost to the defenders. General Franklin saw no alternative to retreat before such a tenacious defense, and returned with his troops to New Orleans. His estimate of the fort's armament, as seven and nine inch cannon, spoke volumes for their handling which no praise could match.[70]

Reinforcements were rushed to the Beaumont area by General Magruder, who also had the fortifications strengthened and enlarged. By mid October two thirty-pounder Parrot rifles from the *Clifton* had been added to the defenses which were then quite extensive.[71] Banks, however, had given over his desire to capture Sabine Pass in favor of cutting off Confederate trade through Mexico and the Rio Grande Valley.

Landing at Brazos Santiago on November 2, 1863, Banks soon took Brownsville with a force of 7000 men. Having been reinforced by another division he sailed up the coast, intent on closing other Texas ports to blockade runners by capture and occupation. While Magruder began concentrating his forces to meet the new threat, Banks reached Mustang Island off Corpus Christi by November 17, 1863. There he landed part of his infantry which captured Captain William N. Maltby's battery of three guns after two hours of skirmishing. Maltby's cannon, twelve, eighteen, and twenty-four-pounders mounted to cover the sea approaches of Corpus Christi Bay, were engaged by the steamer *Monongahela* until their surrender.[72]

Continuing across St. Joseph Island on November 21, Major General Cadwallader C. Washburn, commanding the division ashore, crossed to Matagorda Island and moved against Fort Esperanza. The fort, an enlarged version of Shea's original works on the island's northern extremity, was garrisoned in the fall of 1863 by 500 men with eight heavy guns. Its batteries, two twelve-pounders, five twenty-four-pounders, and a ten-inch Columbiad, were mounted mainly to protect against naval attack. But with parapets ten feet high and fifteen feet thick, flanked by water on both sides, the fortification presented an awesome sight to Washburn's infantry as it loomed through the fog before them

70. Lieutenant R. W. Dowling's report. September 9, 1863, *Official Records,* Series I, Vol. XXVI, Part 1, 311–312; Major General W. B. Franklin's report, September 11, 1863, *ibid.,* 294–297.

71. Major General J. B. Magruder to Lieutenant General E. Kirby Smith, September 22, 1863, *ibid.,* Series I, Vol. XXVI, Part 2, 247–248; Assistant Inspector General Benjamin Allston to Lieutenant General E. Kirby Smith, October 14, 1863, *ibid.,* 318–321.

72. Major General N. P. Banks to Commodore H. H. Bell, November 17, 1863, *Official Records, Navies,* Series I, Vol. XX, 680–681; Houston *Tri-Weekly Telegraph,* December 15, 1863; A. T. Mahan, *The Gulf and Inland Waters* (New York, 1883), 188.

on November 27, 1863. Beset by a Texas norther, rain, sleet, and snow, the Federals dug in and brought up artillery which played on the fort during November 29. Yankee troops kept warm and amused themselves to some extent by dodging ponderous shot from the Southern batteries which bounded through their lines. Exploding Confederate magazines after midnight on November 30 gave notice of the fort's evacuation, unprepared as the garrison was for a prolonged siege. Fear of being cut off and captured, or having his position stormed by the daily increasing Union force, also affected Colonel William R. Bradfute's decision to spike his guns and retire to the mainland.[73] Casualties on both sides had been negligible.

Supported by seven warships, Washburn occupied Matagorda Peninsula and Indianola on the mainland. Probing expeditions skirmished with Magruder's forces behind the San Bernard River in December and on into the early spring of 1864, before being withdrawn for the Red River campaign in Louisiana. The delays involved in dislodging Texas' coastal batteries over a period of two weeks had allowed Confederate concentration of five brigades with nine field batteries in the Caney Creek area of Brazoria County, an effective deterrent to further advance.[74]

With the southern half of Texas' coast occupied by Union forces, and the majority of Confederate troops from Texas opposing Banks' Red River expedition in Louisiana as 1864 began, General Magruder found the great majority of the state's population in no real danger, and blockade running on the increase. Keeping those facts in mind, the district commander withdrew Hobby's regiment from the Matagorda Bay-Corpus Christi area as part of his decision to hold only Sabine Pass, Galveston, and Velasco at all costs. Three well fortified ports allowed some opportunity for choice by the fleet of blockade runners operating out of Havana, who had shifted their trade to Texas as other Southern harbors were closed. In May and June, 1864, most of the remaining Federal troops along the Texas coast were removed through New Orleans to support Banks' defeated army in Louisiana.[75]

---

73. Albert O. Marshall, *Army Life; From a Soldier's Journal* (Joliet, Ill., 1884), 308–337; Houston *Tri-Weekly Telegraph,* December 5, 1863; Galveston *Weekly News,* December 9, 14, 1863; Major General C. C. Washburn's reports, November 30, December 1, 6, 1863, *Official Records,* Series I, Vol. XXVI, Part 1, 416–421.

74. Marshall, *Army Life,* 340–361; Commander J. H. Strong to Commodore H. H. Bell, November 29, 1863, January 1, 1864, *Official Records, Navies,* Series I, Vol. XX, 702, 742–743; General Order 217, District of Texas, New Mexico, and Arizona, December 15, 1863, *Official Records,* Series I, Vol. XXVI, Part 2, 509–510.

75. William Watson, *The Adventures of a Blockade Runner; or, Trade in Time of War* (London, 1892); Marshall, *Army Life,* 390–392; Marcus W. Price, "Ships that Tested the Blockade of the Gulf

Velasco's heavy batteries were estimated at six thirty-two-pounders by the blockading fleet, which showed its respect by never engaging them at close range for any period of time.[76] Galveston, where work on the fortifications never entirely ceased, contained nine companies of Cook's regiment manning thirty-one cannon. Five were mounted in South Battery, five in Fort Magruder, seven on Fort Point, five or six on Pelican Spit, and the rest scattered about in smaller works around the harbor itself. Point Bolivar and Virginia Point on the mainland were also fortified and manned by the artillery companies of Hobby's command, creating a veritable ring of fire into which an attacking fleet would have to sail. The additional problem of navigating the harbor's bars without a pilot or buoys for guidance, plus the threat of torpedoes, proved restraint enough through the final months of conflict. At the eastern terminus of Magruder's new line lay Fort Griffin at Sabine Pass, still garrisoned by the Davis Guards and supported by extensive outer works. Included among those was Fort Mannahassett, a small fortification seven miles southwest of the pass where a Federal supply ship of the same name had washed ashore and broken up in a storm.[77]

March saw another short mutiny at Galveston, in protest against parties given by ladies of the city for General Magruder and his officers, while the garrison suffered from poor food and quarters far from their homes. After the death of General Tom Green during the Red River Campaign in Louisiana that spring, the works on Bolivar Point received his name, but far more important to the troops in Galveston was the reappearance of yellow fever in September.[78]

November returns for the district showed another increase in its armament, with forty-one cannon in Galveston, nine at Sabine Pass, and eight guarding Velasco, manned by almost 1500 cannoneers. Galveston's batteries then included three ten-inch Columbiads, five nine-inch Dahlgrens, three heavy rifled cannon, and eleven thirty-two-pounders, many of them unwelcome presents aboard the five Union warships taken by Texans since January, 1863.[79] Protected

Ports, 1861–1865," *The American Neptune*, XII (1952), 154–161, 229–236.

76. Lieutenant Commander G. H. Perkins to Captain John P. Gilles, February 16, 1864, *Official Records, Navies*, Series I, Vol. XXI, 74–75.

77. H. C. Medford (Rebecca W. Smith and Manon Mullins, eds.), "The Diary of H. C. Medford, Confederate Soldier, 1864," *Southwestern Historical Quarterly*, XXXIV, 125; *Official Records*, Series I, Vol. XXXIV, Part 2, 1010, 1044; Captain J. B. Marchand to Admiral Farragut, April 16, 1864, *Official Records, Navies*, Series I, Vol. XXI, 197.

78. Medford, "The Diary of H. C. Medford," *Southwestern Historical Quarterly*, XXXIV, 127; Houston *Daily Telegraph*, May 29, September 19, 1864.

79. *Official Records*, Series I, Vol. XLI, Part 4, 1066, 1117; *ibid.*, Series I, Vol. XLVIII, 1134.

by such greatly strengthened batteries, blockade running into Texas grew to the extent that Gideon Welles, United States Secretary of the Navy, increased the Western Gulf Blockading Squadron off Texas' coast to twenty ships in 1865, as compared with no more than six or seven in previous years.[80] Even after such precautions only the final fall of the South ended blockade running into Texas ports. When defeat came, the surrender terms drawn up and agreed to in New Orleans, were formally signed aboard the Union gunboat *Fort Jackson* by General Edmund Kirby Smith on June 2, 1865, in Galveston harbor, the only major Southern port held by its defenders until that final hour.[81]

----

80. Secretary of Navy Gideon Welles to Acting Rear Admiral Thatcher, March 30, 1865, *Official Records, Navies,* Series I, Vol. XXII, 119; List of Vessels, January 1865 to January 1866, *ibid.,* 14–16.

81. Report of Acting-Rear Admiral Thatcher, June 8, 1865, *ibid.,* 216.

Albumen carte de visite of Major Richard W. "Dick" Dowling, by H. R. Marks, ca. 1865. *Courtesy Lawrence T. Jones III.*

Dick Dowling and the Battle of Sabine Pass

Andrew Forest Muir*

Jefferson Davis described the defense of Sabine Pass in September 1863 as "one of the most brilliant and heroic achievements in the history of this war." Major General John B. Magruder praised the defenders of Sabine Pass as "the greatest heroes that history recorded." In a battle that lasted less than one hour, Lieutenant Richard W. Dowling and the men under his command damaged and captured two enemy gunboats, killed or wounded nearly one hundred Union soldiers, and turned back an invasion force of five thousand men.

In this essay, historian Andrew Forest Muir describes the battle of Sabine Pass in some detail and provides additional information about Dowling, an Irish immigrant saloonkeeper from Houston, and the Davis Guards who defended Sabine Pass. Muir compares the bravery of Dowling and his men with the defense of the Alamo and the military results of the battle with San Jacinto. He criticizes the ineptness of Union commanders, particularly Major General William B. Franklin.

Readers may wish to compare Muir's treatment of the battle with other accounts, especially Frank X. Tolbert, Dick Dowling at Sabine Pass *(New York: McGraw-Hill, 1962); Alwyn Barr, "Sabine Pass, September, 1863,"* Texas Military History, II

* Andrew Forest Muir, "Dick Dowling and the Battle of Sabine Pass," *Civil War History*, IV (Dec., 1958), 399–428. Reprinted with permission of Kent State University Press.

(Feb., 1962), 17–22; and H. L. Sandefer and Archie P. McDonald, "Sabine Pass:
David and Goliath," Texana, VII (Fall, 1969), 177–188.

Dick Dowling's military reputation has overshadowed his other qualities and
performances—he was a shrewd and foresighted businessman, an early oil oper-
ator, and a public-spirited citizen—but his military exploits have never been described in detail. Some years after the end of the Rebellion, Jefferson Davis
remarked in a public address in New Orleans that the Battle of Sabine Pass "was
more remarkable than the battle of Thermopylae, and, when it has orators and
poets to celebrate it, will be so esteemed by mankind."[1] Davis was not the first
to compare Sabine Pass with Thermopylae, for three days after the battle, the
Houston Tri-Weekly Telegraph had remarked editorially, "Sabine Pass is the new
Thermopylae."[2] The present-day obscurity and low repute of the battle is probably the result of its having been treated exclusively by orators and rhymesters
and never by historians.

Out of obscurity, Richard William Dowling appeared, at the age of nineteen,
in Houston, Texas, in 1857. He is said to have been born in Tuam, County Gal-
way, Ireland, some time between May and July, 1838, one of seven children of
William and Mary Dowling. The surviving five of this brood all lived later in
Texas, but how or why or when they got there can not be determined.[3] The first
record of Dick Dowling is his marriage, on November 30, 1857, to Annie Elizabeth (or Elizabeth Ann) Odlum, daughter of Benjamin Odlum, an Irish
Catholic who had participated in the Battle of Refugio against General Urrea
during the Texan Revolution.[4] The young couple exchanged their vows in a private dwelling in Houston before the Reverend N. Feltin, pastor of St. Vincent's
Church.[5] To this union, that appears to have been a singularly happy one, five
children were born, the last twenty-three days before Dowling's death, but

---

1. *Confederate Veteran*, IX (March, 1901), 120. Davis also described the Battle of Sabine Pass as
having "no parallel in the annals of ancient or modern warfare" and as "without parallel in ancient
or modern war." Davis to John F. Elliott, Beauvoir Miss., July 29, 1884, *ibid.*, IX (August, 1901),
367, and Jefferson Davis, *The Rise and Fall of the Confederate Government* (2 vols.; New York: D. Appleton and Co., 1881), II, 239.

2. *Houston Tri-Weekly Telegraph*, September 11, 1863. See also obituary in *Houston Daily Telegraph*,
September 25, 1867.

3. Frances Robertson Sackett, *Dick Dowling* (Houston: Gulf Publishing Co., c1937), pp. 1–5. Another account shows that Dowling was born in July, 1838, but this date does not agree with his age
at the time of death as Sackett's does. See Mrs. R. F. Pray, *Dick Dowling's Battle; An Account of the
War between the States in the Eastern Gulf Coast Region of Texas* (San Antonio: The Naylor Co.,
1936), p. 129.

4. "Benjamin Odlum, Irish Colonist in Texas," *Frontier Times*, XXVIII (April, 1951), 194–96.

5. Marriage records of Harris County, Texas (MSS, County Clerk's office, Houston), C, 443;

Dowling and his wife had the misfortune to bury three of them.[6]

Dowling was a handsome man. He had a fair and rosy complexion, blue eyes, and reddish brown hair. He liked people and got along well with them, and there was always a smile on his lips. Until his death at the age of twenty-nine, he looked boyish, and everyone thought him younger than he was.[7]

Two months before his marriage, Dowling had become the sole owner of a saloon. On October 6, he had purchased the lease and fixtures of the Lone Star Hall, a two-storied building on the southeast corner of Main and Prairie, where Schulte-United is now located. On the ground floor was the bar and above it "a PLEASANT AND CAPACIOUS BILLIARD SALOON, inferior to none in the State." The saloon itself was known as the Shades,[8] in recognition, it is said, of the sycamore and cottonwood trees that lined the two streets.[9] In a newspaper advertisement Dowling stated that he offered the drinking public a choice assortment of champagne, creme de Bouzy, port, claret, and brandy, as well as first-rate cigars.[10] From the first he was a master of press relations. At the end of 1857 he sent a round of eggnog to the employees of the two local newspapers. The editor of the *Houston Republic* reciprocated the gift by commending Dowling as a "worthy young man" and his billiard saloon as "the best in the State."[11] Early in 1859, Dowling inaugurated the use of illuminating gas in Houston by installing gas lights in the Shades at a cost of $675.[12] That he was able to spend so large a sum on improvements suggests that his business was flourishing.

The billiard hall appears to have been a gambling hall, and Dowling soon closed it.[13] Thereafter, the upstairs room was used as an assembly hall for organizations, and Dowling was soon numbered on the rosters of two of these. On

---

Galveston Weekly News, December 8, 1851; Liber Matrimoniorum, Ecclesia Sti Vincenti a Paulo in praesidio Houston, Texas, 1840–1914 (MS, office of pastor, Annunciation Roman Catholic Church, Houston), No. 69, printed in Sackett, *op. cit.,* p. 10.

6. Sackett, *op. cit.,* pp. 12–15.

7. Memorandum made by Dowling's sister, Mrs. J. B. Cato, of Galveston, Texas, courtesy of Dowling's grandnephew, J. A. Collerain, of Houston, November 17, 1950; letter of Margaret L. Watson, Beaumont, August 29, 1899, in *Galveston Daily News,* September 3, 1899.

8. *Houston Republic,* January 30, 1858.

9. S. O. Young, *True Stories of Old Houston and Houstonians; Historical and Personal Sketches* (Galveston: Oscar Springer, 1913), p. 211.

10. *Houston Republic,* January 30, 1858.

11. *Ibid.; Houston Weekly Telegraph,* December 30, 1857.

12. *Houston Tri-Weekly Telegraph,* January 14, 1859. Nine years later a dealer in gas appliances gave Dowling as a reference, and his estate included a set of gas fixtures. *Houston Daily Telegraph,* July 14, 1867; Deed Records of Harris County, Texas (MSS, County Clerk's office, Houston), VII, 284.

13. Young, *op. cit.,* pp. 211–13. Young was unaware that Dowling had owned the Shades.

April 13, 1858, a group of citizens met in the Lone Star Hall to organize a hook and ladder fire company. As the twenty-year-old Protection Fire Company No. 1 was then inactive, the new group chose to call themselves Houston Fire Company No. 1. A short while later, though, Protection came back to life, whereupon the new company selected the name of Houston Hook and Ladder Company No. 1.[14] Dowling became a member of the company, subscribing his name to the constitution and bylaws on April 17,[15] and was appointed to the relief committee charged with visiting sick members and providing them with such monetary relief as they required not to exceed $15.00.[16] The minutes of the company do not reveal the members' interest in fancy uniforms, parades, and balls. At the beginning of 1859 the Houston Light Artillery, one of the many military companies in town that provided an outlet for social ambitions as well as for military interests, selected the Lone Star Hall as its armory.[17] As early as the beginning of 1860, Dowling was a private in this outfit.[18] On May 5 of that year the company gave at the Old Capitol a ball that was described as the "most brilliant affair of the year."[19] On occasion the company marched in parades.[20] The captain was an attorney, William Edwards, who was at the same time the local leader of the Knights of the Golden Circle, an ambitious and visionary secret organization that hoped to establish a slave empire out of southern United States and northern Mexico.[21]

Not all of Dowling's time was devoted to his family, his business, and his fire and military companies, for, during the summer of 1858, he attended a class in electro-biology conducted by one Lawrence Hale, and he joined twenty-two other class members in testifying to Hale's status as a lecturer and a gentleman and to the pleasure, amusement, and instruction he gave the class.[22] Also, Dowling, unlike many other aliens of his time, on July 26, 1858, was admitted to United States citizenship.[23]

In January, 1860, Dowling sold the Shades and opened a new saloon, the

---

14. Minutes Houston Hook & Ladder Company, 1858–1868 (MSS, Houston Public Library, Houston), pp. 3–5.

15. *Ibid.*, pp. 24, 230.

16. *Ibid.*, pp. 7, 18.

17. *Houston Tri-Weekly Telegraph*, February 21, 1859.

18. *Ibid.*, February 1, 1860.

19. *Ibid.*, May 6, 1859.

20. *Ibid.*, February 21, 1859.

21. *Ibid.*, February 1, 1860.

22. *Houston Weekly Telegraph*, July 28, 1858.

23. Probate Minutes of Harris County, Texas (MSS, County Clerk's office, Houston), D, 336.

Bank of Bacchus, farther downtown, on the southwest corner of Main and Congress. At the end of the month he inserted in the newspapers an advertisement that he liked so well he continued to use it as long as he remained in business. In the advertisement he announced himself as president and cashier and offered exchange in brandy, rum, whiskey, champagne, claret, and port.[24] The Bank of Bacchus was located in one of the oldest buildings in Houston, if indeed not the oldest. It was a block-long edifice on the west side of Main Street between Congress and Preston, built in 1837 and known as Long Row. Dowling's saloon was not to remain long in this building, for during the early morning of March 10, a fire broke out in a restaurant, and before the flames were extinguished they had consumed not only the whole building but another block as well.[25] Almost immediately, however, Dowling reopened the Bank at the corner of Fannin and Congress, across the street from the courthouse.[26] Always alert to the value of publicity, he continued to keep the press supplied with refreshments. At the end of April he sent the printers of the *Houston Telegraph* a "round of 'kiss me quick and go,' a new and fancy drink of his mixture, the flavor of which lingers on the palate like the memory of a dream of paradise and houris."[27]

His liquor business at this time was not confined to the Bank. In the summer of 1860 one of his fellow-publicans fell into his debt, and Dowling accepted a lien on the Hudgpeth Bathing Saloon, to which a bar was attached. A few days later Dowling took title to the business,[28] which was located in the neighborhood of the present Southern Pacific passenger station. How long he operated the place cannot be determined from the scanty records.

In the meantime, as Dowling's business interests prospered, growing sectional tension and the mouthing of southern fire-eaters increased the prospect of war. Throughout the South the number of militia companies grew at a great rate. During the summer of 1860 Dowling became associated with a militia company of infantry commanded by his wife's uncle, Frederick H. Odlum. This company, the Davis Guards, was incorporated under a general state law.[29] Its muster

---

24. *Houston Tri-Weekly Telegraph,* February 8, 1860, partially reprinted in Writers' Program of the Work Projects Administration, comps., *Houston; A History and Guide* (Houston: The Anson Jones Press, 1942), p. 69; advertisement, dated January 30, 1860, in *Houston Weekly Telegraph,* October 23, 1860.

25. *Houston Tri-Weekly Telegraph,* March 10, 1860.

26. *Houston Weekly Telegraph,* January 29, 1861.

27. *Ibid.,* May 1, 1860.

28. Deed Records of Harris County, Texas, X, 359–60, 384–85, 394–95.

29. H. P. N. Gammel, comp., *The Laws of Texas, 1822–1897* . . . (10 vols.; Austin: The Gammel Book Co., 1898), IV, 1092–94.

roll for September 15, 1860, listed four officers, eight noncommissioned officers, forty-three privates, and a secretary. Dowling was first lieutenant and as a banker, also the treasurer. In the company were three other of Dowling's relatives, in addition to Odlum: his brother, Patrick Emmett Dowling, and his wife's brother, Edward John Odlum, were privates; and a sister's husband, Patrick H. Hennessy, was second sergeant.[30] By October, the officers had received their commissions from Governor Sam Houston, the treasurer had some $150 on hand, and a local editor expected the company to parade soon in obedience to the state militia act.[31] Dowling's activities during the Rebellion can only be described in terms of the Davis Guards.

Immediately after the election of Lincoln in November, 1860, Dowling shared in the excitement over the fate of the South. With 221 others, he signed a petition calling a public meeting in Houston for November 14. At the meeting held on that date, those assembled requested the governor to convene the legislature.[32] This Sam Houston refused to do, whereupon the people of the state resorted to revolution: They elected a convention that promptly passed an ordinance of secession purporting to take Texas out of the Union. Having deposed Governor Houston, the convention then turned its attention to the United States troops stationed in Texas. One of the areas in which the army had installations was the lower Rio Grande Valley. A call went out from Austin for militia companies to assemble at Galveston and proceed to the Rio Grande to dispossess the Union forces there. Seven companies responded, four from Galveston, one from Fort Bend County, and two from Houston—one of them Captain Odlum's Davis Guards. The several companies, numbering 500 rank and file, were united into a regiment under the command of Colonel John Salmon Ford.[33] Three of the companies, including the Davis Guards, went aboard the "Union Tug" at Galveston, but Captain Odlum concluded that the boat was unseaworthy and promptly removed his men. This action led to a dispute between him and the colonel commanding, but Ebenezer B. Nichols, commissioner appointed by the convention, interposed and ordered the Davis Guards to board the steamship "Gen. Rusk." The six other companies followed the Davis Guards aboard this ship and the schooner "Shark" that it had in tow.

------

30. Deed Records of Harris County, Texas, X, 423.

31. *Houston Weekly Telegraph*, October 9, 1860.

32. *Ibid.*, November 13, 20, 1860.

33. *Galveston News*, February 28, 1861, reprinted in *Houston Weekly Telegraph*, March 5, 1861; *Dallas Herald*, March 6, 1861.

As the ships left the Galveston wharf, a large crowd cheered heartily, and some citizens fired an artillery salute.[34]

The vessels arrived at Brazos Santiago on February 21. There a Union lieutenant surrendered his small body of men, and the seven militia companies disembarked. The Federals lowered the Stars and Stripes, and Lieutenant Sidney A. Sherman, of the Lone Star Rifles, ran up a Texas flag, as the Galveston Artillery fired a thirty-three-gun salute. But Fort Brown at Brownsville refused to surrender until ordered to do so by General David Twiggs in San Antonio. When the Union forces finally surrendered, the Texans moved up from Brazos Island and occupied Fort Brown.[35]

While Colonel Ford was absent from Brazos Santiago, negotiating with the Union authorities, Captain Odlum (solicitous of his men's well-being and exerting a strong personal influence over them despite the fact he was a strict disciplinarian) got into a disagreement over billeting with another of the captains. As a result, Lieutenant Colonel Hugh McLeod disbanded the Davis Guards for mutinous and disorderly conduct, and refused to honor Odlum's request for a court-martial. But Colonel Ford reinstated the company upon his return from Brownsville.[36] During their stay at Brazos Santiago, the Davis Guards added to their numbers, on February 26, two men who had deserted from the Union Army at Ringgold Barracks.[37] The Guards remained in Brownsville until March 13, and on the 18th they arrived back in Houston, having traveled to Galveston by ship and then up to Houston aboard the Galveston, Houston and Henderson Railroad.[38] They returned with the feeling that they had been most unjustly treated.

Following their return from the Rio Grande, the company remained idle in Houston for five months.[39] Seemingly, the difficulties they had become involved in during the expedition had prejudiced state authorities against them,

---

34. Volunteer, "The Davis Guards," in *Houston Weekly Telegraph,* March 26, 1861.

35. *Houston Weekly Telegraph,* March 5, 1861; John S. Ford to J. C. Robertson, Brownsville, February 22, 1861, in *The War of the Rebellion: A Compilation of the Official Records of the Union and Confederate Armies* (Washington: Government Printing Office, 1880–1901), Ser. I, Vol. 53, p. 651; hereinafter cited on *O.R.,* followed by the series number in Roman numerals, the volume number in Arabic, the part number (if any), and the page, as *O.R.,* I, 53, p. 651. See also "Memoirs of John Salmon Ford" (typescript in Archives Division, Texas State Library, Austin), pp. 929–32, 937–38, 998–1002.

36. Volunteer, "The Davis Guards," in *Houston Weekly Telegraph,* March 26, 1861.

37. *Ibid.,* May 5, 1861.

38. *Ibid.,* March 19, 1861; E. B. Nichols, commissioner and financial agent for the state of Texas, to J. C. Robertson, November 3, 1861, in Ernest William Winkler, comp., *Journal of the Secession Convention of Texas, 1861* ([Austin]: Texas Library and Historical Commission, [1913]), p. 348.

39. *Houston Weekly Telegraph,* August 14, 1861.

but in Houston they were well treated by their fellow-citizens. Friars Augustino da San Damiano d'Asti and Felix Zoppa da Connobio, O.S.F., vacated the presbytery attached to St. Vincent's Church and turned it over to the company. In addition, the priests aroused a spirit of patriotism in their flock, many of whom were of alien origin.[40] Houston businessmen and patriotic ladies, including the Ladies Aid Association of Houston, supplied the company with clothing and other necessities, and three local politicians—Francis Richard Lubbock, Peter W. Gray, and A. N. Jordan—wrote the governor and the adjutant general in their behalf. Finally, on August 13, Governor Edward Clark accepted the Guards for service in Van Dorn's regiment.[41] At the time they were described as a fine body of brawny Irish, most of them mature men.[42]

Within two weeks the company was ordered to Galveston, where, on October 26, it became Company F of Cook's (or the First Texas) Regiment, Heavy Artillery, Confederate States Army.[43] On August 27, a number of the company wrote the editor of the *Houston Weekly Telegraph* reporting that they were conducting themselves splendidly, that Galvestonians were treating them fairly, and that they were increasing in numbers and attaining proficiency in drill.[44] The Ladies Aid Association of Houston kept them supplied with wearing apparel, and in addition sent blankets for new recruits.[45] Captain Odlum acknowledged the women's assistance in a newspaper letter in which he assured them that the company

. . . will ever treasure as their richest jewels the memory of the patriotic donors. And whether on the battle field, or enduring the privations of a soldier's life, this noble action on the part of the fair ones of Houston shall animate and impel them to rival the bravest in the fight, and yield to none in calm endurance and soldierlike conduct.[46]

Some time during the late autumn or early winter, the Davis Guards were sent to Fort Hebert on Virginia Point, at the mainland end of the Galveston, Houston and Henderson Railroad causeway. Thinking themselves permanently

---

40. F. H. Odlum, R W. Dowling, W. P. Cunningham, and P. W. Hennessy to Rev. Messrs. Augustin de Aosti [*sic*] and Felix, Galveston, August 28, 1861, *ibid.,* September 4, 1861.

41. Members of the Davis Guards to editor, Galveston, August 27–28, 1861, *ibid.,* September 4, 1861.

42. *Ibid.,* August 14, 1861.

43. Edward F. Witsell, Adjutant General, U.S.A., to writer, August 22, 1949.

44. Members of the Davis Guards to editor, Galveston, August 27, 1861, in *Houston Weekly Telegraph,* September 4, 1861.

45. *Ibid.,* October 30, 1861.

46. F. H. Odlum to E. H. Cushing, Camp at Eagle Grove, November 17, 1861, in *Houston Tri-Weekly Telegraph,* November 25, 1861, and *Houston Weekly Telegraph,* November 27, 1861.

stationed on the island, they had given away their tents earlier, and they now made no attempt to build barracks at the Point, as they might have done had they not expected to return to Galveston Island.

When cold weather came on, their dissatisfaction grew with their discomfort, and Second Lieutenant William P. Cunningham complained to the commanding general that he feared the men would think themselves slighted on account of their religion and national origin.[47] Despite their dissatisfaction, they continued to perform efficiently, and a newspaper correspondent reported that Cook's regiment was the best drilled artillery he had ever seen and that it handled cannon as easily as a hunter handled a rifle.[48] In a muster roll made on the last day of 1861, Captain Odlum reported a total strength of ninety-three, of whom eight privates were sick and one in arrest, while another had died during the month.[49]

In March, 1862, the Davis Guards were back in Galveston,[50] and in July they varied the monotony of military life by fighting a fire in George Ball's kitchen on Tremont Street until the fire department arrived. For this service Ball rewarded them with a gift of $100.[51] Odlum had the confidence of his superiors, and when Colonel Joseph J. Cook and his staff officers were obliged to go up to headquarters, he left Odlum in charge of the Post of Galveston.[52] On the last day of August, Major E. Van Harter reported that the discipline and instruction of Company F were good, the men "active & able bodied," their arms—percussion muskets with bayonets—in good order, their accoutrements complete though the cartridge boxes were imperfect, and their clothing much worn.[53]

At the beginning of October, Companies F and H, with Odlum in command, manned Fort Point, near the present Galveston landing of the Bolivar Point ferry. They had but one gun, a 10-pounder. On the morning of October

---

47. Last page of letter signed Wm. P. Cunningham, 2 Lieut "J Davis Guards" in War Department Coll. of Confederate Records (MSS, National Archives, Washington, D.C.), Rolls of Co. F, 1st Reg., Texas Heavy Art.

48. Sioux [W. P. Doran] to editor, Galveston, December 13, 1861, in *Houston Weekly Telegraph*, January 18, 1862. For Sioux's identity, see *Dallas Morning News*, April 23, 1902.

49. Muster roll for November 30, 1861–December 31, 1861, certified by F. H. Odlum commanding, in War Department Coll. of Confederate Records.

50. *Houston Weekly Telegraph*, March 26, 1862.

51. H. C. B. to editor, Galveston, July 25, 1862, in *Houston Tri-Weekly Telegraph*, July 28, 1862, and *Houston Weekly Telegraph*, July 30, 1862.

52. H. C. B. to editor, Galveston, August 29, 1862, in *Houston Tri-Weekly Telegraph*, September 1, 1862.

53. Endorsement on muster roll for June 30–August 31, 1862, certified by R. W. Dowling, Galveston, August 31, 1862, in War Department Coll. of Confederate Records.

4, five Federal steamers with a mortar boat in tow crossed the bar into Galveston Harbor and turned their twenty guns on the fort. The 10-pounder was soon disabled, whereupon Odlum ordered the gun spiked and the barracks set afire. The two companies then retreated across the low, open country to the city of Galveston.[54] In the next four days, the Confederate military forces on the island moved with their supplies to Virginia Point, and a Federal force assumed command in Galveston. The commander of the occupying troops agreed not to destroy the railroad bridge across West Bay (although he refused to permit any trains to run into town) so that provisions might continue to be brought into Galveston for the civilians who had not fled to Houston.[55] The Confederate troops at Virginia Point, with virtually nothing to do except to watch the railroad bridge, continued in the best of spirits and feasted on chickens that foraging parties into Galveston had pressed into service.[56] During an artillery practice in late December, according to a newspaper correspondent, they proved themselves better gunners than the enemy.[57]

In the meantime, Major General John Bankhead Magruder, at his headquarters in Houston, was planning the recapture of Galveston. On December 31, two cotton-clad steamboats left Trinity Bay for Galveston, and at sundown the land forces at Virginia Point made preparations to set out for the city. The field artillery had been placed on railroad cars that were pushed across the bridge and into the outskirts of the city, where they were unloaded. Though the moon was shining brightly, a column three miles long moved into the city without detection. As the new year began, Federal gunboats started bombarding the Confederate positions. Women in night clothes, dragging screaming children by the hand, fled to the Gulf beach, while dogs set to howling. The superior Federal gunfire forced the Confederates to drop back. At dawn, the cotton-clads arrived and opened fire on the Federal ships. The land forces moved forward, and Cook's regiment stormed Kuhn's Wharf, where the 42d Massachusetts Regiment was quartered. The cotton-clads disabled the Federal ship "Harriet Lane," and soon thereafter the 42d Massachusetts surrendered.

---

54. Joseph J. Cook to R. M. Franklin, Fort Hébert, October 9, 1862, in *O.R.*, I, 15, pp. 151–53, reprinted in O. M. Roberts, "Texas," in Clement A. Evans, ed., *Confederate Military History* (12 vols.; Atlanta: Confederate Publishing Co., 1899), XI, 73–75; F. H. Odlum and T. J. Catching to editor, Virginia Point, October 14, 1862, in *Houston Tri-Weekly Telegraph*, October 20, 1862, and *Houston Weekly Telegraph*, October 22, 1862.

55. F. Flake to the press of Texas, Galveston, October 9, 1862, in *Houston Tri-Weekly Telegraph*, October 13, 1862, citing *Der Union* (Galveston).

56. Sioux to editor, Virginia Point, December 17, 1862, in *Houston Tri-Weekly Telegraph*, December 19, 1862.

57. Sioux to editor, Eagle Grove, December 22, 1862, *ibid.*, December 24, 1862.

The Davis Guards had been in the midst of the action. A newspaper correspondent reported that

... the artillery boys acted nobly and have covered themselves with glory. They manned their guns as nimbly as though they were behind breastworks. Where all did so well, I feel cautious to draw comparisons; the Irish boys surpassed the expectations of their friends.[58]

During the engagement, four men in Company F were wounded: Junior First Lieutenant J. K. Madden with a slight shell wound in the breast; Private John Hassett with a severe shell wound in the same place; Private John Gleason with a slight gunshot wound in the foot; and Private Joseph Wilson with gunshot wounds in the arm and foot. Of these, Gleason died of tetanus on January 11, at the General Hospital in Houston.[59] After the battle, Company F was given passes to Houston and on January 4 a number of them "kicked up a rumpus" on the Houston courthouse square, in which three shots were fired. One of the men was shot through the hand, and another had his leg broken.[60]

The Davis Guards won wide acclaim for the recapture of Galveston, but they received even higher praise for their part in a naval engagement later in January that cleared Union blockading vessels from the outlet of Sabine Lake. The Confederate force in that engagement comprised two steam vessels that had been outfitted at Orange: the "Josiah H. Bell" of about 182 tons and the "Uncle Ben" of about 135 tons. Aboard the "Josiah H. Bell" was a 64-pound rifled gun made by the Tredegar Works in Richmond and hauled overland from Alexandria, Louisiana.[61] This gun appears officially to have been named Magruder, in honor of the commanding general,[62] but the Irish gunners who manned it referred to it affectionately as Annie, in honor of Dowling's wife.[63] Before the scheduled engagement, some 300 men from Pyron's, Spaight's, and Cook's regiments had been sent from Galveston to Orange and put aboard the two ships.[64] Under command of Major Oscar M. Watkins, the expedition steamed down the Sabine River in the late afternoon of January 18. At eight, they anchored in

58. *Ibid.,* January 5, 1863.

59. *Ibid.,* January 5–7, December 16, 1863; *Houston Weekly Telegraph,* January 7, 1863.

60. *Houston Tri-Weekly Telegraph,* January 5, 1863.

61. R. D. Keith, "Sabine Pass, 1861–63," in *Burke's Texas Almanac and Immigrant's Handbook for 1883* ... (Houston: Compiled, Printed, and Published by J. Burke, n.d.), p. 67.

62. Zack Sabel to editor, on board the steamer "J. H. Bell," January 21, 1863, in *Galveston Tri-Weekly News* (Houston), January 26, 1863, and *Houston Tri-Weekly Telegraph,* January 26, 1863, reprinted in *Dallas Herald,* February 4, 1863.

63. *Houston Weekly Telegraph,* February 4, 1863.

64. Zack Sabel to editor, on board the steamer "J. H. Bell," January 21, 1863, cited in n. 62.

Sabine Lake, and within an hour a severe wet norther struck the area with driving winds that blew most of the water out of the lake, leaving the ships stranded.

During the entire next day, the men aboard were cold and damp; and in addition they had but sour and wormy cornmeal to eat. Major Watkins solved the problem of his personal discomfort by commandeering the hospital stores and going on a binge. Captain Charles Fowler, in command of the "Josiah H. Bell," assumed effective though informal command of the expedition. On the morning of the 20th, the weather moderated, and a foraging squad was sent to the prairie, where they shot two beeves. By noon, when the tide had risen sufficiently to float the two ships, they got under way immediately and proceeded down the lake toward the Gulf.[65] Early on the morning of the 21st, they crossed the bar and set out in hot pursuit of two lurking Federal blockaders—the sloop "Morning Light," with a rifled piece on the poop and a battery of eight 32-pounders, and the schooner "Velocity" (also called "Fairy"), with two 12-pound guns variously described as Napoleons, Dahlgrens, and Parrotts. For thirty miles the chase proceeded. The "Josiah H. Bell" was the faster of the pursuing vessels and was the first to come up to the enemy. As Captain Odlum was acting chief of ordnance, the gunners were under the immediate command of Lieutenant Dowling. The men manning the Magruder were entirely exposed, with Dowling in the most dangerous position of all, but not a man flinched. At two and a half miles, Dowling opened up with his rifled gun. After two shots, a third shell was run in, but it stuck in the barrel. Odlum and Dowling, by brute force, soon rammed the shell home, and the bombardment continued. The gunners poured ten or twelve shots into the "Morning Light." The first struck a main yard, another her quarter boat on the port side, a third her deck, and a fourth her main rigging. When the "Josiah H. Bell" got into rifle range, the sharpshooters aboard opened fire, and Captain John Dillingham of the "Morning Light" struck his flag. In the meantime, the "Uncle Ben" overpowered the "Velocity."[66]

Upon boarding the "Morning Light," Dowling seized the master's mate and went down to the magazine, which he found flooded. He ordered the magazine

---

65. Keith, *op. cit.,* p. 67, wherein Watkins is not referred to by name; item by L, a Houston Lady [Adele Lubbock Looscan] in *Houston Daily Post,* May 23, 1895. For the identification of Mrs. Looscan, see Roberts, "Texas," in *Confederate Military History, op. cit.,* XI, 98.

66. The official reports appear in *Official Records of the Union and Confederate Navies in the War of the Rebellion* (Washington: Government Printing Office, 1894–1922), Ser. I, Vol. 19, pp. 553–73; cited hereinafter as *O.R.N.,* followed by the series number in Roman numerals, the volume number in Arabic, the part number (if any), and the page, as *O.R.N.,* I, 19, pp. 553–73. See also Zack Sabel to editor, on board the steamer "J. H. Bell," January 21, 1863, cited in n. 62.

pumped out, and, when it was again dry, he discovered that all of the munitions except for some 200 cartridges were in good order.[67] With the two captured ships in tow, the Confederate vessels returned to Sabine Pass. By this time, Major Watkins had sobered sufficiently to resume command. The "Velocity" was safely taken across the bar into Sabine Lake, but in obedience to Watkins' order, the "Morning Light" was anchored outside for lightering. By the time most of her stores and part of her armament were removed, a new Union blockading fleet had arrived, and the Confederates fired the ship to prevent its recapture.[68]

In Houston, Watkins' first dispatch about the engagement was read from a window of the *Telegraph* office, and the town went wild. The enthusiastic townspeople rent the air with cheers and rang the public and church bells.[69] In the meantime, at Sabine Pass, the men aboard the "Josiah H. Bell" celebrated with a dinner featuring five meats: pork, mutton, roast beef, chicken, and turkey.[70] Major Watkins handsomely commended the Davis Guards in his report,[71] and in the spring the Confederate Congress tendered its thanks for the victory to Watkins and the officers and men under his command.[72]

For one day less than a year following the capture of the "Morning Light," the Davis Guards were stationed at Sabine Pass, and seemingly, for most of the period, they had little to do other than routine chores.[73] Sabine Pass is a strait some six miles long and not quite a mile wide connecting the Gulf of Mexico with Sabine Lake, at the extreme southeastern corner of Texas. Just above the pass at this time was the town of Sabine City, which had been a prosperous and thriving community before the Rebellion. It had had a large hotel run by one Dorman and his wife,[74] a sawmill owned by one Wingate,[75] and a weekly newspaper, the *Sabine Pass Times*.[76] A railroad, the Eastern Texas, had been built

---

67. Zack Sabel to editor in *Houston Tri-Weekly Telegraph*, February 2, 1863.

68. *Ibid.*, January 26, February 2, 1863.

69. *Ibid.*, January 26, 1863.

70. Junius to editor on board C.S. Gunboat "Josiah H. Bell," off Sabine Pass, January 25 [21], 1863, *ibid.*, February 2, 1863, reprinted in *O.R.N.*, I, 19, pp. 570–73.

71. Oscar M. Watkins to E. P. Turner, off Sabine Pass, January 23, 1863, *ibid.*, p. 565.

72. Joint resolution of thanks to Maj. Oscar W. Watkins and the officers and men under his command, approved May 1, 1863, *O.R.*, I, 53, p. 867.

73. Muster roll for February 28–April 30, 1863, certified by F. H. Odlum, Sabine Pass, April 30, 1863, in War Department Coll. of Confederate Records.

74. J. H. to editor, Beaumont, October 21, 1862, in *Houston Tri-Weekly Telegraph*, November 5, 1862.

75. *Ibid.*, November 3, 1862.

76. United States Census, 1860, Texas, Schedule 6, Social Statistics (MS, Archives Division, Texas State Library), Orange and Jefferson counties. This newspaper is neither listed in Historical Records

from a railhead a short distance out of town to within a mile or two of Beaumont.[77] In July, 1862, a British steamer had come through the blockade and docked at the town, and a short while later a yellow fever epidemic was raging in the area.[78] A number of Federal sorties had occurred in the immediate neighborhood,[79] and on October 30, 1862, a Federal ship, in retaliation for having been fired on by a small number of Confederate scouts, shelled the town and caused some $100,000 of damage.[80] The Federal blockade had just about put an end to commerce out of Sabine Lake, but in anticipation of a resumed traffic, Confederate authorities had stockpiled several thousand bales of cotton at Niblett's Bluff, on the Sabine River, a few miles above Orange.[81] The April, 1863, muster roll of the Davis Guards showed the company at Sabine Pass. It aggregated at that time but seventy-three men present and absent, including twenty-one enlisted men assigned to the company on extra or daily duty and seven of its own privates assigned to detached service.[82] In June, the company was aboard the steamship "Josiah H. Bell" in charge of a 24-pound iron gun and a 12-pound mountain howitzer.[83] As the Federal forces had previously de-

---

Survey Program, comp., *Texas Newspapers, 1812–1939* . . . (Houston: San Jacinto Museum of Historical Association, 1941) nor treated in Walter Prescott Webb, ed., *The Handbook of Texas* (Austin: The Texas State Historical Association, 1952). Quotations from the paper appear in *Houston Weekly Telegraph,* August 7, October 30, 1860, February 12, 1861. The same newspaper reported in its issue for January 29, 1862, that the *Sabine Pass Times* had been suspended since the beginning of the Rebellion.

77. A brief and unsatisfactory account of this railroad appears in S. G. Reed, *A History of the Texas Railroads* . . . (Houston: The St. Clair Publishing Co., c1941), pp. 87–89. See *President's Report of Eastern Texas R. R. Co.* ([Cincinnati]: no pub., [1859]) and map of Sabine Pass, showing the railroad, in *O.R., Atlas,* Plate 32, No.3.

78. *Houston Tri-Weekly Telegraph,* September 10, 24, 1862.

79. Engagement at Sabine Pass, Tex., September 24–25, 1862, in *O.R.,* I, 15, pp. 143–45; affair on Taylor's Bayou, Tex., September 27, 1862, *ibid.,* p. 145; destruction of railroad depot near Beaumont, Tex., October 2, 1862, *ibid.,* pp. 14–47; affair at Sabine Pass, Tex., October 29, 1862, *ibid.,* pp. 180–81; affair at Sabine Pass, Tex., April 18, 1863, *ibid.,* pp. 402–4. See also *Houston Tri-Weekly Telegraph,* September 26, 29, 1862; Supplement, October 3, 1862; October 17, 20, 22, 1862.

80. *Houston Tri-Weekly Telegraph,* November 3, 1862.

81. Keith, *op. cit.,* p. 69. For mention of cotton-running out of Sabine Lake and through the Federal blockade, see Mary E. Moore Davis, *Under Six Flags; The Story of Texas* (Boston: Ginn & Co., c1897), p. 163, and E. G. Littlejohn, *Texas History Stories* (Richmond: B. F. Johnson Publishing Co., c1901), p. 218. According to the Toomey, Louisiana Quadrangle, U.S. Geological Survey (N3007.5-W9337.5/7.5), Niblett's Bluff is located on Old River on the southwest quarter of the southeast quarter, Section 10, Township 10 South, Range 13 West, but a widespread rumor suggests that the community of 1861–1865 was not located on the same site.

82. Muster roll for February 28–April 30, 1865, certified by F. H. Odlum, Sabine Pass, April 30, 1863, in War Department Coll. of Confederate Records.

83. C. M. Mason to E. P. Turner, Houston, June 24, 1863, in *O.R.N.,* I, 20, pp. 830–31.

stroyed Fort Sabine, some two miles below Sabine City, Colonel V. Sulakowski, Corps of Engineers, built a new fort, wholly of earth, several hundred yards above the original fort.[84] This earth structure was sometimes called Fort Sabine but more frequently Fort Griffin, in honor of Lieutenant Colonel W. H. Griffin, who commanded the Post of Sabine Pass.[85] It is said that the last of six guns was installed in the fort on September 6,[86] but, whether this statement is correct or not, it seems definite that the Davis Guards had been practicing for some time from the fort. Governor Lubbock later reported that the company had placed two buoys in the channels through Sabine Pass for practice firing.[87]

The Davis Guards were responsible for what was, without question, the most brilliant victory of the Confederate forces in Texas. This was the Battle of Sabine Pass that took place on the Feast of the Nativity of the Blessed Virgin Mary, September 8, 1863. For bravery this engagement ranks with the Defense of the Alamo, and for military results with the Battle of San Jacinto.

After Maximilian and his French troops had occupied the valley of Mexico in 1863, President Lincoln was anxious to re-establish Federal control over Texas so that he might have some nearby base to bolster a stiff representation against the disregard of the Monroe Doctrine by Napoleon III. After the fall of Vicksburg and Port Hudson in July and the re-establishment of Federal control over the entire Mississippi River, the President thought the time was ripe for a movement into Texas,[88] but General Grant and other general officers thought it would be more advantageous to occupy Mobile and begin squeezing the heart of the Confederacy.[89] On August 6, Major General Nathaniel P. Banks, the commanding general of the Department of the Gulf, was ordered to establish Federal authority in some point in Texas to be selected by him.[90] Banks

---

84. Keith, *op. cit.,* p. 67.

85. *Ibid.* See also Chas. Bickley to editor, Fort Griffin, September 21, 1863, in *Houston Tri-Weekly Telegraph,* Supplement, September 25, 1863.

86. *Galveston Daily News,* March 18, 1905.

87. C. W. Raines, ed., *Six Decades in. Texas; or, Memoirs of Francis Richard Lubbock . . .* (Austin: Ben C. Jones & Co., Printer, 1900), p. 507, quoting Henry S. Lubbock.

88. A. Lincoln to U. S. Grant, Washington, August 9, 1863, in *O.R.,* I, 24, pt. 3, p. 584; Carl Sandburg, *Abraham Lincoln; The War Years* (4 vols.; New York: Harcourt, Brace & Co., c1939), II, 394.

89. N. P. Banks to Secretary of War, New York, April 5, 1865, in *O.R.,* I, 26, pt. 1, p. 18; U. S. Grant, *Personal Memoirs . . .* (2 vols.; New York: Charles L. Webster & Co., 1885–1886), I, 578; U. S. Grant, "Chattanooga," in Robert Underwood Johnson and Clarence Clough Beals, eds., *Battles and Leaders of the Civil War . . .* (4 vols.; New York: The Century Co., 1887–1888), III, 679–80; Richard B. Irwin, "The Capture of Port Hudson," *ibid.,* III, 598.

90. H. W. Halleck to Banks, Washington, August 6, 1863, in *O.R.,* I, 26, pt. 1, p. 672.

immediately began laying plans. The Nineteenth Army Corps under Major General William B. Franklin was chosen for the expedition. Although Lincoln had suggested, but not ordered, the occupation of some point in West Texas, Banks saw the possibility of striking at the heart of Confederate Texas.[91]

From almost the beginning of the war, the headquarters of the District of Texas, New Mexico, and Arizona had been in Houston. This location had been selected because of the several railroad lines radiating out of that city. Before the outbreak of the Rebellion, Houston had been served by five railroads. The Buffalo Bayou, Brazos and Colorado ran from Harrisburg to Alleyton on the Colorado River; the Houston and Texas Central from Houston to Millican above Navasoto; the Galveston, Houston and Henderson from Houston to Galveston; the Houston Tap and Brazoria from Houston to East Columbia on the Brazos River, connecting with the B.B.B. & C. at what is now Pierce Junction; and the Texas and New Orleans from Houston to Beaumont (track had also been laid from Beaumont to Orange, but no motive power or rolling stock was ever run on this segment; long before Appomattox, the ties had rotted out and the rails had rusted). At Beaumont, the T. & N.O. was but a mile or two from the railroad of the Eastern Texas that ran almost, but not quite, to Sabine City.[92] Banks knew from his intelligence reports that the Confederate forces in Texas were few and that if the United States Army could reach the line of the T. & N.O., it could push without much opposition into Houston, from which point it could recapture Galveston by a rear attack and could also fan out through the most populous portion of the state. The plans were impeccable and fitted the facts. Had they been executed with a reasonable degree of efficiency, there can be no question that most of Texas would have been returned to the bosom of the United States in September, 1863.

Knowing that Confederate troops had fortified Sabine Pass, Banks laid out a tactical plan by which the Union force would be landed on the hard sand beach skirting the Gulf of Mexico at a point some twelve miles southwest of Sabine Pass. From that point, the army would move overland across Jefferson, Chambers, and Liberty counties to the railroad at or near the town of Liberty. After the fortification at Sabine Pass had been softened by a joint naval and army attack, Banks would send in additional troops to occupy Beaumont and to join the force at Liberty for a push into Houston.[93] Like the over-all plan, these tac-

---

91. Banks to Secretary of War, April 5, 1865, *ibid.,* pp. 18–19; Hdqrs., Department of the Gulf, New Orleans, Special Orders No. 216, August 31, 1863, *ibid.,* I, 53, p. 569.

92. See incomplete map, *ibid.,* I, 26, pt. 1, p. 291.

93. Banks to Secretary of War, April 5, 1865; *ibid.,* pp. 18–19; Banks to William B. Franklin, New Orleans, August 31, 1833, *ibid.,* pp. 281–88; Banks to President, New Orleans, October 22, 1863, *ibid.,* pp. 290–93.

tical arrangements were without fault. Had the commanding general of the expedition not proved himself both incompetent and cowardly, the expedition doubtlessly would have been a brilliant success.

The assembling of a large force in New Orleans could hardly be kept a secret from Confederate authorities, and as early as September 4, Major General Magruder warned that a force was outfitting at New Orleans for a demonstration against the Sabine Pass area. He ordered Colonel Sulakowski to strengthen the fortifications of the pass,[94] but before the Colonel could take action, the Federal expedition had arrived.

Over 5000 infantry and five batteries of artillery, under command of Major General Franklin, assisted by three brigadier generals, left New Orleans on the evening of September 4, and on the 6th the force was joined at the entrance to Berwick Bay by a number of gunboats. The expedition then numbered twenty-seven craft. This force began assembling off Sabine Pass about midnight of the 6th, but as a result of one lieutenant's losing his way, it was not until the 7th that the principal attacking unit reached the area.[95]

Lieutenant Colonel Griffin, in command of the Post of Sabine Pass, was absent,[96] and Captain Odlum was in temporary charge of headquarters at Sabine City[97] and Lieutenant Dowling in immediate command of the Davis Guards at Fort Griffin.[98] At two o'clock on the morning of the 7th, the sentry at Fort Griffin detected signal lights flashing in the Gulf. He informed Dowling, who put the fort in readiness for attack,[99] and for the remainder of the night the men lay on their arms.[100] During the day that followed, Captain Odlum sent

----

94. W. T. Carrington to V. Sulakowski, Headquarters near Millican, Tex., September 4, 1863, *O.R.N.,* I, 20, p. 555.

95. Acting Volunteer Lt. Frederick Crocker. On the expedition, see Wm. B. Roe to G. B. Drake, New Orleans, February 2, 1864, in *O.R.,* I, 26, pt. 1, p. 293; Franklin to Banks, on board the steamship *Suffolk,* September 11, 1863; *ibid.,* pp. 294–95; G. Weitzel to Wickham Hoffman, on board the steamer *Suffolk,* September 11, 1863, *ibid.,* pp. 298–99.

96. Interview of Margaret L. Watson with J. M. Chasten in *Galveston Daily News,* September 3, 1899.

97. F. H. Odlum to A. N. Mills, Sabine Pass, September 9, 1863, in *Houston Tri-Weekly Telegraph,* September 11, 1863. See also Odlum to Mills, September 8, [1863], in *O.R.,* I, 26, pt. 1, p. 309; Odlum to Mills, September 9, 1863 (not same as letter of 9th cited above), *ibid.,* pp. 309–10; Headquarters, Eastern Sub-District of Texas, Houston General Orders No. 39, September 13, 1863, referred to in *Houston Tri-Weekly Telegraph,* January 2, 1865, quoting *Galveston News.*

98. Odlum to Mills, September 8, 1863, in *O.R.,* I, 26, pt. 1, p. 309.

99. R. W. Dowling to Odlum, Fort Griffin, September 9, 1863, *ibid.,* p. 311.

100. "The Battle of Sabine Pass" in *The New Texas Reader, Designed for the Use of Schools in Texas* (Houston: Published by E. H. Cushing, 1864), p. 95. According to the *Houston Tri-Weekly Telegraph,* November 4, 1863, the account was written by a participant in the battle, but he was not named.

one or more couriers to Beaumont to notify the military commander there, and headquarters in Houston, of an impending attack. The message could not possibly have reached Beaumont in less than six hours, and actually it was not until the morning of the 8th that the Beaumont forces were alerted. Meanwhile, on the 7th, Odlum made additional preparations for the defense of Fort Griffin. Ammunition for the guns at the fort was stored in a house some distance away, and it was necessary to reassemble the wagon of a neighborhood man in order to transport the ammunition to the fort.[101] Captain Odlum stationed Captain Andrew Daly's scouts under Lieutenant Charles Harris behind some sand dunes near the old fort[102] and sent Captain R. D. Keith's company under Lieutenant Joseph O. Cassidy to serve as sharpshooters aboard the steamboat "Uncle Ben."[103] Throughout the day the Federal fleet hovered at the pass.[104] That night, no doubt, the Davis Guardsmen said their Hail Marys with more than ordinary fervor in anticipation not only of impending battle but also of the birthday of the Mother of God.

At 6:30 on the morning of the 8th, six steamers began sounding the bar, and two gunboats of their number came up and fired twenty-six rounds of shot at the fort, without eliciting a reply. The gunboats then retired.[105] At eleven, the "Uncle Ben" steamed down the lake toward the fort, and one of the Federal ships fired three rounds at her.[106]

The apprehension and bungling of the Federal forces pass description. No attempt whatsoever was made to land at the point designated in Banks's plan. Also, Franklin failed completely to exercise ordinary prudence. There is not one suggestion among the records of the action that he sent ashore a single scout to ferret out information of the Confederates' location and number, although he almost certainly could have sent a number of them ashore at dark (if indeed not during daylight) without detection. Completely disregarding the unoccupied

---

101. Statement of David Fitzgerald, private in Odlum's company, in *Houston Daily Post*, March 17, 1905.

102. Account of battle by W. P. Doran in *Dallas Morning News*, September 5, 1897, reprinted *ibid.*, April 23, 1902.

103. Leon Smith to E. P. Turner, Sabine Pass, September 8, 1863, in *Houston Tri-Weekly Telegraph*, September 14, 1863, and *Houston Weekly Telegraph*, September 15, 1863, *O.R.*, I, 26, pt. 1, p. 308.

104. Dowling to Odlum, Sabine Pass, September 9, 1863, in *O.R.N.*, I, 20, pp. 559–60.

105. "The Battle of Sabine Pass," in *The New Texas Reader*, p. 96; *Houston Tri-Weekly Telegraph*, September 9, 1863; Odlum to Mills, September 8, 1863, in *O.R.N.*, I, 20, p. 557.

106. *Ibid.*, p. 559; Uncle Ben to editor, Sabine Pass, September 13, 1863, in *Houston Weekly Telegraph*, September 22, 1863.

and uninhabited beach along the Gulf, he concentrated all of his attention on Sabine Pass. A cursory inspection showed that both shores of the pass were salt marshes and that the shallow water of the pass flowed over a bottom of silt that had washed down from the rivers flowing into the lake. Both the marshy shores and the muddy bottom made a landing in the pass difficult if not impossible. But instead of simply going around the point into the Gulf, Franklin finally fixed on a small inlet immediately above the old fort. This place he was sure had a sandy bottom and certainly had a sandy beach. But the position was well within range of Fort Griffin. With Lieutenant Frederick Crocker, in command of the naval forces, he laid out a plan for diverting the fire of the fort so that 500 troops under Brigadier General Godfrey Weitzel could land. A shallow oyster reef divided the pass into two channels, one along the Texas shore and the other along that of the Louisiana. By sending a gunboat up the Texas channel, he would draw the fire of the fort. Then, when the pieces were laid, two gunboats would go up the Louisiana channel. The gunners would have to re-lay their pieces. When they had done so, the gunboat in the Texas channel would steam at maximum speed up the Texas channel, all the while pouring a fire into the fort. Behind the first gunboat in the Texas channel, and protected by another gunboat, would come a transport, which would land Brigadier General Weitzel's troops at the designated point.[107]

In the meantime, on the morning of the 8th, Acting Volunteer Major Leon Smith, in command of the marine department, at Beaumont, received Odlum's dispatches of the former day. After wiring headquarters in Houston and communicating with the forces at Orange and Niblett's Bluff, he sent the troops at Beaumont aboard the steamboat "Roebuck" and started them down the Neches River. But as nine hours were required to steam to Sabine City and only six to ride, Smith, with Captain W. S. Good, of the ordnance department, set out by horseback. It was about nine o'clock in the morning when they, as well as the "Roebuck," left Beaumont.[108] At about the same time the ships "Josiah H. Bell" and the "Florilda" (belonging to the T. & N.O. Railroad), both with troops aboard, left Orange.[109]

Meanwhile, at Fort Griffin the Davis Guards, though alert, were calm. The earthwork fort had bastioned sides on the east, south, and west, and a redoubt

---

107. Franklin to Banks, on board the steamship "Suffolk," September 11, 1863, in *O.R.,* I, 26, pt. 1, p. 295.

108. Smith to commanding officer, Eastern Sub-District of Texas, September 8, 1863, in *O.R.N.,* I, 20, p. 555; Smith to Turner, Sabine Pass, September 8, 1863, in *O.R.,* I, 26, pt. 1, pp. 307–8.

109. Smith to Turner, Sabine Pass, September 8, 1863, *ibid.*

on the north,[110] in which the men whiled away the time playing cards.[111] The total armament of the fort comprised six guns—two 32-pound smoothbores, two 24-pound smoothbores, and two 32-pound howitzers—mounted *en barbette*.[112] Both junior lieutenants of the Davis Guards were absent,[113] and Captain Odlum assigned Lieutenant Nicholas H. Smith, Corps of Engineers, to assist Dowling. They were augmented by Assistant Surgeon George H. Bailey, who had left the hospital at Sabine City "to administer Magruder pills to the enemy," as Dowling later wrote.[114] In addition to the three officers, forty enlisted men were in the fort.[115] The garrison was also assisted and encouraged by the townspeople of Sabine City, who knew that their safety depended upon the handful of men at Fort Griffin. Neal McCaffey butchered a beef, and Increase Burch dug up a patch of sweet potatoes. The ladies cooked the beef and potatoes, baked bread, biscuits, and cake, and brewed coffee. At noon, a Mrs. Vosburg took the food out to the fort in Mrs. Kate Dorman's buggy.[116]

At three o'clock Major Smith and Captain Good arrived at Sabine City from Beaumont after a hard thirty-four mile ride.[117] Within half an hour the Federal forces went into action.

At about 3:30, the Union gunboat "Clifton," followed by the gunboat "Granite City" and the transport "Gen. Banks" (with Weitzel's troops aboard), started up the Texas channel and the gunboats "Sachem" and "Arizona" up the

---

110. Statement of E. P. Alsbury, participant, in John Thomas Scharf, *History of the Confederate States Navy* . . . (New York: Rogers & Sherwood, 1887), p. 524.

111. Interview by Margaret L. Watson of J. M. Chasten in *Galveston Daily News,* September 3, 1899.

112. Account of battle by W. P. Doran in *Dallas Morning News,* April 23, 1902.

113. *Ibid.*

114. Dowling to Odlum, Fort Griffin, September 9, 1863, in *O.R.,* I, 26, pt. 1, p. 311.

115. In his report, Dowling wrote, "We captured with 47 men. . . ." It would appear that in this number he included every person within the fort at any time during the battle, as he had thereinbefore enumerated Leon Smith, Odlum, Good, and Doctor Murray's presence for a short while. Thus it would appear that a total of forty-three was in the fort throughout the battle. Of these, three were officers: Dowling, N. H. Smith, and Bailey. The remaining forty were men and noncommissioned officers. The number of rank and file varies in secondary accounts, and the various rosters of the company as engraved on monuments and recorded in newspapers, including Major General Magruder's general orders, do not agree in either total number or individual names. At this late date it is probably impossible to determine the names of the men and noncommissioned officers who were present.

116. Interview of Margaret L. Watson with J. M. Chasten in *Galveston Daily News,* September 3, 1899; account of battle by W. P. Doran in *Dallas Morning News,* April 23, 1902.

117. Smith to Turner, Sabine Pass, September 8, 1863 in *O.R.,* I, 26, pt. 1, p. 308.

Louisiana channel. Six transports—the "Suffolk" (serving as headquarters), "St. Charles," "Landis," "Exact," "Laurel Hill," and "Thomas"—lingered at the bar. For an hour, as the Federal gunboats ascended the channels, they fired at Fort Griffin. Their range and marksmanship obviously was deficient, for only one shot hit the fort, damaging the elevating hand wheel of one gun.[118] The fort made no reply. Its defenders were in the "bomb-proofs" behind, while Dowling himself stood concealed in one corner of the bastion, watching the progress of the Federal ships.[119] In the meantime, the Federal forces could see dense smoke toward the head of the lake, and they believed that gunboats were on their way to the pass. The smoke came not from gunboats but from the "Roebuck," the "Josiah H. Bell," and the "Florilda," bearing down at full speed ahead with the aid of pine knots blazing beneath their boilers.[120]

At about 4:30, the two Federal gunboats leading the parade up the two channels reached the buoys at which the Davis Guardsmen had been doing practice firing.[121] Dowling immediately summoned his men to their stations, and he himself fired the first round. Exposed from the waist up, the men poured a deadly fire of 137 rounds into the boats without stopping to swab their guns. The shelling lasted thirty-five minutes. The thumbstalls of two gunners burned away and seared their flesh to the bone. The guns, indeed, became so hot that it was not until three o'clock the next day that one could lay one's hand on their barrels without discomfort.[122] During the firing, one of the howitzers went off its platform. One or two shots alone were required to get range, and thereafter, it was said, not a shot was wasted.[123] Lieutenant Smith, in command of the two 24-pounders, had assigned one to Michael McKernan, and it was McKernan who put a round of shot through the steam drum of the "Sachem." The guns were then turned on the "Clifton." At this point, Major Smith, Captains Odlum and Good, and Acting Assistant Surgeon J. G. D. Murray, a civilian Scot physician of Sabine City, arrived at the fort. In token of the disabling of the "Sachem," Major Smith and Lieutenants Dowling and Smith mounted the parapet and waved the garrison flag. Dowling asked the visiting officers for reinforcements, since his men "were becoming exhausted by the rapidity of . . .

---

118. Account of battle by W. P. Doran in *Dallas Morning News,* April 23, 1902.

119. Statement of E. P. Alsbury in Scharf, *op. cit.,* p. 525.

120. Keith, *op. cit.,* p. 668.

121. Raines, *op. cit.,* p. 501.

122. *Galveston Daily News,* March 18, 1905.

123. Account of battle by W. P. Doran in *Dallas Morning News,* April 23, 1902.

[their] fire," and he had no replacements. Immediately, the officers retired to fetch back new troops that had just arrived at Sabine City.[124] Before they had gone far, a round of shot carried away the tiller rope of the "Clifton," thereby turning her into a sitting duck, and a few minutes later another round went through her steampipe. By now, the "Sachem" had raised a white flag, and some unauthorized person aboard the "Clifton" struck her flag.[125] Her men, thinking the ship was about to explode, plunged overboard; Dowling, in the fort, thought that the Federal force was putting out a landing party and immediately prepared to change his fire to grape and canister. The gunboats behind the "Sachem" and "Clifton" were either damaged or demoralized, and immediately they, as well as the "Gen. Banks," backed out to the bar.

By this time some eighty men who had jumped overboard from the "Clifton" arrived at the shore, with hands upraised, and Dowling went to the water's edge to receive their surrender. An officer aboard the ship hailed Dowling and asked for a surgeon. Dowling replied that he had no boat, whereupon one was sent out from the ship. Dowling and Surgeon Bailey returned in it to the "Clifton." Aboard ship, Lieutenant Crocker presented his sword in surrender to Dowling, who then inspected the magazine as Bailey set to work relieving the wounded. Having finished aboard the "Clifton," Bailey went to the "Sachem" to minister to her wounded. (He was the first Confederate to board the ship.) The bursting of the ship's steam drum had frightfully scalded a number of men, whom he treated by placing them in flour.[126]

In the meantime, the remaining Federal force had crossed the bar and set out posthaste for New Orleans. Though no ship was in pursuit, the panic-struck men aboard the transports lightened their craft by throwing overboard everything within reach. Some 200,000 rations were tossed out of the transport "Crescent," and 200 hobbled mules were pushed out of the "Laurel Hill."[127] When the force finally reached New Orleans, Major General Banks reported the disaster to the General-in-chief and blamed it upon the "misapprehension of the naval authorities of the real strength of the enemy's position."[128] Had justice been done, Major General Franklin would have been broken to the ranks

---

124. Uncle Ben to editor, September 13, 1863, in *Houston Tri-Weekly Telegraph*, September 16, 1863; Dowling to Odlum, Fort Griffin, September 9, 1863, *O.R.*, I, 26, pt. 1, p.312.

125. Frederick Crocker to H. H. Bell, Houston, September 12, 1863, *ibid.*, p. 302.

126. Account of battle by W. P. Doran in *Dallas Morning News*, April 23, 1902; interview by Margaret L. Watson of J. M. Chasten in *Galveston Daily News*, September 3, 1899.

127. Franklin to Banks, on board the steamship "Suffolk," September 11, 1863, in *O.R.*, I, 26, pt. I, p. 297.

128. Banks to Halleck, New Orleans, September 13, 1863, *ibid.*, p. 288.

for incompetence and then shot for cowardice.

The signal officer aboard the "Sachem" soon afterwards wrote for the *New York Herald* an account of the battle in which he set down a conversation with Dowling at the time the men aboard the "Sachem" went ashore. Although not a shorthand transcript, Lieutenant Henry C. Dane's statement was that of a communications officer accustomed to transcribing messages and is therefore likely to be accurate. Nothing in the conversation is more impelling than the evidence of Dowling's modesty, unless it be Dane's lack of hatred for the enemy.

And are you the Shaughram [Dane asked] who did all of that mischief? How many men and guns did you have?

We had four thirty-two-pounders, and two twenty-four-pounders, and forty-three men.

And do you realize what you have done, sir?

No, I don't understand it at all.

Well, sir, you and your forty-three men, in your miserable little mud fort in the rushes, have captured two Yankee gunboats, carrying fourteen guns, a good number of prisoners, many stands of small arms and plenty of good ammunition, and all that you have done with six popguns and two smart "Quakers." And that is not the worst of your boyish trick. You have sent three Yankee gunboats, 6000 troops and a General out to sea in the dark. You ought to be ashamed of yourself, sir.

What was the matter with you fellows, anyway? Why didn't they come up and take us, as we expected they would?

I am very sorry, sir, that you have been so sadly disappointed, but, truly, I am unable to inform you why you have been treated so discourteously and in so emphatic a manner. My impression is that it was owing to a sudden attack of homesickness.[129]

The elation of the Confederate authorities and troops was tempered by a conviction that the Federal force at the bar of Sabine Pass would land elsewhere in the neighborhood, All available forces—and Texas was almost depleted by the great number of men it had sent east of the Mississippi—were rushed to the pass, and Major General Magruder and the Acting Brigadier General Commanding the Eastern Sub-District of Texas went themselves to whip the motley forces into shape.[130] The engineer corps drove piled obstructions into the two channels and threw up intrenchments below Fort Griffin and three redoubts and two redans between the Gulf and Lake Night, near the place that Major General Banks had planned for the Federal troop-landing.[131] But the preparations were unnecessary, for, other than blockading craft, the pass remained quiet

129. *Dallas Morning News*, April 23, 1902, quoting the *New York Herald.*

130. See correspondence and orders in *O.R.*, I, 26, pt. 2, pp. 215 ff.

131. Map, *ibid., Atlas*, Plate 32, No. 3.

for the remainder of the Rebellion.[132] In accordance with President Lincoln's original suggestion, a more successful Federal force soon afterwards occupied the western littoral from Matagorda Peninsula to the Rio Grande.[133]

Commendations for the victory at Sabine Pass poured in upon the Davis Guards. In the two days following the battle, Major General Magruder commended the gallant defenders of the fort in a special order and in a proclamation asking every man able to bear arms to hasten to the defense of his country.[134] On September 13, from Sabine Pass, he issued a lengthy general order in which he listed the members of the Davis Guards by name and conferred on them the privilege of having embroidered upon their caps the word "SABINE" enclosed within a wreath.[135] On the same day, the Acting Brigadier General Commanding the Eastern Sub-District of Texas, in which Sabine Pass was located, congratulated the company for its signal victory.[136] Congress passed a commendatory resolution, which President Davis signed on February 8, 1864, describing the battle as "one of the most brilliant and heroic achievements in the history of this war" and holding up the Davis Guards "to the gratitude and admiration of their country."[137]

Major General Magruder made a formal visit to Fort Griffin on September 12. He entered the fort with uncovered head and made a brief address in which he commended the Irish as soldiers and the defenders of Sabine Pass as "the greatest heroes that history recorded."[138] Two days later, the ladies of Sabine

---

132. *Houston Tri-Weekly Telegraph,* September 11, October 2, 1863; *Galveston Tri-Weekly News* (Houston), September 18, 1863.

133. The Rio Grande Expedition and operations on the coast of Texas, October 27–December 2, 1863, in *O.R.,* I, 26, pt. I, pp. 395–447.

134. Headquarters, District of Texas, New Mexico and Arizona, Houston, Special Orders No. —, September 9, 1863, in *Houston Tri-Weekly Telegraph,* September 11, 1863; J. Bankhead Magruder to the Men of Texas, Beaumont, September 10, 1863, *ibid.,* September 16, 1863.

135. Headquarters, District of Texas, New Mexico and Arizona, Confederate (late U.S.) steamer *Clifton,* Sabine Pass, General Orders No. —, September 13, 1863, *ibid.,* September 18, 1863; also issued in circular form.

136. Headquarters, Eastern Sub-District of Texas, Houston, General Orders No. 39, September 13, 1863, in *Houston Tri-Weekly Telegraph,* Supplement, September 25, 1863, reprinted, *ibid.,* January 2, 1865.

137. *Journal of the Congress of the Confederate States of America, 1861–1865* (7 vols.; Washington: Government Printing Office, 1904–1905), III, 478, 678, 698; VI, 518, 531; James M. Matthews, ed., *The Statutes at Large of the Confederate States of America, Passed at the Fourth Session of the First Congress; 1863–4* . . . (Richmond: R. M. Smith, Printer to Congress, 1864), p. 242, reprinted in Scharf, *op. cit.,* p. 526 n.; *O.R.N.,* I, 20, pp. 526–63; *O.R.,* I, 26, pt. I, pp. 312, 915; *Bellville* [Tex.] *Countryman,* March 17, 1864.

138. Uncle Ben to editor, Sabine Pass, September 15, 1863, in *Houston Tri-Weekly Telegraph,* Sep-

City, through a Protestant minister donated a garrison flag to the company.[139] In Houston, local musicians and amateur actors gave a series of benefit performances for the Davis Guards that netted at least $3380.[140] Friar Felix Zoppa da Connobio pushed a movement to provide silver medals for the men and officers.[141] A few weeks later each was presented with a medal fabricated by Charles Gottchalk: Suspended from a green ribbon was a shaven silver dollar containing on one side an engraved Maltese cross and the letters "D G" and on the other the words and figures "Battle of Sabine Pass, September 8, 1863." One of the medals was forwarded to President Davis, and he carried it on his person until he was relieved of it while he was a prisoner in Fortress Monroe after the Rebellion.[142] Dowling reciprocated, in part, the honors conferred on him and his men by forwarding to the editor of the *Houston Telegraph* a collection of shot and shell fragments as battle trophies.[143]

The Battle of Sabine Pass was the last in which the Davis Guards participated. And as a result of idleness, their subsequent military record was marred by numerous desertions to the enemy. On Christmas Eve, 1863, five of them—Private Patrick McDonald, Patrick Malone, Patrick Murray, John Fitzpatrick, and James O'Neil—went over to the enemy,[144] and on January 8, 1864, three more—Sergeant Timothy McDonagh and Privates John Flood and Daniel McMurray—followed.[145] The first group of deserters had forced Private Patrick

---

tember 18, 1863, and *Houston Weekly Telegraph,* September 22, 1863; *Galveston Daily News,* March 18, 1905.

139. "Address of the Rev. J. J. Loomis, at the presentation of a (Garrison) Flag to the Davis Guards, at Fort Sabine, Sept. 14, 1863," in *Houston Tri-Weekly Telegraph,* October 16, 1863.

140. Charles O. Otis to E. H. Cushing, *ibid.,* September 16, 1863; T. W. House to editor, *ibid.,* October 12, 1863; Odlum to editor, Fort Griffin, September 26, [1863], *ibid.,* October 14, 1863; see also issues for October 2, 5, 9, 1863. One of the promoters of the performances was Henry Weatherby Benchley, conductor on the Houston and Texas Central Railroad and grandfather of the late humorist Bob Benchley.

141. *Ibid.,* September 18, 21, 1863. In error, W.P.A., comps., *Houston; A History and Guide, op. cit.,* p. 77, states that Friar Felix headed the movement at the request of the Houston city council.

142. *Houston Daily Post,* August 22, 1880; account of battle by W. P. Doran in *Dallas Morning News,* April 23, 1902; *Galveston Daily News,* March 18, 1905; *Houston Daily Telegraph,* May 12, 1875. On May 15, 1875, while Jefferson Davis was in Houston to attend the Sixth Texas State Fair, the survivors of the Davis Guards—three of them—presented him with the medal that had been originally presented to Dowling's brother, Patrick Emmett Dowling, who was not, however, at the battle. *Ibid.,* May 16, 1875.

143. *Houston Tri-Weekly Telegraph,* September 21, 1863.

144. Muster roll for December, 1863, certified by Dowling, December 31, 1863, in War Department Coll. of Confederate Records.

145. Muster roll for December 31, 1863–February 29, 1864, certified by Odlum, February 29, 1864, *ibid.;* B. to editor, Sabine Pass, January 9, 1863, in *Houston Daily Telegraph,* January 12, 1864.

Martin to accompany them, but as they were crossing the lake, Martin plunged into the water and swam over a mile and a half back to his company. Major General Magruder issued a special order commending Martin for "his noble fidelity and devotion worthy of the gallantry and heroism displayed by the Davis Guards on the memorable 8th of September" and directed that the order be read at the head of every company in the district.[146] On January 20, 1864, the company moved back to Galveston.[147]

In March, Dowling was appointed recruiting officer of Cook's regiment and announced that he would accept volunteers at Liberty on the 23d, at Beaumont on the 26th, at Sabine Pass on the 28th, at Wiess's Bluff on April 2d, at Jasper on the 5th, and at Newton on the 7th.[148] The muster roll for September 30, 1864, showed the company stationed at Camp Gillespie,[149] probably at Hampstead, to which place five companies of Cook's Regiment had been ordered on May 9.[150] Dowling was then absent on a sixty-day furlough.[151] On February 16, 1865, at which time his company was back in Galveston, Dowling was on detached service at Houston,[152] and shortly afterwards, possibly during the breakup when promotions were handed out in geat numbers, he became a major. As such he was paroled by the United States Army at Houston on June 21.[153]

Dowling lost no time in getting back into the saloon business. On the same day that the Federal Army occupied Galveston, "June 'Teenth," he ran, after a lapse of four years, his advertisement of the Bank of Bacchus, which was back on its original site at Congress and Main in a new building.[154] Until the first

---

146. Headquarters, District of Texas, New Mexico and Arizona, Galveston, General Orders No. 255, December 31, 1863, in *Houston Tri-Weekly Telegraph,* January 4, 1864.

147. Muster roll for December 31, 1863–February 29, 1864. On September 30, October 14, and December 31, 1863, the company had been reported at Sabine Pass. *O.R.,* I, 26, pt. 2, pp. 281, 320, 563, 565. On January 11, 1864, Dowling wrote to Frank H. Bailey, post adjutant, from Fort Griffin. War Department Coll. of Confederate Records.

148. *Houston Daily Telegraph* and *Tri-Weekly Telegraph,* March 25, 1864. Wiess's Bluff was located on the east bank of the Neches River, in Jasper County, immediately north of the mouth of Village Creek. *Houston Post Map of Texas for 1882* (Houston: Gail B. Johnson & Co., c1882).

149. Muster roll for September, 1864, certified by Odlum, September 30, 1864, in War Department Coll. of Confederate Records.

150. *O.R.,* I, 34, pt. 3, p. 813.

151. Muster roll for September, 1864.

152. Edward T. Witsell, Adjutant General, U.S.A., to writer, August 22, 1949. A deserter who left Virginia Point, March 21, 1865, reported that Co. F was stationed at the battery on Galveston Island below the bridge. *O.R.,* I, 48, pt. 2, p. 116.

153. Witsell to writer, see n. 152.

154. *Houston Tri-Weekly Telegraph,* June 19, 1865.

week of August, there was no ice in Houston, so the imbibers of mixed drinks must have had them in the interval at room temperature.[155] Saloons multiplied rapidly in town,[156] and their proprietors served the poorest quality of liquors[157] and circumvented the law. While they closed their front doors on Sundays, as the law required, they kept their back doors open for use by customers,[158] and doubtlessly also they sold liquor to enlisted men despite a specific order to the contrary.[159] Certainly the military liquored up and from time to time created disturbances on the streets. Dowling may not have resorted to all the practices of his fellow-publicans, but on December 18, 1865, the Harris County grand jury brought in three indictments against him for retailing liquor on Sunday.[160] Five months later he pleaded guilty to two of the indictments, whereupon the court fined him $15.00 in each of them, and the district attorney *nolle prosequied* the third.[161]

One Houston newspaper commended Dowling's saloon:

The Bank of Bacchus under the charge of Dick Dowling, is open and ready to issue drinks of the various liquors as fast as called for. Dick says that having "taken the oath" he is prepared to administer it to the multitude. Before the war he was always a favorite. In the war, he proved as good a fighter as he was a mixer of drinks. At the battle of Sabine Pass he won the biggest victory of the war on either side. Mind, we don't advise anybody to drink, but if people will drink, we had as soon see them drink Dick's liquor as anybody's.[162]

The Bank's business flourished, and its prosperity is certified by one robbery[163] and two attempts at felonious entrance.[164]

Always alert to good public relations, Dowling kept the press supplied with news of his activities. He called attention to a new liquor, Chestnut Grove Whisky,[165] and to Gray Jacket Bitters that would "produce an enlargement of

---

155. *Ibid.*, August 9, 1865.

156. *Ibid.*, July 10, 1865.

157. *Ibid.*, November 6, 1865.

158. *Ibid.*, July 17, 1865.

159. *Ibid.*, July 28, November 18, 1865; Headquarters, Post of Houston, Special Orders No. 55, October 19, 1865, *ibid.*, October 20, 1865.

160. Minutes of the 11th District Court (MSS, District Clerk's office, Houston), K, 285.

161. *Ibid.*, p. 375.

162. *Houston Tri-Weekly Telegraph,* June 26, 1865.

163. *Ibid.*, July 17, 1865.

164. *Ibid.*, August 2, 1865; *Galveston Tri-Weekly News* (Houston), November 20, 1865.

165. *Houston Tri-Weekly Telegraph,* October 18, 1865.

good humour,"[166] and he supplied one editor with several bottles of Texas wine.[167] During the excitement attendant upon the execution of Maximilian in Mexico, he gave a Mexican peso to an editor.[168] In March, 1868, the *Rusk Observer* commented about Dowling:

> R. W. Dowling, cashier and director of the Bank of Bacchus, Houston, is the veritable Dick who whipped the United States, England and France, at the attack of Sabine City, and would have whipped the balance of the world at the same time, had it had courage to back against him just then. Dick keeps up the fight with becoming gallantry and vigor, but on a modified principle—using soft slugs, flavored with nectar, and always lodging them in the bowels, taking immediate effect in the head. Everybody visiting Houston should give Dick a call, as a proper means of perpetuating Southern valor.[169]

A short while later a newspaper remarked that Dowling served up an elegant midday lunch with a glass of ale for only two bits.[170]

Of good cheer and a generous heart, very much the local hero and public-spirited citizen (though in 1867 he was refused registration for voting),[171] Dowling was always prominent in every attempt to ameliorate the condition of the distressed and to improve the community. Shortly after the war he tendered his display window for the exhibition of a handsome set of silver that was raffled off for the benefit of a war widow,[172] and later he donated $50.00 toward the purchase of a steam fire engine.[173] He also resumed his membership in Houston Hook and Ladder Company No. 1.[174] As a hero Dowling played a larger part in the company's activities than he had before the Rebellion. He served on a committee of invitations for a ball, on a committee of arrangements for a general parade of the several fire companies in Houston, and on a committee to meet with the board of engineers and representatives of the volunteer fire department.[175] He was less successful, however, in getting himself elected an officer of the company. In April, 1866, E. L. Hopkins defeated him for the office of first assistant foreman.[176] On December 23, 1865, upon the nomination of his some-

166. *Galveston Tri-Weekly News,* January 22, 1866.

167. *Ibid.,* February 26, 1866.

168. *Houston Daily Telegraph,* July 23, 1867.

169. *Houston Evening Star,* March 28, 1866.

170. *Houston Daily Telegraph,* June 22, 1867.

171. *Ibid.* June 21, 1867.

172. *Galveston Tri-Weekly News,* November 27, December 15, 1865.

173. *Houston Tri-Weekly Telegraph,* February 5, 1866.

174. Deed Records of Harris County, Texas, III, 474.

175. Minutes Houston Hook & Ladder Co., 1858–1868, pp. 157–58, 182, 273.

176. *Ibid.,* p. 171.

time junior first lieutenant, William P. Cunningham, Dowling was elected an honorary member of the Houston Lyceum by acclamation.[177] In the spring of 1866, he was a member of the Houston committee assembled to entertain General James B. Longstreet at a picnic at Dickinson's Bayou,[178] but a delay in Longstreet's arrival prevented Houstonians' attending, and the picnic then became no more than a Galveston celebration.[179]

The Bank prospered even though Dowling paid a monthly rental of $300 in gold for the premises.[180] In addition to insuring his life for $10,000,[181] Dowling invested his profits in an assortment of enterprises. He trafficked heavily in real estate,[182] became local agent of the Douglas Brick-Making Machine,[183] was a stockholder in the Houston Gas Light Company and the Young Men's Building Association, and had an interest in a Galveston bonded warehouse.[184] Also, he owned a half interest in a small steamboat, the "Job Bob No. 1," on the Trinity River.[185] In August, 1887, he was a member of a firm, later incorporated as the Houston City Railway Company, that contracted with the city of Houston to build four streetcar lines in that portion of town south of Buffalo Bayou,[186] and earlier he had been a stockholder and incorporator of the Houston & Harrisburg Turnpike Company that was chartered to build an eighty-foot roadway to Harrisburg and the town of San Jacinto, adjacent to the San Jacinto battleground.[187]

Dowling's most forward-looking investment was the oil business. As early as March, 1866, he entered into partnership with one John M. Fennerty, and two months later they admitted John Riordan into the firm. Fennerty agreed to supply the necessary machinery and to manage the partnership until production

177. Minutes of Houston Lyceum, May 27, 1854–March 7, 1878 (typescript in Houston Public Library), p. 152.

178. *Houston Evening Star,* April 19, 1866; *Houston Tri-Weekly Telegraph,* April 20, 1866.

179. *Ibid.,* April 25, 30, 1866.

180. Deed Records of Harris County, Texas, VII, pp. 282–83; Probate Records of Harris County, Texas (MSS, County Clerk's office, Houston), T, 254.

181. *Houston Daily Telegraph,* September 28, 1867.

182. Deed Records of Harris County Texas, III, 306–7, 604–5; IV, 118, 137, 162, 174, 175, 341; V, 118–19, 252–53; Vll, 54–42; Probate Pecords of Harris County, Texas, T, 255–56.

183. *Houston Daily Telegraph,* June 12, 13, 1867; Probate Records of Harris County, Texas, T, 255.

184. *Ibid.*

185. *Ibid.,* p. 296.

186. Deed Records of Harris County, Texas, V, 407–10; Vl, 606–7; *The Laws of Texas, op. cit.,* VI, 34–36.

187. *Ibid.,* V, 1254–56; Deed Records of Harris County, Texas, V, 572–73, 711–12, 795; Deed Records of Fort Bend County, Texas (MSS, County Clerk's office, Richmond), H, 412; J, 529.

began. The firm acquired mineral leases in Harris, Fannin, Bexar, McLennan, Hardin, Liberty, Polk, and Jefferson counties.[188] The activities of this firm beyond the leasing of land cannot be detennined, but it is certain that it discovered no oil and doubtful even that it drilled.

Ex-Confederates of Irish origin could always engage in their favorite sport, twisting the tail of the British lion. No sooner had they lain down their Confederate arms than they began agitating for Irish independence. There were Fenians in Houston as early as October, 1865,[189] and on November 25, they organized Davis Circle, with Captain Odlum as chairman.[190] In the following June, Colonel Patrick Condon, inspector general of the Fenian brotherhood (later he was sentenced to death for participation in an uprising in Ireland, but his sentence was commuted because he was an American national), visited Houston and made a public address.[191] This visit was probably a part of a recruiting drive for the force that attacked Canada later in the year. In addition to its avowed purpose of emancipating Ireland, the organization was a nucleus for the social activities of Irish expatriates. In Houston the Fenians wore green neckties on St. Patrick's Day and sang "Wearing of the Green" whenever the spirit moved them.[192] There can be little question that Dowling was a Fenian.[193]

In August, 1867, yellow fever made its appearance in Galveston, and immediately the citizens of Houston prepared for an epidemic. They reactivated the Howard Association and organized the Fireman's Charitable Association.[194] Dowling was certainly a member of the second organization.[195] The first yellow fever death in Houston occurred on August 11,[196] and within a few days a large proportion of the population was abed with the disease. The city of Houston

---

188. Deed Records of Harris County, Texas, II, 541, 566–67, 598–600, 622; III, 4–5, 87–89; Deed Records of Hardin County, Texas (MSS, County Clerk's office, Kountze), D, 412–16, 469–73; Probate Records of Harris County, Texas, T, 256; C. A. Warner, *Texas Oil and Gas Since 1543* (Houston; Gulf Publishing Co., c1939), pp. 8–9, 113; Carl Coke Rister, *Oil! Titan of the Southwest* (Norman: University of Oklahoma Press, 1949), p. 8.

189. *Houston Tri-Weekly Telegraph,* October 9, 1865.

190. *Galveston Tri-Weekly News,* December 1, 1865.

191. *Houston Evening Star,* June 9, 14, 16, 20, 1866.

192. *Galveston Tri-Weekly News,* November 27, 1865; February 16, 1866.

193. Dowling ought not to be confused with another Richard (Dick) Dowling (1814–January 11, 1908), an English Baptist, Freemason, and cotton-buyer, whose name appears on the monument of Holland Lodge No. 1, A. F. & A. M., on Lots 52–53, Section C, Glenwood Cemetery, Houston. *Houston Daily Post,* January 13, 14, 1908.

194. *Houston Daily Telegraph,* August 5, 10, 1867.

195. *Ibid.,* September 24, 1867.

196. *Ibid.,* August 18, 1867.

opened a yellow fever hospital under Dr. E. L. Massie[197] and initiated the burning of tar and pine wood at street eorners to purify the air of miasma.[198] Up to September 14, there had been 105 deaths from yellow fever.[199] Dowling generously opened up his store of liquors and gave out brandy to any of the sick who required it. Toward the end of August he too came down with the disease, but by September 7 a newspaper was able to announce his rapid recovery.[200] Two days later he was reported on his feet again,[201] and on the 13th he appeared on the streets "looking well and daily gaining strength."[202] But on the 17th he suffered a relapse. The *Houston Daily Telegraph* advised, "Take better care of yourself next time, Dick. Houston cannot afford to lose such men as you."[203] Despite the skill of his physician, Dr. Andrew J. Hay, he sank quickly and died on the evening of September 23d (not the 24th, as usually given).[204] On the following afternoon the local fire companies turned out to escort his remains to their grave in St. Vincent's Cemetery.[205] A newspaper concluded an obituary with the remark, "The far-off echoes of the guns of Fort Griffin have served as funeral salvos for the warm-hearted hero DICK DOWLING."[206]

Shortly after the Battle of Sabine Pass, the name Dowling was given to a short street in the A. C. Allen Addition to the city of Houston.[207] When a re-platting of the addition made this street a continuation of an older and longer street, the name Dowling was assigned to what theretofore had been East

---

197. *Ibid.,* August 15, 18, 30, 1867.

198. *Ibid.,* August 23, 28, 29, 1867.

199. *Ibid.,* September 15, 1867.

200. *Ibid.,* September 7, 1867.

201. *Ibid.,* September 9, 1867.

202. *Ibid.,* September 13, 1867.

203. *Ibid.,* September 19, 1867.

204. Obituary by Tom Vapid [Charles Bickley], *ibid.,* September 28, 1867. For Bickley's identity, see *ibid.,* October 19, 1867. See also *ibid.,* September 25, 1867.

205. *Ibid.* Dowling's grave is not marked, but its almost exact position can be determined from the description given by F. Lee Schwander, John White, and C. C. Beavin, Sr., in the *Houston Post,* August 4, 1899.

206. Obituary by Tom Vapid. Captain F. H. Odlum died in Houston, October 22, 1867. *Houston Daily Telegraph,* October 24, 1867. Dowling's widow, born in 1842, married Walter R. Daniel (1840–1916) in Galveston on February 14, 1870. She died in Dallas, Tex., on May 13, 1918, and her remains are buried in the State Cemetery in Austin. Marriage Records of Galveston County, Texas (MSS, County Clerk's office, Galveston), D, 327; *Austin Statesman,* May 15, 1918; tombstone, Row 4, North Johnston, State Cemetery.

207. Plat of Blocks 63–64, Allen's Addition, City of Houston, by C. G. Forshey, reorded about April 9, 1864, in Deed Records of Harris County, Texas, I, 389.

Broadway in the main axis of the city.[208] In 1958 this street, which ends a short distance from the site of Dowling's home, is the principal Negro business thoroughfare of Houston. In 1889, a proposal to create Dowling County out of Pecos County was before the Texas legislature, but nothing came of it.[209] Richard William Dowling and his men are today commemorated by a stained glass window in the Confederate Museum in Richmond, Virginia, and by statues at Sabine Pass and in Hermann Park in Houston.

---

208. Cf. E. F. Gray, *Plan of the City of Houston and Environs, Texas* (New York: Miller's Lith., [1858] with *Full Composition Tax Map of the City of Houston and the Houston Independent School District* ([Houston: City of Houston], n.d.).

209. Petitions of R. W. Mussey, county judge, and 24 others, n.d., and of R. W. Mussey, county judge, and 14 others, February 12, 1889, and R. W. Mussey to G. B. Stevenson, Fort Stockton, February 7, 1889, in Memorials and Petitions (MSS, Archives Coll., Texas State Library); *Journal of the House of Representatives, Being the Regular Session, Twenty-First Legislature Begun and Held at the City of Austin, January 8, 1889* (Austin: Smith, Hicks & Jones, 1889), pp. 294, 296, 403, 470. On March 5, 1889, a medal was presented to Dowling's daughter, Annie, in one of the legislative chambers. *Ibid.*, pp. 553, 613–15.

José Agustín Quintero y Woodville, from José Manuel Carbonell, *Los Poetas de "El Laúd del Desterrado"* (Havana: Imprenta "Avisador Comercial," 1930). Quintero was a Confederate agent in northern Mexico during the Civil War. *Courtesy Benson Latin American History Center, University of Texas at Austin.*

Cotton on the Border, 1861–1865

Ronnie C. Tyler*

The Union navy maintained a blockade of the Texas coast throughout the war. Although the blockade was never totally effective (see L. Tuffly Ellis, "Maritime Commerce on the Far Western Gulf, 1861–1865," Southwestern Historical Quarterly, LXXVII [Oct., 1973], 167–226, and Robert W. Glover, "The West Gulf Blockade, 1861–1865: An Evaluation" [Ph.D. diss., North Texas State University, 1974]), the Union naval action prevented much of the rich Texas cotton crop from being exported through Texas ports.

To get their cotton to eager European buyers, Texas planters developed a lucrative trade through the Mexican city of Matamoros on the Rio Grande. Hundreds of wagons loaded with Texas cotton rolled through South Texas to Brownsville, Laredo, and Eagle Pass and across the Rio Grande to Matamoros. From there the cotton was loaded on river steamers and taken to the village of Bagdad on the coast for transshipment to ocean-going vessels.

In this article Ron Tyler, formerly curator of history at the Amon Carter Museum and currently director of the Texas State Historical Association, describes the Texas cotton trade through Mexico and the various problems relating thereto. He points

---

* Ronnie C. Tyler, "Cotton on the Border, 1861–1865," *Southwestern Historical Quarterly*, LXXIII (Apr., 1970), 456–477.

out that the Rio Grande trade was essential to the Confederate war effort. It also en-
riched a number of individuals and "became the basis of financial empires on both
sides of the river."

For more on the Mexican trade see Tyler's Santiago Vidaurri and the Southern
Confederacy *(Austin: Texas State Historical Association, 1973); James W. Daddys-*
man, The Matamoros Trade: Confederate Commerce, Diplomacy, and Intrigue
(Newark, Del.: University of Delaware Press, 1984); James A. Irby, Backdoor at
Bagdad: The Civil War on the Rio Grande *(El Paso: Texas Western Press, 1977);*
and Fredericka Meiners, "The Texas Border Cotton Trade, 1862–1863," Civil War
History, *XXIII (Dec., 1977), 193–306.*

When he later recalled his wartime escapades, John Warren Hunter realized that
as a teamster on a cotton wagon en route to Brownsville he had participated in
a significant aspect of the Civil War. Hoping to write an interesting and accurate account of his experiences during the conflict, the farmer, newspaper editor, and amateur historian reflected upon some of his youthful adventures and
concluded that war had been very profitable for several residents of the lower
Rio Grande Valley. Although only fourteen when the war began, he vividly recalled "a never ending stream of cotton pouring into Brownsville." After he
crossed into Mexico, he saw "ox trains, mule trains, and trains of Mexican carts,
all laden with cotton coming from almost every town in Texas," converging on
what had been the only open port in the Confederacy since the Union navy had
blockaded all the harbors. "Brownsville became the greatest shipping point in
the South," he concluded; and "Matamoros became a great commercial center,"
with "cotton and other commodities . . . pouring into her warehouses."[1]

The primary product in this burgeoning exchange, of course, was cotton, the
fiber that had sustained the industrial revolution in Great Britain, that had provided the bulwark of America's economy for over half a century, and that had
relentlessly bound Negro slavery on the southern United States. Cotton was the
"glittering attraction" that kept the commerce moving. It was expected to work
miracles for the new Confederacy; it was to bring hundreds of foreign ships to
southern ports gasping for the staple so necessary for the textile mills of Europe;
it was to insure the international success of the South as a nation. In short, cotton was king.[2]

1. John Warren Hunter, "The Fall of Brownsville on the Rio Grande, November, 1863" (typescript, Biographical File, Barker Texas History Library, University of Texas, Austin), 4–5. For discussions of Matamoros during the Civil War, see Robert W. Delaney, "Matamoros: Port for Texas
during the Civil War," *Southwestern Historical Quarterly,* LVIII (April, 1955), 473–487, and Avila
Larios, "Brownsville-Matamoros: Confederate Lifeline," *Mid-America,* XL (April, 1958), 67–89.

2. The best account of Confederate diplomatic operations is Frank Lawrence Owsley, *King Cotton*

But the Confederate strategy became an unintentional perversion of this plan. When the European powers did not immediately recognize the South's independence, President Jefferson Davis and his cabinet agreed that the method by which they would achieve their goal would be withholding cotton from the international market. They hoped that the ensuing shortage would force Great Britain to intervene in the war, or at least recognize their government. Some planters refused to export their cotton even before the Union blockade became effective, then they burned it, still trying to provoke British intervention.[3]

The most significant dissenter from this policy was Secretary of State Judah P. Benjamin, who initially agreed with Davis, but soon advocated hypothecation of the cotton—a plan whereby cotton would be set aside as security for bonds sold in Europe. By storing the cotton at government expense, instead of holding it off the market or burning it, Benjamin hoped to build up southern credit in Europe.[4]

From the beginning of the conflict, the idea that cotton should be withheld from the world market was unpopular in Texas. Most Texans agreed with the overall policy of their government, but felt that they should be allowed to continue shipping the fiber to Mexico, because Matamoros offered such an easy—and profitable—outlet. And the Confederate Congress consented. When it voted to prohibit cotton shipments from southern ports, it specifically exempted shipment into Mexico, ostensibly because the trade supplied several mills there. Two North Texas companies, those of Colonel Middleton T. Johnson and the Rhyne brothers, shipped the first big load of cotton, some 3,000 bales, to Mexico for exportation to Europe.[5]

When the Confederate authorities became aware of the economic possibilities that Mexico offered, they were forced to revise their plans. President Davis had expected Mexico to be a significant, perhaps determining, factor in south-

Diplomacy: Foreign Relations of the Confederate States of America (2nd ed. rev.; Chicago, 1959). Also see Stuart Bruchey (ed.), *Cotton and the Growth of the American Economy: 1790–1860* (New York, 1967), 73–75; and Henry Blumenthal, "Confederate Diplomacy: Popular Notions and International Realities," *Journal of Southern History,* XXXII (May, 1966), 151–171. Quote is in H. P. Bee to S. S. Anderson, November 30, 1862, in *The War of the Rebellion: A Compilation of the Official Records of the Union and Confederate Armies* (130 vols.; Washington, 1880–1901), Series I, XV, 882; hereafter cited as *O.R.A.*

3. J. M. Callahan, *The Diplomatic History of the Southern Confederation* (Baltimore, 1901), 102–159; Owsley, *King Cotton Diplomacy,* I, 43–50; Blumenthal, "Confederate Diplomacy," 154–171; San Antonio *Weekly Herald,* September 14, November 9, 1861.

4. Owsley, *King Cotton Diplomacy,* 362–392. Apparently this is the plan referred to in Tom Lea, *The King Ranch* (2 vols.; Boston, 1957), I, 188.

5. Owsley, *King Cotton Diplomacy,* 31; Hunter, "Fall of Brownsville," 5.

ern independence.[6] But he had given no consideration to the importance of
Mexico as a trading partner or outlet to other markets. This was brought forcefully to his attention by José Agustín Quintero, a secret agent whom Secretary
Benjamin had sent to northern Mexico. Quintero's original mission had been to
seek the friendship of Santiago Vidaurri, governor of Nuevo León y Coahuila,
who had controlled the frontier since 1855. He was to promise southern cooperation in resolving any disputes that might arise and to elicit similar assurances
from Vidaurri.[7]

Quintero was a particularly able diplomat. A Cuban by birth, but a southerner by choice, he had spent several years in Texas, where he worked in jour-
nalism, studied law, and served as assistant clerk of the legislature. He was a
shrewd, loyal Confederate, who had the insight and tenacity necessary to serve
his government well. In 1859 Quintero had met Governor Vidaurri in Austin,
and they had maintained a sporadic correspondence.[8] He received unexpected
encouragement from the governor on this mission.

During a series of interviews in July, 1861, Vidaurri not only offered any
quantity of powder, lead, copper, bronze, saltpeter, and foodstuffs in trade, but
also he suggested that the Confederacy annex the two north Mexican states of
Nuevo León y Coahuila[9] and Tamaulipas, a proposal that Davis could not real-
istically consider, but one that indicated that close cooperation was possible.
Davis was so impressed with Quintero's work—and Vidaurri's potential—that
he appointed the Cuban permanent agent in Monterrey, the Nuevo León y
Coahuila capital.[10] The trade with Mexico had started slowly, but with Quintero in Monterrey, it rapidly increased.

---

6. Davis felt that some European power, probably France, would invade Mexico after the Civil
War began, thus intentionally violating the Monroe Doctrine and forcing the United States to challenge the intervention. The European invader then would assure the independence and success of
the Confederacy by seeking an alliance with the South. Kathryn Abbey Hanna, "The Roles of the
South in the French Intervention in Mexico," *Journal of Southern History*, XX (February, 1954), 5–7.

7. William M. Browne to Quintero, September 3, 1861, in James D. Richardson (ed.), *A Compilation of the Messages and Papers of the Confederacy Including the Diplomatic Correspondence, 1861–1865*
(2 vols.; Nashville, 1906), II, 77–80.

8. *Daily Picayune* (New Orleans), September 8, 1885; *Times Picayune* (New Orleans), January 25,
1937; Walter P. Webb and H. Bailey Carroll (eds.), *The Handbook of Texas* (2 vols.; Austin, 1952), II,
424; J. Fred Rippy, *The United States and Mexico* (New York, 1927), 230–251.

9. Vidaurri had combined the two states of Nuevo Leon and Coahuila under his jurisdiction.
The united state was called Nuevo León y Coahuila. Edward H. Moseley, "Santiago Vidaurri,
Champion of States' Rights: 1855–1857," *West Georgia College Studies in the Social Sciences*, VI (June,
1967), 74–80.

10. Quintero to R. M. T. Hunter, August 19, 1861; Quintero to Browne, June 1, 1861, John T.
Pickett Papers (Library of Congress, Washington, D.C.); Quintero to Edward Clark, July 11, 1861,

A number of merchants in Matamoros and Monterrey were eager to profit from the hardships of war. Late in 1861 Quintero reported that the Monterrey firm of Lorenzo Oliver and Brothers probably was in the best position to supply the Confederacy. The company already had contacts all over northern Mexico and considerable experience in Texas and New Orleans. The Oliver Brothers offered lead, blankets, shoes, sulphur, saltpeter, and firearms at what Quintero considered reasonable prices. Assistant Secretary of State William M. Browne authorized Quintero to negotiate, but José Oliver was so anxious to sign a contract that he left for Richmond with samples of his goods.[11]

The Confederacy could make no deal with Oliver, because he would not promise to deliver the goods, although he insisted that he be paid in advance with cash or cotton. Secretary Benjamin concluded that Oliver was "fearful of responsibilities." Still he recommended that the southern authorities continue negotiations with him because of his potential use to the country.[12]

Quintero did not wait to hear about Oliver before making other commercial agreements. Patricio Milmo, Governor Vidaurri's son-in-law, was anxious to trade flour for cotton. Other merchants presented favorable contracts, and Quintero reported in November that he could purchase rifle and cannon powder at a fair price, but suggested instead that the Confederacy buy saltpeter and sulphur, because the Mexican powder was not as dependable as that made by the Confederacy. Later he wrote that he could trade for "everything with the exception of small arms."[13]

As the war progressed, more merchants sought contracts with the South. In addition to Milmo, other large firms—such as Woodhouse and Company; Attrill and Lacoste; Droege, Oetling and Company; Bellot, De Mermes and Company; and Marks and Company, most with headquarters either in Matamoros or Monterrey—approached Quintero trying to buy southern cotton. On one occasion, Droege, Oetling and Company tried to get a large share of the cotton business by dealing with Major Charles Russell, the Confederate quartermaster at Brownsville. Oetling offered forty dollars in specie per bale of cotton, plus all the freight costs. Although Russell apparently favored the proposal, Quintero

---

Governors' Letters (Archives, Texas State Library, Austin); Owsley, *King Cotton Diplomacy*, 116–117.

11. Quintero to Hunter, November 4, 11, 1861; Quintero to Browne, November 6, 1861, Pickett Papers; Quintero to Francis R. Lubbock, November 9, December 2, 1861, Governors' Letters; Browne to Quintero, December 9, 1861, in *Official Records of the Union and Confederate Navies in the War of the Rebellion* (31 vols.; Washington, 1894–1927), Ser. II, III, 308; hereafter cited as *O.R.N.*

12. Benjamin to Mansfield Lovell, March 22, 1862, *O.R.A.*, Ser. I, VI, 863–864.

13. Quintero to Hunter, November 11, 1861, Pickett Papers.

rejected it, saying that better deals were available. Oetling, nevertheless, prospered during the war. Lieutenant Colonel Arthur J. L. Fremantle noted that "Mr. Oetling is supposed to have made a million of dollars for his firm by bold speculations" by 1863.[14]

Quintero felt that he had made a promising beginning in northern Mexico. He had negotiated several significant trade agreements, and he had facilitated contracts among government agents, private producers, and area companies. He also had established what appeared to be a firm friendship with Vidaurri, who was exceptionally open to discussions regarding any problem. To Assistant Secretary Browne, Quintero indicated that "we have gained an ally" in Vidaurri. He wrote Texas Governor Edward Clark that, "I have been entirely successful in my mission."[15]

But there was unforeseen trouble. Planters endured endless natural difficulties to get their cotton to a free port. Starting from remote points in Texas or Arkansas, hundreds of cotton wagons rumbled toward the Mexican border at an agonizingly slow pace. Huge amounts of cotton rolled through Alleyton, just east of Houston, because the railroad line ended there. When Lieutenant Colonel Fremantle saw the town in 1863 it was no more than a "little wooden village . . . crammed full of travelers and cotton speculators," but it had grown tremendously in the past three years because it was on the main route to Brownsville. From Alleyton the cotton was hauled by ox cart or wagon to Richard King's ranch, where, according to John Hunter, "all roads from every cotton section of the state in the direction of Brownsville converged." Between the ranch, which soon became an official cotton depot, and Brownsville was a "long stretch of 125 miles [which] became a broad thoroughfare along which continuously moved two vast, unending trains of wagons; the one outward bound with cotton, the other homeward bound with merchandise and army supplies."[16] It was a difficult journey because much of the trip was made over semi-arid or desert country.

San Antonio was the focal point for another, even more desolate route.

---

14. Bee to Edmund P. Turner, August 27, 1863, *O.R.A.*, Ser. 1, XXVI, pt. 2, 184–186; W. A. Broadwell to C. G. Memminger, January 28, 1864, *O.R.A.*, Ser. I, LIII, 955–957; Quintero to Benjamin, January 30, September 16, 1863, Pickett Papers; Arthur James Lyon Fremantle, *The Fremantle Diary: Being the Journal of Lieutenant Colonel Arthur James Lyon Fremantle, Coldstream Guards, on His Three Months in the Southern States*, ed. by Walter Lord (Boston, 1954), 12; Owsley, *King Cotton Diplomacy*, 118. In some sources Droege is spelled Dredge.

15. Quintero to Browne, February 9, 1862; Quintero to Benjamin, July 5, 1862, Pickett Papers; Quintero to Clark, July 11, 1861, Governors' Letters.

16. Fremantle, *Diary*, 49; Hunter, "Fall of Brownsville," 6; LeRoy P. Graf, "The Economic Histo-

"Hundreds of huge Chihuahua wagons were . . . seen 'parked' with military precision outside" San Antonio, wrote Mrs. Eliza Moore McHatton Ripley, "waiting their turn to enter the grand plaza, deliver their packages of goods, and load with cotton" for the return trip to Mexico. As early as March, 1862, H. M. Smith, a San Antonio merchant, advertised "Mexican Goods" for sale: bagging, baling rope and twine, blankets, leather, lead, various foodstuffs, and "segars." Another Alamo City merchant, H. Mayer & Company, offered for sale Mexican flour from the Taylor and Black mills of Monclova, Coahuila.[17]

Hoping to profit from the cotton traffic that came through San Antonio, various merchants in Texas and Mexico advertised for cotton. From Eagle Pass Adolfo Duclos, a French immigrant, offered to accept cotton delivered there, then sell it in Mexico on commission, or for goods. Later, Guilbeau and Herman of Monterrey advertised a similar arrangement. They would pay freight, other expenses, and duties in Mexico, if the planter would consign his crop to them. Another merchant offered "Mexican mares" in exchange for cotton.[18]

The routes connecting San Antonio with Laredo or Eagle Pass were perhaps the roughest portions of the road. Mrs. Ripley, who claimed to have been one of the few women to make the trip during the war, described land near the Rio Grande as being "so barren that the only growths were prickly-pear and mesquite." John S. ("Rip") Ford, no stranger to the borderland himself, concurred in her judgment, indicating that around the "water holes" he found "hundreds of domestic animals, dead, their flesh seemingly dried up on their bones." And the situation worsened following the scorching drought of 1863–1864. L. M. Rogers, a friend of Ford's, claimed that "you cannot imagine how desolate, barren, and desert-like this country is; not a spear of grass, nor a green shrub, with nothing but moving clouds of sand to be seen on these once green prairies." [19] Nor did the road improve on the Mexican side of the river.

Most of the wagons went to Brownsville, which was the nearest point to the Gulf of Mexico; and they wrought a complete transformation in the "twin cities of the border" in just a few months. In 1858 a writer for the Nueces Valley described Brownsville as having "busy peopled streets and fully-occupied houses,"

ry of the Lower Rio Grande Valley, 1820–1875" (2 vols.; Ph.D. dissertation, Harvard University, 1942), II, 496.

17. Eliza Moore McHatton Ripley, *From Flag to Flag: a Woman's Adventures and Experiences in the South during the War, in Mexico, and in Cuba* (New York, 1889), 95–96; see San Antonio *Daily Herald*, September 21, 1861, March 18, 1862, for advertisements.

18. San Antonio *Daily Herald*, October 4, November 7, 1862.

19. Ripley, *Flag to Flag*, 81; John S. Ford, *Rip Ford's Texas*, ed. by Stephen B. Oates (Austin, 1963), 347–348.

which made Matamoros, with empty streets and "apathetic poor people," a dismal comparison. But in just a few years William Watson, the famous blockade runner, saw Matamoros actually "blocked up with goods." Admiral Raphael Semmes described it as a "quaint old Spanish town" that "presented the very picture of a busy commercial mart."[20]

In Matamoros the cotton was loaded onto one of the many river steamers built especially for the Rio Grande traffic, and taken to Bagdad (a village of almost 2,000 inhabitants in 1863) for transshipment to an ocean-going vessel in the gulf. This operation, too, presented a number of problems. Located approximately thirty miles from the coast, Matamoros did not provide easy access to the sea. Bagdad could be reached by wagon, or by winding some sixty-five miles down the Rio Grande in a boat, a trip that easily consumed twelve hours, and sometimes twenty-four if the captain could not keep the craft from running aground.[21]

After the cotton arrived at Bagdad, it might still wait months before being loaded on ocean-going vessels. Captain George G. Randolph, of H.M.S. *Orlando*, complained in January, 1863, that some thirty ships awaited approximately 10,000 bales of cotton. It frequently required from two to three months to load a vessel, wrote Randolph, because the small steamboats used to transport the cotton could not cross the bar in the harbor when the water was low. During the winter the tide allowed the shippers to work only about one day out of fourteen,[22] but this was the best route to the gulf.

There was a great deal of trade in Laredo as well, until the Union army under General Nathaniel P. Banks captured Brownsville in November, 1863.[23] Normal-

20. W. H. Chatfield (comp.), *Twin Cities of the Border, and the Country of the Lower Rio Grande* (New Orleans, 1893), 2; *Nueces Valley* (Corpus Christi), January 10, 1858; William Watson, *The Adventures of a Blockade Runner; or, Trade in Time of War* (London, 1892), 23, 25–26; Raphael Semmes, *Memoirs of Service Afloat during the War Between the States* (Baltimore, 1869), 792–793.

21. Harbert Davenport, "Notes on Early Steamboating on the Rio Grande," *Southwestern Historical Quarterly*, XLIX (October, 1945), 286–289; Fremantle, *Diary*, 6–7.

22. Randolph to [Commander Dunlop], January 1, 1863, Foreign Office Papers (F.O. 50/378, Public Record Office, London).

23. Santos Benavides to Vidaurri, May 8, July 12, 1862; Vidaurri to Benavides, May 14, 1862, December 29, 1863, Correspondencia Particular de D. Santiago Vidaurri (Archivo General del Estado de Nuevo León, Monterrey); Quintero to Benjamin, November 4, 26, 1863, Pickett Papers; Nannie M. Tilley (ed.), *Federals on the Frontier; the Diary of Benjamin F. McIntyre* (Austin, 1963), 239–259; Lea, *King Ranch*, I, 205–214. Most of the papers in the Correspondencia de Vidaurri are filed alphabetically according to who corresponded with Vidaurri. Some, however, are filed under a subject. In the latter instance the *expediente* number is given.

ly the cotton would have been shipped via Laredo, but many freighters feared that General Banks would try to extend his control up the river. In fact, he did, but Colonel Santos Benavides beat him back in a furious battle on February 19, 1864. With the Brownsville route closed and Laredo in danger, cotton buyers and agents alike moved to Eagle Pass. One Little Rock, Arkansas, merchant brought 100 wagons of cotton through Eagle Pass, and the customs inspector, Jesse Sumpter, noted that "there was scarcely a day that hundreds of bales were not unloaded . . . and crossed [over] . . . as fast as possible."[24]

The Eagle Pass merchants were prepared to take advantage of their windfall. Adolfo Duclos expanded his business to include wholesaling, dry goods, and groceries. He advertised that cotton consigned to him in San Antonio would be shipped from there to Eagle Pass without cost to the planter, that he had connections with the best houses in Matamoros, and that he would rebale all the fiber with his new cotton press. Sappington & Owings and William Stone competed with Duclos by offering similar terms. This influx soon created a large surplus of cotton in Piedras Negras, opposite Eagle Pass on the Rio Grande.[25]

In addition to the natural obstacles, there was political trouble that Quintero had not anticipated. He immediately faced severe problems that threatened the very fabric that he had labored so diligently to weave. When he returrned to Richmond to report Governor Vidaurri's reactions in person, he left what appeared to be a rather tranquil situation. Upon his return, however, he found a raging civil war in Tamaulipas. When the Confederate sympathizer Jesús de la Serna was declared the legally elected governor, the opposing candidate, Cipriano Guerrero, denounced the election and pronounced against Serna. Serna turned to General José María Jesús Carvajal, longtime filibuster and old nemesis of Vidaurri, for military aid.[26]

The conflict became critical for the South when Vidaurri was appointed governor and military *comandante* of Tamaulipas. Mexican President Benito Juárez, fearing that the combined British, French, and Spanish army might land at Matamoros or Tampico as a result of the London Convention, moved to strengthen the defenses along the northern coast, even if it meant giving more

24. Jesse Sumpter, *Paso del Águila: A Chronicle of Frontier Days on the Texas Border*, ed. by Ben E. Pingenot (Austin, 1969), 87. See also *Frank Leslie's Illustrated Newspaper*, April 30, 1864, pp. 88–89; Ford, *Rip Ford's Texas*, 355–357.

25. San Antonio *Herald*, December 24, 1864; James P. Newcomb, *Sketch of Secession Times in Texas and Journal of Travel from Texas through Mexico to California, Including a History of the "Box Colony"* (San Francisco, 1863), pt. 2, p. 4.

26. Arturo Gonzalez, *Historia de Tamaulipas* (Ciudad Victoria, 1931), 81–82; Gabriel Saldivar, *Historia compendiada de Tamaulipas* (Mexico City, 1945), 212; Quintero to Hunter, October 18, 1861, Pickett Papers.

power to the self-willed Vidaurri.[27] But when he attempted to take control of his newly acquired territory, Vidaurri met opposition from Carvajal, who sought refuge in Texas from his longtime friend, Colonel "Rip" Ford, commander of the Confederate garrison at Brownsville. Vidaurri threatened retaliation unless the South refused protection to Carvajal.[28]

Before the South ended the partisanship of its officials in Brownsville, Vidaurri acted. On April 8 Colonel James N. Langstroth, a Confederate sympathizer from Monterrey, told Quintero that Vidaurri had closed the port of Mier because of Carvajal's raids. At Quintero's request the border was soon reopened, but the duty on cotton was doubled, from one cent per pound to two cents. Vidaurri justified the increase on the grounds that a loan from the merchants had proved insufficient to support his occupation of Tamaulipas, but Quintero suspected that it was retaliation for Ford's support of Carvajal. Quintero finally secured a reduction of the tariff, and the Confederacy avoided serious trouble by enforcing neutrality, but Vidaurri had proved that he was the South's most valuable ally in Mexico.[29]

Shipment of cotton was further hampered by the U.S.S. *Montgomery* that waited off the coast of Brownsville, enforcing the recently effected blockade of the Texas coast. There was so much cotton in Texas, and so many merchants willing to go to great lengths to sell it, that some of the "white gold" even found its way southward to the port of Tampico, situated on the Rio Pánuco, about 250 miles directly down the coast from Matamoros. Tampico was not as good a port as Matamoros, but some cotton was shipped from there, a fact that Union Consul Franklin Chase considered "gratifying evidence . . . [of] the efficiency of the blockade."[30]

---

27. *Boletín Oficial* (Monterrey), January 14, 1862; Vidaurri to Juárez, January 14, 1862, in Santiago Roel (ed.), *Correspondencia particular de D. Santiago Vidaurri, gobernador de Nuevo León (1855–1864)* (Monterrey, 1946), 107. Signed on October 31, 1861, the London Convention called for occupation of ports and military points in Mexico until Mexico paid the debts owed the three countries. Ralph Roeder, *Juárez and His Mexico* (2 vols.; New York, 1947), I, 342.

28. Quintero to Hunter, February 1, 1862, Pickett Papers; *Boletín Oficial* (Monterrey), January 24, 26, February 1, 1862. It appeared to Quintero that Ford actually was aiding Carvajal and he appealed to various authorities to enforce neutrality. Quintero to Browne, March 4, 28, 1862, Pickett Papers; Quintero to Lubbock, March 10, 23, 1862, Governors' Letters. Vidaurri also appealed for enforcement of neutrality. Vidaurri to Jefferson Davis, January 25, 1862, Correspondencia de Vidaurri.

29. Quintero to Vidaurri, April 21, 1862, Correspondencia de Vidaurri; Quintero to Lubbock, April 13, 1862, Governors' Letters; Quintero to Browne, April 17, 1862, Pickett Papers.

30. *La Bandera* (Brownsville), July 31, 1862; Watson, *Blockade Runner*, 125–126; Chase to William Seward, August 6, 1861, Despatches from United States Consuls in Tampico, 1824–1906: January 10, 1860-January 26, 1863, General Records of the Department of State (Record Group 59, National Archives, Washington; microfilm copy in Texas Christian University Library, Fort Worth).

After Quintero settled the troubled situation in Tamaulipas, there were no apparent obstacles to the trade. A friendly governor controlled the tier of border states stretching from the Gulf of Mexico to the Big Bend region of Texas, and the cotton was ready. American Consul Leonard Pierce, Jr., reported from Matamoros that the southerners had a "large pile of cotton" on the wharves at Brownsville that they would ship at the first possible opportunity. Prominent Texas merchants such as Charles Stillman and Richard King regained their confidence in the trade.[31]

And Governor Vidaurri continued to be helpful. When Major Simeon Hart, Confederate quartermaster in San Antonio, asked for adequate vessels and protection for cotton shipments once they reached the Mexican side of the river, Vidaurri worked out a satisfactory arrangement with Quintero, allowing the merchants either to take their cotton downriver immediately, or deposit it in Monterrey until they found a market for it. No charge except the regular tariff would be levied, which meant that Monterrey would be a free deposit station.[32]

There was little to keep the commerce from thriving. The "trade is immense," claimed Quintero. It "grows larger every day." The American consul in Monterrery, M. M. Kimmey, warned that it had reached "enormous proportions," that "large trains" carrying "goods of all kinds" were departing for Texas daily. The road from Matamoros was "one vast and almost unbroken line of wagons and carts carrying cotton to the gulf shore." But the boat crews could not keep pace with the demand. Lieutenant Colonel Fremantle saw some "seventy vessels. . . . constantly at anchor outside" Bagdad, with "their cotton cargoes being brought to them . . . by two small steamers." Acting Rear Admiral Theodorus Bailey counted between 180 and 200 waiting ships from various nations. And there were "endless bales of cotton" along the coast for an "immense distance" waiting to be loaded.[33]

Cotton seemingly was more desirable than money. Major Hart visited Mexico and purchased more than $1,000,000 worth of military supplies and foodstuffs, all to be paid for in cotton. The foreign consuls in Monterrey informed Quintero that their governments would furnish "any amount of specie"

---

31. Pierce to Seward, March 1, 1862, Despatches from United States Consuls in Matamoros 1826–1906: Vols. 7–9, January 1, 1838–December 28, 1869 (RG 59, NA; microfilm copy, TCU Library); Stillman to King, March 18, 1862, quoted in Lea, *King Ranch*, I, 187.

32. Quintero to Benjamin, August 30, 1862, September 16, 1863, Pickett Papers.

33. Quintero to Benjamin, September 24, October 19, 1862, Pickett Papers; Kimmey to Seward, October 29, November 21, 1862, in Despatches from United States Consuls in Monterrey, Mexico, 1849–1906 and Volume 2, November 15, 1849–December 9, 1869 (RG 59, NA; microfilm, TCU Library); Kimmey to Seward, October 29, in *O.R.A.*, Ser. III, II, 949–951; Fremantle, *Diary*, 6; Bailey to Gideon Wells, April 2, 1863, in *O.R.N.*, Ser. I, XVII, 403; Hunter, "Fall of Brownsville," 7.

for southern cotton in the interior or on the frontier, and they claimed that they could soon have 500 wagons ready to haul the goods.[34]

Despite the fact that the cotton trade was one of the more profitable enterprises for the South, there were many obstacles that remained to threaten it, sometimes practically halting it. One of the most infuriating, as far as Quintero was concerned, was an attempt by the influential merchants in Matamoros to control the market. "No transactions are taking place," wrote the editor of the Fort Brown Flag, because the "prices offer[ed] . . . and demanded are so wide apart." The companies were hoping to buy cotton at a low price—eighteen to twenty cents specie per pound—and sell high on the world market. The planters, of course, held out as long as they could. Some even doubted the wisdom of selling cotton in Mexico, particularly in view of the Confederacy's overall policy of withholding the fiber from the European markets. But there was little chance of their success. After surveying the situation, the editor of the *Flag* concluded that there was "neither buyer nor seller" in the Matamoros market.[35]

Quintero hoped the planters would hold out. Of course, the small producers would have to sell quickly because they had no capital; but perhaps the larger planters could keep their cotton off the market until the Matamoros buyers had to "call for it." This would give the Texans the opportunity to set the price. It was a complex tangle that Quintero feared the planters could not win. The only hope, as he saw it, was for the Confederate government to regulate the cotton trade.[36]

He was convinced that government regulation was the only solution as he viewed problems that the Confederates themselves created, but refused to solve. Confusion and disorganization pervaded southern efforts to get cotton to the Mexican market, and then return the supplies to the war zone. Quintero immediately realized that there would be trouble when he was swarmed by Confederate contractors and purchasing agents, Mexican merchants, and private companies from both sides of the river. Even Sam Houston, Jr., and Charles Power (his uncle) visited Monterrey, armed with a recommendation from "the Raven" himself, and solicited the aid of Quintero and Vidaurri in disposing of their cotton. Major Hart had such difficulty getting cotton to Brownsville to supply General Hamilton P. Bee's command, that Bee simply contracted with Mifflin Kenedy and Company to get enough cotton for supplies. Quintero summed up the situation for the State Department: there was no unity, little

---

34. Quintero to Benjamin, October 18, 1862, Pickett Papers.

35. *Fort Brown Flag* (Brownsville), April 17, 1862; San Antonio *Herald*, November 16, 1861; Quintero to Benjamin, June 19, 1863, Pickett Papers.

36. Quintero to Benjamin, June 19, 1863, Pickett Papers.

cooperation, and, therefore, waste, inefficiency, speculation, and competition all along the line. The "multiplicity of purchasers, speculators . . . competition and confusion," he wrote Benjamin, were "detrimental to the interests of the government."[37]

Clear-cut cases of mismanagement or bungling were common. A shipment of some 15,000 rifles first was delayed for a year, then finally cancelled because of the disorganization among government agents trying to buy it. Quintero reported that the Belgian ship *Jane*, carrying this valuable cargo, arrived at an island off the coast of Honduras, either because the captain simply lacked instructions or because he refused to deliver the cargo to Matamoros. After more than a year, the captain sold the guns to pay expenses and left. When the *Sea Queen*, a British vessel, arrived at Matamoros with another cargo of rifles, Major Hart could not gather enough cotton to pay off the contractor.[38]

After the Union forces captured Brownsville the situation worsened considerably. As the Confederate army retreated northward "every bale [of cotton] that came within reach . . . was rolled off [the wagon], the bailing [sic] wire cut, and the match applied." John Hunter described one particularly "pathetic incident." A group of neighbors from Arkansas had combined their cotton to make up a train of about twenty-five wagons. "Old, white-haired men, young boys, and a few old trusted Negro uncles," all suffering from extreme poverty, had coaxed the teams as far as the King Ranch, where they met General Bee's retreating veterans. Hunter arrived after the confrontation, but in time to behold the "rarest spectacle" that he had ever seen "among his own countrymen."

The air was yet laden with the odor of burning cotton and the pall of smoke that hung over the landscape. The dismantled wagons, and the half-consumed, yet burning cotton bales, the forlorn and woeful look of the teamsters—all these gave mute evidence of the fearful ravages under the thin guise of expediency. [The] old men [were] sitting around as if in a stupor, while the boys wandered aimlessly about, silent, morose, as if trying to comprehend the enormity of the calamity that had engulfed them in general ruin.[39]

The Confederates burned the cotton, of course, to keep it from falling into the hands of the Union forces at Brownsville. That probably was unnecessary,

---

37. Quintero to Hunter, February 1; Quintero to Browne, March 4, 1862; Quintero to Benjamin, January 30, 1863, Pickett Papers; Sam Houston to Vidaurri, April 20, 1863, Santiago Roel Papers (closed manuscripts owned by Santiago Roel, hijo, Monterrey, and used by his permission); Lea, *King Ranch*, I, 197–199, 404–405.

38. Quintero to Benjamin, January 30, 1863, Pickett Papers; James L. Nichols, *The Confederate Quartermaster in the Trans-Mississippi* (Austin, 1964), 56–57.

39. Hunter, "Fall of Brownsville," 19–22.

because, other than raiding parties, General Banks' forces never successfully penetrated further than Brownsville. General Bee brought upon himself severe criticism for his haste in burning the precious fibers.[40]

Even when the government finally decided to regulate the commerce, monumental problems contributed to the failure of the regulation. The Confederate authorities in Texas had been impressing cotton, paying the owners with bonds, and shipping it to the border. But impressment angered cotton producers. Their upset combined with other grievances to create widespread unrest throughout the western states with the government in Richmond.[41] Some felt that those with influential friends or extensive properties could have their cotton exempted from impressment, again raising a problem crucial to the war effort: more people felt, in the words of "Rip" Ford, that they were involved in a "rich man's war, [but] a poor man's fight!" Some contractors hesitated to accept impressed cotton, for fear that the owner would follow it to Mexico and successfully reclaim it. This happened on occasion, much to the chagrin of the Confederate authorities who had worked so hard to get the fiber safely across the river.[42]

At the request of influential citizens in the West, a conference was held at Marshall, Texas, in August, 1863, to propose solutions for the many problems facing the Trans-Mississippi Department, particularly the one involving cotton. The resulting plan called for the government to purchase one-half the planter's crop with "cotton bonds." If the planter sold half his crop, he would be guaranteed that the other half would not be impressed.[43]

The arrangement might have worked had it not been in competition with a similar program worked out by Texas. In January, 1862, Texas had established the State Military Board for the primary purpose of negotiating some government bonds obtained from the United States as a part of the Compromise of

---

40. Richard Fitzpatrick, the Confederate commercial agent in Matamoros, was particularly critical of Bee's conduct. See Fitzpatrick to Benjamin, March 8, 1864, in *O.R.A.*, Ser. I, XXXIV, pt. 2, 1030–1032. See also Tilley, *Federals on the Frontier*, 255–256; Lea, *King Ranch*, I, 206–209.

41. Part of the discontent was caused by scarcity of and high prices for household goods. San Antonio *Herald*, October 11, 1862; Rena Maverick Green (ed.), *Samuel Maverick, Texan: 1803–1870* (San Antonio, 1952), 372–374.

42. Ford, *Rip Ford's Texas*, 357; Quintero to Benjamin, September 16, 1863, Pickett Papers; Nichols, *Quartermaster*, 56–57; Bee to E. P. Turner, July 29, 1862, in *O.R.A.*, Ser. I, XXVI, pt. 2, 113–114, 123; Watson, *Blockade Runner*, 28–30.

43. E. Kirby Smith to Jefferson Davis, September 11, 1863, in *O.R.A.*, Ser. I, XXII, pt. 2 1003–1010; Francis R. Lubbock, *Six Decades in Texas; or Memoirs of Francis Richard Lubbock, Governor of Texas in War-Time, 1861–1863*, ed. by C. W. Raines (Austin, 1900), 493–500; Graf, "Lower Rio Grande," II, 510–511; Joseph Howard Parks, *General Edmund Kirby Smith, C.S.A.* (Baton Rouge, 1954), 315.

1850. Confederate Secretary of State Benjamin got Texas Governor Francis R. Lubbock to turn in these bonds—634 of them, each worth $1,000 and drawing 5 percent interest, payable semiannually—and accept 8 percent Confederate bonds in their place. After the Military Board had disposed of all the state's bonds, however, it soon turned to the only other asset which could bring in cash or trade goods, cotton. The state had no cash to pay the planters, of course, but it worked out a plan whereby it would buy cotton with the 8 percent bonds.[44]

Obviously the Confederate plan was more advantageous than the Texas plan, because a planter's cotton still might be impressed after he had sold part of his crop to the state. Under the Confederate plan half his cotton would be guaranteed against impressment, leaving him the opportunity of selling that cotton in Mexico for specie. But after Governor Pendleton Murrah took office, Texas offered another program. The state would contract for all the planter's cotton, thereby insuring it against impressment. It would transport the cotton to the border, where half of it would then be given back to the planter for him to dispose of as he pleased. This plan not only guaranteed that the cotton would not be impressed, but it also relieved the planter of the worry of shipping his cotton to the border. The Cotton Bureau set up in 1863 by General E. Kirby Smith, commander of the Trans-Mississippi Department, to procure a sufficient amount of the staple to provide his forces with supplies, could not compete on these terms.[45] The end result was the chaos and confusion that Quintero witnessed from his vantage point in Monterrey.

The tangled overlap and disorganization eventually led to a confrontation with Governor Vidaurri and a halt in the Mexican trade. Patricio Milmo had traded with the Confederacy ever since the war began and he accumulated a credit of hundreds of thousands of pounds of cotton. He substantially inflated this credit by taking over claims of other companies such as Attrill and Lacoste, and Droege, Oetling and Company, and by financing several agents who participated in the trade, such as A. Urbahan of San Antonio.[46]

The man responsible for getting the cotton to the merchants was the beleaguered Major Hart. He had a complicated, if not impossible, task. First, he had

---

44. Charles W. Ramsdell, "The Texas State Military Board, 1862–1865," *Southwestern Historical Quarterly*, XXVII (April, 1924), 253–262.

45. Nichols, *Quartermaster*, 68; Graf, "Lower Rio Grande," II, 513–514.

46. See rather lengthy correspondence on this issue: Hart to George Williamson, December 24, 1863; George T. Howard to Hart, September 10, 1863; Hart to Milmo, November 17, 1863; and Hart to Williamson, December 28, 1863, in *O.R.A.*, Ser. I, LIII, 933–942; Owsley, *King Cotton Diplomacy*, 125–126.

to find cotton to ship. That was not easy with the Cotton Bureau, the State Military Board, and speculators voraciously competing for each bale. Then he had to transport it to Brownsville for payment on the Confederate debt. Unknown to him, however, Major Charles Russell confiscated the cotton Hart had collected and applied it to debts that his own command had accumulated. Hart's bills thus not only went unpaid, but increased with each additional purchase.[47]

Milmo protested unsuccessfully on several occasions, but also looked for an opportunity to collect his cotton. That chance came when Confederate Treasury agent Clarence C. Thayer arrived in Matamoros on November 6, 1863, with $16,000,000 worth of treasury notes intended to relieve the money shortage in the Trans-Mississippi Department and restore confidence in the Confederate notes. Not knowing who the ranking officer was, Thayer disclosed the purpose of his mission to Russell. He wanted to place the notes in the hands of a reliable company to be shipped to Eagle Pass.[48] Russell, apparently hoping to make some money himself, recommended Milmo's company, then saw to it that Milmo knew that the seven boxes placed in his possession contained a large amount of treasury notes. On December 11 Milmo informed Major Hart that he had confiscated the shipment, and that it was being held in lieu of the entire debt owed him.[49]

Milmo was dealing with more than just Major Hart; he had endangered the currency of the entire Trans-Mississippi Department. When Quintero protested to Governor Vidaurri (who undoubtedly sanctioned Milmo's seizure because Vidaurri and Milmo were business partners), he was told that he had recourse to the courts of Nuevo León y Coahuila. Court action displeased Quintero for several reasons, however, and he wrote Hart indicating that the problem was the Major's to handle as best he could.[50] Then he recommended to General Smith that all shipments from Texas cease, thereby cutting off Vidaurri's major source of income, the customs house at Piedras Negras. General Smith went even further. On January 12, 1864, he issued Special Order Number 8 freezing all Mexican assets in Texas until an agreement could be worked out. He also appointed Judge Thomas J. Devine, Colonel T. F. McKinney, and Captain Felix Ducayet

---

47. Owsley, *King Cotton Diplomacy*, 125–126.

48. Quintero to Benjamin, December 23, 1863, Pickett Papers; Thayer to Smith, December 20, 1863, in *O.R.A.*, Ser. I, LIII, 931–932.

49. Milmo to Hart, December 11, 1863; Milmo to [Quintero], [December, 1863], Expediente 343, Correspondencia de Vidaurri; Milmo to Thayer, Decemoer 17, 1863, in *O.R.A.*, Ser. I, LIII, 933.

50. Quintero to Benjamin, December 23, 1863, January 25, 1864; Quintero to Hart, December 20, 1863, Pickett Papers; Quintero to Vidaurri, December 17, 1862, Correspondencia de Vidaurri.

to go to Monterrey and negotiate with Vidaurri.[51]

Governor Vidaurri was under considerable pressure to settle the dispute. Quintero estimated that losses from the import duties alone would total $50,000 to $60,000 per month. Vidaurri, however, was also being pressured internally. The French had forced President Juárez to flee Mexico City, and he was moving northward, just ahead of the invaders under General Achille François Bazaine. Having never been a friend or ally of the President, Vidaurri feared Juárez as much as he did the French. And if the French occupied Matamoros, he would be forced to relinquish his control over Tamaulipas and probably over the cotton trade as well.[52]

Under these conditions a solution was quickly agreed upon, with the Confederacy promising to pay Milmo in full, and Milmo releasing the seven cases of treasury notes.[53] Now Vidaurri and the Confederacy were back on friendly terms, but the South had lost time and an untold amount of trade because of the seizure and embargo, primarily a result of disorganization and the inefficient government regulation of commerce.

Seemingly there were countless other problems that continually kept the cotton trade from reaching its full potential. Just after Quintero arrived in Monterrey he had to play a favorite Mexican game—customs manipulation—which Vidaurri frequently used to gain the cooperation of the Confederacy. On occasion Vidaurri allowed internal politics to dictate the tariff, but usually he worked it to his advantage.[54] Quintero also had to negotiate the duty that was charged on trade goods coming from Mexico into Texas, for it changed depending upon who controlled Tamaulipas. General Juan B. Tranconis raised the tariff when he was appointed military *comandante* in October, 1862, but Albino López lowered it when he became governor less than a month after Tranconis had ordered the increase.[55]

---

51. Quintero to Benjamin, January 25, February 1, 1864, Pickett Papers; Smith to [members of the commission], January [12], 1864, in *O.R.A.*, Ser. I, LIII, 949–950; Smith to Vidaurri, January 12, 1864, Roel Papers; W. J. Hutchins to Devine (copy), January 21, 1864, Thomas J. Devine Papers (Archives, University of Texas Library, Austin); Parks, *Kirby Smith*, 302–305, 352–353.

52. Quintero to Benjamin, January 25, 1864, Pickett Papers; Vidaurri to Smith (copy), February 2, 1864; Manuel G. Rejón to Vicente Garza (copy), February 2, 1864, Devine Papers; Carlos Pérez-Maldonado, "La Pugna Juárez-Vidaurri en Monterrey, 1864," *Memorias de la Academia Mexicana de la Historia*, XXIV (January-March, 1965), 56–91.

53. Quintero to Benjamin, February 28, 1864, Pickett Papers; [Devine] to Smith (copy) February 24; Devine to Hart (copy), July 24, 1864, Devine Papers.

54. Quintero to Browne, April 17, 1862; Quintero to Benjamin, August 14, 30, 1862, Pickett Papers.

55. Quintero to Benjamin, September 24, October 12, November 2, 1862, Pickett Papers.

Another troublesome problem was bandits, who raided on one side of the border, then fled to the other bank for protection. Stories such as, "murdered— near Brownsville . . . a wagoner who had delivered cotton . . . accompanied by a boy about fifteen years of age, who was seriously wounded,"[56] regularly appeared in the Texas press. General Carvajal continued raiding even after his band was refused protection by "Rip" Ford in 1861. In March, 1862, he and 500 men crossed the border into Mexico and attacked Reynosa and several other villages. When another party crossed the river and sacked the Nuevo León village of Guerrero, Vidaurri threatened to terminate all commerce if the southerners did not control the outlaws within their borders.[57]

More serious were the Union sympathizers and refugees who gathered in the Mexican border towns in rebellious groups.[58] Some famous politicians such as E. J. Davis and Andrew J. Hamilton provoked violent reaction from the Confederates in Brownsville, which again threatened the trade. Reportedly Davis, William Montgomery, and others would stand just across the river each evening and shout insults at the southerners. Whatever the case, patriotic Confederates could not tolerate Hamilton and Davis residing in Matamoros, openly recruiting men to raid in Texas. On March 14 a group of men crossed the river and seized a number of Yankees, including Davis.[59] This blatant violation of Mexican neutrality brought an immediate, and surprisingly hostile, reaction in Matamoros. Governor López threatened to close the border to all trade and arrest all Confederate officers in Matamoros if the prisoners were not released. Because of rumors that López had not made sufficient demands of the Confederacy, he was "hissed at" when he attended the theater by a populace that had just come from a street parade in which they sang patriotic songs and shouted *vivas* for the Lincoln government. General Bee concluded that even Davis was not that coveted a prisoner, so he ordered the captives released. William Montgomery could not be returned, however, for he had been hanged from one of the wispy mesquite

---

56. San Antonio *Herald*, May 24, 1862.

57. Quintero to Browne, March 24, 28, 1862, Pickett Papers; Quintero to Lubbock, March 24, 28, 1862; Vidaurri to Lubbock, April 6, 1862, Governors' Letters; *Fort Brown Flag* (Brownsville), April 17, 1862. See also August Santleben, *A Texas Pioneer: Early Staging and Overland Freighting Days on the Frontier of Texas and Mexico*, ed. by I. D. Affleck (New York, 1910), 22, 32–33.

58. The Union consuls in Monterrey frequently complained that they were "overrun with" the refugees. C. B. H. Blood to Seward, June 9, 1862; Kimmey to Seward, September 21, 1863, in Despatches from U.S. Consuls in Monterrey (RG 59, NA; microfilm, TCU Library); Sumpter, *Paso del Águila*, 93; Thomas North, *Five Years in Texas: or, What You Did Not Hear During the War from January 1861 to January 1866* (Cincinnati, 1871), 172.

59. Fremantle, *Diary*, 7–9; Quintero to Benjamin, March 21, 1863, Pickett Papers.

trees near the town.[60]

Quintero also possessed reliable information that the Union consul in Mata-moros, Leonard Pierce, Jr., was supporting refugee raids into Texas.[61] He at-tempted to prove that a foray on December 18, led by Octaviano Zapata, one of Juan N. Cortina's lieutenants, was inspired by Pierce. Zapata and his men had crossed the Rio Grande at Las Cuevas, attacked a Confederate wagon train, killed three teamsters, then returned to Mexico. But Quintero failed to prove that Pierce was implicated in the raids, and only secured a promise from Gover-nor López that he would do his best to preserve peace along the river. López, a merchant himself, wanted nothing to interfere with the trade.[62]

A final hazard, over which Quintero had no control, was one that plagued any boom area. Speculators and swindlers quickly reaped unfair and excessive profits from the exchange, at the expense of and despite all the efforts of the Confederate authorities. On February 20, 1863, for example, Henry Safford, formerly a resident of Galveston, smuggled $50,000 in counterfeit Confederate notes into Texas. It was not until one of his helpers tried to pass $2,000 of the worthless note that he was exposed and arrested. Perhaps most irritating were the parasites who hovered near the border entry ports, taking legal advantage of the trade. Major Hart was shrewdly duped when he purchased a wagon train from G. F. Justiniana with the understanding that the purchase price included a $272 bond. When Hart tried to take the train back into Mexico, the customs collector demanded that a bond be paid. Justiniana had been refunded the bond money when he returned to Mexico without the train.[63]

The most serious threat to the profitable international commerce was the French invasion of Mexico. In February, 1864, President Juárez, attempting to organize the resistance, confronted Governor Vidaurri in Monterrey. Then Vidaurri received an ultimatum from General Bazaine, giving him the choice of joining the intervention or fighting. Hoping to live for another and more glori-ous day, Vidaurri fled to Texas, leaving Juárez and Bazaine to settle the dispute

60. Quintero to Benjamin, March 21, April 6, 20, 1863, Pickett Papers; Fremantle, *Diary*, 8.

61. Quintero to Benjamin, August 30, October 19, 1862, January 24, 1864, Pickett Papers; Ford, *Rip Ford's Texas*, 351; Quintero to Vidaurri, November 23, 1863, Correspondencia de Vidaurri.

62. Quintero to Benjamin, January 30, 1863, Pickett Papers; Benavides to Vidaurri, February 1, 1863, Correspondencia de Vidaurri; *Boletín Oficial* (Monterrey), January 30, 1863; Emilio Velasco, Ygnacio Galindo, and Antonio García Carillo, "Investigating Commission of the Northern Fron-tier," in *Report of the Committee of Investigation Sent in 1873 by the Mexican Government to the Fron-tier of Texas* (New York, 1875), 67–68.

63. Hart to Quintero, November 4, 1863; Quintero to [Vidaurri], November 20, 1863; Silva to Lorenzo Castro, October 27, 1863, Expediente 343, Correspondencia de Vidaurri.

themselves.[64] Juárez immediately occupied Monterrey, and Quintero negotiated a trade agreement with him. But the advancing French army under General Armard Alexandre Castagny compelled Juárez to continue his flight to Chihuahua.[65]

Then Quintero successfully dealt with Castagny. The Confederates also established good relations with the French in Matamoros. There was a new boom in the cotton trade with contractors like Richard King trying to offset any losses that they incurred during the bleaker days of the war. Quintero's agreement with Castagny led him to conclude that "we have never before been in such a favorable condition . . . in regard to our intercourse with Mexico."[66]

Even with the enemy in sight, the most important element to everyone was the trade. Southerners once more held Brownsville, with Union troops still occupying the island of Brazos Santiago; both imperialist and *Juarista* forces were scattered throughout Matamoros. Union General Lew Wallace, a special envoy from General U. S. Grant, visited Port Isabel, a few miles up the coast from Brownsville. There he conferred with southern General James E. Slaughter and Colonel Ford. They agreed that any fighting they did would have no effect on the ultimate outcome of the war, so they called a truce; and the trade continued. "Goods come in as fast as possible," wrote Quintero in his last dispatch to Richmond. The speculators were trying to market the last of their cotton before the war ended and all the southern ports reopened to the cotton trade.[67]

Despite the truce, there was one more scrap in the lower Rio Grande Valley before the southerners laid down their guns. Many speculators had been caught with hundreds of bales of cotton in Brownsville and Matamoros. After Generals Lee and Grant had agreed upon surrender terms at Appomattox Court House,

64. Vidaurri returned to Mexico in September, 1864, and joined the French. He served in the Emperor Maximilian's cabinet; he was captured and executed by General Porfirio Díaz in June, 1867. Pérez-Maldonado, "La Pugna Juárez-Vidaurri," 68–75; Bazaine to Vidaurri, February 15, 1864, in *Boletín Oficial* (Monterrey), March 3, 1864; Benavides to James E. Slaughter, April 10, 1864, in *O.R.A.*, Ser. I, LIII, 980–981; *Daily Telegraph* (Houston), May 23, 1864; *La Gaceta* (Monterrey), September 7, 11, 1864; Santiago Roel, *Nuevo León: apuntes historicos* (11th ed.; Monterrey, 1963), 172–179, 188–189; Vito Alessio Robles, *Monterrey en la historia y en la leyenda* (Mexico City, 1936), 245–251.

65. Quintero to Benjamin, February 1, April 3, June 1, 1864, Pickett Papers; Quintero to Pedro Santicilia, January 29, 1864, in Jorge L. Tamayo (ed.), *Benito Juárez: documentos discursos y correspondencia* (13 vols.; Mexico City, 1966–present), VIII, 575–577; *La Opinión* (Monterrey), May 5, 12, 1864; José Fuentes Mares, *Juárez y el imperio* (Mexico City, 1963), 87.

66. Quintero to Benjamin, September 5; Quintero to Smith, October 21, 1864, Pickett Papers; *Daily Telegraph* (Houston), October 1, 1864; Lea, *King Ranch*, I, 233–234. Quote is in Quintero's despatch of October 21.

67. Ford, *Rip Ford's Texas*, 388–389; Quintero to Benjamin, December 7, 1864, Pickett Papers.

Union Colonel Theodore H. Barrett, believing that the Confederates knew of Lee's surrender and would not fight, ordered the occupation of Brownsville. He had not counted on the determination of "Rip" Ford, who led his ragged troops into what he thought would be the last battle of the war. "From the number of Union men I see before me, I am going to be whipped," Ford thought. But he drove the Yankees back to Brazos Santiago, defending the truce—and the bales of cotton piled high on the banks of the Rio Grande.[68]

"Old Rip" had indeed fought the last engagement of the war. The southerners laid down their arms and returned to their homes and families. Texas had escaped the most serious ravages of the war, but had suffered economically. Only the points along the Mexican border prospered far beyond their normal means. But the border region very quickly returned to *status quo ante bellum.* Bagdad again became a dusty little village that attracted no particular attention. Matamoros, which might have had as many as 30,000 inhabitants in March, 1865, declined as well.

The Rio Grande trade had been essential to the war effort in the Trans-Mississippi Department. John Warren Hunter recalled that cases of Enfield rifles marked "Hollow ware," gun powder barrels labeled "bean flour," and cargoes of percussion caps branded "canned goods" were shipped into Texas in large quantities. General John S. Marmaduke, in Little Rock, received a load of 4,000 Enfield rifles that had been purchased in England, then shipped through Bagdad, Matmoros, and Brownsville before reaching Little Rock.[69] Other items such as dry goods, hardware, foodstuffs, tobacco, and liquor came in through Matamoros. The South also tried to import other military supplies and drugs.[70] At the height of the conflict General Kirby Smith admitted that the Rio Grande was the "only channel" through which the Confederacy could obtain many necessities. The trade was so extensive that several influential members of President Lincoln's cabinet advocated the conquest of Texas, primarily to disrupt the Mexican trade. But the exchange flourished until the war ended and southern ports were reopened.[71]

---

68. Ford, *Rip Ford's Texas,* 389–393; Lea, *King Ranch,* I, 234–235; Barrett to [?], August 10, 1865, in *O.R.A.,* Ser. I, XLIII, pt. 1, 265–267.

69. Hunter, "Fall of Brownsville," 7–8.

70. Frank E. Vandiver (ed.), *Confederate Blockade Running Through Bermuda, 1861–1865: Letters and Cargo Manifests* (Austin, 1947), 110, 130; Stuart L. Bernath, "Squall Across the Atlantic: The Peterhoff Episode," *Journal of Southern History,* XXXIV (August, 1968), 382–383; Bee to Anderson, November 30, 1862, in *O.R.A.,* Ser. I, XV, 882.

71. Smith to John B. Magruder, July 27, 1863, in *O.R.A.,* Ser. I, LIII, 885; Ludwell H. Johnson, *Red River Campaign: Politics and Cotton in the Civil War* (Baltimore, 1958), 6–17.

Perhaps one of the most lasting effects of the trade was the economic prosperity that accompanied it and remained to become the basis of financial empires on both sides of the river. Men in the cotton business accumulated "vast
and immense fortunes," wrote Hunter: in Texas, Richard King, Charles Stillman, Mifflin Kenedy, and many others; on the Mexican side of the border perhaps Patricio Milmo was the most notable, but there were others. Merchants in
Monterrey garnered profits that became the economic foundation of present-
day Monterrey, the third largest city in Mexico and the financial capital of the
north.[72]

---

72. Hunter, "Fall of Brownsville," 5; Delaney, "Matamoros: Port For Texas," 486–487; Horacio
Garduñio García, *Nuevo León, un ejemplo de protección a la industria de transformación* (Mexico
City, 1958), 40; Isidro Viscaya Canales, *Los orígenes re la industrializatión de Monterrey (1867–1920)*
(Monterrey, 1969), xix.

Carte de visite of General Edmund Kirby Smith by Gurney & Son, New York, ca. 1860s. *CN 08604. Courtesy Center for American History, University of Texas at Austin.*

Texas and the Confederate Army's Meat Problem

Frank E. Vandiver*

In his classic account of the Confederate soldier, The Life of Johnny Reb *(Indianapolis: Bobbs-Merrill Co., 1943), Bell Wiley noted that "food was undoubtedly the first concern of Johnny Reb" (p. 90). When the war began there appeared to be an abundance of food, but within several months serious shortages, particularly of fresh meat, developed. Although antebellum southern production of beef and pork was extensive, distribution problems compounded by enemy military operations placed enormous burdens upon the Confederate commissary department. As a result, Rebel armies, particularly in Virginia, were often without fresh beef and pork.*

In recent years military historians have paid increased attention to the logistical support required by modern armies. Frank Vandiver, one of the nation's foremost Civil War historians, was one of the first to focus attention on the problems faced by the Confederacy in feeding its armies. In this article, published when he was only eighteen years of age, Vandiver discusses efforts of Commissary General Lucius B. Northrop to bring herds of cattle from Texas to Virginia. Lack of suitable forage en

---

* Frank Vandiver, "Texas and the Confederate Army's Meat Problem," *Southwestern Historical Quarterly,* XLVII (Jan., 1944), 225–233.

route made cattle driving difficult. The fall of Vicksburg and other Mississippi posts added to the problem. Although thousands of Texas cattle did reach Virginia the number was not sufficient to relieve all the food needs of Confederate armies east of the Mississippi. Vandiver speculates that had better communication existed between the Trans-Mississippi department and the eastern Confederacy, the Civil War might have been prolonged.

For other studies of logistical matters in Texas and the Trans-Mississippi, see James L. Nichols, The Confederate Quartermaster in the Trans-Mississippi *(Austin: University of Texas Press, 1964); Allan C. Ashcraft, "Confederate Beef Packing at Jefferson, Texas,"* Southwestern Historical Quarterly, *LXIII (Oct., 1964), 259–270; and Charles W. Ramsdell, "The Texas State Military Board, 1862–1865," ibid., XXVII (Apr., 1924), 253–275.*

The vital issues contingent upon supplying an army with munitions of war were illustrated in the British Eighth Army's pursuit of Rommel from El Alamein to Tunis. Food is one of these munitions of war. To keep the "British Eighth" advancing, food as well as ammunition and gasoline had to reach the front. Manifestly the Tunisian campaign was, if not the greatest, one of the greatest miracles of supply in modern war. It is not to be forgotten, however, that the armies of the southern Confederacy were confronted with a problem of supply; theirs was the harder to solve because ways had to be found of getting food out of the steadily contracting areas of the Confederacy, while the African problem was that of transporting subsistence across a desert. Importation of food being negligible, the Confederate Government was forced to rely on the output of the southern farmer and cattleman.

To an army whose personnel was from a section of the country which raised large numbers of hogs and beef, meat was a vital part of the ration. It is obvious that a study of all the problems concerning meat which weighed on the South would require much more than the space available; therefore, the present inquiry will be confined, for the most part, to beef. It is further hoped that this article may shed some light on all the problems facing the Confederate Commissariat after the loss of the Mississippi.

The Commissary-General, L. B. Northrop, found that his troubles began in the early part of the war as 500,000 pork hogs were considered necessary to feed the southern armies for a year. Northrop did not think that that number could be obtained in the Confederacy.[1] While he had his troubles in procuring meat, the fact remains that the basic ration on which the southern soldier lived was

---

1. Ella Lonn, *Salt as a Factor in the Confederacy* (New York, 1933), 16.

corn and beef.[2] In the early part of the war, some, at least, of the Rebel camps fared well in the matter of meat.[3] With all the meat the soldiers consumed, there were still 40,000 cattle ready for packing in the Confederacy at the end of 1861.[4] This indicates that the South started with something. The real pinch began to be felt in early 1863 when Lee's chief commissary informed him that he would not be able to make the supply of beeves last through the month of January. The condition of the beeves issued to the Army of Northern Virginia was so bad that Lee recommended they be sent somewhere to fatten in the spring. In lieu of the ration of beef he hoped his chief commissary had enough salt meat to issue.[5] Two weeks later his available supply had dwindled to four days' fresh beef. Following his usual practice, he refused to resort to impressing any meat which the civilians in the vicinity of the army might have. He told the Secretary of War that it would gain the army little and would anger the people,[6] and even if he had resorted to commandeering, it would have afforded only temporary relief. He could not remedy a condition which the Government could not, or would not remedy. That condition was faulty transportation. The transportation system of the South was the main adverse factor working against the commissary and quartermaster officials. The sad, and steadily deteriorating, condition of southern rail lines played a major part in holding back the flow of provisions to Lee's army and to all other Confederate forces.[7] The Government seemed powerless to do anything about the railroads and the armies continued to live on shorter rations. Another adverse factor, during the latter part of the war, was the Federal blockade, which was becoming steadily more efficient. Confederate coastwise shipping, which, early in the war, had been transporting subsistence, could no longer do so with any security.[8] The shortage of wagons also told on any effort to collect supplies situated around the bivouac of troops.

2. Bell I. Wiley, *The Life of Johnny Reb* (New York, 1943), 97.

3. George M. Lee to "Dear Sister" (Mrs. Sallie C. Taylor), Jan. 16, 1862, MS. letter. This letter, with several others, is in the possession of Mrs. Sallie Lee Boner of Austin, Texas. This collection, edited by the writer, will appear in the *Louisiana Historical Quarterly*.

4. *Official Records of the Union and Confederate Armies* (Washington, 1880-1901, 130 vols. Cited hereafter as *O. R.*), Series IV, vol. 2, 192.

5. *Ibid.*, Ser. I, vol. 51, pt. 2, 669. For the problems involved in salting meat in the South see Ella Lonn, *Salt as a Factor in the Confederacy*.

6. *O. R.*, Ser. I, vol. 25, pt. 2, 597.

7. Charles W. Ramsdell, "The Confederate Government and the Railroads" in *The American Historical Review*, XXII, 810.

8. Evidence of coastwise shipping is contained in Claiborne to Branch, April 23, 1862. MS. letter in the writer's possession.

The amount of rations to be taken on the march sometimes had to be reduced, because the capacity of the commissary wagons was not sufficient to carry the total.[9]

All these factors, combined with the breakdown of Confederate finances, continuously weakened the commissary department, and Lee became so acutely aware of the pressing need for food that he wrote Longstreet, in the west: "The great obstacle everywhere is scarcity of supplies. That is the controlling element to which everything has to yield."[10]

General Joseph E. Johnston must have found this to be true when the Secretary of War informed him that he should not draw supplies from Atlanta or other depots which were considered general reserves for all the armies.[11] Johnston, it was hoped, could get sufficient food from the country around his army. This scheme originated in the mind of the Commissary-General and seems to have been one of his favorites.

While the Commissary-General was employing all shifts to husband the shrinking stores of food, his eyes, as well as those of the Secretary of War, turned to North Carolina. The latter, J. A. Seddon, felt this state to be the main reliance of the South for foodstuffs, even though the enemy controlled the main food producing counties.[12]

Then came the fall of Vicksburg, July 4, 1863. The Government's worries after that date, if they had been great before, were crushing. The Confederacy no longer controlled the Mississippi River, and Arkansas, western Louisiana, Indian Territory, and Texas no longer were in direct connection with the eastern Confederacy. The loss of Texas beef at once caused the number of cattle east of the Mississippi to fall off; Northrop, as a result of this, had to recommend a reduction of the meat ration in late July.[13] The Army of Northern Virginia got temporary relief by invading Pennsylvania, but the only significant acquisition of beef cattle on this campaign was that of General R. S. Ewell, who on the way to Carlisle captured and sent to the main column some 3000 head. General John

---

9. MS. Statement of Commissary Transportation, Sept. 24, 1862, Reid Collection, Confederate Army Papers, Louisiana State University Archives. For shortage of wagon transportation see C. W. Ramsdell, "General Robert E. Lee's Horse Supply, 1862-1865" in *The American Historical Review*, XXXV, 758-77.

10. *O. R.*, Ser. I, vol. 52, pt. 2, 648. Lee to Longstreet, March 28, 1864.

11. *Ibid.*, 426. J. A. Seddon to J. E. Johnston, Feb. 23, 1863.

12. *Ibid.*, vol. 51, pt. 2, 681-2. Seddon to Maj. Gen. S. G. French, Feb. 20, 1863.

13. C. W. Ramsdell, "The Control of Manufacturing by the Confederate Government" in *The Mississippi Valley Historical Review*, VIII, 247; *O. R.*, Ser. I, vol. 61, pt. 2, 738; and Howard Swiggett (ed.), *A Rebel War Clerk's Diary* (New York, 1935), I, 385.

B. Imboden, on guard detail with Lee's retreating wounded train after Gettysburg, said that he had "a small lot of fine fat cattle" which he had taken on the way to that place.[14]

Regardless of what little additions there were to the number of beeves by captures and the like, the amount of meat on the eastern side of the Mississippi in December was enough for only twenty-five days. Virginia had nothing, of course, above the absolute wants of Lee's troops.[15] Even after cutting the issue of salt meat to a fourth of a pound, Lee had only three days' supply.[16]

By November, the attention of most commissary officers was directed toward Florida, which was generally recognized, since the loss of the Texas source, as the last remaining area from which beef might be drawn, as all other beef-producing areas east of the Mississippi were in Federal hands or were being devastated by raiding. Major J. F. Cummings, charged with supplying Bragg's army, had written to Major P. W. White, the chief commissary of Florida, on October 5, urging that he should forward beef, as all other sources were exhausted. Cummings was totally dependent on Florida for Bragg's beef supply. On the 20th his letter said that the troops under Bragg were getting half rations of beef and he feared that in a few days they would be living on bread alone. Georgia was equally dependent on Florida; the chief commissary of that state, Major J. L. Locke, confessed that his only hope was in Major White. South Carolina was in the same condition; Major Millen, at Savannah, felt that the weekly collections by purchasing commissaries would have to be relied on. This was doubly so in his case, as he had killed up all the beef cattle in his area and was reduced to killing stock herds.[17]

This alarming state of affairs seemed to jolt the Commissary-General out of his lethargy and he made more strenuous efforts to obtain beef. One of these was to try to swim beeves across the Mississippi River. The cooperation of General E. Kirby Smith, commanding the trans-Mississippi Department, was solicited in order to establish contact with General J. E. Johnston and arrange the times and localities for crossing the cattle.[18] While this was going on, Northrop,

---

14. R. U. Johnson and C. C. Buel (eds.), *Battles and Leaders of the Civil War* (New York, 1887), III, 426.

15. D. S. Freeman, *R. E. Lee* (New York, 1934), III, 246-7.

16. *O. R.*, Ser. I, vol. 33, 1061. Lee to Davis, Jan. 2, 1864. Northrop, it will be recalled, recommended this ration in July, 1863, see *supra*.

17. *O. R.*, Ser. I, vol. 35, pt. 2, 394-5. Later it would have been impossible to kill up stock herds as the Confederate Congress forbade the impressment of these animals. See C. W. Ramsdell (ed.), *Laws of the Last Confederate Congress* (Durham, N.C., 1941), 151.

18. *O. R.*, Ser. I, vol. 53, 914. Seddon to E. K. Smith, Nov. 19, 1863.

by intercepting a communication from two Florida men to the Secretary of War,[19] cost the Confederate States a million pounds of salt beef. The Floridians, who owned the only steamboats in their section of Florida, would have been willing to sell the beef to the Government at a reduced price because it was exposed to raiding, and would have transported it to the main rail line themselves. Since they did not wish to deal with Northrop, they left Richmond as soon as it came to their ears that he had intercepted their letter, without the Secretary of War having heard of their proposal.[20] Thus Northrop defeated himself. It is beyond the scope of this paper to attempt to give a picture of the Confederate Commissary-General, but suffice it to say that he seemed actually to enjoy the commanders' complaints of food shortage, for these gave him opportunities to write long missives stating that he had foreseen that the army would be reduced to that state, and in one case he absolved himself "from all responsibility" for a shortage of supplies in Lee's army.

At Christmas time, luckily for them, Longstreet's troops were encamped near Morristown, Tennessee, and according to Longstreet, himself, the country was heaven so far as food was concerned; all varieties of victuals, long since forgotten to the Rebels, were to be found in abundance.[21] What a time those ill-fed veterans of Lee's must have had!

In striking contrast to this was the Department of South Carolina, Georgia and Florida, commanded by General P. G. T. Beauregard. On January 12, 1864, Morris Island was reported out of meat for several days, and Northrop was forced to comment that ante bellum South Carolina had been dependent on external sources for food and that under war conditions it was certainly no different. The troops stationed there had to be fed on provisions shipped in. The chief commissary of that state, Major H. C. Guerin, indicated his desperation when he said: "Purchases and impressments will be attempted . . . but the main dependence for meat next summer is Florida."[22] It is little wonder that this was the case. By October, 1863, the number of beef cattle in the eastern Confederacy had fallen from the 40,000 of 1861 to less than half that number, and Major P. W. White reported on April 15, 1864, that the supply of beef in Florida was running low because of lack of rail transportation.[23]

---

19. The Secretary of War is not specifically mentioned but the terminology would seem to indicate that J. A. Seddon is meant; see *A Rebel War Clerk's Diary*, II, 109.

20. *Ibid.*

21. James Longstreet, *Manassas to Appomattox* (Philadelphia, 1896), 621.

22. *O. R.*, Ser. I, vol. 35, pt. 1, 615. Indorsement to Taliaferro to Jordan, Feb. 16, 1864.

23. *Ibid.*, Ser. IV, vol. 2, 969; *ibid.*, Ser. I, vol. 35, pt. 2, 431.

The severe privation which seemed to be staring the army in the face focused the attention, once more, of General Beauregard. Help was so urgently needed in the collection of supplies of beef in Florida that Beauregard offered to pardon deserters in certain areas of that state if they would report to commissary officers for duty.[24] This measure was all the more necessary because the number of beef cattle in the east had fallen to 5,959 in the spring of 1864,[25] and the main area of reserve stores had been reduced to Georgia, Virginia and North Carolina.[26] One of these areas was soon to be the objective of General Sherman; on September 2, 1864, he entered the main Confederate supply base of Atlanta. After Hood had started his disastrous Tennessee campaign, Sherman began his "March to the Sea," with the purpose of destroying the area from which Lee's army was drawing so much of its food.[27] This marked the beginning of the end for the Confederate States. With a good portion of Georgia devastated by Sherman's "bummers," Northrop, contrary to his usual attitude, was optimistic in reporting to the Secretary of War, J. C. Breckinridge, February 9, 1865, on the condition of the meat supply. He went into some detail on this subject. Among other things, he said:

Some thousands of beeves have been obtained within the past few months by swimming the Mississippi, and when the river is again in a suitable state and the season admits of it, the proceeding should be continued.

In the same report he said that Florida had supplied a good number of beeves and that he expected to get 20,000 more from that source.[28]

Whether or not Northrop obtained the beeves he seemed confident of getting the records do not show, but one thing is clear: the history of the Confederate food supply during the last months of the war is one long string of pleas

---

24. *Ibid.*, Ser. I, vol. 35, pt. 2, p. 331. Proclamation of Amnesty, March 4, 1864.

25. *Ibid.*, Ser. IV, vol. 3, 379. The Government, wishing to aid its impressing officers, and obviously thinking that the "Act to Regulate Impressments," 3rd. Sess., 1st Cong. (James M. Matthews (ed.), *Statutes at Large of the Confederate States of America*, St. III, Chap. X) was not specific enough, passed another act which specifically authorized the impressment of meat for the army ("An Act to authorize the impressment of meat for the army, under certain circumstances," *ibid.*, St. IV, Chap. LII). This could not have been of much help, for it must have followed the path of all other Confederate impressment acts, and broken down. See Frank L. Owsley, *State Rights in the Confederacy* (Chicago University Press, 1925), 4, 242.

26. *O. R.*, Ser. I, vol. 46, pt. 2, 1297; also MS. Reminiscences of Major R. J. Moses, 51, 70. Major Moses had been chief commissary of Longstreet's Corps and was later made chief commissary of Georgia. These Reminiscences are in the possession of Major Moses' granddaughter, Mrs. S. Silverman, Austin, Texas. The writer is much indebted to her for allowing him the use of them.

27. O. O. Winther (ed.), *With Sherman to the Sea* (Louisiana State University Press, 1943), 134, note 7.

28. *O. R.*, Ser. I, vol. 46, pt. 2, 1222.

from commissary officers for funds or transportation. With these requisites they were certain they could maintain the armies;[29] without them they were helpless. Because neither of these requisites could be supplied, the eastern Confederate armies, especially Lee's, ended the war practically starved.

The one remaining question is: What help would the trans-Mississippi Department have been, if the Mississippi had been a southern river after 1863? The inquiry would be incomplete if we overlooked this most important of beef-producing areas. This was certainly the most prolific part of the country for beef, since Texas comprised most of the department. Northrop, himself, pointed out that Texas had been one of the main sources of beef and that he had obtained large numbers of animals from there.[30]

During the period of 1862–3 Northrop tried to bring herds from Texas and put them on Virginia grasslands, but the lack of good forage en route caused this attempt to fail. Later attempts proved more successful, as Northrop, in his report to the Secretary of War mentioned above, said that thousands had been obtained by swimming them over the Mississippi.[31]

The trans-Mississippi Department was not only concerned with shipping beef to the east, but also with subsisting the large numbers of troops stationed within its own limits. To feed these men, cured meat, in all forms, had to be supplied. Various ways of packing beef were practised, as evidenced by Northrop's statement that large quantities of pickled beef came from the west.[32] The great center of Jefferson, Texas, besides being an important quartermaster depot,[33] was the site of a number of commissary activities. One of these enterprises was the meat-packing establishment of J. B. Dunn. In late 1863 this firm entered into a contract with the Confederate States to slaughter and pack 150 beef cattle per day. The manner of packing was specifically stated: "The hind quarter . . . with the bone extracted to be smoked and dried the balance of the beef (or Such parts as are usually used in making a prime article of mess beef) to be pickled in the best manner . . ." Major W. H. Thomas, chief commissary of the trans-Mississippi Department, was to furnish 440,000 pounds of New Iberia salt to Dunn to enable him to cure the beef and to pack it. Major Thomas was also to furnish Dunn with 4,000 head of beef cattle before the

29. *Ibid.*, 1220–21, 1297; Longstreet, *Manassas to Appomattox*, 689.

30. *O. R.*, Ser. I, vol. 46, pt. 2, 1222.

31. See *supra*, note 28.

32. *Ibid.*

33. See the papers of Capt. N. A. Birge, A. Q. M., Jefferson, Texas, in The University of Texas Archives.

10th of January, 1864.[34] This is but one indication of the importance of the Texas beef supply.

Five days before all the beef should have been delivered, Kirby Smith directed that a "Board of Survey" should convene in Major Thomas' office to investigate the quality of beef packed by Dunn. The board, on the same day, reported the meat to be in good condition.[35]

The soldier, himself, was much more concerned with what he was issued in the way of meat than with how it was packed or by whom. And luckily the boy in butternut west of the Mississippi fared generally very well. He might complain of the quality of the beef given him, but rarely of the quantity, for he usually had plenty.[36] As the war dragged on and the east suffered more and more, the troops in the west continued in moderate comfort. Texas, as late as January of 1865, had abundant herds of beef, but the commissary officials found that they were hampered in getting them because the people refused to accept the currency which the commissaries were forced to use.[37]

The foregoing evidence clearly shows that the trans-Mississippi Department—of which Texas was the major part—could have been of immeasurable help to the eastern Confederacy had the two been in direct communication. It would certainly be too much to claim that such communication might have turned the tide in favor of the South, but it is not too much to say that it would have been of great instrumentality in prolonging the conflict.

---

34. MS. Contract between Major W. H. Thomas, representing the Confederate States and J. S. Dunn, Sept. 19, 1863, in the Confederate Army Papers, Department of Archives, Louisiana State University.

35. Special Orders No. 2, Hdqrs. Trans-Miss. Dept., Shreveport, La., Jan. 5, 1864, and appended report of the Board of Survey. MSS. in the Reid Collection of the Confederate Army Papers, L.S.U. Archives. There is some doubt about the date of the board's report, but the date given in the text is probably correct.

The quality of the packing by Dunn must have fallen off later, as it caused widespread complaint. MS. Letter, Maj. W. H. Thomas to Maj. John Reid, Jan. 11, 1865, in Reid Collection, *loc. cit.*

36. MS. Letter, E. Jefferson Lee to "Sister Sallie," Aug. 26, 1864. In Mrs. Sallie Lee Boner's collection, see *supra*, note 3; also B. I. Wiley, *The Life of Johnny Reb*, 95.

37. MS. Letter, Maj. W. H. Thomas to J. S. Magruder, Jan. 11, 1865, Reid Collection, Confederate Army Papers, L.S.U. Archives.

"Old Time Slaves—Austin County." The lives of these two men, like those of thousands of other slaves, were changed forever by the Civil War, though to many in Texas the war seemed a distant and almost irrelevant conflict. *CN 01427. Courtesy Center for American History, University of Texas at Austin.*

Slaves and Rebels: The Peculiar Institution in Texas, 1861–1865

James Marten*

There were nearly two hundred thousand African American slaves in Texas when the Civil War began. This number was increased thirty to forty thousand during the war by the influx of slaves from Louisiana, Arkansas, and Missouri brought in by refugee planters escaping Federal occupation of their states.

The majority of Texas slaves continued to work on farms and plantations without interruption as the war went on. Some went off to war with their masters as servants, a few ran away to join the Union army, and others escaped to Mexico while serving as teamsters in the cotton trade. In this article James Marten, associate professor of history at Marquette University, notes that although some Texas slaveowners believed they detected deterioration of slave behavior, most slaves did not seriously challenge the slave system during the war. Randolph B. Campbell, whose An Empire for Slavery: The Peculiar Institution in Texas *(Baton Rouge: Louisiana State University Press, 1989) is the most thorough study of slavery in the Lone Star State,*

* James Marten, "Slaves and Rebels: The Peculiar Institution in Texas, 1861–1865," *East Texas Historical Journal*, XXVIII (Spring, 1990), 29–36. Reprinted with permission of the East Texas Historical Association.

writes that *"slaves in Texas generally knew what the war meant, but they did relatively little to hinder the Confederate military effort or contribute to Union victory"*
(p. 247).

For more on the role of Texas slaves in the war see James Marten, Texas Divided:
Loyalty and Dissent in the Lone Star State, 1856–1874 *(Lexington: University
Press of Kentucky, 1990); Cecil Earl Harper Jr., "Slavery without Cotton: Hunt
County, Texas, 1846–1864,"* Southwestern Historical Quarterly, *LXXXVIII (Apr.,
1985), 386–405; and Drew Gilpin Faust, "Trying to Do a Man's Business; Gender
Violence and Slave Management in Civil War Texas," in Faust,* Southern Stories in
Peace and War *(Columbia: University of Missouri Press, 1992), 174–192.*

That the Civil War changed the lives of southern blacks forever is a truism that
tends to obscure the drama that slaves experienced during the war. The Confederate surrender dealt the institution of slavery its final blow, but the war years
already had seen drastic changes in the lives and status of slaves. All over the
South thousands of slaves flocked to areas occupied by Northern armies seeking
long-denied education in missionary schools, proving themselves in the federal
army, and broadening their economic opportunities.[1] Far from the liberating
Union lines, Texas slaves endured a different kind of war than did blacks east of
the Mississippi River. "White man," said a former Texas slave to a WPA inter-
viewer long after the Civil War had ended, "we 'uns didn't know dere am de
war. We seed some sojers at de star[t], but dat all." Indeed, although many
black Texans extended the boundaries of their bondage, they usually had no
choice but to wait out the war with their masters, while the masters had no
choice but to rely on their slaves even more than they had in peace time.[2]

    This may have been difficult in light of the Lone Star State's recent history.
Six months before Texas seceded from the Union, the "Texas Troubles"—a wave

---

1. See Benjamin Quarles, *The Negro in the Civil War* (Boston, 1953); Harvey Wish, "Slave Disloyalty Under the Confederacy," *Journal of Negro History* (October 1938), pp. 435–450; C. Peter Ribley,
Slaves and Freedmen in Civil War Louisiana (Baton Rouge, 1976); Clarence L. Mohr, *On the Thresh-
old of Freedom, Masters and Slaves in Civil War Georgia* (Athens, 1986); Robert Francis Engs, *Freedom's First Generation: Black Hampton, Virginia, 1861–1890* (Philadelphia, 1979), pp. 3–79; Ronald L.
F. Davis, *Good and Faithful Labor: from Slavery to Sharecropping in the Natchez District, 1860–1890*
(Westport, Conn., 1982), pp. 60–73; Willie Lee Rose, *Rehearsal for Reconstruction: The Port Loyal Experiment* (New York, 1964); and James H. Brewer, *The Confederate Negro: Virginia's Craftsmen and
Military Laborers, 1861–1865* (Durham, 1969).

2. George Rawick (ed.), *The American Slave: A Composite Autobiography* (Westport, Conn., 1972),
p. 140. Despite the spelling errors and phonetic exaggerations inflicted upon black oral testimony by
1930s researchers, I have retained them as they appear in Rawick's splendid compilation of interviews of former slaves.

of arson and alleged poisonings—convinced white Texans that meddling Northern preachers and peddlers had instigated a massive slave insurrection. Most of the business district of Dallas burned down on July 8, 1860, and fires broke out in a number of other north Texas towns. Rumors flew around the state that the slaves had planned a general uprising for August 6 and town meetings hastily organized vigilance committees to patrol rural areas and keep an eye on suspicious strangers. Members of the Chatfield Vigilance Association pledged to defend their families, as well as their "honor and property" against the "robbers, murderers, assassins, traitors . . . and thieves" at large in the land. To that end, vigilantes hanged at least ten white men and nearly thirty blacks. Relative peace returned to Texas by early autumn.[3]

Texans did not often discuss the faithfulness of their slaves during the next five years; perhaps the latent but ever-present potential for violence within the slave system caused them to reassure themselves with silence. "The negroes, as a general thing," reported the *Marshall Texas Republican* after the shooting had stopped, "have acted very well towards their owners and the white residents of the South, during the disturbed condition of the country for the last four years." A few joined "the invaders," but only because of their "ignorance and the superior control of the white man." With a confidence that belied whites' later reactions to blacks during Reconstruction, the Republican asserted that the "war has demonstrated . . . that the idea of negro insurrections, once so prevalent, is a humbug."[4]

The war-time behavior of many Texas slaves supported the editorialist's assertion. Slave members of a Marshall Methodist Church hosted a supper for the minister and other guests early in 1865, while blacks in Houston raised $40 for sick soldiers with a "grand ball" in July 1862. James Hayes, a slave on a plantation near Marshall, validated the popular image of the faithful slave after his master marched off to the army. Whenever Hayes returned from town with the mail, his mistress "run to meet me, anxious like, to open de letter, and was skeert to do it." One day he "fotcher a letter and I could feel it in my bones; dere was trouble in dat letter." Young Master Ben—the oldest son, who had

---

3. William W. White, "The Texas Slave Insurrection of 1860," *Southwestern Historical Quarterly* (January 1949), pp. 259–276; *Navarro Express*, August 11, 1860. See also Wendell G. Addington, "Slave Insurrections in Texas," *Journal of Negro History* (October 1950), pp. 408–434; Bill Ledbetter, "Slave Unrest and White Panic: The Impact of Black Republicanism in Antebellum Texas," *Texana* (1972), pp. 342–348; and Donald E. Reynolds, "Smith County and its Neighbors During the Slave Insurrection Panic of 1860," *Chronicles of Smith County* (Fall 1971), pp. 1–8.

4. *Marshall Texas Republican*, June 2, 1865.

gone off to war with his father—had been killed in action; "all de ole folks, cullud and white, was cryin' . . . When de body come home, dere's a powerful big funeral and after dat, dere's powerful weepin's and sadness on dat place."[5]

Many slaves went to war as horse-tenders, nurses, or personal servants to their masters. Rube Witt enlisted in the Confederate army but reached Mansfield, Louisiana, after Confederate forces had turned back General Nathaniel P. Banks' Yankee troops, while James Cape helped rob a Yankee train and suffered a shoulder wound while fighting in Tennessee. Some slaves went to great lengths to prove their loyalty. William Byrd walked all the way from Virginia to Texas after his master became a Federal prisoner and waited until after the war to be freed. Henry Smith marched beside his master's son in the Texas Brigade until the latter was killed at Petersburg, then buried him and carried his belongings back to his family in Texas.[6]

Slaves who remained at home frequently demonstrated their loyalty when they "kept de work on de plantations going, for dey had to keep on livin' an' some one had to do dis work." The slaves on Burke Simpson's plantation "jis stayed an' took keer of things for de Master while [he] wuz away to de war." When Union troops invaded South Texas and tried to entice slaves away from the King Ranch, a Houston newspaper proudly reported, they "remained with their mistress . . . proving true to the last." Few blacks considered escaping from the Bexar County ranch on which Felix Haywood worked, because "we was happy." Life "went on jus' like it always had before the war . . . We get layed-onto time on time, but gen'rally life was . . . just as good as a sweet potato." Slaves were not unaware of the threat they posed to Southern society, however. "If every mother's son of a black had thrown 'way his hoe and took up a gun to fight for his own freedom along with the Yankees," Haywood believed, "the war'd been over before it began." Nevertheless, "we couldn't help stick to our masters. We couldn't no more shoot 'em than we could fly."[7]

Life did not continue unbroken on every Texas plantation. James Hayes recalled that although day to day life went on "like always . . . some vittles was scarce." The war "sho' did mess us up," according to Mollie Dawson of Navarro County. Since much of the plantation's produce went toward feeding and clothing Confederate soldiers, "we did'nt have as much ter eat as we had been having

5. *Marshall Texas Republican*, January 6, 1865; *Houston Tri-Weekly Telegraph*, July 30, 1862; *The American Slave*, v. 4, pt. 2, pp. 126–129.

6. *The American Slave*, v. 5, pt. 4, p. 20; v. 4, pt. 1, pp. 194–196 and 182–184; suppl. 2, v. 9, pt. 8, pp. 3609–3623.

7. *The American Slave*, suppl. 2, v. 9, pt. 8, p. 3561; *Houston Tri-Weekly Telegraph*, January 11, 1864; *The American Slave*, v. 4, pt. 2, pp. 131–134.

and our clothes and shoes had ter last us longer." Masters bound for the army often found overseers to take their place. Andy Anderson's master hired a man named Delbridge, and "after dat, de hell start to pop." Delbridge "half starve us niggers," Anderson remembered, "and he want mo' work and he start de whippin's . . . I guess dat Delbridge go to hell when he died, but I don't see how de debbil could stand him." The fighting reached other slaves, as well. Philla Thomas' father, laboring on Confederate breastworks, died during a Yankee bombardment of Galveston, and when Federal gunboats lobbed shells into Corpus Christi, "all de folks . . . takes to de woods and sev'ral am still gone." Slave children were warned against going into the woods by themselves. Manuel Armstrong, a young boy during the war, recalled that deserters from the Confederate army hid in a nearby forest. Fearing that "de chillen would tell on 'em," the fugitives would "ketch dem an' whip dem an' scare dem an' sen' dem home so they wouldn't come back no mo!"[8]

In the face of these hardships, Texas slaves could hardly ignore the war, although whites tried to prevent them from hearing news from the front. One plantation mistress remembered that "the white men didn't talk the situation around where the niggers could hear . . . knowing that the nigger is a natural news ferret, and the biggest gossiper that ever was." Nevertheless, she recalled, "they knew that everything they said finally reached the niggers' ears." Few slaves "in the whole South ever let on that they knew anything . . . They just kept their mouths shut, and their eyes and ears open." Former slave J. W. King said that "some of de men on de plantation would slip up to a open winda at de big house at night and . . . lissen whut was read f'om a letter." Bad news for the Confederacy fueled the slaves' hopes. Despite their distance from the battlefields, they instinctively grasped what was at stake in the white men's war. Around late-night fires, Abram Sells recalled, the older men would crouch, "stirrin' the ashes with the pokes and rakin' out the roas' taters. They's smokin' the old corn cob pipe and homemade tobacco and whisperin' right low and quiet like what they's gwineter do and whar they's gwineter go when Mister Lincoln, he turn them free."[9]

Despite the fairly normal war-time relations between whites and blacks in Texas, those whispered conversations around late-night fires—combined with the absence of a large percentage of the white adult male population—helped

---

8. *The American Slave*, v. 4, pt. 2, pp. 116–119; suppl. 2, v. 4, pt. 3, p. 1141; v. 4, pt. 1, pp. 14–16; v. 5, pt. 4, p. 92; v. 5, pt. 3, p. 249; suppl. 2, v. 2, pt. 1, p. 64.

9. *The American Slave*, suppl. 2, v. 10, pt. 9, p. 4335; suppl. 2, v. 6, pt. 5, pp. 2213–2214; v. 5, pt. 4, p. 14.

inspire the surliness that some Texans detected in their slaves. A Houston news-paper complained in January 1865 about the insolence of the city's blacks. They uttered obscenities in the presence of children, refused to yield roads or side-walks to white ladies, and bought illicit liquor from white merchants. The edi-tor declared that local slave owners were "altogether too lenient . . . and too regardless of their [slaves'] behavior." Likewise, the *San Antonio News* reported in mid-1864 that blacks were "pulling on important airs" on that city's streets. A "general negrow row" ensued in Nueces County when a female slave stole about $2000 and distributed it among her black and Hispanic friends. Authorities re-covered only $700. A Harrison County black allegedly plundered the home of a Mrs. Manson, whose husband was off fighting the war, then burned it down to escape detection. A few whites also reported aberrant behavior among slaves on their plantations. Jack, a slave on John B. Walker's plantation, ran away three times during the summer of 1864. Once he left after having "refused Authority," and on another escapade he "borrowed" a mule.[10]

Mrs. Lizzie Neblett recorded the deterioration of slave behavior on her Grimes County plantation in a series of letters to her husband Will, who was away in the army for much of the war. She complained late in 1863 that most of the slaves would not do anything unless they were told, and that "I find I must think continually for them." Several slaves resisted whippings from the overseer or ran away, part of a disturbing trend of insolence and misbehavior among slaves in the neighborhood. The situation had gotten so bad that many owners were afraid to flog their slaves. One slave, threatened with a beating by one of Mrs. Neblett's elderly neighbors, "cursed the old man all to pieces, and walked off in the woods." He came back only after his master promised not to punish him. Another neighbor's slaves rode his horses all over the county during their nocturnal adventures, and she doubted whether her own slaves were much bet-ter: "I believe if I was to tell [the overseer] to whip one of the negroes they would resist & it would make matters no better so I shall say nothing, and if they stop work entirely, I will try & feel thankful if they let me alone." Fear had also entered her relationship with the slaves: "I won't sleep with my doors open, any more, & if they break open either door or window I'll have time to be bet-ter prepared for them & will fight till I die." She continued in this vein in a lat-

10. *Houston Tri-Weekly Telegraph*, January 24, 1865; quoted in Robert L. Kerby, *Kirby Smith's Con-federacy: The Trans-Mississippi South, 1863–1865* (New York, 1972), p. 401; Rufe Byler to Martha Byler, May 15, 1863, Dobie-Byler Family Papers, Barker Texas History Center; *Marshall Texas Repub-lican*, March 5, 1863; John B. Walker Plantation Book, March 30, and August 13, 14, 16, 1864, Barker Texas History Center.

er letter when she wrote, "I would not care if they killed me, if they did not do worse."[11]

The large migration of blacks into Texas from other states added a unique dimension to the story of slavery in Civil War Texas. Thousands of them were shipped from more distressed portions of the Confederacy during the course of the war. Many came from nearby Louisiana and Arkansas, but planters from as far away as Virginia also brought their slaves to Texas. Late in the war, Elvira Boles came to Texas with her master, "a dodgin' in and out, runnin' from de Yankees" all the way from Mississippi. Somewhere along "dat road," Elvira's baby died and was buried in an unmarked grave. Tempe Elgin was a toddler when her master brought her mother and sister to Texas from Arkansas; her father, who belonged to a different owner, followed them for sixty miles, imploring his wife to escape with him. She refused, "so pappy rode away on his hoss and mammy never did see him again." The odyssey of Josh Miles began when his owner decided to leave Virginia early in the war. They reached Texas two years later after lengthy stays in Nashville, Memphis, and Vicksburg were interrupted by invading Yankee armies. Another former slave told of moving to Texas from Franklin, Louisiana, with about 300 other slaves, while Van Moore, who grew up in Texas, recalled his mother's stories of how, as a band of slaves and their masters set out for Texas from war-torn Virginia, the "white folks" encouraged the slaves by telling them that in Texas "de lakes [were] full of syrup and covered with batter cakes, and dey won't have to work so hard." Other masters showed less concern for their slaves' states of mind. Litt Young journeyed west from Vicksburg in 1863 under an armed guard who tied the male slaves to trees at night.[12]

Some Texas slaves, reversing the migratory process, hurried the day of freedom by escaping from their masters and a handful—forty-seven—joined the Union army. Some slaves on a Williamson County plantation ran away—despite the nearly automatic "whippin' at de stake" that would greet them if caught—when a cruel overseer took over for their master, who had gone to fight in the war. Susan Ross' brother, after refusing to go to the army, fled his master's plantation after a beating so severe that "you couldn't tell what he look like." Although the war years did see an apparent escalation in the number of runaway slaves, escape held little chance of success, at least according to one

---

11. Lizzie to Will Neblett, November 4, August 13 and 18, 1863, Lizzie Neblett Papers, Barker Texas History Center.

12. Kerby, *Kirby Smith's Confederacy*, 255; *The American Slave*, v. 4, pt. 1, p. 108; suppl. 2, v. 4, pt. 2, pp. 1292–1294; v. 5, pt. 3, pp. 79–80, 29–31, 129; v. 5, pt. 4, pp. 227–231.

Burleson County ex-slave. "I never seen any slaves that tried to run away until after the war," said John Mosley, "but . . . they never got very far at that." At least one master had "all de quarters move up close to de big house, so if we tries to make de run for it in de night he can catch us." Punishment was sure and swift for captured escapees. Lee McGillery saw "a few slaves try to run away to the north after the war started and when the white folks of the south find them they would most of the time jest shoot them. Some few they never did find."[13]

Most of the slaves attempting to escape exploited the traditional sympathy between Mexicans and blacks by making their way to Mexico. Felix Haywood declared that "in Mexico you could be free. They didn't care what color you was, black, white, yellow, or blue." Haywood claimed that hundreds of slaves fled to Mexico, and "got on all right," becoming in effect, Mexicans, and raising their children to speak only Spanish. At one point Mexicans on the south bank of the Rio Grande rigged up a flatboat in the middle of the river. Once a fugitive reached the boat he could easily pull himself across to freedom. Jacob Branch reported that slave patrols "rid[e] de Mexican side [of] dat river all de time, but plenty slaves git through, anyway." Sallie Wroe's father hauled a load of Travis County cotton to the border. Upon reaching his destination, he and a number of other drivers paddled a bale of cotton over the river to Mexico. When he returned to his family after the war, he told them "he done git 'long fine with Mexico. He learnt to talk jes' like them." Similar instances led the *Houston Tri-Weekly Telegraph* to warn its readers against taking even "their trusty negroes" to Matamoros on business. The booming border town was "overrunning with these trusty, now insolent negroes." "Loose colored women" and escaped slaves with plenty of spending money would lure otherwise faithful slaves into the welcome anonymity of the city.[14]

As a non-citizen, even the least faithful slave legally could not be charged with disloyalty. A Confederate district judge ruled in May 1863, that since slaves "are not members of the body politic—& do not owe allegiance to the Govt.,"

---

13. Frank Smyrl, "Unionism, Abolitionism, and Vigilantism in Texas, 1856–1865" (Master of Arts thesis, University of Texas, 1965), pp. 146–160; *The American Slave*, v. 4, pt. 1, pp. 14–16; v. 5, pt. 3, p. 256; suppl. 2, v. 7, pt. 6, p. 2801; v. 5, pt. 3, p. 249; v. 7, pt. 6, p. 2495. In Tennessee, where Union lines were always relatively close and where masters had far more to worry about than a few unruly bondsmen, slaves aggressively forced a relaxation of controls and often ran away. See John Cimprich, *Slavery's End in Tennessee, 1861–1865* (University, 1985).

14. *The American Slave*, v. 4, pt. 2, p. 132; v. 4, pt. 1, p. 141; v. 5, pt. 4, p. 224; *Houston Tri-Weekly Telegraph*, December 29, 1864. For the best survey of racial tension between Hispanics and Anglos in Texas—including Mexican attitudes about slaves—see Arnoldo DeLeon, *They Called Them Greasers: Anglo Attitudes Toward Mexicans in Texas, 1821–1900* (Austin, 1983).

they could not be tried for treason. Nevertheless, the state legislature responded to the potential threat of rebellious slaves and Northern invaders by passing several laws aimed at preventing slave insurrections—especially those instigated by marauding Yankee troops or their emissaries. An act passed on March 5, 1863, condemned persons convicted of selling, giving, or loaning, any sort of weapon or ammunition to a slave to up to five years hard labor, while another established a penalty of from five to fifteen years for any officer of the United States armed services guilty of "inciting insurrection or insubordination." In addition, "any person of color" captured while invading Texas could be enslaved, a fate suffered by at least a few black Yankees, and it was illegal to leave slaves alone without "free white" supervision or to allow a slave to pretend to own or to control property. Other "disloyal" slaves fell outside the bounds of the law. Late in 1864, three railroad workers took eight hours to beat a black man to death for allegedly stealing three yards of homespun cloth, while another slave suspected of murdering his master was captured in Rusk County, brought home to Tyler, and burned at the stake. Vigilant Texans near La Grange hanged an escaped slave named Yorick—two weeks after General Robert E. Lee surrendered at Appomattox—when he was found "endeavoring to accomplish a purpose too horrid to mention" upon a "German girl."[15]

Despite the problems caused by some Texas slaves during the Civil War, neither the war nor the behavior of their chattel property led Texas Confederates to question the desirability of retaining the peculiar institution. Some masters hurried to the frontier of Texas late in the war, hoping to outrun the Yankees and establish themselves far beyond the effective boundaries of emancipation. A Travis County slave owner relocated in Robertson County, according to one of his bondsmen, "cause he done figured de Yankees can't git up dere." As late as May 1865, owners of runaway slaves still offered rewards of up to $500 in Confederate currency, and J. L. Maxwell of Collin County offered to exchange his small farm for "Negro property" that same month. Even after the remnants of

---

15. H. P. N. Gammel (comp.), *The Laws of the State of Texas,* v. 5 (Austin, 1898), pp. 601–603, 608–610, 484, 762–763; Gary Wilson, "The Ordeal of William H. Cowdin and the Officers of the Forty-Second Massachusetts Regiment: Union Prisoners in Texas," *East Texas Historical Journal* (Spring 1985) pp. 16–26; May 30, 1863, William Pitt Ballinger Diary, Barker Texas History Center; *Marshall Texas Republican,* December 23, 1864; Kerby, *Kirby Smith's Confederacy,* p. 257; *San Antonio Herald,* copies in the *Marshall Texas Republican,* May 19, 1865. Slaves' liability under the Confederate treason laws rarely came up during the war. The only opinion issued by the Confederate Attorney General that dealt with slaves established the parameters of the government's financial liability for damage to slaves working on government projects. Rembert W. Patrice (ed.), *Opinions of the Confederate Attorneys General, 1861–1865* (Buffalo, 1950), pp. 51–53.

the Confederate presence in Texas had been surrendered, the *Marshall Texas Republican* confidently predicted that Southerners would be allowed to keep their slaves in some form of perpetual servitude. Emancipation "naturally" would be followed by "vagrancy, filth, disease, and crime" among the freedmen; masters should be kind to their servants, motivated by "an attachment for the race, by a grateful remembrance for past services."[16]

The experiences of masters and slaves in Texas during the Civil War flowed out of two conflicting pre-war situations: the general faithfulness of most slaves counterpointed to the constant threat that they posed to the institution. While some Texas slaves confirmed Southern fears of that threat by taking advantage of war-time tumult to expand the boundaries of their lives, most did not, in any meaningful way, challenge the restrictions placed on their lives by the peculiar institution. In fact, at least one free black voluntarily gave up his freedom during the war. George, a "free man of color," petitioned the Collin County District Court to become the slave of James B. Thomas. As Martin Jackson's father told him, "the War wasn't going to last forever, but . . . our forever was going to be spent living among the Southerners after they got licked." Reconstruction would, in many ways, fulfill Jackson's prophecy.[17]

---

16. *The American Slave*, v. 5, pt. 4, p. 125; *Marshall Texas Republican*, May 19 and June 16, 1865.

17. Collin County District Court, Civil Minutes, 1858–1864, vol. B, p. 466; *The American Slave*, v. 4, pt. 2, p. 189. The Seventh Legislature passed a law allowing free blacks to select their own masters and become slaves early in 1858. Gammel, *The Laws of Texas*, v. 4, pp. 947–948. The most useful surveys of blacks in Reconstruction Texas are James Smallwood's *Time of Hope, Time of Despair: Black Texans During Reconstruction* (Port Washington, New York, 1981), and Jesse Dorsett's "Blacks in Reconstruction Texas, 1865–1877" (Doctoral Dissertation, Texas Christian University, 1981).

"A Group of Contrabands," stereo card, ca. 1864. *Courtesy Lawrence T. Jones III.*

$\mathcal{A}$ Texas Cavalry Raid: Reaction to Black Soldiers and Contrabands

ANNE J. BAILEY*

Confederate treatment of captured African American soldiers in the Union army was one of the dark chapters in the Civil War. Many southerners declared they would show no quarter to captured blacks and their white officers. In his Pulitizer Prize-winning Battle Cry of Freedom *(New York: Oxford University Press, 1988), 793, James M. McPherson points out that "many black prisoners never made it to prison camp." Dozens of African Americans were killed at Milliken's Bend, Fort Pillow, Poison Spring, Petersburg and elsewhere.*

Unfortunately, Texans were involved in several such affairs, including Milliken's Bend and Poison Spring. Another incident occurred in northern Louisiana three weeks after Milliken's Bend. On this occasion African Americans were killed by members of Colonel William H. Parsons's Texas cavalry brigade in a raid along the Mississippi. Anne J. Bailey, associate professor of history at the University of Arkansas and a leading authority on the Civil War in the Trans-Mississippi, describes the affair in this essay. She concludes that the reaction of these Texas cavalrymen to black troops "stemmed from their cultural heritage, the separateness of their

---

* Anne J. Bailey, "A Texas Cavalry Raid: Reaction to Black Soldiers and Contrabands," *Civil War History,* XXXV (June, 1989), 138–152. Reprinted with permission of the Kent State University Press.

department from the rest of the Confederacy, and, probably most decisive, their strong desire to protect their families in Texas from the ravages of war."

For more on this subject, see Bailey, Between the Enemy and Texas: Parsons's Texas Cavalry in the Civil War *(Fort Worth: Texas Christian University Press, 1989); Bailey, "Was There a Massacre at Poison Spring?"* Military History of the Southwest, *XX (Fall, 1990), 157–168; and Joseph T. Glatthaar,* Forged in Battle: The Civil War Alliance of Black Soldiers and White Officers *(New York: Free Press, 1990).*

In June 1863 when Major General Ulysses S. Grant's army bottled up the Confederates in Vicksburg, the Union campaign to gain control of the Mississippi River moved into its final stage. As summer began many Southerners feared the army defending the town could not hold out much longer. Nevertheless, Confederate troops on the west side of the river displayed guarded optimism that they still might offer some support to their besieged comrades. Early in June, therefore, Texas infantry assaulted enemy positions on the Louisiana bank opposite Vicksburg and late in the month Texas cavalry raided Federal strongholds in the same region. The former, an attack on Milliken's Bend, has often been utilized by historians to point out atrocities that accompany war. The latter, a cavalry raid just over three weeks later, had much the same result, but has never been examined carefully. Neither of these forays, however, effected any military significance. The major result of the fighting "was to publicize the controversy surrounding northern employment of black troops."[1]

Events in the Trans-Mississippi have never received the same recognition as those in other theaters. Perhaps one reason little is known of the Texas cavalry raid in Louisiana is because any account of Southern brutality toward blacks fades in comparison with Nathan Bedford Forrest's infamous assault upon Fort Pillow in April 1864. Forrest's biographer, Robert S. Henry, correctly observed, "Fort Pillow was the 'atrocity' of the war." Certainly, historians have evaluated and reevaluated the incident over and over.[2]

---

1. James M. McPherson, *Battle Cry of Freedom* (New York and Oxford: Oxford Univ. Press, 1988), 634.

2. Robert Selph Henry, *"First With The Most" Forrest* (1944; reprint, Wilmington, N.C.: Broadfoot Publishing Co., 1987), 248; John Cimprich and Robert C. Mainfort, Jr., "Fort Pillow Revisited: New Evidence About an Old Controversy," *Civil War History,* 28 (Dec. 1982):293–306; Albert Castel, "The Fort Pillow Massacre: A Fresh Examination of the Evidence," ibid., 4 (Mar. 1958):37–50; idem, "Fort Pillow: Victory or Massacre," *American History Illustrated,* 9 (Apr. 1974):4–11, 46–48; Charles W. Anderson, "The True Story of Fort Pillow," *Confederate Veteran,* 3 (Nov. 1895):326; John L. Jordan, "Was There a Massacre at Fort Pillow?" *Tennessee Historical Quarterly,* 6 (June 1947):122–32.

The use of former slaves as soldiers in the United States Army often aroused heated emotions. With enmity widespread, it is surprising there were not more violent racial incidents. James M. McPherson, who has masterfully chronicled the uphill struggle of blacks during the Civil War, concluded: "The southern response to emancipation and the enlistment of black troops was ferocious—at least on paper and, regretably [*sic*], sometimes in fact as well."[3] Without the sensitive issue of Confederate treatment of contrabands, the cavalry raid along the Louisiana shore—less than a week before Vicksburg's surrender—would have scant importance.

To Confederates along the Mississippi, Vicksburg was only a fragment of a much larger picture—Federal forces threatened vital areas of Louisiana. To meet this emergency, soon after Lieutenant General Edmund Kirby Smith had assumed command of the Trans-Mississippi Department early in 1863 he had started concentrating available troops to reinforce Major General Richard Taylor's District of Louisiana. By June Major General John Bankhead Magruder, in charge of the District of Texas, reported he had forwarded almost five thousand men across the Sabine River.[4] From Arkansas Lieutenant General Theophilus H. Holmes sent Major General John G. Walker's Texas Infantry Division.[5] These reinforcements did not arrive in time to prevent a Federal push up the Red River toward Alexandria, but after occupying the town Major General Nathaniel P. Banks halted his advance. Urged by Grant to take part in a joint campaign along the Mississippi, Banks concentrated his men near the Confederate stronghold of Port Hudson. By late May Banks had moved to a position outside the fortification while Grant threatened Vicksburg.

The Confederate situation along the river was critical. Taylor had to utilize most of his available troops to confront Banks's army. Moreover, Taylor recognized the futility of offering substantial support to Vicksburg. He later pointed out, however, that "public opinion would condemn us if we did not *try to do something*."[6] Thus, to exhibit concern for the defenders in Vicksburg, Confederates raided Union positions in northeast Louisiana. These movements, too late

3. McPherson, *Battle Cry of Freedom*, 565.

4. Report of J. B. Magruder, 8 June 1863, *The War of the Rebellion: A Compilation of the Official Records of the Union and Confederate Armies*, 128 vols. (Washington, D.C.: GPO, 1880–1901), ser. 1, vol. 26, pt. 2:58 (hereafter cited as *OR*; citations are to series I unless otherwise noted).

5. E. K. Smith to T. H. Holmes, 14 Apr. 1863, ibid., 15: 1041; E. K. Smith to T. H. Holmes, 15 Apr. 1863, ibid., 1042–43; E. K. Smith to T. H. Holmes, 19 Apr. 1863, ibid., 22, pt. 2:828; Richard Taylor, *Destruction and Reconstruction* (London: William Blackwood and Sons, 1879), 178–79; John D. Winters, *The Civil War in Louisiana* (Baton Rouge: Louisiana State Univ. Press, 1963), 198.

6. By June Taylor believed that he should place his major emphasis on relieving the Confederates at Port Hudson rather than operating opposite Vicksburg. Taylor, *Destruction and Reconstruction*,

and ineffectual to alter the outcome of Grant's campaign, scarcely concerned the Federal commander, but the Texans' alleged murder of blacks did produce a reaction.

Early in June Walker's division of Texas infantry assaulted Milliken's Bend, a Federal supply depot on the Mississippi. One important detail, often overlooked by historians, is that this was the first actual combat situation for many of these Texans, and their reaction to fighting blacks in Federal blue only reinforced what Bell I. Wiley believed—most Southerners "felt as the Mississippian who wrote his mother: 'I hope I may never see a Negro Soldier,' he said, 'or I cannot be . . . a Christian Soldier.'" Many blacks were brutally murdered; one Federal officer claimed the slaughter at Milliken's Bend was "butchery." When Rear Admiral David Porter arrived on the scene he had described "quite an ugly sight. The dead negroes lined the ditch inside of the parapet, or levee, and were mostly shot on the top of the head."[7] The charges of atrocity coupled with the stubborn resistance of the black troops only served to help relieve widespread prejudice against blacks in combat. Charles Dana, assistant secretary of war, believed the bravery of the soldiers in the fight "completely revolutionized the sentiment of the army with regard to the employment of negro troops."[8]

Yet the foray had brought no military rewards, and Taylor considered transferring Walker's command south of the Red River to assist his troops around Port Hudson. When Kirby Smith disapproved, Taylor decided instead to hold the force in the northeastern part of the state until the events at Vicksburg developed.[9] To harass Union positions along the river Walker needed mounted re-

---

179. Also see Robert L. Kerby, *Kirby Smith's Confederacy: The Trans-Mississippi South, 1863–1865* (New York: Columbia Univ. Press, 1972), 112–15.

7. Bell Irvin Wiley, *The Life of Johnny Reb: The Common Soldier of the Confederacy* (1943; reprint, Baton Rouge: Louisiana State Univ. Press, 1987), 314; Report of Abraham E. Strickle, 9 June 1863, *OR*, vol . 24, pt. 2:453–54; Report of David D. Porter, 7 June 1863, *OR*, vol. 24, pt. 2:453–54. See also Herbert Aptheker, "Negro Casualties in the Civil War," *The Journal of Negro History*, 32 (Jan. 1947):10–80.

8. Charles Dana quoted in Dudley Taylor Cornish, *The Sable Arm: Negro Troops in the Union Army, 1861–1865* (1956; reprint, New York: W. W. Norton & Co., Inc., 1966), 145.

9. Jackson Beauregard Davis, "The Life of Richard Taylor," (Master's thesis, Louisiana State University, 1937), 75–76; Report of Richard Taylor, 11 June 1863, *OR*, vol. 24, pt. 2:461–62; Report of J. G. Walker, 10 July 1863, ibid., 466. For a detailed account of confederate operations west of the Mississippi River see Edwin C. Bearss, "The Trans-Mississippi Confederates Attempt to Relieve Vicksburg," *McNeese Reviews*, 15 (1964):46–70, 16 (1965):46–67. Walker's Division consisted of the brigades of Henry McCulloch, Horace Randal, and James Hawes. An excellent narrative of Walker's operations along the Mississippi River can be found in Norman D. Brown, ed., *Journey to Pleasant Hill: The Civil War Letters of Captain Elijah P. .Petty, Walker's Texas Division, C.S.A.* (San Antonio: Institute of Texan Cultures, 1982), 234–45.

inforcements; therefore, Kirby Smith ordered Holmes to forward a mounted brigade toward Louisiana where the troops were to raze locations under Federal control. "All such should be destroyed," he instructed, "and the negroes captured."[10]

Holmes ordered a brigade of Texas cavalry commanded by Colonel William Henry Parsons to Louisiana. He decided not to send the entire brigade, however, for fear he might weaken his own defenses around Little Rock. Holmes released the 12th and 19th Texas cavalries and one section of the 10th Texas Field Battery, but kept the remainder of the brigade in Arkansas.[11] These men were seasoned veterans—the 12th Texas had been among the first regiments to arrive in Arkansas in 1862 and had since earned the reputation as an outstanding fighting unit. The 19th Texas and the battery had just returned from Missouri after taking part in Major General John S. Marmaduke's unsuccessful raid upon Cape Girardeau.

Colonel Parsons, who viewed this opportunity to assist the defenders at Vicksburg with solemn regard, recognized that to be effective with his small force he must carefully plan his strategy. Over a year's experience assaulting enemy supply trains and patrols in Arkansas had taught him the necessity of careful planning. Thus he preceded his men to Louisiana in order to personally reconnoiter the situation. When the two regiments crossed the Louisiana border late in June, the colonel had already determined the enemy's strengths and weaknesses. He had, according to a member of the 12th Texas in a letter to a Houston newspaper, scouted "single-handed and alone, on his own hook, thro' the swamps, keeping his own counsel and learning the whereabouts of the Federals, and finding the best point for striking a telling blow; which self-imposed task, as the sequel proved, he accomplished most successfully."[12]

Parsons reunited with his men June 27 near Lake Providence where he told them what he had learned during the reconnaissance. He spoke of the planned campaign, and his manner of deliverance strengthened the men's loyalty and

---

10. S. S. Anderson to T. H. Holmes, 4 June 1863, *OR*, vol. 22, pt. 2:856–57.

11. Not accompanying Colonel Parsons to Arkansas were Colonel George W. Carter's 21st Texas Cavalry, several companies in a battalion under Major Charles L. Morgan, and a section of the battery under Major Joseph H. Pratt. T. H. Holmes to Sterling Price, 13 June 1863, ibid., 866; W. B. Blair to Sterling Price, 9 June 1863, ibid., 864: T. H. Holmes to Sterling Price, 9 June 1863, ibid. Special Orders, No. 71, 2 June 1863, *OR*, vol. 22, pt. 2:851.

12. "Col. Parsons' Cavalry Raid in the Valley of the Mississippi, nearly opposite Vicksburg . . ." by Soldat, *Houston Weekly Telegraph*, 4 Aug 1863 (hereafter Soldat, "Parsons' Cavalry Raid"). Soldat, sometimes spelled Solidat, was a member of the 12th Texas probably on the colonel's staff who wrote numerous articles for the Houston paper. His letters, which have proved quite accurate, provide information on events not otherwise recorded.

their determination to follow him in battle. Henry Orr, a private in the 12th Texas, recalled that the colonel addressed the troops "in an eloquent and patriotic strain, gave the soldiers great encouragement, and said he was glad that we are privileged to strike a blow for Vicksburg."[13] Another member of the 12th who listened to the "stirring, eloquent speech" observed "it forcibly struck me, much as a father would talk to his boys, of whom he was proud." Parsons told "them of the brave garrison at Vicksburg . . . that he could not take them there, but that he would take them where they would hear the sullen boom of the Vicksburg cannon. . . ." The men, he observed, "resolved to follow where he would lead, and nobly do or die for Vicksburg."[14]

Just after sunrise the next morning the troops, stimulated by Parsons's enthusiasm, left on the scout toward Lake Providence in the "highest spirits." A member of the 19th Texas pointed out: "Under the leadership of our deservedly popular and able commander (for he's nothing less) we proceeded so cautiously and securely. . . ."[15] When the troops stopped to rest in the camps of Walker's division, J. P. Blessington, a private in the 16th Texas Infantry commented: "As they passed by us, I could not but admire their horsemanship; they all appeared to be excellent horsemen, and at a distance their general appearance was decidedly showy and gallant." Although he noticed their uniforms "contained as many colors as the rainbow" the rifles and swords just issued to the command impressed him. Of this flashy force he noted, "their arms consisted mostly of Enfield rifles, slung to their saddles, while around the waist of each was buckled a heavy cavalry sword, which clattered at every movement of their horses. A pair of holster pistols attached to the pommels of their saddles completed their equipment."[16]

Parsons joined Walker's infantry on a raid through the region between Milliken's Bend and Lake Providence. "The object of the expedition," a member of the 19th Texas reported to the *Dallas Herald*, "proved to be to break up a nest of federals who were cultivating cotton and corn in the valley of Bayou Mason

---

13. Ibid.; Henry Orr to Father, 27 June 1863, John Q. Anderson, *Campaigning With Parsons' Texas Cavalry Brigade, CSA: The War Journals and Letters of the Four Orr Brothers, 12th Texas Cavalry Regiment* (Hillsboro, Tex.: Hill Junior College Press, 1967), 110–11.

14. Soldat, "Parsons' Cavalry Raid."

15. Henry Orr to Father, 27 June 1863, Anderson, *Campaigning With Parsons' Texas Cavalry Brigade*, 110–11; "Letter from Burford's Regiment" from J. E. T., 18 July 1863, *Dallas Herald*, 5 Aug. 1863 (hereafter J. E. T., "Letter from Burford's Regiment"). J. E. T. was probably James E. Terrell, adjutant of the regiment, who died at Jackson, Mississippi, in November 1863 while on his way to Richmond.

16. J. P. Blessington, *The Campaign of Walker's Texas Division by a Private Soldier* (New York: Lange, Little & Co., 1875), 113–14. Blessington mistakenly dated this account May instead of June.

[Macon] and on the Miss. on the free labor system that is to say with hired ne-groes." Walker had left on this march in late June and had broken up several plantations, burning the picked cotton, and had returned numerous slaves to their owners.[17]

Parsons had authorization to lead an independent action against Federal gar-risons near the Mississippi. After leaving Walker's camp on Monday, June 29, Parsons's two regiments joined Brigadier General James C. Tappan's Arkansas brigade and Colonel Horace Randal's Texas brigade, both infantry, accompa-nied by their scouts, Colonel Isaac F. Harrison's Louisiana cavalry. The latter was temporarily placed under Parsons's command along with two batteries, one from Mississippi and the other from Louisiana.[18]

Parsons divided his force. Harrison's cavalry accompanied by one of the bat-teries took a road leading toward Goodrich's Landing on the Mississippi be-tween Milliken's Bend and Lake Providence. Parsons headed his Texans along with the other battery toward a fortified position built on an old Indian mound. The infantry followed with the intention of reinforcing where needed.[19]

The cavalry's first objective was a fort manned by black troops under the command of white officers. Located about ten miles below Lake Providence and about one and one-half miles from the Mississippi, this stronghold, built on the top of an ancient Indian burying ground, supplied protection for the Federal plantations. Stationing black troops along the fertile regions of the Mississippi served a dual purpose; they not only safeguarded former slaves working on the plantations, but their presence released white soldiers from this duty.[20]

As the Texans emerged from the dense undergrowth of bushes and briers, the position, identified by one Texan as De Soto Mound, presented an impressive appearance. Rising about eighty to one hundred feet from an extensive open field, it was described by George Ingram, a lieutenant in the Twelfth Texas, as "the most peculiar looking mound I ever saw. . . ."[21]

---

17. J. E. T., "Letter from Burford's Regiment"; Report of J. G. Walker, 10 July 1863, *OR*, vol. 24, pt. 2:466; Winters, *The Civil War in Louisiana*, 203; Brown, *Journey to Pleasant Hill*, 234–45.

18. Winters incorrectly identified Parsons's command as "two Arkansas regiments to Tappan's cav-alry. . . ." Winters, *The Civil War in Louisiana*, 203.

19. Soldat, "Parsons' Cavalry Raid."

20. For a complete account of the decision to station troops along the Mississippi River see Cor-nish, *The Sable Arm*, 115–19, 163–69. A description of life on a Federal plantation is found in Thomas W. Knox, *Camp-fire and Cotton-field: Southern Adventure in Time of War. Life with the Union Armies and Residence on a Louisiana Plantation* (New York: Blelock and Co., 1865), 305–90, 417–54.

21. Soldat, "Parsons' Cavalry Raid"; George W. Ingram to Martha Ingram, 18 July 1863, Henry L. Ingram, comp., *Civil War Letters of George W. and Martha F. Ingram 1861–1865* (College Station: Texas A&M University Press, 1973), 55–56.

The main fort was situated on the summit which, measuring around thirty or forty feet square, was only accessible by a single pathway on the south side. To discourage anyone from trying to storm the slope the Federals had loosened the dirt for a distance of fifteen to twenty feet from the top so that anyone attempting to climb would lose his footing.[22]

The soldiers at the garrison had made preparations for an assault. The first line of defense was a secure trench surrounding the entire position some two and one-half to three feet deep with the dirt thrown up in front to provide a light breastwork. Waiting in the ditch were troops of the 1st Arkansas Volunteers (African descent), adequately armed with Enfield rifles. Upon the top of the mound were other blacks poised behind heavy timbers placed there for the purpose of rolling them down on anyone rash enough to try to scale the precipitous sides if the first line broke.[23] There was no artillery although the Federals had attempted to fabricate a cannon. Upon approaching the fortification, however, the Texans realized what had appeared to be a formidable eight-pounder was only a wooden log with a "vicious looking hole, some three inches in diameter, bored in one end of it."[24]

Parsons formed his men into a line of battle. The 12th Texas took the right, the 19th Texas the left, and the battery the center. When eight hundred yards from the Federal position, Parsons ordered a halt and instructed the battery to open fire. Lieutenant Ingram informed his wife that the blast from the four Confederate guns "caused the rascals in the fort to hide their heads." As the Texans cautiously neared the garrison, Parsons ordered the 12th to form at right angles to the 19th.[25]

Parsons judged he could not storm the fort without great loss of life. The colonel detailed some of his men as sharpshooters in order to pick off the enemy exchanging rifle fire with the Confederates, and a company from the 19th Texas deployed on the top of a smaller mound about one hundred fifty yards from the main location. As the two sides traded fire, Federal riflemen killed one Texan and wounded several.[26] Fortunately, the timely arrival of the infantry un-

---

22. J. E. T., "Letter from Burford's Regiment"; Soldat, "Parsons' Cavalry Raid."

23. Winters, *The Civil War in Louisiana*, 203–4; J. E. T., "Letter from Burford's Regiment"; Soldat, "Parsons' Cavalry Raid."

24. Soldat, "Parsons' Cavalry Raid."

25. George W. Ingram to Martha Ingram, *OR*, July 1863, Ingram, *Civil War Letters*, 55–56; J. E. T., "Letter from Burford's Regiment"; Soldat, "Parsons' Cavalry Raid."

26. James J. Frazier to Mother, Brothers, & Sisters, 7 July [1863], Frazier Family Papers, Barker Texas History Center, Austin, Texas; J. E. T., "Letter from Burford's Regiment"; Soldat, "Parsons' Cavalry Raid."

der Tappan provided the cavalry with reinforcements. With his number greatly increased Parsons recognized, and the officers atop the mound quickly realized, that resistance by the Federals was futile. Just as Parsons ordered the men to form a line of battle he directed a flag of truce toward the enemy demanding unconditional surrender.[27]

The fort capitulated without further bloodshed. The white officers acceded on the promise their captors would treat them as prisoners of war but requested to surrender the armed blacks unconditionally. Since Brigadier General Tappan had arrived, Parsons consulted with him before accepting the terms, then one hundred thirteen blacks and three white officers grounded their arms.[28]

The problem of black prisoners exacerbated acrimony on both sides. Walker reported: "I consider it an unfortunate circumstance that any armed negroes were captured. . . ." And Taylor had already received a warning from Grant. After hearing rumors that Walker's troops were guilty of hanging several black soldiers as well as a white captain and a white sergeant at Milliken's Bend, Grant wrote Taylor he hoped there was "some mistake in the evidence" or that "the act of hanging had no official sanction, and that the parties guilty of it" would be punished. "It may be you propose a different line of policy toward black troops and officers commanding them, to that practiced toward white troops," observed Grant. "If so, I can assure you," he warned, "that these colored troops are regularly mustered into the service of the United States. The Government and all officers serving under the Government are bound to give the same protection to these troops that they do to any other troops." Yet Private John Simmons of the 22d Texas Infantry wrote that as the foot soldiers escorted the prisoners back to camp about "12 or 15" blacks died before they arrived.[29]

Actually facing former slaves in blue uniforms was a new experience for many of the Texans. Parsons, who disliked the necessity of engaging black soldiers, had declared, "I would not give one of my brave men for the whole of them." Yet another participant had indicated surprise with the obstinate stand of the black troops when he observed: "These negroes were *well drilled*, and used their

27. J, E. T., "Letter from Burford's Regiment"; Soldat, "Parsons' Cavalry Raid."

28. Winters, *The Civil War in Louisiana*, 203–4: J. E. T., "Letter from Burford's Regiment"; Soldat, "Parsons' Cavalry Raid."

29. Report of J. G. Walker, 10 July 1863, *OR*, vol. 24, pt. 2:466; U. S. Grant to Richard Taylor, 22 June 1863, ibid., pt. 3:425–26; Richard Taylor to U. S. Grant, 27 June 1863, ibid., 443–44; U. S. Grant to Richard Taylor, 4 July 1863, ibid., 469. For a detailed discussion see Cornish, *The Sable Arm*, 163–73. John Simmons to Nancy Simmons, 2 July 1863, "The Confederate Letters of John Simmons," Jon Harrison, ed., *Chronicles of Smith County, Texas*, 14 (Summer 1975):33–34.

guns with a precision equal with any troops, and here were killed three of the four men we lost."[30]

Parsons, nevertheless, had no desire to remain at the mound any longer than necessary and he quickly resumed his raid. As the Texans rode toward the Mississippi they burned houses, gins, cotton, and captured all the black field hands they came upon. Brigadier General Alfred W. Ellet, commanding the Union's Mississippi Marine Brigade (an army unit despite its name), observed the destruction the next morning. "In passing by the negro quarters on three of the burning plantations," he reported, "we were shocked by the sight of the charred remains of human beings who had been burned in the general conflagration. No doubt they were the sick negroes whom the unscrupulous enemy were too indifferent to remove. I witnessed five such spectacles myself in passing the remains of three plantations that lay in our line of march and do not doubt there were many others on the 20 or more other plantations that I did not visit which were burned in like manner." Perhaps the Texans felt much as McPherson astutely describes Forrest, as showing "a killer instinct" for "blacks in any capacity other than slave."[31]

The brutality of these Confederates toward blacks was not an isolated incident. An important point to note is that this is not the first time there were charges against Parsons's 12th Texas for murdering blacks. When the regiment had raided a Federal supply train at L'Anguille River in northeastern Arkansas in 1862, there were reports they killed several refugee slaves accompanying the detachment. A Wisconsin soldier had claimed after the fighting: "The rebels . . . took possession of the camp, and with the most fiendish barbarity murdered many negroes, both men and women, plundered and burned the train, and then, with forty-seven prisoners besides negroes, returned, as rapidly as they came. . . ."[32]

But in Louisiana in 1863, blacks were not the only ones to feel the wrath of the Texans—Union sympathizers also suffered at the hands of the Southern

---

30. Soldat, "Parsons' Cavalry Raid." It should be pointed out that the black troops had also received what James McPherson described as "a somewhat left-handed compliment" from their Confederate adversaries after the fighting at Milliken's Bend. James M. McPherson, *The Negro's Civil War: How American Negroes Felt and Acted During the War for the Union* (New York: Vintage Books, 1965), 186–87. Also see the Report of Henry E. McCulloch, 8 June 1863, *OR*, vol. 24, pt. 2:467–70.

31. Soldat, "Parsons' Cavalry Raid"; Alfred W. Ellet to D. D. Porter, 3 July 1863, *Official Records of the Union and Confederate Navies in the War of the Rebellion*, 30 vols. (Washington, D.C.: GPO, 1894–1922), ser. 1, 25:215–16 (hereafter cited as *ORN*; citations are to series 1 unless otherwise noted); McPherson, *Battle Cry of Freedom*, 402.

32. William De Loss Love, *Wisconsin in the War of the Rebellion* (Chicago: Sheldon & Co., 1866), 557.

raiders. As the Confederates moved south, they razed all the homes they suspected of housing traitors. Ellet recalled he had "found the road strewn with abandoned booty. . . ." Rear Admiral David D. Porter listed among the plunder such items as "furniture, pianos, pictures. . . ." Ellet concluded, however, the Southerners' primary objective was not pillaging but securing "the negroes stolen from the plantations along the river, some hundreds of whom they had captured."[33]

The path of destruction led from the Indian mound toward Lake Providence. Parsons hoped to arrive at the town before local Unionists spread news of his coming. Anxious to employ the element of surprise, he urged his troops to speed. The men in the 19th Texas, whose mounts had not yet recovered from the raid into Missouri with Marmaduke just a few weeks before, could not keep the pace and fell behind. When the Confederates neared the little town the 12th Texas was well in advance of the rest of the force.[34]

News of the advance had preceded the Southerners and Federal soldiers had prepared a reception. As the Texans emerged from a skirt of timber interspersed with heavy undergrowth they rode into an ambush. Parsons promptly formed the 12th Texas into a line of battle and a man near the colonel recalled: "I don't know whether I was scared or not, but I do know that I was not too *badly* scared to observe him closely. I know that he was not scared. He watched every movement and gave his orders as deliberately as though he was in no danger." In the midst of the firing Parsons rode everywhere, "and though the balls rattled all around him, he gave his orders and directions as coolly as if he was on a drill."[35]

The battle, although fierce, proved short. Parsons, in front of his men, gave orders to dismount all but one squadron. Armed with recently arrived rifles, the Texans rushed toward the enemy on foot fighting "Indian or Texas fashion."[36] As the dismounted cavalrymen drove the troops of the 1st Kansas Mounted Regiment back in a "pretty hot fight" about two to three hundred yards, Parsons ordered one squadron to charge on horseback.[37]

---

33. Alfred W. Ellet to D. D. Porter, 3 July 1863, *ORN*, 25:215–16; Report to David D. Porter, 2 July 1863, ibid., 212–14.

34. The 19th and 21st Texas along with Morgan's companies and Pratt's Battery had joined Marmaduke on his raid upon Cape Girardeau, Missouri, from 17 Apr. until 2 May 1863. For more on the expedition see Stephen H. Oates, *Confederate Cavalry West of the River* (Austin: Univ. of Texas Press, 1961), 121–31.

35. J. E. T., "Letter from Burford's Regiment."

36. George W. Ingram to Martha Ingram, 18 July 1863, Ingram, *Civil War Letters*, 55–56; J. E. T., "Letter from Burford's Regiment"; Soldat, "Parsons' Cavalry Raid."

37. Henry Orr to Sister, 2 July 1863, Anderson, *Campaigning with Parsons' Texas Cavalry Brigade*, 111–13.

For a second time in the day the fortuitous arrival of reinforcements saved further destruction. As the 19th Texas rode up Parsons ordered them to charge. A participant recalled with pride one should "have heard the real Texan yell they sent forth and seen those brave determined men, as they dashed off, urging on their jaded horses, you would have cried with me, the 'Lone Star' is in hands of which she may well be proud; and thus the exciting race continued for five miles, and within a mile of the town of Providence. But the Federal horses, being fresh, outran our horses and the jaded condition of both man and beast" forced Parsons to call a halt. Brigadier General Hugh T. Reid, commanding Federal troops in the vicinity of the town, reported his men had found the rebels "too strong, and had to fall back, skirmishing to within 3 miles of town, where the progress of the enemy was stopped."[38]

The cavalry headed back to join the main infantry force. But a gunboat, the *Romeo*, along with a transport mounting two guns on the hurricane deck, the *John Raine*, shelled the Confederate column as it marched down the levee.[39] One Texan observed, "their shells burst harmlessly above and around us, doing no other damage than killing three negroes." Porter claimed the gunboat pursued the Confederate column for fifteen miles but was unable to prevent further destruction of houses and property.[40]

The Confederates left the fertile land in ruin. All around them columns of black smoke rose from burning houses, the red flames casting a sullen glow on the horizon. When the boom of signal guns bore the news of the fighting one of Parsons's men proudly noted that the cannon informed the Confederates at Vicksburg "that a blow had been struck for [them]," and to "the besiegers, that a blow had been struck against them." As twilight fell the strange scene, enhanced by the sobs of hundreds of black captives, observed the writer, was "grand, gloomy and peculiar."[41] Union commander Hugh Reid observed the

38. Soldat, "Parsons' Cavalry Raid"; Report of H. T. Reid, 6 July 1863, *OR*, vol. 24, pt. 2:450.

39. Porter reported to the secretary of the navy that the *John Raine* had arrived "as the rebels were setting fire to the so-called Government plantations, and supposing her to be an ordinary transport they opened fire on her with fieldpieces, but were much surprised to have the fire returned with shrapnel, which fell in among them, killing and wounding a number." The *Raine* was soon joined by the gunboat *Romeo* which commenced shelling the enemy troops. Report of David D. Porter, 2 July 1863, *ORN*, 25:212–14.

40. Soldat, "Parsons' Cavalry Raid"; Report of David D. Porter, 2 July 1863, *ORN*, 25:212–14.

41. A member of Parsons's Regiment watching the scene described it as "the grandest sight I ever witnessed, and, were I to live threescore years and ten more, perhaps will never see again." Soldat, "Parsons' Cavalry Raid."

damage and confirmed, "it was a part of Parsons' brigade of cavalry which did the mischief in this vicinity."[42]

Federal pursuit came immediately. By two the following morning Ellet had debarked his entire force at Goodrich's Landing—infantry, artillery, and cavalry; at sunrise he started in search of the raiders. Sending the cavalry in advance of the main force Ellet's mounted men found the Confederates resting on the west bank of Tensas Bayou where spirited firing erupted. Parsons, directing his men in person, attempted to cross the bayou and turn Ellet's right flank but an advance line of Union skirmishers repulsed the assault. One Texan believed the Federals were "afraid to come out into an open space and give us a fair fight. . . ." Ellet, however, insisted the arrival of his artillery, which opened up on the Confederate position, convinced the Southerners to "precipitately" retreat.[43] But before leaving, Parsons ordered the bridge burned. Then, in obedience to Walker's orders, the Texas cavalry began to fall back covering the infantry's rear.

Porter's reaction to the raid was matter-of-fact. "I am much surprised that this has never been attempted before," he observed, as "the temptation to plunder is very great, and there is nothing but the black regiments to protect the coast." Porter criticized the plantation system by pointing out its excessive cost to the government. Moreover, he believed unobstructed navigation of the Mississippi under this arrangement required a large army of white soldiers and gunboats to safeguard the blacks whom he believed had proved unable to protect themselves.[44]

The raid, although successful, brought few material benefits. On the positive side, the Confederates had captured between thirteen and fifteen hundred blacks, over four hundred horses and mules, cattle, and camp equipage, and— important to the department—Southern wagons now held over two hundred Federal arms. But retaining Confederate troops opposite Vicksburg late in June offered no military rewards. As Richard Taylor later observed, "The time wasted on these absurd movements cost us the garrison of Port Hudson, nearly eight thousand men," he conceded, "but the pressure on General Kirby Smith to *do something* for Vicksburg was too strong to be resisted."[45]

In reality the Confederates in Louisiana could do nothing to aid their comrades across the river. Walker informed Kirby Smith on July 3: "If there was the

---

42. Report of H. T. Reid, 6 July 1861, *OR*, vol. 24, pt 2:450.

43. Alfred W. Ellet to D. D. Porter, 1 July 1863, *ORN*, 25:215–16; Soldat, "Parsons' Cavalry Raid."

44. Report of David D. Porter, 2 July 1863, *ORN*, 25:212–14.

45. Soldat, "Parsons' Cavalry Raid"; J. E. T., "Letter from Burford's Regiment"; Taylor, *Destruction and Reconstruction*, 181; Kerby, *Kirby Smith's Confederacy*, 115.

slightest hope that my small command could relieve Vicksburg, the mere probability of its capture or destruction ought not, and should not, as far as I am
concerned, weigh a feather against making the attempt, but I consider it absolutely certain, unless the enemy are blind and stupid, that no part of my command would escape capture or destruction if such an attempt should be made."
Walker noted that at no time did his force amount to more than 4,700 men
and with the bad weather and "deleterious effect of the climate" the number
was reduced to barely 2,500 fit for duty. Although he had been reinforced by
Tappan there were never more than 4,200 effectives.[46] And when Pemberton,
besieged by Grant's army, ceased fighting the next day, Private Orr of the 12th
Texas wrote his sister: "The news of the surrender [of] Vicksburg was received
with regret . . ."[47]

Although the raid made no significant military difference, few would have
predicted it would bring the issue of blacks to the forefront. Moreover, public
opinion in the South often condoned such acts. Kate Stone, a young Louisiana
refugee living in East Texas, noted in her diary in June of Walker's fight at Milliken's Bend: "It is hard to believe that Southern soldiers—and Texans at that—
have been whipped by a mongrel crew of white and black Yankees. There must
be some mistake. . . . It is said the Negro regiments fought there like mad
demons, but we cannot believe that. We know from long experience they were
cowards." On September 1 she wrote: "There are quite a number of Yankee
prisoners at Tyler [Texas], captured while in command of black troops. It does
seem like they ought to be hanged. . . . The detestable creatures!"[48]

What happened to the captured blacks? Confederate soldiers seldom mentioned them in their correspondence and the question is difficult to answer
since they were treated as captured property. That status was clear in an order
Colonel Parsons issued on August 16 which prohibited soldiers from keeping or
selling any property taken during raids—specifically "mules or negroes."
Significantly, Parsons (whose birthplace was New Jersey) owned only one slave,
an old woman who had apparently come with his wife upon their marriage.[49]

---

46. Report of J. G. Walker, 10 July 1863, *OR*, vol. 24, pt. 2:466; Winter, *The Civil War in Louisiana*, 203–5; Kerby, *Kirby Smith's Confederacy*, 115.

47. Henry Orr to Sister, 15 July 1863, Anderson, *Campaigning with Parsons' Texas Cavalry Brigade*, 113–14.

48. Kate Stone diary, 10 June, 1 Sept. 1863, John Q. Anderson, ed., *Brokenburn: The Journal of Kate Stone, 1861–1868* (Baton Rouge: Louisiana State Univ. Press, 1955), 218–19, 239.

49. Special Order No. 2, 16 Aug. 1863, Special Order Book of Parsons' Brigade, Collection of Parsons' Brigade Association Texas Cavalry, Sims Library, Waxahachie, Tex. Parsons had been born in New Jersey of Puritan ancestors. His family, however, had moved to Montgomery, Ala., when he

Nevertheless, fighting along the Mississippi had brought the disagreeable question of black prisoners into the spotlight for both sides. Not only had Grant cautioned Taylor about the treatment of black soldiers opposite Vicksburg, persistent rumors of murdered blacks in the fighting around Port Hudson surfaced. Although in May the United States War Department had taken a stand on the position of troops of African descent in the army, Southerners seldom worried about punishment threatened by Abraham Lincoln's government.

In fact, Texans in the Trans-Mississippi simply ignored Washington's warnings of retaliation. For example, in April 1864 the 30th Texas Cavalry, which joined Parsons's Texas Cavalry Brigade shortly before the war ended, would take part in the most publicized massacre of blacks recorded in the department. Within days of Nathan Bedford Forrest's infamous assault on black troops at Fort Pillow, Tennessee, on April 12, 1864, Confederates fighting in Arkansas brutally murdered former slaves wearing Federal uniforms. On April 18 at Poison Spring, the Southerners slaughtered many black soldiers. The historian Robert L. Kerby has concluded: "The so-called battle of Poison Spring was a one-sided massacre: the Union soldiers were torn to shreds" and the Confederates "deliberately drove captured wagons back and forth over the fallen Negro wounded, and execution squads went about the field shooting incapacitated prisoners." Kirby Smith had confided to his wife that the Southerners had taken "some 200 prisoners and left 600 reported dead on the field principally negroes who neither gave or recd quarter. . . . I saw but two negro prisoners." When Private Orr of Parsons's 12th Texas visited the battle site in November he wrote his sister that a "great many Negroes were killed. The Yankees were invited to come and bury them after the battle; three days after they came and threw a little dirt over them, but the hogs rooted them up; I reckon I saw half a wagonload of bones."[50]

To see if there is any consistent attitude toward blacks among these Texas cavalrymen serving in the Trans-Mississippi Department it is necessary to consider all three incidents: L'Anguille River in 1862, the Louisiana raid in 1863,

---

was a small child and he had received his education in the South. There is a great deal of information concerning Parsons's ancestors as his younger brother Albert moved north following the war, and was among those executed for the killings at Chicago's Haymarket Square Riot in May 1866. Lucy E. Parsons, ed., *Life of Albert R. Parsons* (1889; reprint, Chicago: Lucy E. Parsons, 1903), 12–15; Philip S. Foner, ed., *The Autobiographies of the Haymarket Martyrs* (New York: Humanities Press, 1969), 27–29; Paul Avrich, *The Haymarket Tragedy* (Princeton: Princeton Univ. Press, 1984), 3–5; Carolyn Ashbaugh, *Lucy Parsons, American Revolutionary* (Chicago: Charles H. Kerr Pub. Co., 1976), 13–14.

50. Kerby, *Kirby Smith's Confederacy*, 312; Henry Orr to Sister, 12 Nov. 1864, Anderson, *Campaigning with Parsons' Texas Cavalry Brigade*, 149–50.

and Poison Spring in 1864. The atrocities committed against blacks along the banks of the Mississippi in northern Louisiana in 1863 were no different from those committed by Texans in Arkansas in 1862 and what they would continue to do in 1864. Moreover, it is important to look at the men involved. In each encounter, many of the Confederates were members of the 12th, 19th, or 30th Texas cavalries. For example, James Frazier, a private in the 12th Texas who took part in the Louisiana raid had one brother serving in the 19th Texas Cavalry and another serving in the 30th Texas. The majority of the troops in these regiments came from North Central Texas—an area settled predominantly by families from the Upper South, an area without plantations and little cotton production, and an area where numerous inhabitants did not record ownership of any slaves in the 1860 Federal census.[51]

Why then did these Texans, many nonslaveholders from the Texas frontier, react as they did toward blacks? There appear to be three reasons. First, the majority of these Texans shared a common heritage—as Southerners they acted as many Southerners would have in the same situation. In 1862, when they first encountered contrabands following the Union soldiers, they responded as their culture had taught them—an almost natural wartime reaction to seeing blacks in any other capacity than that of slave. Second, since all of the incidents described occurred in the Trans-Mississippi there was not as great a chance of publicity or condemnation. By the time of the raid along the Mississippi in 1863 the troops had long since realized that the hierarchy in Richmond generally overlooked or even ignored their department. Finally, these Texas cavalry regiments served most of the war as scouts and raiders on the fringe of Union occupied areas; they had a strong determination to prevent Federal soldiers from reaching their home state. When the United States Army amassed a two-front assault toward Texas in the spring of 1864, the Texans had to halt the advance or possibly concede North Texas to the enemy. The thought that soldiers, black soldiers, could have marched toward their homes sent fear and anger through the Texans, and the result was the massacre at Poison Spring. The reaction of Texas cavalrymen serving in the Trans-Mississippi to black soldiers and contrabands, therefore, stemmed from their cultural heritage, the separateness of their department from the rest of the Confederacy, and, probably most decisive, their strong desire to protect their families in Texas from the ravages of war.

---

51. Frazier Family Papers, Barker Texas History Center; Frazier Papers, Confederate Research Center, Hillsboro; 1860 Census, Hill Co., Texas; Terry G. Jordan, "The Imprint of the Upper and Lower South in Mid-Nineteenth Century Texas," *Annals of the Association of American Geographers,* 57 (1967):667–90.

Sixth-plate ambrotype of Captain J. F. M. Robinson, Company A, 33rd Texas Cavalry, ca. 1860s. This regiment spent much time in the field rounding up conscripts and deserters. Robinson was wounded at the Battle of the Nueces on August 10, 1862. *Courtesy Lawrence T. Jones III.*

Conscription and Conflict on the Texas Frontier, 1863–1865

DAVID P. SMITH*

Conflict between state and Confederate authorities occurred often during the American Civil War. The concept of state rights was strong in the South, and state officials jealously guarded their powers and prerogatives. In some states, particularly North Carolina and Georgia, disagreements over martial law, conscription, civil liberties, and military matters were frequently bitter. In general, Texas officials cooperated with Confederate political and military leaders in carrying on the war effort. Governors Edward Clark (1861) and Francis R. Lubbock (1861–1863) were consistent supporters of the Davis administration. Pendleton Murrah, the last Confederate governor of the state (1863–1865), was more prone to question Richmond decisions than his predecessors, but was usually supportive of Confederate policies.

One area of major disagreement between Texas and the Confederate government was over frontier defense. Texans believed that Confederate authorities failed to understand the concerns of frontier residents over Indian incursions. Efforts by Texas authorities to maintain state forces for frontier protection resulted in conflicts relating to Confederate conscription laws.

* David P. Smith, "Conscription and Conflict on the Texas Frontier, 1863–1865," *Civil War History*, XXXVI (Sept., 1990), 250–261. Reprinted with permission of Kent State University Press.

In the following essay, David P. Smith, author of Frontier Defense in the Civil
War: Texas' Rangers and Rebels *(College Station: Texas A&M University Press,
1992), discusses the conflict between Texas and Richmond over frontier defense. He
concludes that "the state-rights conflict with the Confederate government perhaps
helped retain for the frontier a measure of protection it would never have received
from the Confederacy." For additional insights on this matter the reader is referred
to the various secondary studies cited in Smith's article.*

The state-rights thesis once expounded by the disciples of historian Frank
Owsley and later in its modified form by David Donald has rightly come under
ardent scrutiny by modern-day critics. The most current extended look came in
a recent, controversial book that included a historiographical survey of Confederate failure, and provided insightful new perceptions which, if not always con-
vincing, were always intriguing.[1] The present work will consider only one facet
of the Owsley thesis, that dealing with a single state's posture on conscription,
in an attempt to shed further light on the long-enduring question of whether or
not the Confederacy "Died of State Rights." The example of Texas, while similar in many regards to the other Confederate states, encompassed a unique situation: the complete abrogation of the Confederate conscription laws for the last
eighteen months of the war over a region of Texas the size of the state of North
Carolina—the state's frontier counties with an 1860 population of nearly fifty
thousand.

That such a circumstance could exist can be comprehended only by an understanding of the state government's determination to protect its Indian frontier at all hazards. In 1861 it was natural for the state to look to the Confederate
government for protection of its Indian frontier, but recalling the difficulties of
the United States Army in the same task since the Mexican War, Texans saw little to convince them that Confederate responsibility could solve the problem.
Part of the problem, indeed, lay in the belief by most non-Texan Confederate
authorities that the Indian menace simply did not require the military might or
expenditure that Texans demanded.

Confederate Secretary of War Leroy P. Walker in 1861 echoed United States
authorities of the 1850s when he called the Indian threat "merely predatory" and
believed that one regiment of cavalry should suffice on the frontier.[2] This same

---

1. Richard E. Beringer, et al., *Why the South Lost the Civil War* (Athens, Ga., 1986).

2. Leroy P. Walker to John Hemphill, April 11, 1861, *The War of the Rebellion: A Compilation of the
Official Records of the Union and Confederate Armies* (1880–1901; 70 vols. in 128 books, rpt., Harrisburg, Pa., 1971), ser. I, 1:1621–22 (cited hereafter as *OR*).

attitude existed on the part of the Confederate government throughout the war. In one sense they were correct; if damage done to life and property was the sole standard upon which to base the degree of military force required, then one regiment should have been sufficient. One estimate gives a total of approximately eight hundred Texans killed by Indians from the summer of 1862 to 1868, which would result in approximately four hundred Texans killed, wounded, and made captive for the four years of the Civil War.[3] These losses scarcely compare with the total of Confederate casualties suffered in even a single medium-sized battle of the war, but what those back east failed to appreciate was the nature of the warfare waged on the Texas frontier. The Texans who witnessed the results of countless Indian raids throughout the 1850s and 1860s could scarcely imagine more savage and inhumane conduct than that practiced by their old adversaries, a war in which so often the victims were old men, women, and children. Especially infuriating was the brutal manner in which the Plains Indians ravaged, killed, and mutilated women and children—actions made even more galling when one considers that most of those kidnapped had almost no chance of safe return. It is the image of this type of warfare, one that easterners could scarcely comprehend, that drove Texans to persist in their efforts to guard the Indian frontier and exterminate hostile Indians found in their midst. No quarter was asked and none was given.[4]

When it was rumored that the Confederate cavalry regiment stationed on the frontier in 1861 would be withdrawn in early 1862, the legislature created the state-supported Frontier Regiment, a unit of Rangers, to take its place. Commanded by Texans familiar with the frontier, the legislature sought to muster it into Confederate service, with the proviso that it not be withdrawn by Confederate authorities from the frontier. This would have been the culmination of what Texans had wanted from a national government since the early years of statehood, a force of Rangers on the frontier paid for and provisioned by the government but under the direction of Texans. The Confederate Congress agreed to such a proposal, but President Jefferson Davis vetoed the idea as unconstitutional.[5] In the meantime, in the spring of 1862, Jefferson Davis asked the Confederate Congress to pass the first military draft law in American history. The ensuing act was to conscript all white males between eighteen and thirty-five to three years of service; a supplemental law passed later that year raised

---

3. Carl Coke Rister, "Fort Griffin," *West Texas Historical Association Year Book*, I (June 1925), 16.

4. It is difficult to find a better narrative on the clash of culture between Comanches and Texans, and the nature of their warfare, than T. R. Fehrenbach, *Comanches: The Destruction of a People* (New York, 1974).

5. Jefferson Davis to the Congress of the Confederate States, Jan. 22, 1862, *OR*, 53:770–71.

the age limit to forty-five. An exemption and substitute system accompanied the acts, but it left no doubt that the central government, not the states, would be responsible for raising units for Confederate service.[6] For nearly two years Texas bore the burden of funding the Frontier Regiment while attempting to persuade Confederate authorities to accept it into Confederate service stationed permanently on the frontier.

The subject of frontier defense and the fate of the state-supported Frontier Regiment played a major role in deliberations of the Tenth Legislature in November and December of 1863. While newly elected Governor Pendleton Murrah and the legislators seemed willing to transfer the regiment to the Confederacy, even with no restrictions, theirs was a single-minded determination to assure the best protection possible for the frontier counties.

The legislature responded with a plan similar to one proposed by Governor Francis Richard Lubbock during the previous session of the legislature.[7] The new law passed the legislature as "an Act to Provide for the Protection of the Frontier, and turning over the Frontier Regiment to Confederate States Service," and as such, represented the last major modification of frontier defense by the State of Texas during the Civil War. The new plan created what became known as the Frontier Organization, an organizational structure that functioned in the frontier counties not only until the surrender of the Trans-Mississippi Confederacy but for some months afterward. Enacted by the legislature on December 15, 1863, the law declared that all persons liable for military service who were actual residents of the frontier counties of Texas were to be enrolled and organized into companies of not less than twenty-five and not more than sixty-five men. The act defined the frontier line and instructed Governor Murrah to divide the designated counties into three districts and to appoint a major of cavalry to take charge of the organization of mounted companies within each district.[8]

Of the entire force raised in such manner, the major of each district was to require that one-fourth of his men, on a rotation basis, be in service at any one time, with provisions that the governor could set forth extraordinary circumstances by which the entire force could be called out. That the Frontier Organization was to be used to protect the frontier from Indian incursions was not

---

6. Albert B. Moore, *Conscription and Conflict in the Confederacy* (New York, 1924), 52–53; Emory M. Thomas, *The Confederate Nation: 1861–1865* (New York, 1979), 152–53.

7. Lubbock's administration is identified with harmonious and complete cooperation with Confederate authorities in any state-national clash. In 1864 he became adviser to President Davis on Trans-Mississippi affairs and was captured with Davis in May of 1865. Murrah took office in Nov. 1863 with a devotion to prevent further subversion of state sovereignty.

8. H. P. N. Gammel, comp., *Laws of Texas, 1822–1897*, 10 vols. (Austin, 1898), vol. 5, 677.

stated in the bill, but rather was an understood prerequisite. The law emphasized, however, that all members of the organization were to take an oath that they would use the best of their abilities to arrest and deliver to the nearest authorities every person reported or known to be a deserter, either from the state or Confederate States army, including all persons known to be avoiding conscription.[9]

Section 12 of the new law stated that, upon the completion of the new organization, the governor was to turn over the Frontier Regiment to Confederate authorities. In this manner authorities hoped that the frontier would have adequate protection, even if the Confederate-controlled Frontier Regiment left to counter a threat elsewhere. Just as importantly, this protection would come from those who lived on the frontier, from men presumably motivated to give their best effort to protect their families and property.

Under the Texas Legislature's "Act to Provide for the Defense of the State," also passed in December 1863, Governor Murrah proceeded in January 1864 to retain in the state militia for a six-month period all able-bodied men not in Confederate service or exempted by state law.[10] This stance by Texas, combined with the fact that the legislature simultaneously exempted men in all or part of fifty-nine counties in the frontier districts to enable them to enroll in the Frontier Organization, led inevitably to a state-rights clash over the issue of conscription. This conflict, through subsequent debate between Texas and Confederate officials, held ramifications that affected the structure of the Texas State Troops and threatened the existence of the Frontier Organization.

General John Bankhead Magruder, commander of the Military District of Texas, New Mexico, and Arizona, reacted unfavorably to the state militia law, but his initial concern dealt with that part of the law that proposed to offer three-month furloughs to one-third of the militia on a rotation basis. The general did not wish to see any reduction in the militia strength of ten thousand men, subject to Confederate control within Texas, that he had struggled so hard to gain from Governor Lubbock and the legislature in the summer of 1863. In early January 1864, General Magruder had Colonel John Sayles, his judge advocate general, present his views to Governor Murrah on the conflict between Confederate conscription laws and the new militia law. Murrah's spirited response left no doubt that he would not be as compliant on the issue of conscription and Confederate authority as his predecessor in office. The governor maintained that Texas called these troops into being under the sovereign will of

9. Ibid., 677–78.

10. Gammel, *Laws of Texas*, vol. 5, 698–99; Moore, *Conscription and Conflict in the Confederacy*, 247.

the state; as such, the militia should be seen as volunteer aid to the Confederacy and Magruder had no right to assume command over them unless the government of Texas gave him that right.[11]

General Edmund Kirby Smith, commander of the Trans-Mississippi Confederacy, likewise soon brought the issue to Governor Murrah's attention, then pointed out that in regard to the conflict between the legislature's actions and the Confederate conscription law then in effect, only President Davis could suspend conscription in any locale, such as the frontier counties of Texas. Smith complained that "it is to be regretted that the Legislature should have passed an act so well calculated to produce an unpleasant issue between State and Confederate authorities."[12] Not only did General Smith question the legality of suspending Confederate conscription laws in the frontier districts, but he doubted particularly whether the men of the Frontier Organization were even needed for frontier protection.

In an attempt to clarify the fate of the Texas militia, Generals Smith and Magruder met with Governor Murrah in Houston to try to arrive at an amicable arrangement. Instead, Murrah insisted upon state control of the "conscript element," and compromised only so far as to allow those of conscript age who wished to do so to enter either new or old companies in Confederate Army service. To complicate matters, the Confederate Congress at this time, in an attempt to raise the number of men needed against the growing Northern armies, passed a new draft law on February 17, 1864. The law in question conscripted for the duration of the war all white men between the ages of seventeen and fifty. Those in the army between eighteen and forty-five remained under their current organizations, while men of seventeen to eighteen and forty-five to fifty constituted a reserve corps to be used for military service within their home states.[13]

The debate, chiefly a matter of semantics and interpretation of the Confederate Constitution, might in peacetime merely have been an intellectual exercise, but not so now, for in February and March of 1864, Union armies in the Trans-Mississippi began their spring offensives, the most serious of which was General Nathaniel P. Banks's Red River Campaign, aimed seemingly at east Texas. Mur-

---

11. Magruder to Murrah, December 18, 1863, Governor Pendleton Murrah Records, Archives Division, Texas State Library, Austin, Texas (all references to the archives of the Texas State Library will hereafter be cited as TSL-A); Murrah to Magruder, Jan. 12, 1864, *OR*, 53: 926–30. Murrah's twelve-page, handwritten copy of this letter is found in the Governor Pendleton Murrah Records, TSL-A.

12. Kirby Smith to Murrah, Jan. 18, 1864, *OR*, 34, pt. 2: 886.

13. Magruder to W. R. Boggs, Feb. 16, 1864, ibid., 973–75; Wilfred Buck Yearns, *The Confederate Congress* (Athens, Ga., 1960), 88.

rah, in the face of pressure by Magruder to release the militia completely to his control, offered only to turn them over by brigades under Murrah's six hand-picked brigadier generals of state troops, rather than by companies as prescribed by the Confederate Army. Magruder declined the offer as contrary to Confederate regulations.[14]

By the first week in April Magruder was nearly frantic in his effort to solidify the defenses of Texas with the state militia to take the place of those troops forwarded to Louisiana. He daily expected to hear of the fall of Shreveport, Kirby Smith's headquarters, and the occupation of most of northeast Texas by federal troops advancing through Louisiana and Arkansas. On April 5 Magruder made a last urgent appeal to Murrah to organize the state troops in the face of such an emergency that federal forces under General Frederick Steele in Arkansas were only sixty miles from Texas, while General Banks and his army were less than that distance away at Pleasant Hill, Louisiana.[15] Under such conditions Governor Murrah's objections gave way:

I shall be forced, in view of the dangers surrounding the State and country, to co-operate with you in organizing [the militia] under the recent law of Congress. I shall take upon myself the responsibility . . . of calling upon the State troops to look no longer to an organization under the State laws.[16]

Magruder felt no ill will toward Murrah for his stand in the conflict, but attributed his actions to patriotic motives and the belief that Murrah felt himself "trammelled by a law of the Legislature in relation to the conscripts." By the following month the Texas Legislature worked to conform the state's militia laws with Confederate conscription laws, and by July transferred nearly seventy-five under-strength companies to Confederate service.[17]

But the issue over conscription in Texas was not resolved by Murrah's April

---

14. The correspondence between Murrah and Magruder concerning this matter in Feb. and Mar. 1864, is found in *OR*, 34, pt. 2: 1087–95.

15. Magruder to E. S. Nichols, Apr. 2, 1864, ibid., pt. 3: 726–27; Magruder to Murrah, Apr. 5, 1864, ibid., 735. There was also a small federal force in south Texas, the remnants of Banks's invasion at Brazos Santiago the previous November.

16. Murrah to Magruder, Apr. 7, 1864, ibid., 747. The best secondary account of the militia controversy is found in Robert L. Kerby, *Kirby Smith's Confederacy: The Trans-Mississippi South 1863–1865* (New York, 1972), 276–79, but brief and accurate discussions of the controversy above are also found in Moore, *Conscription and Conflict in the Confederacy*, 247–48; and Allan Coleman Ashcraft,"Texas: 1860–1866, The Lone Star State in the Civil War" (unpublished doctoral dissertation, Columbia University, New York, 1960), 200–202. Ashcraft concludes that it was well that the Confederate Army took control of raising the troops, because the state conscription law and militia organization had been a failure.

17. Magruder to Colonel H. B. Andrews, Aug. 16, 1864, Texas State Military Board Records, TSL-A. Magruder expressed almost identical sentiments in an earlier letter to General Smith, when

decision, for the governor still did not admit that Confederate conscription laws were in force in the frontier districts. It was here that the enrollment of men for frontier service held priority, based on the legislative act passed the previous December, a point almost neglected by Smith and Magruder at the time and by historians ever since. In January and February of 1864, as the frontier district commanders enrolled the men of their districts for service, they attempted to enroll only men who could prove their citizenship in the frontier county in question and who were not then in active Confederate service.[18] Even so, Major William Quayle, commander of the First (Northern) Frontier District, reported that the men were in "a continual state of excitement," that Confederate enrolling officers were about to enter the districts to take away those of conscript age not exempted by the Confederate law of February 17.[19]

Confusion over the conscript status of the men of the frontier districts mounted when General Elkanah Greer, head of the Bureau of Conscription, Trans-Mississippi Department, issued Special Orders Number 40. These orders declared that men in the frontier districts could form "temporary organizations" for the defense of the Texas frontier, but that Confederate enrolling officers would also organize them into Confederate companies detailed for frontier protection "whilst their presence is necessary."[20] This arrangement was not exactly what the legislature had in mind. State and Confederate authorities differed not only between each other, but among themselves, in interpreting how to proceed in the matter of enrollment in the frontier counties. General Henry E. McCulloch gave specific conditions that applied to those parts of the First and Second Frontier Districts located within his Confederate Northern Sub-District of Texas. He stated that all men enrolled as conscripts before the legislature passed the frontier protection bill should be sent to camps of instruction and enrolled for Confederate service. Some of the more energetic Confederate enrolling officers, however, attempted to enroll all men on the frontier not exempted by Confederate law. Major Quayle would have nothing of it:

---

he mentioned that Murrah's actions, "trammeled as he was by the State law, were prompted by the loftiest patriotism." Magruder to Kirby Smith, Apr. 23, 1864, *OR*, 34, pt. 3:788; Gammel, *Laws of Texas*, vol. 5, 773–75; Kerby, *Kirby Smith's Confederacy*, 279.

18. George B. Erath to D. B. Culberson, Jan. 18, 1864, Adjutant General's Records, TSL-A; Erath to Culberson, Feb. 22, 1864, ibid.; William Quayle to Culberson, Feb. 4, 1864, William Quayle Papers, Rare Book Room, University of Alabama, Tuscaloosa, Alabama (all references to this collection will be cited hereafter as Quayle Papers, UAL).

19. Quayle to Culberson, Feb. 25, 1864, Quayle Papers, UAL.

20. Special Orders Number 40, Mar. 12, 1864, Quayle Papers, UAL. A copy is also found in *OR*, 48, pt. 1:1376.

I hereby notify you that I claim the conscripts in this Frontier Dist. they having been mustered into this service under the instructions of the Adjutant General of the State and I cannot give them up except by an order from the Governor of the State.

Quayle pointed out the chief reason why the state refused to allow Confederate conscription in the frontier counties: that to give up his district to Confederate conscription would be to remove from it all reliable men who could be counted upon to arrest deserters and fight Indians; their removal would leave behind "a class of persons" that would make the frontier "a resort of Disloyalty and Treason."[21]

In the midst of this state-rights clash over the Frontier Organization, President Jefferson Davis replied to Governor Murrah's request that the frontier counties be relieved from the operation of the Confederate Act of Conscription. Davis could give no such relief, but he offered Murrah the next best thing, a move anticipated by General Greer's earlier order. The president said that for the time being he would direct General Smith to enroll the men of the frontier counties, then have them detailed and left for the defense of the frontier.[22] If not a victory for Murrah and the legislature, this at least sounded like a more permanent arrangement than that found in the wording of Greer's Special Orders Number 40.

During the special session of the legislature in May of 1864 Murrah vowed that the officers of the frontier districts would continue to exclude from their muster rolls all deserters and men who left other parts of the South to avoid military service, and would embrace only those who were there in good faith before the passage of the frontier protection bill. To promote that end, Murrah proclaimed that further immigration into the frontier counties of Texas was now forbidden, and all men found there between the ages of eighteen and forty-five who were not residents of their district prior to July 1863 were to be turned over to Confederate military authorities. Over two months after the legislature met, however, Major Quayle reported that rumors were still afloat in his district that the Frontier Organization was to be disbanded, rumors fed largely by General Greer's pronouncement months earlier that led some frontier citizens to flee the frontier to avoid Confederate conscription officers.[23] Murrah

---

21. McCulloch to Quayle, Mar. 16, 1864, Quayle Papers, UAL; Quayle to John W. Hale, Enrolling Officer, Wise County, Apr. 24, 1864, Quayle Papers, UAL; Quayle to Greer, Apr. 24, 1864, Quayle Papers, UAL.

22. Jefferson Davis to Govr. P. Murray [sic], Apr. 26, 1864, Dunbar Rowland, ed., *Jefferson Davis, Constitutionalist: His Letters, Papers and Speeches*, 10 vols. (Jackson, Miss., 1923), vol. 6, 235–36.

23. James Day, ed., *Senate and House Journals of the Tenth Legislature, First Called Session, May 9, 1864–May 28, 1864* (Austin, 1965), 19; Gammel, *Laws of Texas*, vol. 5, 773; Quayle to Murrah, Aug. 22, 1864, Quayle Papers, UAL.

assured him that the frontier districts would not be interfered with—he had General Smith's word on that.

At least he thought he did; instead, the Frontier Organization found itself assailed once more in the fall and winter of 1864–65, this time by Trans-Mississippi Army authorities who sought to break up the organization in order to call upon the manpower on the frontier they believed to be unnecessary for its defense. If Governor Murrah thought that General Smith's relative silence on the subject had meant acquiesence, he soon discovered otherwise. Kirby Smith's assistant adjutant general, Charles S. West, opened the offensive in October. He attacked the Frontier Organization as a structure that precluded conscription, one that produced an interminable conflict between Texas and Confederate authorities. There should be no reason for exemption from conscription, he said, for anyone because of geographic location; the Frontier Organization did just that for over three thousand men, men who should be turned over at once to the Confederate Army. West then pointed out the standard argument against the organization, that it encouraged deserters and others anxious to evade their duty to congregate in the frontier counties of Texas, so that by adding such men to the total, West estimated that approximately four thousand men resided on the Texas frontier who should then be in Confederate service. He then repeated something quite familiar to skeptical Texans: "It is the duty of the Confederate Govt. & not of the State of Texas to protect the Indian frontier."[24] West directed that the men of the frontier districts should be turned over to the Confederacy, whereupon General Smith would immediately order the Frontier Regiment to the Texas frontier, supported by local militia—a process, according to West, that would give adequate protection to the Texas frontier and release not less than three thousand greatly needed men to fill the depleted ranks of the army.[25] In General Smith's view, the frontier counties were "a grand city of refuge where thousands of able-bodied men have flocked to escape service in the Confederate Army."[26]

24. C. S. West to Murrah, Oct. 19, 1864, Governor Pendleton Murrah Records, TSL-A. This letter, with an occasional change of wording, and without paragraph indentation, is found in West to Murrah, Oct. 19, 1864, *OR*, 48, pt. 1:1376–77.

25. West to Murrah, Oct. 19, 1864, Governor Pendleton Murrah Records, TSL-A. Four companies of the Frontier Regiment never left the Fort Belknap vicinity, west of Decatur, in the first Frontier District in 1864 and 1865, except for a short period from Aug. to Oct. of 1864. Also part of the permanent frontier defense force was the Border Regiment, under Colonel James A. Bourland, stationed on both sides of the Red River, to protect the exposed northwestern section of organized counties. For an analysis of the policy and process of the various elements that guarded the frontier of Texas see, David Paul Smith, "Frontier Defense in Texas, 1861–1865" (Ph.D. diss., University of North Texas, 1987).

26. Kirby Smith to Maj. C. S. West, Oct. 7, 1864, *OR*, 41, pt. 3:987.

Murrah received West's letter while the Texas Legislature met in a special session in the fall of 1864 with the status of the Frontier Organization at stake. Governor Murrah then placed General Smith's views before the legislature, but its members refused to change the law. Even when faced with a recently received letter from President Davis, which stated that he could not continue to exempt men from the conscription law, the lawmakers provided necessary funds to continue the frontier districts, and maintained steadfastly that the Frontier Organization should not be interfered with by Confederate authorities.[27] Murrah wrote that Smith's plan to order the Frontier Regiment back to the frontier would not strengthen the frontier defenses of Texas, but would only be an exchange of forces, an inequitable exchange for Texas. There remained the unalterable fact that once the Frontier Regiment became a Confederate Army unit, it was subject to recall at any time to meet emergencies elsewhere, which is exactly what happened only three months after its transfer when Magruder ordered Colonel James McCord and the six southern companies of the regiment to the interior. Moving the regiment to the frontier, coupled with ordering local militia to support the regiment, would give barely two thousand men to guard a frontier over five hundred miles in length and some 125 miles in breadth. Such an attempt to break up the Frontier Organization without substituting an adequate alternative plan could not be tolerated, Murrah said. With the firmness of conviction, Murrah defended the latest evolution of frontier defense in Texas:

The testimony, as I am informed, is almost unanimous from the frontier counties, that the present Organization affords better protection to that exposed portion of the State, than any mode of defense ever before adopted. By its exertions and influence, disloyal combinations have been broken up, deserters arrested and sent to their post of duty, and quiet order and satisfaction restored to those counties.[28]

If "quiet order" in the frontier counties was more than a small exaggeration, Murrah at least had the backing of the legislature and many of those who lived on the frontier that the Frontier Organization should be maintained. The new commander of the First Frontier District, future Texas governor James Webb Throckmorton, urged him to "maintain it at all hazards & to the last extremity," and stated unequivocally that should the Frontier Organization be broken up, not only would Indians and renegades continue to do serious damage in his district, but the entire frontier would be overrun by deserters, draft dodgers,

---

27. James M. Day, ed., *Senate and House Journals of the Tenth Legislature, Second Called Session, October 15, 1864–November 15, 1864* (Austin, 1966), 14, 17, 124–25; Murrah to Kirby Smith, Nov. 23, 1864, Governor Pendleton Murrah Records, TSL-A.

28. Murrah to Smith, Nov. 29, 1864, Governor Pendleton Murrah Records, TSL-A.

and traitors, and the frontier line would be thrown back upon a new line of counties. As for General Smith, he worked no further to break up the Frontier Organization, but submitted his arguments to President Davis in February of 1865 and awaited his decision. Davis, caught up in the maelstrom of events that soon led to the fall of Richmond, never replied, and the Frontier Organization continued in existence until the war's end.[29]

The fate of the Frontier Organization in the fall and winter of 1864–65 has been virtually ignored, much as has the story of the organization itself.[30] The most recent study of Murrah's administration does not view Murrah as quite the obstructionist that earlier historians saw, but rather one who placed the interests of the Confederacy ahead of state ones when necessary; the analysis, however, fails to place his stand on the Frontier Organization within the larger context of the search for a viable system of defense for the frontier, in the face of repeated failures by the United States and Confederate States to maintain it effectively. In the most perceptive and thorough study of the Trans-Mississippi Confederacy, Robert L. Kerby limits his discussion of the conscription dilemma in Texas to the militia debate in the spring of 1864, stating that "the belated capitulation of Texas removed the last official obstacle to the efficient prosecution of the draft west of the Mississippi," noting that at the time "the government of Texas virtually abdicated its claimed autonomy in favor of the army's authority." The most recent overview of the situation appears in a study of the Confederate war governors.[31] In this work, Ralph A. Wooster offers an excellent synopsis of the major problems and goals of the three war governors of Texas. He likewise adds that Murrah's concession in the militia debate in 1864 ended the controversy over the general question of conscription, but he at least includes three sen-

---

29. Throckmorton to Murrah, Dec. 9, 1864, Governor Pendleton Murrah Records, TSL-A; Kirby Smith to Jefferson Davis, Feb. 10, 1865, *OR*, 48, pt. 1:1373–74.

30. Robert Chellis Overfelt, "Defense of the Texas Frontier: 1861–1865" (M.A. thesis, Baylor University, 1968), 73, devotes one paragraph to the debate, all based on Day, ed., *Senate and House Journals of the Tenth Legislature, Second Called Session.* William Royston Geise, "Kirby Smithdom, 1864: A Study of Organization and Command in the Trans-Mississippi West," *Military History of Texas and the Southwest,* 15, No. 4 (1979), 29–30, allots one paragraph to a discussion of the militia debate in the spring of 1864, and includes two sentences on the debate over the fate of the Frontier Organization, which he bases on *OR*, 48, pt. 1:1373–77. James Farber, *Texas, C.S.A.* (New York, 1947), 180–84, deals with the militia debate in the spring of 1864, but makes only one observation on the issue of the Frontier Organization and conscription: "[Murrah] shortsightedly failed to see that by nullifying the Confederate draft laws by exempting all border residents from service in the Confederate Army, he was hamstringing victory."

31. Fredericka Ann Meiners, "The Texas Governorship, 1861–1865: Biography of an Office" (Ph.D. diss., Rice University, 1975); Quotations from Kerby, *Kirby Smith's Confederacy,* 279, 433; Wilfred Buck Yearns, ed., *The Confederate Governors* (Athens, Ga., 1985).

tences on the struggle over conscription in the frontier districts. Thus, the stance of Texas to preclude conscription in the frontier counties has received scant heed, just as Texans believed the frontier itself never received adequate attention from the national government.

A more cooperative spirit shown by the Texas legislators and Governor Murrah would almost certainly have led to a reduction in military strength for frontier protection, a state of affairs that Texas leaders would not contemplate. The people who lived along the Texas frontier never relented in their appeals to the state government for better protection, and in this instance, at least, the state-rights conflict with the Confederate government perhaps helped retain for the frontier a measure of protection it would never have received from the Confederacy. And in its struggle to obtain that protection, Texans revealed a frontier state's unique response to a national problem.

General Hamilton P. Bee. *CN 03266. Courtesy Center for American History, University of Texas at Austin.*

Hamilton P. Bee in the
Red River Campaign of 1864

FREDERICKA MEINERS*

In the spring of 1864 Union forces in Louisiana commanded by Major General Nathaniel P. Banks began a major drive up the Red River toward Shreveport and East Texas. Various Texas cavalry units were rushed to Louisiana to reinforce the outnumbered Confederates opposing Banks's advance. Among these Texas horsemen were several regiments commanded by Hamilton P. Bee, Laredo merchant, Mexican War veteran, and longtime state legislator.

Bee was relatively inexperienced in military command. He handled his cavalry fairly well in the battles of Mansfield and Pleasant Hill (although he was criticized by Major General John G. Walker), but at Monett's Ferry he withdrew his troops from a strong position, allowing Federal forces to slip away from an encirclement planned by his superior, Major General Richard Taylor. For this failure Bee was relieved from command.

In this essay Fredericka Meiners describes Bee's role in the Red River campaign. While she admits that Bee made errors, she points out that the Confederates lacked the manpower to carry out Taylor's plan. Given the speed and size of the Federal

* Fredericka Meiners, "Hamilton P. Bee in the Red River Campaign of 1864," *Southwestern Historical Quarterly*, LXXVIII (July, 1974), 21–44.

move, Bee may have acted properly in withdrawing his forces and avoiding destruction of his command.

For other views on Bee's action and the Red River campaign see Ludwell H.
Johnson, Red River Campaign: Politics and Cotton in the Civil War *(Baltimore:*
Johns Hopkins Press, 1958); Richard Taylor, Destruction and Reconstruction:
Personal Experiences of the Late War *(New York: Longman's, Green, and Co.,*
1955); T. Michael Parrish, Richard Taylor: Soldier Prince of Dixie *(Chapel Hill:*
University of North Carolina Press, 1992); and J. P. Blessington, Walker's Texas
Division *(reprint; Austin: State House Press, 1994).*

In the priorities of the United States for areas of action against the enemy in the
Civil War, the Trans-Mississippi ranked a poor third to the eastern and western
theaters. This was especially true after Vicksburg fell and the Union gained con-
trol of the Mississippi River. Even though General Nathaniel P. Banks's
Brownsville expedition of November, 1863, had shown the flag to the French in
Mexico and had gained a foothold on the Rio Grande, expanded operations in
Texas had not followed. The administration in Washington seemed satisfied
with what had been done and did not give Banks any men to continue the cam-
paign, even though trade between Texas and Mexico had not been halted.
Federal activities in December, January, and February of 1863–1864 consisted of
patrols and occasional raids on the Texas coast, but little more. Action in the
Trans-Mississippi Department, however, did not come to an end. General-in-
Chief Henry W. Halleck was determined to mount an offensive up the Red
River to take Shreveport. He thought this action would be the best defense for
Louisiana and Arkansas and would provide a base of operations against Texas.
Other considerations also offered reasons for a campaign. A vast storehouse of
southern supplies would be eliminated; Union strength would be further
demonstrated to the French; large quantities of cotton would be made available
for northern use. Preferring the more militarily desirable object of Mobile, the
commander of the Department of the Gulf, General Banks, objected at first,
but he yielded in February, 1864, to Halleck's plan.[1]

It was an involved scheme calling for combined movements in Arkansas and
Louisiana and for naval cooperation. Frederick Steele was to march on

---

1. Fred Harvey Harrington, *Fighting Politician: Major General N. P. Banks* (Philadelphia, 1948),
128–130, 151–153; Ludwell H. Johnson, *Red River Campaign: Politics and Cotton in the Civil War*
(Baltimore, 1958), 3–49; John D. Winters, *The Civil War in Louisiana* ([Baton Rouge], 1963),
324–326; J. C. Randall and David Donald, *The Civil War and Reconstruction* (2nd ed.; Boston,
1961), 452; H. L. Landers, "Wet Sand and Cotton—Banks' Red River Campaign," *Louisiana*
Historical Quarterly, XIX (January, 1936), 153; Richard Hobson Williams, "General Banks' Red River
Campaign," ibid., XXXII (January, 1949), 103–105.

Shreveport from Little Rock as one arm of a pincer movement. Banks, with his own men and 10,000 on loan from William T. Sherman's Army of the Tennessee, was to make his way up the Red with aid from Commodore David D. Porter's river gunboats. The two were to meet at Shreveport, the headquarters of the Trans-Mississippi Department.[2]

On March 12 the expedition started up the Red River, the long lines of soldiers staying close to the river and the comforting presence of the transports and gunboats. The Confederates under General Richard Taylor fell back before them. Taylor had no choice but to retreat. The Yankees numbered about 30,000, and he had only about 7,000 men, with no cavalry.[3]

More troops were on the way from Texas. General Edmund Kirby Smith, commander of the Confederate Trans-Mississippi Department, and Taylor had been watching the enemy concentration closely, and it was not difficult to determine that the large Federal army was meant for a drive on the Red River. On March 5 Kirby Smith ordered General John B. Magruder, commanding the District of Texas, New Mexico, and Arizona, to send General Thomas Green's Texas cavalry to Alexandria. A few days later he ordered all troops possible to Louisiana. Hamilton P. Bee's command was part of this exodus to stop the enemy.[4]

Bee was a Texan of long standing, having come to the state in 1837 at age fifteen to be with his father, Barnard E. Bee, who had held several offices in the Republic, including that of secretary of state. Hamilton worked at various positions before 1846—clerk to the comptroller Francis Lubbock, secretary on a treaty commission to the Comanches, and secretary of the first state Senate in 1845. During the Mexican War he served in Captain Benjamin McCulloch's company of cavalry in the battle at Monterrey and, under Mirabeau B. Lamar, helped bring the Laredo area under United States and Texas control. After the war Bee settled in Laredo as a merchant and served in the state House of Representatives from 1849 to 1858. He was speaker for the sixth session,

2. Harrington, *Fighting Politician*, 151–153; Johnson, *Red River Campaign*, 81–85; Joseph H. Parks, *General Edmund Kirby Smith, C.S.A.* (Baton Rouge, 1954), 374–376.

3. Troop returns, *War of the Rebellion: A Compilation of the Official Records of the Union and Confederate Armies* (130 vols.; Washington, D.C., 1880–1901), Series I, XXXIV, pt. 1, pp. 167–168; Richard Taylor, *Destruction and Reconstruction: Personal Experiences of the Late War*, edited by Charles P. Roland (Waltham, Massachusetts, 1968), 153. The *Official Records* are hereafter cited as *O.R.A.*, and, unless otherwise indicated, reference will be to Series I.

4. Samuel S. Anderson to Magruder, March 5, 1864, *O.R.A.*, XXXIV, pt. 2, p. 1027; William R. Boggs to Magruder, March 11, 1864, ibid., 1034; Boggs to Magruder, March 12, 1864, ibid., pt. 1, p. 494; Special Orders, No. 72, March 12, 1864, ibid., pt. 2, pp. 1037–1038; Special Orders No. 76, March 16, 1864, ibid., 1048; Johnson, *Red River Campaign*, 87; Parks, *Kirby Smith*, 372.

1855–1856. Although fairly prominent in state Democratic politics, he chose to retire in 1858 from both the business world and active political life. The speaker's chair had brought with it too many political enemies, and his tentative feelers found no support for a bid for Congress. He settled at Woodstock, his plantation on the San Antonio River in Goliad County, and tried to concentrate on raising cotton.[5]

When the Civil War came, Governor Edward Clark appointed Bee state-militia general, in June, 1861, probably because of his political connections. Bee was responsible for the Twenty-Ninth Militia District, a ten-county area including Karnes, Refugio, and Nueces counties. In March 1862, he received a commission as brigadier general in the Confederate army. His command, the Sub Military District of the Rio Grande, sometimes called the Western Sub-District, was large, stretching from Matagorda Bay to Brownsville to Eagle Pass to Fredericksburg to San Antonio. Bee made his headquarters in Brownsville in early 1863 and attempted to bring some order to the chaos on the border. The area had become a swirling mass of speculators, bandits, Unionists, deserters, spies, and Confederate agents, as Matamoros became the port of entry for Texas. Bee tried to regulate the cotton trade, keep on friendly terms with Mexico, and provide for the military defense of the border, while following sometimes conflicting orders from Magruder, Kirby Smith, and government officials at Richmond. He seemed to be making some progress in this difficult situation when, in November, Banks and his Union forces landed at the mouth of the Rio Grande. Bee, a very inexperienced military commander, panicked, abandoned the city, and fled northward. The winter of 1863–1864 was a cold one for him, spent trying to defend the bleak Texas coast from another invasion, which never came.[6]

Bee received Major General Magruder's order to proceed to Alexandria on March 12, 1864. He reported that he had to leave some of his command in position on the coast, but had six regiments on the march.[7] Magruder first told him to take all his transport with him, but to move with the least amount of baggage possible. By March 23, fearing that the state was being stripped of wagons, the major general had reduced to fifteen the number of wagons allowed a cavalry regiment. This created some difficulty for more commanders than Bee, and

---

5. Fredericka Meiners, "Hamilton Prioleau Bee" (M.A. thesis, Rice University, 1972), 1–6. Indications exist that Bee was involved in some kind of settlement for the estate of Gideon K. Lewis in Corpus Christi. See Tom Lea, *The King Ranch* (2 vols.; Boston, 1957), I, 137, 438 n.

6. Meiners, "Bee," 9–40, 48–83, 91–123, 129–157.

7. Special Orders, No. 72, March 12, 1864, *O.R.A.*, XXXIV, pt. 2, pp. 1037–1038; Bee to Magruder, March 13, 1864, ibid., 1040.

General Taylor complained to Kirby Smith. Troops had to bring their own provisions and forage because those items and wagons were scarce in Louisiana.[8]

By April 1 Bee was at Sabinetown in Louisiana, with his command strung out and separated on the road. The General did not know the whereabouts of some of his regiments, but thought he had enough men to "cut" his way to Taylor if the enemy came between them.[9] Bee reported to Taylor at Mansfield on the fifth with X. B. Debray's, A. Buchel's, and A. W. Terrell's regiments. He was given a division consisting of two brigades under Debray and Buchel in General Tom Green's Cavalry Corps.[10]

Taylor had steadily fallen back before the enemy, but he was tired of retreating. Now that reinforcements were arriving, he thought of giving battle, even though still seriously outnumbered. The fresh troops would bring his forces to only 9,000. Enemy occupation of Mansfield, however, would put Banks at the junction of three roads to Shreveport and a number of ways west to Texas, and Taylor had to prevent that situation.[11]

Banks was at Natchitoches, having occupied that city on April 1. The Union general did not expect Taylor to make a stand yet, and this assumption led him to blunder. From Natchitoches and Grand Ecore two routes led to Shreveport—one by the river and the other to the west through Pleasant Hill and Mansfield. Banks did not know of a road along the water route and did not look for one. Instead, he chose the road to the west away from the river and naval protection.[12]

From Natchitoches to Mansfield the land changed character markedly—from rich plantations to smaller places surrounded by dense pine thickets on sandy hills. Water was very scarce, and the rain that fell on the seventh of April served only to turn the red-clay-and-sand road to mud, rather than to quench the thirst of men. The road Banks picked was narrow and, at times, sunken, and it wandered over the hills and through ravines, offering a dismal view of a dreary countryside.[13]

By now Union strength had been somewhat reduced, as detachments were left behind to occupy Alexandria and other points. At Natchitoches, Banks sent 2,500 more away from the main force to go upriver with the navy. After that

8. Special Orders, No. 72, March 12, 1864, ibid., 1037–1038; Magruder to Bee, March 23, 1864, ibid., 1075; Taylor to Boggs, April 2, 1864, ibid., pt. 1, p. 518.

9. Bee to James E. Slaughter, April 1, 1864, ibid., pt. 3, pp. 722–723.

10. Bee to Simeon Hart, report, April 10, 1864, ibid., pt. 1, p. 606.

11. Taylor, *Destruction and Reconstruction*, 154–157.

12. For a complete discussion of Banks's decision, see Johnson, *Red River Campaign*, 113–114.

13. Ibid., 118.

assignment he still had about 19,000, more than enough to crush any Rebel opposition. On the sixth of April the Federals marched out of Natchitoches for Shreveport with their inexperienced cavalry in the van. They met the Confederates at Pleasant Hill on the seventh.[14]

A portion of Green's cavalry waiting for the Yankees put up a brisk fight, finally halting the Union advance at Carroll's Mill, some eight miles on the road to Mansfield. Bee was ordered up in reserve with Debray's, Buchel's, and Terrell's regiments and put his forces into line of battle, where they remained for the night.[15]

At daylight Green returned to Mansfield with James P. Major's Division and all of the artillery, leaving Bee to contest the enemy advance.[16] This Bee did by forming the regiments in "successive lines of battle," at intervals of five hundred yards, holding each line as long as possible, and then retiring to the next. In the heavily wooded country the Confederate cavalry was able to consume seven hours in its retreat of seven miles to Taylor's waiting position.[17]

While Bee was delaying the Federal advance, Taylor had prepared his battle lines about three miles outside of Mansfield.[18] His men occupied the northern side of a large clearing, eight hundred yards across by twelve hundred from east to west, straddling the road. A hill ran down the middle parallel to the long sides of the clearing, and the enemy following Bee took the crest as the skirmishers fell back. Discovery of the Confederate line of battle led to hurried attempts to bring forces to the front. Banks had committed an error in choosing the Mansfield road, but that in itself was not a fatal mistake. His order of march, however, was disastrous, because immediately following the cavalry was

14. Banks to Grant, report, April 13, 1864, *O.R.A.*, XXXIV, pt. 1, p. 181; Johnson, *Red River Campaign*, 110–111; Harrington, *Banks*, 154.

15. Bee to Hart, April 10, 1864, William T. Mechling Subcollection, Jeremiah Y. Dashiell Papers (Archives, University of Texas Library, Austin); Bee to Hart, report, April 10, 1864, *O.R.A.*, pt. 1, p. 606.

16. _____ to Bee, April 8, 1864, Mechling Subcollection.

17. Bee to Hart, report, April 10, 1864, *O.R.A.*, XXXIV, pt. 1, pp. 606–607; Bee to Hart, April 10, 1864, Mechling Subcollection.

18. More complete descriptions of the battle of Mansfield, upon which this account is based, may be found in Johnson, *Red River Campaign*, 101–145; Winters, *Civil War in Louisiana*, 330–347; Landers, "Wet Sand," 162–180; Williams, "Red River," 118–122; Taylor, *Destruction and Reconstruction*, 159–162; Richard B. Irwin, *History of the Nineteenth Army Corps* (New York, 1892), 299–312; Harrington, *Fighting Politician*, 151–157; Jackson Beauregard Davis, "The Life of Richard Taylor," *Louisiana Historical Quarterly*, XXIV (January, 1941), 84–90; Robert Selph Henry, *The Story of the Confederacy* (Indianapolis, 1931), 341–346; Parks, *Kirby Smith*, 386. The Yankees called the battle Sabine Crossroads.

its train of 320 to 350 wagons, which stretched out for almost three miles. Despite the pleas of the cavalry commander, Albert L. Lee, neither Banks nor William B. Franklin, leading the Nineteenth Corps, would change the designated order or give him much infantry assistance. When Lee found the Rebels and drew what forces he had into line, therefore, all he could muster on the field by three-thirty in the afternoon was about 4,800 effectives, half of whom were dismounted cavalry.[19]

Bee, on arriving at the position about noon, was ordered by Taylor to the extreme right flank, next to John G. Walker's infantry division. Debray's regiment was placed in reserve, but then brought up into line, and Taylor ordered Terrell's regiment to help reinforce the left, thinking the enemy was massing on that side.[20]

At four o'clock Taylor ordered the attack opened on the left. When the action was well underway, he sent the right into motion. Walker was to move forward and turn the enemy's left while Bee swept around and gained the rear.[21] The cavalry, however, had to make its way through the dense timber at the end of the clearing, and its progress was slow. While the infantry drove the enemy before them, Bee and his men fought trees and swamps. Before Bee managed to disentangle his command from the undergrowth, the Yankee lines had broken. The battle turned into a rout, causing one Rebel soldier to remark that the Federals were "making Bull Run time"[22] as they fled, leaving all their equipment and the wagon train to the exultant Confederates.

When Bee and his men finally met the enemy, just before nightfall, it was at a place called Pleasant Grove, a small clearing with a fenced farm and a creek. The Yankees were no longer running. General William H. Emory's First Division of the Nineteenth Corps had hurried to the front and was drawn up to halt the Confederate advance and avert a complete Federal disaster. The southerners were disorganized after the long two-mile pursuit, but they attacked immediately.[23]

---

19. Irwin, *Nineteenth Corps*, 309; Johnson, *Red River Campaign*, 125–139.

20. Taylor, *Destruction and Reconstruction*, 159, Taylor to Anderson, report, April 18, 1864, *O.R.A.*, XXXIV, pt. 1, pp. 563–564

21. Taylor to Anderson, report, April 18, 1864, *O.R.A.*, XXXIV, pt. 1, pp. 564–565; Taylor, *Destruction and Reconstruction*, 159–161.

22. Rebecca W. Smith and Marion Mullins (eds.), "The Diary of H. C. Medford, Confederate Soldier, 1864," *Southwestern Historical Quarterly*, XXXIV (January, 1931), 218.

23. Bee to Hart, report, April 10, 1864, *O.R.A.*, XXXIV, pt. 1, p. 607; Bee to Hart, April 10, 1864, Mechling Subcollection. Bee called this final action of the day the battle of the Peach Orchard and considered it distinct from the battle of Mansfield.

Their charge ran into intense rifle fire at point-blank range. Neither side had artillery; it had been left behind in the rush. Bee's men tried to turn the Federal left after an attack on the enemy right had failed, but the Yankee lines there held also. Confederate pressure in the twenty-minute action was sufficient, however, to force the Union men back some four hundred yards and give the Rebels possession of the creek, the only source of water on the battlefield. Bee and his men slept that night on their final positions. The enemy retreated.[24]

At dawn on the ninth, a bright spring day, Taylor ordered the cavalry in pursuit of the retreating enemy. Bee followed George T. Madison's and George W. Baylor's regiments of James P. Major's Division along a road strewn with burnt-out wagons, abandoned arms, and dead or wounded men. The Confederates captured many stragglers, whom they sent quickly to the rear. At nine o'clock that morning, the leading detachments encountered the enemy drawn up in line a mile outside of Pleasant Hill.[25]

Since he was the ranking general in the advance, Bee assumed command and put his troops into position with Buchel on his left and other regiments as they arrived, to the right. A reconnaissance informed him that the enemy line was long, extending for a mile between two patches of timber. Bee had thought that he was chasing a routed and retreating enemy, and "this extraordinary show of force on the part of the enemy" surprised him. He quickly concluded that his "irregular cavalry would have no business to charge such a line of battle."[26] General Green soon arrived and took command, and the cavalry, except for some skirmishing, made no moves against the enemy. While the Confederates waited for the remainder of the army to come up, they studied the position.[27]

Pleasant Hill was a large clearing on the top of a slight plateau containing a number of buildings which made up a summer resort. Surrounding the hill were tracts of pine woods and thickets; a number of roads—to Mansfield, the Sabine, Fort Jesup, Natchitoches, and Blair's Landing—ran through the battlefield. The Federal line extended in a shallow "u" in front of the village between the woodlands and across the roads to Mansfield and the Sabine.

Action did not begin until three in the afternoon because Taylor wanted to give his tired infantry a couple of hours rest after their long march from

24. Taylor, *Destruction and Reconstruction*, 161; Taylor to Anderson, report, April 18, 1864, *O.R.A.*, XXXIV, pt. 1, p. 565; Emory to Hoffman, report, April 12, 1864, ibid., 389–392.

25. Bee to Hart, report, April 10, 1864, ibid., 607–608; Bee to Hart, April 10, 1864, Mechling Subcollection; Alwyn Barr (ed.), "William T. Mechling's Journal of the Red River Campaign, April 7–May 10, 1864," *Texana*, I (Fall, 1963), 367.

26. Bee to Hart, report, April 10, 1864, *O.R.A.*, XXXIV, pt. 1, pp. 607–608.

27. Ibid.; Bee to Hart, April 10, 1864, Mechling Subcollection; Barr (ed.), "Mechling's Journal," 367.

Mansfield. Cavalry was posted on the right flank to cover Thomas J. Churchill's infantry divisions. Walker was placed to left of center, with Bee on his left on the Mansfield road. The far side of the line consisted of Major's Division, dismounted, with Camille de Polignac's infantry division in reserve behind Bee. Taylor planned to open with Churchill in a flanking movement trying to roll up the Federal left. Walker was to attack when he heard the sound of Churchill's guns, pulling the battle to the left. When the attack on the right "disordered" the enemy, Bee, with Buchel's and Debray's cavalry, was to charge straight up the road and through the village on the top of the hill, while Major took possession of the road to Blair's Landing on the Red River.[28]

At three Churchill started his men moving, but he did not swing far enough right to flank the enemy, and his attack was stalled for a short time. Walker, hearing the battle on his right, put his own brigades into motion. When Green saw this and heard Churchill's guns, he supposed the enemy to be in retreat as planned and ordered Bee's cavalry to make their charge. It was about four-thirty in the afternoon.[29]

Bee and his troopers rode out toward the Yankee lines in columns of fours, Debray's regiment in the lead. Bee intended to deploy and charge when closer to the enemy, but before he could give the order the Federals opened fire from an ambush fifty yards away. The Twenty-fourth Missouri had concealed itself in a deep gully filled with a thick growth of young pine trees which was behind a fence parallel to Bee's line of march. They waited until the Rebels came within point-blank range and then hit them broadside from the left. This unexpected volley wreaked havoc in the cavalry columns. Men and horses went down, falling in all directions. Frightened animals reared and ran, some dragging their wounded riders by the stirrup. Men screamed, some in agony, others trying to give directions. Those who could, picked themselves up and made for cover in some pine ravines close by. There they found a haven of sorts from the fire now coming from the front as well as the left.[30]

28. Taylor, *Destruction and Reconstruction*, 163–165; Taylor to Anderson, report, April 8, 1864, *O.R.A.*, XXXIV, pt. 1, pp. 566–568.

29. Bee to Hart, April 10, 1864, Mechling Subcollection; Bee to Hart, report, April 10, 1864, *O.R.A.*, XXXIV, pt. 1, p. 608; Taylor to Anderson, report, April 18, 1864, ibid., 566–567. For more complete descriptions of the battle of Pleasant Hill, see Johnson, *Red River Campaign*, 146–169; Winters, *Civil War in Louisiana*, 348–355; Taylor, *Destruction and Reconstruction*, 163–173; Williams, "Red River," 123–125; Irwin, *Nineteenth Corps*, 313–322; Frank Moore (ed.), *The Rebellion Record: A Diary of American Events* (20 vols.; New York, 1862–1871), VIII, 535–567; Harrington, *Fighting Politician*, 157.

30. Bee to Hart, April 10, 1864, Mechling Subcollection; Bee to Hart, report, April 10, 1864, *O.R.A.*, XXXIV, pt. 1, p. 608; Johnson, *Red River Campaign*, 156.

Buchel managed to pull his regiment back in time to avoid the ambush. Dismounting, he quickly led his men behind the fence and attacked the Federal rear, driving the Yankees back to their own lines. In so doing the Prussian was wounded fatally. Bee had two horses shot from under him, but rallied his men and brought them back to their own lines, receiving praise from Taylor for withdrawing his men "with coolness and pluck" and retiring last himself.[31]

Fighting, by now, extended to the extreme end of the line. Bee dismounted the remainder of his men and joined forces with Major to continue the battle. He led Buchel's men into action himself. In the attacks on the Federal entrenchments Bee received two slight wounds in the face, but continued to take part until darkness brought an end to the battle. With no artillery, the Confederates on the left had been unable to force the enemy works.[32]

Pleasant Hill was not a victory for the South. While Bee and his companion had been holding the left, the Confederate force on the right had been attacked by the enemy reserve. The Union advance which followed drove Churchill's men back to the woods past their positions at the beginning of the battle. The Confederate withdrawal could have been turned into a rout, but, because of darkness, heavy losses, and unfamiliar terrain, the Federals did not pursue.[33]

In order to obtain water, since there was none on the field, Taylor ordered his troops to fall back to the nearest source some six miles away. He left Bee on the field with two companies of Buchel's regiment and two companies of Debray's regiment to keep contact with the enemy. Bee set up his camp some eight hundred yards from the village and entertained important visitors. Taylor had remained with him, and about eight o'clock Kirby Smith arrived from Shreveport. The three men had coffee at Bee's campfire and listened to the sounds of wagons and other movement that testified to enemy departure. Before he left at ten, Taylor told Bee to return to the battlefield and picket the enemy lines. This Bee did, with some of Buchel's men, and quickly established that the enemy had not moved yet from his forward lines. Picket fire soon died down, and after midnight all that could be heard were the groans and cries of the wounded still on the field.[34]

---

31. Taylor, *Destruction and Reconstruction*, 167.

32. Bee to Hart, April 10, 1864, Mechling Subcollection; Bee to Hart, report, April 10, 1864, *O.R.A.*, XXXIV, pt. 1, pp. 608–609; Taylor to Anderson, report, April 18, 1864, ibid., 567; Taylor, *Destruction and Reconstruction*, 167; Barr (ed.), "Mechling's Journal," 367–368.

33. Johnson, *Red River Campaign*, 157–164.

34. Barr (ed.), "Mechling's Journal," 368; Bee to Hart, report, April 10, 1864, *O.R.A.*, XXXIV, pt. 1, pp. 608–609; Taylor to Anderson, report, April 18, 1864, ibid., 568; Taylor, *Destruction and Reconstruction*, 165–168; Parks, *Kirby Smith*, 388–391.

Hamilton Bee probably felt fairly pleased with himself that night. He had met the enemy in open combat and had acquitted himself gallantly. He had received praise from the commander of the army, Richard Taylor. He had been privy to the highest councils when Kirby Smith visited his camp. His excitement showed in his reports, which were considerably more "eloquent" than his letters from Brownsville had been. Bee was generous with his praise for his men and modest in his accounts of his own actions.[35]

But Bee did not escape criticism. John G. Walker, commanding the infantry division which Bee's cavalry was to support at Mansfield, did not consider him fit for command of a large body of troops because of his conduct. In that battle Bee had failed to accomplish his designated purpose when his men became entangled in the woods and were unable to attack the enemy rear. This failure and Bee's "general want of appreciation of the necessities of the moment" were the reasons why the Confederates had not captured Banks's entire transportation and artillery, according to Walker. The infantry commander claimed that Bee had "failed on the eighth to take any share in the engagement, or in any manner to contribute to the success of the day. . . ." And as if that were not enough, he charged that Bee had not been "eager to retrieve his mistake on the following day." When ordered to be in line of battle before daylight, he was not ready until a half hour after sunup, by which time others were already in pursuit of the enemy.[36]

It must be pointed out that Walker was wounded in the last stages of the battle at Pleasant Hill and knew nothing of Bee's activities of that day. Although that certainly would not erase any previous mistakes, it might have influenced Walker to be a little more lenient. Whether anyone could have brought cavalry through the dense pine woods on time is impossible to determine, but the general does not seem to have taken the terrain into account in his criticism. The infantry had a clear field. Bee had been at Pleasant Grove and had taken part in the fighting there, but there had been much confusion in the disorganized commands, and Bee, who usually mentioned the generals he met, did not indicate even seeing Walker on the field.

Bee gave no indication that he received an order from Walker to be in line of battle before daylight, only that at dawn he was ordered to pursue the enemy. If Bee did receive an order from Walker, it could easily have been vague as to time. "Dawn" or "daylight" mean different things to different people. Bee had no

---

35. Bee to Hart, report, April 10, 1864, *O.R.A.*, XXXIV, pt. 1, pp. 608–610; Bee to Hart, April 10, 1864, Mechling Subcollection.

36. Walker to Boggs, August 15, 1864, *O.R.A.*, XLI, pt. 2, pp. 1066–1067.

idea, at least in his reports, that he had not followed this order or that Walker was displeased about his actions that morning or the previous day. Walker was also writing after the action at Monett's Ferry and may have been influenced by Bee's conduct there. With no real evidence to the contrary, Walker's judgment that an important command for Bee would be a "public calamity,"[37] based on his actions on the eighth and morning of the ninth, seems harsher than necessary. If nothing else, Bee's tardiness could be blamed on inexperience, not nonaggressiveness. Bee wanted to fight.

In February, 1864, Bee had been appraised in an inspection report as an "excellent man," although one with "but little service."[38] The battles of Mansfield and Pleasant Hill were his first real face-to-face encounters with the enemy since the Mexican War—he had not stayed long enough to fight at Brownsville—and his reports indicated a certain naive attitude toward the enemy. His surprise at the "extraordinary show of force" by the Yankees drawn up before Pleasant Hill was too great.[39] He was too willing to assume from the remnants of retreat and rout that the enemy was incapable of battle. He also seemed to make too quickly assumptions that the enemy would do what he wanted him to do. But Bee was not the only one with these tendencies. Taylor also had thought the enemy more demoralized than he really was. The test for Bee would come when he was on his own again.

Hamilton Bee, on the field at Pleasant Hill, did not hear any criticism or consider his own shortcomings. He was convinced both battles had been victories and all had behaved gallantly. He and his men remained at their forward posts through the cold night of the ninth of April. At dawn, when they advanced, they learned that the enemy had indeed retreated from the field, and without taking their wounded with them. Bee moved into the village with his men and went to the house which Banks had occupied the night before, according to the "kind lady" who owned it. He sent word of the retreat back to Taylor and dispatched his cavalry in pursuit of the enemy, who were moving to Grand Ecore. The troopers, under W. O. Yager in place of the fallen Buchel, followed for twenty miles without firing a shot before coming on the Federal rear guard.[40]

Bee meanwhile stayed in Pleasant Hill, where he was soon visited by a num-

---

37. Ibid.

38. Inspection report, February 16, 1864, ibid., XXII, pt. 2, p. 1131.

39. Bee to Hart, report, April 10, 1864, ibid., XXXIV, pt. 1, p. 607.

40. H. P. Bee, "Battle of Pleasant Hill—An Error Corrected," *Southern Historical Society Papers*, VIII (April, 1880), 184–186; Barr (ed.), "Mechling's Journal," 368; Bee to Hart, report, April 10, 1864, *O.R.A.*, XXXIV, pt. 1, p. 609.

ber of Union surgeons who had been left behind to care for the wounded of their army. The general did not consider them prisoners of war, but offered them what assistance he could, within the limitations of his facilities. General Green arrived and took command, and the rest of the day was spent caring for the wounded and burying the dead.[41]

On the eleventh Bee and his command, consisting of several brigades from his and Major's divisions, were sent out to keep a close eye on the Yankees and to apply constant pressure to enemy lines. For a week the cavalry skirmished in front of Grand Ecore. During this time General Tom Green was killed at Blair's Landing while contesting the passage of a Union ship headed for Grand Ecore. Command of the cavalry corps passed to Bee for a few days until John A. Wharton arrived and took over.[42] Bee, reinforced by the remainder of Major's Division and Debray with two regiments, continued to harass the enemy until April 20,[43] when he turned over command of the position in front of Grand Ecore to William Steele and moved south.

Just below Grand Ecore, Cane River, originally the main channel of the Red River, leaves the larger stream, parallels it on the south, and rejoins it about thirty straight-line miles downstream. The road downriver to Alexandria goes through the island formed by the two rivers, crossing the Cane at Grand Ecore on the north end and at Monett's Ferry on the south. Steep, pine-clad hills arise from the water on the south bank of the ferry, offering a good view of the other side, which is low and relatively flat.[44]

Bee, with five regiments and one battery, moved into this area from Natchitoches, after receiving orders to place guns on the Red River for operations against Union transports and gunboats carrying supplies. The command camped that night on the Cane, and the next day, the twenty-first, they crossed

---

41. Bee, "Pleasant Hill," 184–186 (quotations); Barr (ed.), "Mechling's Journal," 368; Taylor, *Destruction and Reconstruction*, 206; Bee to Lubbock, May 9, 1864, Mechling Subcollecton.

42. Bee, General Orders, No. 1, April 15, 1864, in Houston *Daily Telegraph*, April 22, 1864. When Bee took over from Green, Harvey C. Medford, a private in Lane's Texas Cavalry, Major's Division, wrote, "I am sorry he is in command too, for I do not believe that General Bee has the ingenuity or the military skill to effect anything against the enemy. Brig. Gen. Major surpasses him in every particular, and all of the characteristics incident to a military man. It is a pity that rank should supercede knowledge, experience and known abilities." Smith and Mullins (eds.), "Medford Diary," 229–230.

43. Bee to Francis R. Lubbock, May 9, 1864, Mechling Subcollection; Barr (ed.) "Mechling's Journal," 369–371; Taylor, *Destruction and Reconstruction*, 177–179; Winters, *Civil War in Louisiana*, 357–361.

44. Taylor, *Destruction and Reconstruction*, 179; [Xavier B. Debray], *A Sketch of the History of Debray's 26th Regiment of Texas Cavalry* (Austin, 1884), 21; Johnson, *Red River Campaign*, 222.

the Twenty-four Mile Ferry onto the island and marched to a point a mile or so below Cloutierville. The village was the only settlement on the island, about three-fourths of the way to Monett's Ferry. Engineers scouted the Red River and found a place for the battery, but it was too late in the day to establish the guns. The men, tired after being in constant service since Mansfield, settled down that night for a much needed rest. Word that Mosby M. Parson's brigade had been driven back to Double Bridges, twenty miles southeast of Pleasant Hill, worried Bee. He posted pickets six miles from camp up the island on the Natchitoches road, but he did not expect trouble.[45]

At two o'clock the next morning the pickets were driven in by a large Union cavalry detachment. The tired men were awakened and formed into line, but the enemy did not appear until sometime after daylight. Bee had already sent his train to Monett's Ferry, some six miles away, and when he saw that the Federals were in force, he followed, skirmishing as he went. There he met General Major in position on the hills on the south side of the river with his small group of men and three batteries. The two generals prepared to defend the crossing from what Bee thought was a force sent down to prevent his taking position on the Red River. It was not until the next day, the twenty-third, that he looked down from the hill and realized "that Banks's whole army was upon me."[46]

General Banks had decided on April 18 to retreat from Grand Ecore, Alexandria, and the Red River. The river was falling, and Porter's boats could no longer operate in the shallow water. U. S. Grant wanted the return of Sherman's troops which he had loaned to Banks. Under the circumstances, with no naval protection and the depletion of his forces, and with no word from Arkansas that Steele was advancing on Shreveport, Banks ordered withdrawal. He did not know that Kirby Smith had taken most of Taylor's troops away from him to combat the northern threat, but thought that the Confederates had 25,000 men. Taylor actually had left only some 2,000 infantrymen under Polignac and about 3,000 cavalry under Wharton. Banks had 17,000 to 20,000, and he could have pushed forward to Shreveport without too much trouble, if he had had the nerve to try.[47]

---

45. Bee to Lubbock, May 9, 1864, Mechling Subcollection; Barr (ed.), "Mechling's Journal," 372; Bee to B. F. Weems, report, May 14, 1864, *O.R.A.*, XXXIV, pt. 1, p. 610

46. Quoted in Bee to Weems, report, May 14, 1864, *O.R.A.*, XLXIV, pt. 1, p. 612; Bee to Lubbock, May 9, 1864, Mechling Subcollection.

47. Johnson, *Red River Campaign*, 214–221; Harrington, *Fighting Politician*, 157–159; Winters, *Civil War in Louisiana*, 359–361; Banks to Grant, report, April 17, 1864, *O.R.A.*, XXXIV, pt. 1, pp. 187–188; Banks to Grant, report, April 30, 1864, ibid., 189–192.

On April 19 A. J. Smith led the way to Natchitoches, and then on the twen-ty-first the Union army set off on the road to Cloutierville and Monett's Ferry. A report came in that the Confederates also were heading for the ferry to cut off the retreat, and the march was quickened to an exhausting pace which left many stragglers behind. Leading units camped three miles south of Cloutierville the night of the twenty-second, and advanced on the ferry before dawn on the twenty-third. They found Bee already in possession of the ford.[48]

When he arrived on the twenty-second, Bee had positioned his men, defer-ring to Major's suggestions, since Major had been there longer and had a better knowledge of the ground. Most of Bee's troops were put into line, the majority on the right of tne ferry, but Terrell's and Yager's regiments were sent back to Beasley Plantation to the west to guard the depot of supplies and Bee's train there. Beasley's was thought to be open to attack from Cloutierville. A. P. Bagby's brigade, reinforced by Debray's regiment under Captain J. L. Lane, held the right side of the line, and Major and the artillery, with P. C. Woods's regi-ment, were in the center covering the ferry. On the left, under Debray at first and Colonel George W. Baylor later, was W. P. Lane's brigade, consisting—from center to left—of Baylor's, Isham Chisum's, Lane's, and George T. Madison's regiments and the First Battalion of Louisiana State Troops.[49]

Although Bee's total complement amounted to only 2,000 men, he had one important advantage. He was occupying a naturally strong position. The steep hills on the right looked out over a low swampy area with trees only on the river banks. Open fields led to the crossing and offered no cover from attack. To the left on Bee's side stretched timbered hills protected by more swamps, lakes, streams, and ravines that appeared impassable. The river itself was supposed to be fordable only at the ferry, and Bee, expecting the attack there, massed what strength he had at that point.

A light rain fell about daylight on the morning of the twenty-third, cleaning the air of dust so that Bee had a clear view of the enemy from a hill about two miles on the left of the ferry. As more and more Federals appeared Bee estimat-ed that by ten o'clock fully 15,000 opposed his center. The Union generals had obviously decided not to attack the ferry for a time, because Bee could see

48. William B. Franklin to George B. Drake, report, April 29, 1864, ibid., 262; William H. Emory to Wickham Hoffman, report, April 28, 1864, ibid., 395–397; Richard Arnold to Assistant Adjutant General, report, May 5, 1864, ibid., 460–461.

49. Bee to Lubbock, May 9, 1864, Mechling Subcollection; Baylor to ———— Ogden, report, April 18, 1864, O.R.A., XXXIV, pt. 1, p. 619; for more on the Federal side, see Johnson, *Red River Campaign*, 206–241; and Winters, *Civil War in Louisiana*, 361–365.

detachments being sent off to feel for other approaches to or around his position. A cavalry column was sent downriver to the Confederate right, and some infantry regiments upriver to the Confederate left. Bee could do nothing but watch. He did not have the men to assume anything more than a defensive posture, and, if the river lived up to its reputation of being unfordable, then he was in a good place to inflict much damage on the Union army.[50]

Unfortunately, as the Red River had dropped, so had the Cane, and the enemy infantry was able to find a ford about two miles upriver from the ferry. Low water in the rivers also meant a semi-dry condition in land that was usually marsh. Federal forces were able to make their way through the wooded country to the position held by Baylor's brigade on the hills.[51]

When scouts brought report of the enemy crossing, Baylor was sent a section of artillery, two rifled guns, from M. V. McMahan's Battery. When the enemy appeared the guns opened up with some effect and soon drew the fire of Union artillery across the river. As it became clear that the Federals were moving in force there, Major gave Baylor command of the left wing, but left his regiment in position at the ferry. Baylor immediately asked for reinforcements. Woods's regiment was pulled out of the center and sent to him. In spite of all efforts to hold, Madison's, Lane's, and Woods's men and the Louisianians could not maintain their first positions and were forced to fall back to a line of fences and thick undergrowth.[52]

To mask the crossing and movement upriver, the Union forces had started an artillery duel at the ferry, but neither side hurt the other much as they blazed away. Bee had watched this carefully for signs of impending attack, but as more reports arrived from the left, he became uneasy about that end of the line. When it appeared that the right was in no danger of immediate attack, Bee pulled Baylor's and Chisum's regiments out of line at the ferry and went with them to reinforce Baylor. They arrived just after the retreat to the second line, and Baylor put the regiments in on his right. His line was anchored on the river and extended over the hills, but was in the air at the left end. He did not have enough men to reach Mill Lake, a body of water several miles in length, that would have secured the position. Before he could ask Bee for more troops, however, the latter had gone back to the center at a request from Major.[53]

―――――

50. Bee to Lubbock, May 9, 1864, Mechling Subcollection; Barr (ed.), "Mechling's Journal," 373–374; Bee to Weems, report, May 14, 1864, *O.R.A.*, XXXIV, pt. 1, pp. 610–611.

51. Johnson, *Red River Campaign*, 228.

52. Bee to Lubbock, May 9, 1864, Mechling Subcollection; Bee to Weems, report May 14, 1864, *O.R.A.*, XXXIV, pt. 1, p. 611; Baylor to Ogden, report, April 18, 1864, ibid., 619.

53. Bee to Lubbock, May 9, 1864, Mechling Subcollection; Bee to Weems, report, May 14, 1864,

When Bee arrived at the ferry he was informed that a report had been received from Captain Lane of Debray's regiment on the extreme right. Lane said he was being pushed from place by an enemy force of some numbers. Word had come to Bee earlier of a rumored landing from transports on the Red River below the mouth of the Cane, but it had been discounted or disregarded. Now it appeared to be true. Baylor's message that his flanks would be turned unless he filled the gap between his left and the lake, which some enemy troops had already reached, combined with Lane's report, convinced Bee that both his flanks were about to be turned, and that the "critical moment had come." He could expect an immense frontal attack at any minute and was persuaded of its imminence by another barrage from the enemy artillery at the ferry. With his few troops he could not expect to hold and he determined to abandon the position. He sent word to Baylor to "get out of there the best way" he could, and started his men on the road to Beasley's. He had lost about fifty men.[54]

Bee went to Beasley's to pick up supplies, since the troops were without rations. He expected the enemy forces to take a day to cross the river, during which time he could reprovision and return to harass their progress. But Beasley's turned out to be thirty miles away, and by the time the Confederates

---

O.R.A., XXXIV, pt. 1, p. 611; Taylor to Ogden, report, April 18, 1864, ibid., 619.

54. Bee to Weems, report, May 14, 1864, ibid., 611 (first quotation); Baylor to Ogden, report, April 18, 1864, ibid., 620 (second quotation); Bee to Lubbock, May 9, 1864, Mechling Subcollection. This letter covers the events from April 10 to May 9 and contains much information which apparently has never been published. Bee referred in it to the report of a Yankee landing on the Red River that figured so prominently in his decision to abandon the ferry. According to Alwyn Barr, who edited the journal of W. T. Mechling, Bee's adjutant general for this period, Mechling confirrns a "previously unsupported statement" by Theophilus Noel that Bee had received such a report (p. 364). Barr also states that Bee probably omitted any mention of the report from his own account through "a sense of chagrin" (p. 374n.) because the report had been false. Yet a correspondent for the Houston *Tri-Weekly Telegraph* calling himself "Sioux," who was with Bee's forces at Monett's Ferry, reported in the paper that they fell back because another Yankee column was coming from the Red River. This letter to Lubbock was a report made to the assistant adjutant general, Lubbock, of Wharton's Cavalry Corps. Wharton was Bee's direct commander at that time. Bee may have omitted the information in his report to Taylor from chagrin, as Barr claims. But that report was written on the fourteenth, after Bee had been relieved, and he might have thought either that Taylor had seen his letter of the ninth, or that it would do no good to include the information. The general was too angry to listen. As Barr states, Johnson's *Red River Campaign* does not use the Noel or Mechling accounts. Neither used the Bee-to-Lubbock letter. Theophilus Noel, *A Campaign from Santa Fe to the Mississippi, Being a History of the Old Sibley Brigade*, edited by Martin Hardwich Hall and Edwin Adams Davis (Houston, 1961), 124–126; Barr (ed.), "Mechling's Journal," 364, 374 n.; Johnson, *Red River Campaign*, 206–241; Houston *Tri-Weekly Telegraph*, May 2, 1864; Bee to Weems, report, May 14, 1864, O.R.A., XXXIV, pt. 1, p. 611; Bee to Boggs, report, September 17, 1864, ibid., 613.

reached it, early in the morning of the twenty-fourth, they were exhausted. Bee stayed at Beasley's until two in the afternoon and then marched out again. He did not make contact with the enemy that day.[55]

On the twenty-fifth his forces again began to skirmish with the Federals on Bayou Rapide, near McNut's Hill. They had caught up with the rear guard, but for some reason he did not know, Bee's order to Debray to hurry his men into line was not carried out. Bee did not receive the reinforcements he requested, and he was unable even to slow down the Union rear units.[56]

From the first of May to the eighth Bee and his division pursued the Yankees to Alexandria and were engaged almost constantly in some kind of small fight. They were then ordered to Marksville for the same kind of work against the Federal forces in that vicinity. On May 14 Bee was relieved of his command and ordered by Major General Richard Taylor to report to headquarters at Shreveport.[57]

Taylor was furious and censured Bee strongly for his conduct at Monett's Ferry. Taylor had had big plans for the Union army. Wharton and the remainder of the cavalry not at the ferry had followed Banks onto the island between the Cane and the Red rivers and were applying constant pressure on the rear guard. Polignac, with the infantry, was opposite Cloutierville and ready to give battle if Banks should try to escape in that direction. The Union troops were in a demoralized state and ready to panic, Taylor thought; it would not take much to push them over the edge. But Bee had let the Federals go—at small cost to the enemy and none to himself—after both Taylor and Wharton had impressed upon Bee "the importance of holding the position to the last extremity."[58] Taylor had advised Bee of the enemy's imminent advance on the twenty-first, but Bee had let himself be outmaneuvered.[59] Taylor went so far as to enumerate his subordinate's failings:

Bee's errors were, first, in sending back Terrell's entire brigade to Beasley's to look after a subsistence train, for the safety of which I had amply provided; second, in taking no

55. Bee to Weems, report, May 14, 1864, ibid., 611–612; Barr (ed.), "Mechling's Journal," 374; Bee to Lubbock, May 9, 1864, Mechling Subcollection.

56. Bee to Lubbock, May 9, 1864, Mechling Subcollection.

57. Ibid.; Taylor to Anderson, April 27, 1864, *O.R.A.*, XXXIV, pt. 1, p. 583; Taylor to Anderson, May 6, 1864, ibid., 587.

58. Taylor to Anderson, April 24, 1864, ibid., 580.

59. Taylor, *Destruction and Reconstruction*, 219–220; Taylor to Boggs, June 1, 1864, Edmund Kirby Smith Papers, microfilm, Ramsdell Collection, Roll 209 (Archives, University of Texas Library, Austin); Taylor to Anderson, April 24, 1864, *O.R.A.*, XXXIV, pt. 1, pp. 579–580; Taylor to Anderson, April 24, 1864, ibid., 580–581

steps to increase artificially the strength of his position; third, in massing his troops in the center, naturally the strongest part of his position and where the enemy was certain not to make any decided effort, instead of toward the lakes on which his two flanks rested; fourth, in this, that when he was forced back he retired his whole force thirty miles to Beasley's, instead of attacking vigorously the enemy's colurnn . . . marching . . . through a dense pine woods, encumbered with trains and artillery and utterly demoralized by the vigorous attacks of Wharton in the rear. He displayed great personal gallantry, but no generalship.[60]

For his part, Bee thought he had acted only as he must have acted in the circumstances. Although he stated once that he had been impressed "with the importance of the position at Monett's Ferry,"[61] it appears from later reports that he thought he had been sent to the island to blockade the Red River. He had had no warning that the Union army was on its way to his location, but thought that the skirmishing of the twenty-second was caused by a small Federal scouting detachment. Not until he saw Banks's whole force did he realize his predicament and the importance of holding his place. He had no time to prepare to meet such a horde, and even with ample warning his position was not as strong as it had first seemed, because of the state of the river. Furthermore, the Union army was by no means demoralized. It was a "splendid army spread over the valley of the Cane River as far as the eye could reach," "marching its solid columns with the compactness of self-reliance and conscious strength." "Success was impossible."[62] There were just too many Yankees. When reports had arrived that both flanks had been turned, Bee and his officers, particularly Major and Bagby, had all agreed that the important thing was to save the command. They had fallen back to Beasley's, which they thought only eighteen miles away, because it was the sole place to get rations and some of the men had been without food for over forty-eight hours.[63]

While Bee can most certainly not escape criticism, Taylor's objections to his actions should perhaps have been not quite so strong. Taylor's plan of encirclement and destruction of the Union arrny was audacious, but almost too much so. He just did not have enough men to bring it off. The enemy was not so demoralized as the general wanted to believe. Taylor seemed to be operating

---

60. Taylor to Anderson, April 24, 1864, ibid., 580–581.

61. Bee to Lubbock, May 9, 1864, Mechling Subcollection.

62. Bee to Weems, report, May 14, 1864, O.R.A., XXXIV, pt. 1, p. 611 (first quotation); Bee to Boggs, report, September 17, 1864, ibid., 613 (second quotation); Bee to Weems, report, May 14, 1864, ibid., 611 (third quotation).

63. Bee to Lubbock, May 9, 1864, Mechling Subcollection; Bee to Weems, report, May 9, 1864, O.R.A., XXXIV, pt. 1, p. 611; Bee to Boggs, report, September 17, 1864, ibid., 613.

also on the misapprehension that Bee had several days to examine and prepare his ground, a completely false assumption. Taylor did not realize the speed of the Federal advance, and although he mentioned several times the difficulty of communicating with Bee over the distance of fifty-six miles[64] he assumed that Bee received all his messages and knew Banks was coming.

Bee was correct; the Yankees were going to get by him sooner or later. The low river and the great numbers of Federals precluded stopping them for any significant length of time. He did not know of Taylor's plan, the location of the remainder of the army, the prearranged guard at Beasley's, or the movement of Banks toward the ferry. He arrived at Monett's Ferry on the twenty-second and did not realize what threatened him until the next day; so he had no time to make much preparation that morning. To sacrifice a command when it cannot inflict great damage to the enemy is senseless.

All things considered, the blame for the things that Bee did do wrong must be laid at the feet of inexperience—both his and that of the Texas troops. Evidently no real reconnaissance of the river conditions to the left of the ferry was made; that would have foretold the need for some kind of fortifications on that side of the line. The Yankees started searching for a ford immediately. The Confederates seem to have assumed they would not find one. Bee, furthermore, had had little chance to fight any kind of defensive engagement. At both Mansfield and Pleasant Hill he had been in the attacking force. He was greatly impressed with the immensity and the panoply of the Union army. Therefore, he massed his strength in the center, assuming the attack would come there because the river was supposed to be unfordable and the enemy had massed his forces opposite that point. It was not established whom Lane on the extreme right was fighting; it may have been some wandering Union cavalry looking for a ford. But, as at Brownsville, Bee, influenced by numbers and earlier reports, believed the first information he received. He should have checked on the distance to Beasley's, but he could not have been expected to know the country as Taylor did, and why he did not send back for help is a mystery to which he did not offer a solution. It is to his credit that he did not try to put some of the criticism on Major, who, Bee said in his first report, was the one who ordered Terrell's brigade to Beasley's.

Bee wrote Kirby Smith in August to request a court of inquiry to investigate the facts surrounding Monett's Ferry, He did not like reports in circulation "prejudicial to his character as an officer" and wanted vindication. Kirby Smith told him that a court was unnecessary because he agreed with Bee that a longer

---

64. Taylor to Anderson, April 24, 1864, ibid., 580–581; Taylor, *Destruction snd Reconstruction*, 180.

defense would have led to loss of artillery and perhaps the command. From other friends, Wharton, Bagby, and Major, came assurance that they were willing to make a statement for publication that Bee had remained in position much longer than they would have.[65] This approval of his judgment by superiors did not come immediately, however, and even when it was given, "talk" continued. He did not obtain the court of inquiry.

After he was relieved Bee went back to Texas and spent most of his time in Seguin, probably with his family. He found himself a target for criticism after reports of Monett's Ferry were published in the newspapers. One correspondent who had been with his forces had talked to a Yankee major captured a few days later and reported that the enemy felt they would have been crushed between Wharton and Bee within four hours if Bee had not given way.[66] Bee quite naturally became very tender on the subject. He was quick to take offense and slow to forget those who criticized him. Even as late as April, 1865, he still felt the hurt and humiliation. He was willing to endorse Captain William G. Moseley's conduct at Monett's Ferry, he said, in spite of the fact that Moseley had harshly judged Bee's actions there. Bee told Moseley of his disappointment in the captain, whom he had considered a friend, and took Moseley to task for yielding to "an unjust clamor" and deciding against Bee, even though Moseley could not have known the whole story from his position in line. He would testify to Moseley's gallantry and efficiency as an officer, he said, because it was his duty, "and personal considerations cannot induce me to withhold justice from others, although it may have been denied to me."[67]

No matter how much sympathy or endorsement he received from his friends, Bee still could not get his old command back. From exile he wrote to Kirby Smith requesting reassignment, but none was forthcoming. General Walker censured him for his conduct at Mansfield, as previously stated, and this disapprobation seems to have squashed any chance for active command until December.[68]

In that month Kirby Smith suggested Bee as leader of a brigade under the control of Samuel Maxey, an old friend of Bee's, commanding in Indian Territory. Bee was subsequently assigned to that command. He spent the

65. Weems to Bee, November 18, 1864, O.R.A., XXXIV, pt. 1, pp. 614–615; Wharton to Bee, ibid., 615.

66. Houston Daily Telegraph, May 9, 1864.

67. Bee to Moseley, April 20, 1865, Hamilton P. Bee Papers (Archives, University of Texas Library, Austin).

68. Boggs to Walker, August 12, 1864, O.R.A., XLI, pt. 2, p. 1063; Walker to Boggs, August 15, 1864, ibid., 1066–1067.

remainder of the war stationed in Texas still somewhat under a cloud.[69] Since operations of any importance in the Department ceased, he could do little to redeem his name, and this frustration hurt him deeply. In the aftermath of war, however, it appears that defeat healed most of the wounds inflicted by criticism. The Lost Cause embraced all its defenders as unsullied, gallant heroes.

---

69. Maxey to Kirby Smith, December 2, 1864, ibid., LIII, 1029; Meiners, "Bee," 189–191.

Carte de visite of Colonel John Salmon "Rip" Ford, 2nd Texas Cavalry, by Louis de Planque, Brownsville, Texas, and Matamoros, Mexico, ca. 1865. *Courtesy Lawrence T. Jones III.*

John S. "Rip" Ford:
Prudent Cavalryman, C.S. A.

STEPHEN B. OATES[*]

John S. "Rip" Ford was one of the best-known Texans of the nineteenth century. Lawyer, physician, politician, newspaper editor, Texas Ranger, explorer, and soldier, Ford had a varied career before the Civil War. An active participant in the Texas secession convention in 1861, he was appointed colonel of cavalry in the Army of Texas with orders to take control of Federal property in the lower Rio Grande region even before the firing on Fort Sumter.

In this essay Stephen B. Oates, professor of history at the University of Massachusetts at Amherst and an authority on Confederate cavalry, points out that Ford was highly successful as a military commander. After securing the South Texas region in 1861, he served briefly as superintendent of conscripts with headquarters in Austin. Following the Union occupation of Brownsville in the fall of 1863 Ford was ordered back to the lower Rio Grande. With his newly recruited Cavalry of the West, Ford cleared the area of Federal troops and held the region for the Confederacy the remainder of the war. In the last battle of the Civil War, fought a month after Robert E. Lee's surrender at Appomattox Courthouse, Ford defeated Union troops at Palmetto Ranch.

[*] Stephen B. Oates, "John S. 'Rip' Ford: Prudent Cavalryman, C.S.A.," *Southwestern Historical Quarterly,* LXIV (Jan., 1961), 289–314.

For other works on Ford and the war in South Texas, see Ford's memoirs edited by Oates, Rip Ford's Texas *(Austin: University of Texas Press, 1963); Jerry Don Thompson,* Sabers on the Rio Grande *(Austin: Presidial Press, 1974); and James A. Irby,* Backdoor at Bagdad: The Civil War on the Rio Grande *(El Paso: Texas Western Press, 1977).*

On the morning of February 5, 1861, John Salmon Ford was standing in front of the stage line office in Austin shaking hands with a number of friends who had gathered to see him off. He was forty-five years old, tall and muscular, and his flashing blue eyes and stentorian voice gave him a commanding presence in the small crowd. As he talked his facial expression neither changed nor revealed emotion. His features appeared even more rigid because of a moderately sloping roman nose and a stubby gray beard that framed his wide chin.[1] Though dressed entirely in civilian clothing, he was a colonel of cavalry in the newly-formed Army of Texas with an exceedingly difficult assignment. The Texas Secession Convention had ordered him to recruit a volunteer force in the Houston vicinity and move toward the Lower Rio Grande region to capture all United States property and munitions of war.[2] But as he waved to his friends and climbed into a small coach, Ford was concerned less with the problem of raising troops and capturing forts than with the cold wind howling and churning up dust in the unpaved street that promised to make his ride to Houston a dreary one.

At Hempstead, Colonel Ford left the coach and took a train to Houston, where he set up recruiting headquarters and appealed to loyal "Texians" to take up arms. By February 18 he had about 500 eager volunteers in six companies.[3] At dawn the next day, the troops marched to Galveston, boarded the steamer *General Rusk* and the schooner *Shark* and sailed down the coast to the island Brazos de Santiago, a United States stronghold several miles above Brownsville. Hoping for a fight, the Texans stormed ashore on February 21 to find only twelve defenders who struck their colors without the firing of a shot. The victorious Southerners then converged on the parade grounds to shout and wave

---

1. John S. Ford, Memoirs (7 vols., preserved as typescript copies in the Archives Collection of the Library of the University of Texas), V, 997; Charles L. Martin, "The Last of the Ranger Chieftains," *The Texas Magazine*, IV (January, 1898), 39–40.

2. *The War of the Rebellion: A Compilation of the Official Records of the Union and Confederate Armies* (70 vols. in 128, Washington, 1880–1901), ser. 1, vol. LIII, 650–651. Hereafter cited as *Official Records*.

3. Ford, Memoirs, V, 997; Dudley G. Wooten (ed.), *A Comprehensive History of Texas* (2 vols.; Dallas, 1898), II, 520.

their rifles as the Lone Star Flag was run up the flagpole to the boom of a fif-
teen-gun salute.[4]

Colonel Ford witnessed the change of flags with mixed emotions, for he felt a
loyalty to the United States as well as to Texas. A native of South Carolina, he
had grown up in Tennessee and then set out for Texas in 1836, arriving only
days after San Jacinto. In the early years of the Republic he had successive ca-
reers as a doctor and an Indian fighter on the frontier. The inadequacy of frontier defense and the possibility of another death struggle with Mexico convinced
Ford that Texas' best course was with the United States. Elected to Congress in
1844, he worked hard for annexation, and when war broke out with Mexico, he
enlisted in the United States Army. In the Mexico City campaign, he served as
adjutant and surgeon for a Texas Ranger regiment under Colonel John C. (Jack)
Hays. It was in this capacity that Ford acquired his famous nickname. His main
duty was to make death certificates for troops killed in action. He had the habit
of completing each report with "Rest in Peace" after his signature, but as the
number of fatalities increased, he abbreviated the phrase to "R.I.P." The initials
stuck. Until his death, Ford was known as "Rip" or "Old Rip" by those who
knew and respected him. After the war, Ford became a journalist, but unable to
suppress his love for combat, he soon joined the Texas Rangers to fight the Indians, rising to the rank of senior captain of all state forces in 1858.[5] When war
clouds gathered in 1860, his patriotism to the United States was overcome by a
more powerful devotion to Texas and the slaveholding South. He became a
leading figure at the Secession Convention, helping to fashion the ordinance
that Texans claimed took their state out of the Union.[6] Because of his varied
military experience, he was a logical choice as colonel of cavalry. Because he was
a man of action, Rip Ford had won a Southern victory long before Fort Sumter
and the opening of the Civil War.

---

4. Ford to J. C. Robertson, February 22, 1861, *Official Records*, ser. I, vol. LIII, 651–652; James
Thompson to G. D. Bailey, February 22, 1861, *ibid.*, vol. I, 537–538.

5. One can learn of the details of Ford's many activities up to 1860 by reading the first four volumes of his Memoirs. Short biographical sketches may be found in the *State Gazette* (Austin), January 30, 1858; *The Handoook of Texas* (2 vols., Austin, 1952), I, 617; Sidney Smith Johnson, *Texans
Who Wore the Gray* (Tyler, 1907), 109–110; and Martin, "Last of the Ranger Chieftains," *Texas Magazine*, IV, 33–41. Walter P. Webb's *The Texas Rangers: A Century of Frontier Defense* (Boston and New
York, 1935), 151–161, 175–193, is the most vividly written account of Ford's Ranger service in the
1850's. See also, W. J. Hughes, "'Rip' Ford's Indian Fight on the Canadian [1858]," *Panhandle-Plains
Historical Review*, XXX (1957), 1–26.

6. Ford, Memoirs, V, 940–995; Anna Irene Sandbo, "The First Session of the Secession Convention of Texas," *Southwestern Historical Quarterly*, XVIII (October, 1914), 162–194. For the documents pertaining to the Texas Secession Convention and its agents, see E. W. Winkler (ed.), *Journal
of the Secession Convention of Texas, 1861* (Austin, 1912).

On February 22, 1861, Ford left Lieutenant Colonel Hugh McLeod[7] in command of Brazos Island and went to the mainland to negotiate with the United States force that held Fort Brown just below Brownsville. He was accompanied by Major Edward Waller and E. B. Nichols, commissioner and disbursing agent for the state. At Brownsville the Texans sent the Union commander a communique outlining their objectives and requesting immediate capitulation.[8] They received a belated reply: "You have raised a question upon which my government will doubtless take action in due season." But until then United States troops would not surrender without spilling blood—Texan blood.[9] Such action, the Texans said in a second communique, would bring on "Civil War with all its horrors."[10]

Still seeking peaceful surrender, Ford remained at Brownsville while Nichols sailed for Corpus Christi to get reinforcements. Nichols returned on March 2 with four cavalry companies under Major Benjamin F. Terry, who later commanded the celebrated Terry Texas Rangers.[11] By this time the Union commander had come to terms, agreeing to surrender to Ford all the United States forts from Brownsville to El Paso.[12] Texan troops immediately occupied Fort Brown, whose walls were crumbling and whose surroundings were overgrown with mesquite. On March 13, 1861, the last boatload of Union soldiers departed for New York.[13] Ford's patience and general prudence had avoided blood shed and won for Texas a strategic area and valuable supplies.

Rip Ford was enthusiastic over the achievement of his Texan volunteers. Wearing huge wheel spurs and high black hats ornamented with the beloved Lone Star and armed with six-shooters and bowie knives, they were fearless horsemen.[14]

---

7. A native of New York, McLeod had come to Texas in 1836. He was a West Point graduate with a reputation as a first-rate engineer. He commanded the ill-fated Santa Fe Expedition in 1841 and served as Adjutant General in the Mexican War. Like Ford, he was a firm secessionist and played a conspicuous part in the secession movement in Texas. Later in 1861 he became colonel of the First Texas Infantry. He died of pneumonia on January 3, 1862.

8. Ford to J. C. Robertson, February 25, 1861, *Official Records*, ser. I, vol. LIII, 655; Nichols to B. H. Hill, February 22 and 23, 1861, *ibid.*, vol. I, 538–540.

9. Hill to Nichols, February 23, 1861, *ibid.*, vol. 1, 540.

10. Nichols to Hill, February 22, 1861, *ibid.*, 538.

11. Nichols to J. C Robertson, February 23 and 28, 1861, *ibid.*, 540, vol. LIII, 655.

12. For the documents relating to the surrender of Federal forts on the Rio Grande, see *ibid.*, vol. LIII, 618–666. Terse accounts may be found in the Galveston *Civilian*, March 11, 1861, and the *Texas Almanac, 1862* (Galveston, 1862), 17–18.

13. Ford, Memoirs, V, 1004; *Official Records*, ser. I, vol. LIII, 653–654.

14. Ford, Memoirs, V, 1000; Ford to Robertson, February 25, 1861, *Official Records*, ser. I, vol.

Ford's area of command was a desolate and sprawling one. It extended nearly 1,200 miles along the Rio Grande from Fort Brown through Brownsville, Rio Grande City, Laredo, Eagle Pass, and out to El Paso. It included all the area between the Nueces River and the southern border. Along the coast from Corpus Christi, near the mouth of the Nueces, down to Fort Brown (a distance of about two hundred miles), wave action had formed a series of sand islands and peninsulas which separated the mainland from the open gulf. Padre and Brazos Islands were the longest of these sand bars enclosing several hundred square miles of shallow bays and lagoons. Except for the sand district, an area sixty-five miles wide and a hundred miles long lying between Corpus Christi and Brownsville, the country for some fifty miles inland was marked by low rolling plains covered with grass and mesquite trees. The landscape from Rio Grande City westward was a savanna of chaparral—thick coverts of mesquite and high prickly pear—and short grasses. Around El Paso there were not only plentiful growths of yucca, cacti, and coarse grasses on slopes and plateaus, but also large areas of igneous and sedimentary rock. The drouth-ridden lower Rio Grande region with few inhabitants would be John S. Ford's main theater of operations for the next four years.

One of Ford's first duties as commander of the Rio Grande country was to publish an address to the citizens explaining his objectives. He intended to preserve order and respect civil rights. His chief concern was to avoid "a civil and fratricidal war." He promised protection from Indians and bandits and hoped the people would recognize the "noble ends" that Texas expected to gain as a state in the Confederacy.[15]

The colonel then centered his attention on the Mexicans across the border. He told the Mexican people and General Guadalupe Garcia, commanding the line of the Bravo, that the Confederacy was a friendly nation which had no imperialistic designs in their direction.[16] Since the Federal blockade had sealed off Texas from the outside world, cordial relations with the state of Tamaulipas were extremely important. Matamoros furnished a medium for Confederate-European trade as well as a good market for the sale of cotton and the acquisition of arms and war materiel.[17]

LIII, 655; Thomas North, *Five Years in Texas: or, What You Did Not Hear During the War From January 1861 to January 1866* (Cincinnati, 1871), 104.

15. March 6, 1861, *Official Records*, ser. I, vol. LIII, 654.

16. *Ibid.*, 655.

17. Hamilton P. Bee to L. P. Walker, October 12, 1861, *ibid.*, vol. IV, 119; J. Fred Rippy, "Mexican Projects of the Confederates," *Southwestern Historical Quarterly*, XXII (April, 1919), 291.

Assured of Mexican cooperation, Ford turned to the pressing problem of frontier defense. Since entering the Confederate service as the Second Texas Cavalry on May 23, 1861, his ten companies had occupied Fort McIntosh, Camp Wood, Fort Inge, Fort Clark, Fort Lancaster, Camp Stockton, Fort Davis, and Fort Bliss.[18] Ford ordered each post to send out daily patrols to disperse small bands of renegade Indians, who during the past month had attacked a number of isolated homesteads, burning fields, destroying buildings, and killing and scalping women and children.[19]

But the Indians were not Ford's most serious concern. His old enemy, Juan Nepomuceno Cortina,[20] had gathered a bloodthirsty band of Mexican outlaws and was spreading terror and destruction on both sides of the Rio Grande from Brownsville to Laredo. On May 19 the bandits rode into Zapata County and struck a column of forty men under Captain Santos Benavides, forcing them to retreat at a gallop. Merciless Mexicans then captured and hanged the county judge, leaving his corpse dangling from a tree as a warning to those who defied Cortina. Such brutality spurred the Texans to action. Reinforced by forty-six volunteers from Webb County, Benavides' horsemen rode after Cortina. They overtook the outlaws at Redmond's Ranch and chased them back across the Rio Grande in a wild running fight.[21]

Meanwhile, a second band operating under Cortina's orders swept across the border north of Reynosa to burn farms and attack small towns. As the number of raids increased, Colonel Ford in desperation met with General Garcia, beseeching him to put a stop to the outrages. Garcia told Ford that he was friendly to Texas and the Confederacy and would do what he could. According to an unsubstantiated report, the Mexican officer actually went to Cortina's secret camp where he persuaded the outlaw to retire from the border. However that may be, it is true that bandit raids declined considerably that summer and the terrorized border country enjoyed a temporary period of peace.[22]

In September, Ford received badly needed reinforcements in the form of

---

18. General Orders No. 8, May 24, 1861, *Official Records*, ser. I, vol. I, 574–575.

19. Ford, Memoirs, V, 938.

20. Born in 1824 in Camargo, Tamaulipas, Cortina became well known in the 1840's and 1850's for his outlawry in the border country. In the so called Cortina wars (1859–1860) he twice defeated volunteer Texas organizations and terrorized the area around Brownsville until the spring of 1860 when a force under Colonel Robert E. Lee chased him into the Mexican hills. After the Civil War, Cortina continued his remunerative occupation as a cattle rustler until his death in 1894.

21. Ford, Memoirs, V, 919, 923–924, 1003; W. H. Brewin to Ford, November 7, 1861; Ford to D. C. Smith, November 11, 1861, *Official Records*, ser. I, vol. IV, 131–132, 137.

22. Ford, Memoirs, V, 921–922, 927.

Colonel Philip N. Luckett's two infantry companies and a howitzer battery. The fighting quality of the new troops was greatly reduced in that most of them were hungry Mexicans and soldiers of fortune who would desert for "a few dollars and a little whiskey."[23] To defend adequately the strategic area, Ford needed intrepid men who would die for the Southern cause.

Severe shortages of supplies further impaired the effectiveness of Ford's small army. His men had lived for months on starvation rations of dried beef and flour. They had only a few rounds of ammunition. Almost daily Ford had asked the state quartermaster for supplies, only to be told each time that the colonel must provide for himself. He managed to obtain meat, flour, and some vegetables through contracts with Brownsville merchants, but in amounts scarcely large enough to feed adequately his eight hundred horsemen. For the rest of the summer and the fall of 1861 they performed their duties with empty stomachs and tattered clothing.[24]

On November 1, 1861, Ford received an order to leave his command to Colonel Luckett and return home for a much needed rest. The leisurely days spent with his wife and small children at San Antonio did much to restore the colonel. When his furlough ended in December, he was physically and mentally ready to begin a new assignment. General Henry E. McCulloch, commander of the Western Sub-District, had ordered him to supervise the construction of coastal defenses in the Brownsville area and to negotiate a trade agreement with Mexico.[25]

Ford arrived in Brownsville shortly after Christmas. While his junior officers took charge of fortifications, the colonel obtained a formal trade agreement with the Mexicans and detailed cavalry patrols to guard the wagon trains that rolled back and forth across the drouth-ridden border area.[26]

During the cold winter days of 1862, the colonel frequently took time off from his vortex of paper work to visit isolated outposts above Fort Brown. Around flickering campfires Ford and the lonely pickets would sit and gossip

---

23. A. Buchel to Samuel Boyer Davis, November 30, December 5, 1861, *Official Records*, ser. I, vol. IV, 149–150, 152–153; Oran M. Roberts, "Texas," *Confederate Military History* (ed. by Clement A. Evans, 12 vols., Atlanta, 1899), XI, 54.

24. Texas Adjutant General, *Report, November, 1861* (Austin, 1861), 7–8; Texas Governor (Edward Clark), *Governor's Message to the Senators and Representatives of the Ninth Legislature of the State of Texas, November 1, 1861* (Austin, 1861), 11. Hereafter cited as *Governor's Message, November 1, 1861.*

25. Ford, Memoirs, V, 1007; *Governor's Message, November 1, 1861*, p. 11.

26. Ford, Memoirs, VI, 11; *Official Records*, ser. I, vol. XLVIII, pt. I, 512–513. An excellent discussion of this trade during 1862 may be found in Charles W. Ramsdell, "The Texas State Military Board, 1862–1865," *Southwestern Historical Quarterly*, XXVII (April, 1924), 263–265.

about a variety of subjects from the going price of horses to the events of the war. When asked, the colonel might recount his harrowing experiences as an Indian fighter during the 1850's. One youthful picket Lieutenant Charles L. Martin, was exceedingly impressed by Old Rip's warm and considerate manner, his self-confidence and his ability to lift the morale of his men.[27]

By March 1 Ford's efforts were beginning to show results. The soldiers were in high spirits and work on the forts was coming along satisfactorily. On Brazos Island there were several heavy batteries ably manned; miles down the coast at Fort Brown there were over 400 cavalry and twenty-five cannon of varying poundage and a ten-inch mortar pointing to the open sea.[28] Determined Texans were ready to fight, should the enemy try to invade their homeland.

Colonel Ford's reward for good work in the Brownsville area was a new command. On June 2, 1862, General Hamilton P. Bee appointed him superintendent of conscripts with orders to enforce the draft law in the Western Sub-District.[29] Setting up headquarters in Austin, Ford hand-picked enrolling captains and sent them into the surrounding counties. Each officer had instructions to draft all men subject to military duty between the ages of eighteen and thirty-five.[30] Then Governor Francis R. Lubbock sought to help by directing that brigadier-generals of state militia appoint enrolling officers for counties in their respective districts. These men were to send periodic reports to Austin.[31]

Ford had little taste for his new job, regarding the conscript law as "an unfortunate enactment." He sympathized with the poor man who, unable to get an exemption, met enrolling officers with loaded musket and shouts of "rich man's war, poor man's fight!" He was inclined to despise the man of means who could avoid the army because he owned so many slaves or so many acres of land. But the colonel suppressed a recurrent desire to resign his post and for over a year discharged his duties faithfully.[32]

---

27. Martin, "Last of the Ranger Chieftains," *Texas Magazine*, IV, 38–39.

28. Ford had 524 men all told at Fort Brown, Brazos Island, Ringgold Barracks, and 310 men on patrol duty just north of Brownsville. *Official Records*, ser. I, vol. XI, 706.

29. Roberts, "Texas," *Confederate Military History*, XI, 69–70; J. Bankhead Magruder to W. R. Boggs, May 29, 1863, *Official Records*, ser. I, vol. XXVI, pt. II, 22.

30. John S. Ford, Superindendent of Conscripts, Special Instructions to Enrolling Officers, June 25, 1862, broadside in Oran M. Roberts Papers, Archives Collection of the Library of the University of Texas.

31. *Official Records*, ser. I, vol. XI, 717.

32. Ford, Memoirs, V, 1008; Martin, "Last of the Ranger Chieftains," *Texas Magazine*, IV, 40; North, *Five Years in Texas*, 167. Ford's activities as Superintendent of Conscripts are not mentioned in either John Pattison Felgar, Texas in the War for Southern Independence (unpublished Ph.D. dissertation, University of Texas, 1935), or Margaret N. Goodlet, The Enforcement of the Confederate

His good soldiering did not go unnoticed. Oran M. Roberts thought that while Ford was "well-fitted" for his position at Austin, it was "a shame that he has been . . . kept there." Roberts considered "Old Rip" the best "military man . . . in Texas." He "should have been in the field," where he "would have made his mark."[33] Events that transpired would give Ford a chance to make his mark.

On September 8, 1863, Federal land and naval forces attempted an invasion of Texas through Sabine Pass. Turned back there by the remarkable shooting of Dick Dowling's artillery, the Yankees decided to make a second try at the mouth of the Rio Grande. On November 1, 4,500 troops under General Nathaniel P. Banks and General Napoleon Dana landed on Texas soil and overran Brownsville, cutting off the Confederate trade route through Matamoros. During the next month invading columns pushed up the coast to capture Corpus Christi, Aransas Pass, Cavallo Pass, and Fort Esperanza. Federal commanders exhorted their men to fight harder. Texas was crumbling.[34]

The Confederate generals, Bee and "Prince John" Bankhead Magruder, tried desperately to concentrate their scattered forces to stop the Yankees. Bee and Magruder made frantic appeals to "noble Texas" citizens to help and even threw walking wounded into the battle lines. But the invaders could not be checked. By December 31 they had seized Indianola, Lavaca, and the rest of the Matagorda Peninsula. Confederates wrecked the San Antonio and Gulf Coast Railroad and then retired west of the Colorado. Southern garrisons at Galveston and at the mouth of the Brazos prepared to resist enemy attacks.[35]

Conscription Acts in the Trans-Mississippi Department (unpublished master's thesis, University of Texas, 1914).

33. Quoted in Ford, Memoirs, V, 995. There was at this time some question over Ford's actual military rank. When his regiment entered Confederate service, Ford automatically lost his appointment of colonel of state forces. For some reason he twice refused to hold regimental elections which would have made him colonel. He was never commissioned by the Confederate War Department. On March 1, 1864, the governor appointed him brigadier general of a reactivated state corps to command Brigade District No. 11 (Official Records, ser. I, vol. XXXIV, pt. II, 1011). Ford, however, claimed throughout the war the rank of colonel of cavalry, C.S.A., and Hébert, Magruder, and Walker, successive commanders of the state, recognized him and paid him as such. Magruder to S. Cooper, June 8, 1863, ibid., vol. XXVI, pt. II, 65; S. S. Anderson to Magruder, June 11, 1863, ibid., 47; E. Kirby Smith to McCulloch, November 2, 1863, ibid., 382; Magruder to Pendleton Murrah, December 20, 1863, ibid., 517; Ford, Memoirs, V, 1008.

34. William H. Seward to Edwin M. Stanton, July 16, 1863, Official Records, ser. III, vol. III, 521–522; Dana to James H. Strong, November 4, 1863; Banks to Bell, November 3, 1863; Banks to Herron, December 25, 1863, ibid., ser. I, vol. XXVI, pt. I, 787, 785, 880–881.

35. Magruder's Address, November 27, 1863, in Frank Moore (ed.), The Rebellion Record: A Diary of American Events . . . (12 vols., New York, 1861–1871), VIII, pt. II, 244; Houston Tri-Weekly Telegraph, December 2, 4, 9, 11, 1863, January 11, 13, 20, February 29, 1864.

Meanwhile, a second Yankee column advancing up the Rio Grande occupied Ringgold Barracks. Magruder's worst fears were becoming a reality. Main Federal objectives apparently were to cut off completely the Confederate lifeline of supplies through Mexico and afterwards advance into the interior to attack San Antonio and Austin.[36]

Then Union drives inexplicably stopped. Unknown to the Confederates, Banks had decided to hold what he had in the valley and concentrate most of his manpower on the Red River campaign, which would take Yankee forces up Louisiana and into Texas from the northeast. Federal strength in Texas was reduced to 3,500 men under General Dana and General Benjamin F. Herron.[37]

Magruder, however, still thought the Federals to be committed to the offensive in Texas. The present lull could only mean that they were waiting for reinforcements. Then Magruder decided upon a daring course of action. If his army should take the offensive before the enemy resumed movement, Confederates might save the rest of Texas, might even, in fact, recapture the Rio Grande Valley and renew the invaluable trade through Matamoros. A tough officer with battle experience and organizing abilities would have to command such an operation. The best choice, Magruder decided, was Colonel Ford, who not only met these requirements but knew the country and enjoyed the respect of soldiers and civilians alike.[38]

Receiving the order on December 27, 1863, Ford left Austin and established headquarters at San Antonio. After soliciting the aid of responsible citizens,[39] he began recruiting men for three months duty in "The Cavalry of the West."[40] "Come to the front," he urged potential volunteers, "and aid in expelling the enemy from the soil of Texas!"[41] Loyal men responded and Ford's army grew daily. Even women were enthusiastic over the plan of operations. Citizen committees gathered food and clothing to give to Captain C. H. Merritt, chief

---

36. Magruder to W. R. Boggs, December 22, 1863; Magruder to E. Kirby Smith, December 24, 1863, *Official Records,* ser. I, vol. XXVI, pt. II, 524, 530.

37. Special Orders No. 322, December 24, 1863, *ibid.,* pt. I, 879; Banks to Stanton, April 6, 1864, *ibid.,* vol. XXXIV, pt. I, 194–195; Herron to Charles P. Stone, January 15, 1864, *ibid.,* pt. II, 85.

38. Edmund P. Turner to Ford, December 22, 1863, *ibid.,* vol. XXVI, pt. II, 525–526; Magruder to W. R. Boggs, December 22, 1863; Magruder to E. Kirby Smith, December 24, 1863, *ibid.,* 524, 530.

39. Ford to Magruder, February 21, 1864, Letter Books of John S. Ford (3 vols. [vol. I, February 18 to April 24, 1864; vol. II, September 22 to November 29, 1864; vol. III, August 24 to December 30, 1864], preserved as typescript copies in the Texas State Archives, Austin), I, 12. Hereafter cited as Ford Letter Books.

40. Ford to Turner, December 27 and 29, 1863, *Official Records,* ser. I, vol. XXVI, pt. II, 543–544, 560–561.

41. Ford, Memoirs, VI, 11.

quartermaster.[42] Major A. G. Dickinson, Ford's able assistant, forgot the pain of a running eye wound and traveled to nearby towns to borrow arms and ammunition.[43] By February 1, 1864, the Cavalry of the West numbered 1,000 troops. Ford wrote Magruder that he expected to get a thousand more.[44]

But as the winter days wore on, initial enthusiasm over the enterprise disappeared. Supplies became scarce and many recruits, not wiiling to go hungry, deserted.[45] Nevertheless, Ford and Dickinson were not discouraged. They continued to urge the people to support them "in the name of patriotism, of liberty, and all that is dear to man." They offered fifty dollars apiece to men who would enlist and "defend their homes & property, their wives and their little ones against the brutal assaults of an enemy who respects neither age, sex or condition, who plunder . . . the homestead."[46]

Slowly the number of volunteers returned to a thousand. Ford continued to call for men. By mid-March there were 1,300 poorly armed troops and the colonel was ready to move, hoping that additional recruits could be picked up on the march. "With the help of God," he would drive the Yankees into the Gulf.[47]

At daybreak on March 18, 1864, the Cavalry of the West trotted out of San Antonio to seek out the enemy troops, who were reported to be holding a line from Ringgold Barracks to Corpus Christi.[48] Because of the lack of forage, movement was in two columns, one under Ford, the other under Lieutenant Colonel Daniel Showalter. The line of march carried them southward to a point near Pleasanton, then along the meandering Atascosa River to its confluence with the Rio Frio and Nueces, and finally down to Camp San Fernando, a Confederate outpost commanded by Major Mat Nolan.[49]

While encamped at San Fernando, Ford received the alarming report of a Yankee raid on Laredo, the headquarters of Colonel Santos Benavides' regiment

---

42. Ford to Turner, December 25, 1863, *Official Records*, ser. I, vol. XXVI, pt. II, 535; Ford to Theodore Heermann, February 21, 1864, *ibid.*, vol. XXXIV, pt. II, 979–980.

43. Dickinson to W. A. Alston, December 26, 1863, *ibid.*, vol. XXVI, pt. II, 540–541.

44. Ford to Turner, February 7, 1864, *ibid.*, vol. XXXIV, pt. II, 948–949; Ford to Heermann, February 21, 1864, *ibid.*, 979–980.

45. Ford, Memoirs, VI, 11–12; Ford to Turner, February 5, 1864, *Official Records*, ser. I, vol. XXXIV, pt. II, 946–947.

46. Ford to Mat Nolan, March 5, 1864, Ford Letter Books, I, 48; San Antonio *Weekly Herald*, March 19, 1864.

47. *Official Records*, ser. I, vol. XXXIV, pt. II, 947, 1074–1075.

48. San Antonio *Weekly Herald*, March 19, 1864.

49. Roberts, "Texas," *Confederate Military History*, XI, 123.

and the center of the Mexican trade at that time. The report stated that at 3 P.M. on March 19, 200 Federal cavalry led by Colonel E. J. Davis galloped with pistols blazing down the streets of the town to swamp Benavides' sixty Texans, who fired from behind crude barricades in the plaza. Hot fighting, much of it hand-to-hand, lasted until nightfall, when the Confederates crying the "Texan yell" repulsed a final enemy charge. Such determination convinced the Yankees that they would do well to retire for the night and try again in the morning.

At 2 A.M. a Confederate column arrived from Lapata, twenty-five miles to the north. Ecstatic civilians met the new troops with hoarse cheering, "the ringing of churchbells and blowing of trumpets." To the enemy encamped three miles away, so much rejoicing could mean but one thing—Confederates had been heavily reinforced. Little could be done except retreat and the Federals mounted and galloped southward toward Rio Grande City. At daybreak Captain Refugio Benavides took a Confederate scout to reconnoiter, returning to report that beleaguered Laredo was saved. Several hours later more reinforcements arrived— Lieutenant Colonel George H. Giddings' 150 men from Eagle Pass.

The report of the battle ended on a discordant note. Colonel Benavides was certain that the enemy, determined to stop the Mexican trade, would quite soon strike him with a more powerful force. To prevent this, he suggested that Colonel Ford move his cavalry to the Rio Grande and attack the Union rear. In this event the Yankee invader would indeed find himself in "a bad fix."[50]

Ford thought the suggestion to be a good one, but he was not disposed to execute it immediately. The country between the Nueces and the border was not conducive to swift movement. The drouth of 1863 and 1864 had dried up water holes and left the land a barren waste without a green shrub or a spear of grass existing beneath moving clouds of dust. Ford would not ride until extra supplies, canteens, and horses arrived from San Antonio. He told Benavides that for the time being Laredo must be held without the aid of the Cavalry of the West.[51]

The colonel then turned his attention to a report carrying news of hostile activity to the south of Camp San Fernando. He called on Mat Nolan, a "sprightly boy" who had been his bugler in the Indian wars,[52] to take a company and

---

50. Benavides to Ford, March 21 and 25, *Official Records*, ser. I, vol. XXXIV, pt. I, 647–649. Benavides was born in Laredo on November 1, 1827, and for a number of years was procurador and mayor of the city. After the Civil War he organized a mercantile business with his brother, Cristobal Benavides. Santos served in the Sixteenth, Seventeenth, and Eighteenth Legislatures from 1879 to 1884. He died in 1891.

51. Ford, Memoirs, VI, 13–14; Roberts, "Texas," *Confederate Military History*, XI, 124–125.

52. Ford, Memoirs, V, 1010; VI, 1051.

investigate. Riding down the Nueces, Nolan and his horsemen learned from ranchers and farmers that Federal raiding parties were plundering the country-side, seizing beef and cotton to be sent back to Union headquarters at Brownsville. The most ruthless of these units was a company of Mexican guerillas led by Cecilio Balerio, a border bandit who held a captain's rank in the Second Texas (Union) Cavalry. Balerio was supposed to be operating near Patricio and the Texans galloped off to find him. Having searched the area for hours, they stumbled upon the Mexican camp hidden in a grassy arroyo and quietly surrounded it. Then drawing knives and pistols and whooping and shouting the Texans swept over the unsuspecting Mexicans, scattered them, and captured "a number of horses and small arms and ammunition."[53] But the main prize, Balerio, managed to escape. That evening the Confederates rode back to San Fernando to report. News of the victory spread rapidly, bringing new hope to the war-weary people of South Texas. "Bully for the Expeditionary Forces," savored the San Antonio *Herald*.[54]

But the small victory did not encourage Colonel Ford, who knew that the campaign actually was bogging down because of a number of "problems" that had inexplicably arisen. For one thing, his fear of moving without substantial supplies had caused him to lose the vital element of surprise—friendly Mexicans had told him that Yankee cavalry, reinforced by Mexicans from Camargo, were concentrated around Ringgold Barracks waiting to meet Confederate thrusts. Then there were the many messages from embattled frontiersmen in Blanco and adjoining counties crying for protection against blood-drenched Indian bands. Colonel Benavides' dispatches, too, came almost daily warning that Laredo would fall unless Ford moved immediately. To complete the list of problems, supplies still had not come; arms were "of a very inferior quality"; and inactive men were complaining of hunger—already many of them had quit complaining and headed for home on stolen horses.

The last week in March passed with the situation growing worse instead of better. Messages of Indian depredations came more regularly and desertions occurred daily. Something had to be done, and done immediately, or the campaign would fail before it really started. Colonel Ford and his lieutenants held a war council in which they agreed that the campaign must be resumed, despite the shortages of provisions and the strength of the enemy. When the soldiers received the order to move, they cheered loudly—their colonel was ready to

---

53. *Ibid.*, VI, 25-29; San Antonio *Weekly Herald*, March 19, 1864.
54. San Antonio *Weekly Herald*, March 19, 1864.

fight.[55] As they mounted and waited, Ford wrote a short message to Major Dickinson at San Antonio: "We must take the enemy in the rear, and force him out of the up country. . . . Scouts are out. We are active and cheerful . . . And I trust the smiles of providence. A just cause and courage will give us victory."[56] The colonel went outside, mounted, and gave the order to move. The Cavalry of the West with the Stars and Bars snapping in the warm April breeze rode out of Camp Fernando heading south.

The ride over the desolate country to the Rio Grande was accomplished without bloodshed but with "much suffering to the men and teams." On April 17 the force reached Ringgold Barracks to find that their worst fears had been groundless. Yankee cavalry had left the up country and retired toward Brownsville. As a result, the area from Ringgold Barracks to El Paso, except for scattered Mexican outlaws and Indian bands, was free of hostile forces.[57]

Had the Confederates pushed on to the Gulf at this time, they might have won a decisive victory. Federal strength in the region had been considerably weakened by the transfer of troops to Louisiana, a situation which had compelled the enemy commander to call most of his mounted units back to Brownsville.[58] But once again Rip Ford allowed overcaution and the fear of defeat to dictate his plans. Because rumor placed enemy strength at three to four thousand, the colonel decided against a general movement toward Brownsville and divided his command into smaller, more mobile units to protect the trade through Laredo and Eagle Pass. During the next seven weeks or so, these units skirmished with Federal and Mexican detachments at Ranchos Como se Llama, La Jura, Tajitos, and the Suaz.[59] The largest skirmish occurred on June 25, when 250 Confederates led by Ford himself met an equal number of Federals at Ranchos Las Rucias, about twenty-five miles above Fort Brown. Desperate close quarter fighting about the ranch grounds was followed by a running battle in which the yipping Confederates chased the Yankees along the chaparral and

---

55. Ford, Memoirs, VI, 1036–1040; Ford to Turner, March 25, 1864, *Official Records*, ser. I, vol. XXXIV, pt. II, 1083–1084.

56. Ford Letter Books, I, 83–84.

57. Ford to S. Benavides, April 7, 1864; Ford to E. P. Turner, April 9, 1864; Ford to Mat Nolan, April 10, 1864; Ford to Daniel Showalter, *ibid.*, 98, 107–108, 110, 114–115; Ford, Memoirs, V, 1012; Roberts, "Texas," *Confederate Military History*, XI, 125.

58. L. G. Aldrich to Ford, March 21, 1864, *Official Records*, ser. I, vol. XXXIV, pt. II, 1068; Hubert Howe Bancroft, *History of the North American States and Texas* (2 vols., San Francisco, 1886–1889), II, 466–468.

59. Ford to J. E. Slaughter, June 15, 1864, *Official Records*, ser. I, vol. LIII, 1001.

across the shallow waters of the Rio Grande.[60] This victory, plus news of the Federal rout along the Red River in Louisiana, did much to lift the morale of Ford and his Texans. General Magruder wrote them: "Your course and efforts meet with most perfect satisfaction none could have conducted the operations with greater success."[61]

Because of the turn of events, Ford threw caution aside and determined to move against Brownsville. On July 25 he led his cavalry past Palo Alto and into Dead Man's Hollow on the outskirts of the border city. A bugle sounded as the horsemen formed in line and cheered loudly in anticipation of a cavalry charge in the grand manner. Then white puffs of smoke appeared on the roofs of nearby buildings, followed by the crack of gunfire and whizzing bullets. A deeper boom rose above the spatter of skirmishing indicating that Yankee field guns were coming into action. With shells exploding all around, the prudent Ford decided that a cavalry charge was out of the question. He ordered his troops to dismount and wait for the enemy to come out in the open to fight. But the Yankees did not oblige them and for five days there was almost continuous skirmishing as Confederates peppered away at the enemy, and got peppered in return.

On July 30 a scout galloped into the Confederate camp to report that the Yankees were making an escape toward Fort Brown. Weakened from a sickness that had plagued him since the opening of the campaign, Ford named Lieutenant Colonel Showalter acting commander with orders to take his regiment and Giddings' battalion to investigate. An hour later Showalter's column trotted down Brownsville's main street to find at the square a group of loyal Confederate citizens under Major E. W. Cave, who had organized to protect the city until the liberators should arrive. Deciding to wait for the colonel, Showalter sent Captain W. N. Robinson's company to harass the Federals as they retired. Robinson pursued them for fifteen miles below the city killing two and taking two prisoners.

Late that afternoon Colonel Ford with the remainder of the cavalry entered the city. They were met by jubilant civilians.[62] "Confidence has been restored," Ford wrote General James E. Slaughter, "our people are returning to their

---

60. Confederate casualties were three killed and four wounded. Ford to Slaughter, July 2, 1864, *ibid.*, vol. XXXIV, pt. I, 1054–1056. Federal losses were two killed, five wounded, and twenty-three missing. F. J. Herron to William Dwight, June 26, July 2, 1864, *ibid.*, pt. II, 1053–1054.

61. Quoted in Ford, Memoirs, V, 1011–1015.

62. *State Gazette* (Austin), August 24 and 31, 1864; James H. Fry to W. G. Tobin, August 4, 1864, *Official Records*, ser. I, vol. XLI, pt. I, 185–186; Ford, Memoirs, V, 1013–1018.

homes, and commerce is being reestablished, and our relations with the Mexican authorities are of the most friendly character."[63] By mid-August his Texans had forced the enemy to abandon all of the Rio Grande Valley except Brazos Island. Once again the lifegiving supply trains from Matamoros were rumbling through Brownsville moving north.[64]

In token of their appreciation for gallant work, the ladies of Brownsville presented Rip Ford with a Confederate flag. Admiring the symbolic gift, he assured them that it would be "upheld by the expeditionary forces as long as human endurance can allow a stout arm to wield a keen blade."[65]

The occasional skirmishing in the Brownsville area during August, 1864, was only a sidelight to the power struggle between the French and the Mexicans south of the border. On August 24 5,000 French legionnaires landed at Bagdad at the mouth of the Rio Grande and drove Juan N. Cortina's Republican troops of Mexico back to Matamoros.[66] The arrival of Maximilian's forces occasioned much rejoicing among the Confederates who carried a bitter hatred of Cortina, the ex-border bandit. Colonel Ford immediately established friendly relations with the French commander who promised to protect Southern citizens and their property should his army take Matamoros.[67]

A Texan doctor in Matamoros warned Ford that this action had infuriated Cortina. Believing that the Confederates were going to fight with the loathed French, the Mexican leader had sought Yankee aid (another report said that he had requested a general's commission in the Union Army) and planned within a fortnight to attack Brownsville.[68] Ford knew Cortina well enough to believe the doctor's message. There was grave danger that a reign of terror might come which would take lives ruthlessly and reduce to ashes the peaceful communities along the Rio Grande. The colonel alerted his cavalry patrols, then urged General John Walker, newly appointed commander of Texas, to send reinforcements in a hurry.[69] In the place of men and materiel, Ford received a belated order

---

63. *Official Records*, ser. I, vol. XLI, pt. II, 989.

64. General Orders No. 166, August 16, 1864, *ibid.*, 1068–1069; Ford to J. E. Dwyer, August 29, 1864, *ibid.*, 1088–1089.

65. Ford to H. P. Bee, September 21, 1864, Ford Letter Books, III, 81.

66. Bancroft, *History of North Mexican States and Texas*, II, 468; *State Gazette* (Austin), September 7, 1864.

67. Ford to A. Vernon, August 24, 1864; Vernon to Ford, August 25, 1864, *Official Records*, ser. I, vol. XLI, pt. II, 1089; Ford to J. E. Dwyer, August 29, 1864, *ibid.*, 1088.

68. C. B. Combe to Ford, September 5 and 6, 1864, *ibid.*, pt. III, 912.

69. Ford to J. E. Dwyer, September 3, 1864; Ford to J. E. Slaughter, September 6, 1864, *ibid.*, 909, 911; San Antonio *News*, September 3, 1864.

that Cortina, if captured, was to be treated as "a robber and murderer, and executed immediately."[70] With anxious eyes watching the events across the border, the Confederates had all but forgotten the strong Federal force on Brazos de Santiago.

After dark on September 15, 1864, a column of Union cavalry from Brazos Island galloped up the Rio Grande to swarm over a Confederate patrol under Lieutenant Colonel Showalter. Heavily outnumbered the Southerners had to take cover at Palmetto (Palmito) Ranch where for several hours they managed to check repeated Federal attacks. But at dawn Showalter's Texans were blasted by artillery hidden on the Mexican side of the Rio Grande (one of Cortina's batteries from Matamoros). Caught in a deadly crossfire, the Confederates decided to run for it. They mounted, and riding at a killing gallop through singing bullets, broke into the clear. Two hours later they trotted their lathered horses through the gates of Fort Brown.[71] That evening the blurred figures of Mexican cavalry were sighted along the horizon south of Brownsville. Inside the city, frantic citizens prepared to evacuate.[72]

With hostile forces pressing him from three directions, Ford sought aid from the French, only to be told: "Our position of perfect neutrality towards the United States as well as towards the Confederacy prevents us from doing the service you request."[73]

Riders then set out for San Antonio and Austin to get help. But no reinforcements were available. What could Ford do? Suppressing the ever-present urge to be cautious, the colonel divided his force. Against heavy odds he was going on the offensive.

While 900 Confederates demonstrated along the Rio Grande near Brownsville, Lieutenant Colonel Giddings led 400 handpicked horsemen toward Palmetto Ranch. Early on September 9 they struck a Yankee-Mexican force of over 500 men at San Martin Ranch, driving the superior force across the Rio Grande at a gallop. Three days later, Giddings left a small outpost at Palmetto Ranch and returned to Brownsville to give Ford the details of the victory.[74]

---

70. See J. G. Walker to J. E. Slaughter, October 1, 1864, *Official Records*, ser. I, vol. XLI, pt. II, 972.

71. Ford to A. P. Root, September 22, 1864, Ford Letter Books, II, 1–2; Ford, Memoirs, V, 1024–1025.

72. *State Gazette* (Austin), September 21, 1864.

73. Ford, Memoirs, V, 1026.

74. Confederate losses were reported at one dead, one wounded. *Ibid.*, 1026–1027; James H. Fry to G. H. Giddings, September 12, 1864, Ford Letter Books, III, 66. Federal casualties were reported at eighty-six in dead, wounded, and missing. *Official Records*, ser. I, vol. XLI, pt. I, 742.

Cortina was not long in seeking to avenge the battle of San Martin Ranch. With 3,000 Mexicans and sixteen cannon he attacked French forces just below Matamoros early on September 15. By nightfall the Frenchmen were in head-long flight toward Bagdad.[75] Cortina then gazed across the Rio Grande at the flickering lights of Brownsville and at the faint glimmer of Confederate camp-fires just above Fort Brown. The next day he would satiate his burning hunger to kill Rip Ford and his Texans and to ravage the accursed city of Brownsville.[76] There was a rumble of thunder from the low hanging clouds. Soon it began to rain.

The Texans were prepared to fight, knowing well that they would receive no quarter when the attack commenced. About 1,000 of them with a few howitzers were deployed in line from Brownsville down to a point near Fort Brown. An-other hundred or so were near the Boca Chica watching the Federals on Brazos Island. On the outskirts of Brownsville, inside a small shack Colonel Ford sat at a table reviewing his situation. He prepared a statement to be delivered to Cortina asking if he intended to declare war on the Confederacy. About mid-night Ford tried to get some sleep, but the steady beat of the rain on the roof and the concern for his wife and children at Brownsville allowed him no rest. Just before dawn he slipped into his uniforrn, and forcing himself to smile, Rip Ford went outside to talk to his men, saying "Hallo boys . . . get ready. We have to go out and meet the enemy to-day."

The sight of their commander, still weakened from illness, standing there in the cold rain, smiling, determined to give battle despite the odds, this time oblivious to caution or prudence, moved some of the Texans to tears, gave them all courage.

"Hurrah boys!" shouted one man, "by G-d, Old Rip is going to fight!"

Artillery opened up across the river. A skirmish line became barely visible in the drizzly dawn. An order was shouted. Confederate howitzers returned the Mexican fire. Then the Texan riflemen commenced to shoot across the water at crouching figures in the tall weeds along the river bank. Suddenly, from the south of the Mexican position, came the deep boom of heavy field guns and the steady sputter of 5,000 muskets—the French army, heavily reinforced and com-manded by General Tomás Mejía himself, was counter-attacking.[77]

Outflanked on their right and stubbornly contested on their front, the Mexi-

---

75. Bancroft, *History of North American States and Texas*, II, 468.

76. Ford said that his old enemy hated "all" Texans and Americans and bore a grudge against Brownsville. Ford to J. E. Dwyer, September 3, 1864, *Official Records*, ser. I, vol. XLI, pt. III, 909.

77. Ford, Memoirs, V, 1024; VI, 1129; Ford to [?], [n.d.], Ford Letter Books, III, 83-84; Ford to A. P. Root, September 22, 1864, *ibid.*, II, 4.

cans retreated to Matamoros. As the French legions tramped along the southern bank of the Rio Grande following Cortina, the Texans across the water stood and cheered. Three days later, on September 29, Cortina surrendered his Mexican army to Mejía. That evening the forces of Emperor Maximilian marched triumphantly through the streets of Matamoros.[78]

The fall of Cortina called for three days of lavish celebrations and public gatherings in Matamoros. Rip Ford was on hand cultivating a strong friendship with Mejía as well as working out neutrality agreements and making arrangements for the rendition of marauders, deserters, and criminals. Afterwards the colonel returned to Brownsville where he was warmly received by soldiers and civilians.[79] One junior officer was certain that in a larger sphere of action his gallant commander would have been "the Murat of the Confederacy."[80]

There was little evidence that the lower Rio Grande was a battlefront during the winter of 1864 and 1865. Union troops at Brazos Island and Confederates in the Brownsville vicinity were content with watching each other and exchanging only an occasional shot. Most of the fighting in this period was between Colonel Ford and General James E. Slaughter, recently appointed commander of the Western Sub-District. Probably what precipitated the feud that soon raged between the two officers was jealousy on the part of Rip Ford. Having done more than any one man to keep the Valley in Confederate control and to maintain the Mexican trade, the colonel no doubt wanted command of the sub-district and highly resented the appointment of Slaughter, who, in Ford's opinion, had done little for Texas or the Confederacy and who was not extremely popular with the soldiers. The two men feuded constantly over Mexican policy and military strategy, over problems of logistics and defense, even over such trivia as who should command patrols and where they should operate.[81] It was fortunate for Confederate Texas that a Yankee offensive similar to the one of November, 1863, did not come at this time.

The smouldering feud was fanned into open flames in February, 1865, when General Lew Wallace of the Federal Army came to Brazos Island to discuss with

---

78. Thos. F. Drayton to Asst. Adj. Gen. of J. G. Walker, September 26, 1864, *Official Records*, ser. I, vol. XLI, pt. III, 957; H. M. Day to George B. Drake, October 9, 1864, *ibid.*, 721–722; *State Gazette* (Austin), October 12, 1864.

79. Ford to Nestor Maxon and F. W. Lathan, October 17, 1864; Ford to Aldrich, October 28, 1864, Ford Letter Books, III, 118–119, 135.

80. Captain W. H. D. Carrington's statement in John Henry Brown, *History of Texas From 1685 to 1892* (2 vols., St. Louis, 1893), II, 435.

81. Felgar, *Texas in the War for Southern Independence*, 198; Wooten, *Comprehensive History of Texas*, II, 556; Roberts, "Texas," *Confederate Military History*, XI, 127–128.

Confederate commanders "some matters pertinent to the then existing war." After a heated argument, Slaughter and Ford on March 1 agreed to meet Wallace in the living room of a local residence at Port Isabel. For hours the three men engaged in lively discussion, the liveliest of it between Ford and Slaughter. There were many points covered in the conference but the main result was that the two Confederates left believing that the fighting was over in the Rio Grande area. Another result was that Ford became more firmly convinced of the incompetence of his superior officer.[82]

March and April passed quietly as Yankees and Confederates lived in peaceful coexistence. The inactivity had an adverse effect on Slaughter's small force, for tired and hungry men with no fighting to keep them occupied laid down their arms and went home. By March 1 Confederate forces in the Valley tallied less than 1,5000 men.[83] When news that Richmond had fallen reached Texas, two hundred of these deserted, leaving only a skeleton force to fight the last battle of the war at Palmetto Ranch.[84]

On the evening of May 11, 1865, 250 men of the Sixty-Second United States Colored Infantry and fifty-two men of the Second Texas (Union) Cavalry under Lieutenant Colonel David Branson left Brazos Island and crossed the Boca Chica in a blinding rainstorm. After a circuitous march through the chaparral the column at 8:30 A.M. the next day met a Confederate battalion led by Captain W. N. Robinson at Palmetto Ranch. After about an hour of skirmishing the Confederates retreated into the thickets leaving to their protagonists a number of horses and cattle and some supplies. Having set fire to the ranch, the Yankees retired to White Ranch, where they bivouacked for the night. Sometime during the early morning of May 13, some 200 reinforcements led by Colonel Theodore H. Barrett reached Branson's camp.[85]

Meanwhile, Robinson's cavalry had taken a position about a mile above Palmetto Ranch. At 10 P.M., May 12, a rider set out for Brownsville to get help. For the next twelve hours or so the Confederates skirmished lightly with Federal pickets near Palmetto Ranch.[86]

When Slaughter and Ford got Robinson's message they had barely 300 men

---

82. There is prodigious material extant on the conference. An account by Sam H. Dixon is in the Houston *Post,* June 25, 1922. The documents are in the *Official Records,* ser. I, vol. XLVIII, pt. I, 1166–1167, 1275–1276, 1279–1282; pt. II, 458–463.

83. *Official Records,* ser. I, vol. XLVIII, pt. I, 1456–1457.

84. Carrington's report of the Battle of Palmetto Ranch in Brown, *Texas,* II, 431.

85. Branson's report, May 18, 1865, *Official Records,* ser. I, vol. XLVIII, pt. I, 267, 268; Barrett's report, August 10, 1865, *ibid.,* 265–266.

86. Ford, Memoirs, VII, 1174–1180; Ford's article in the San Antonio *Express,* October 10, 1890.

at Brownsville. The rest of the command was scattered over the sub-district. The two officers held a conference in which they agreed to forget their feud temporarily and try to work in unison to meet the exigency. While Slaughter concentrated the scattered forces at Brownsville, Ford with the available troops and six field guns moved east toward the battlefront.[87]

At 3 p.m., on May 13, Ford's column reached Robinson's new position in a thicket on the river bank about two miles north of Palmetto Ranch. A Federal offensive was about to open. Ford quickly deployed his horsemen in line of battle. Anderson's battalion under Captain D. W. Wilson held the Confederate right; a section of O. G. Jones' battery of light artillery, the center; and Giddings' battalion and two infantry companies, all under Robinson, the left.[88] A bugle blared over the swell. There was a hoarse cheering and the Yankees came swarming through the thickets. Over the noise of exploding shells and humming bullets could be heard the shouts of officers exhorting their men to die. Soon the Federals retired to regroup and try again to overrun the Confederate position.[89]

During the momentary lull, Rip Ford became once again the impulsive Indian fighter of the 1850's and determined to counter attack. He rode up and down the line shouting: "Men, we have whipped the enemy in all our previous fights! We can do it again!"

"Rip!" "Rip!" his soldiers shouted back.

Ford raised his six-shooter.

A piercing Texan yell resounded across the chaparral.

"Forward!"

"Charge!"[90]

The Confederates surged forward shooting at everything that moved. The Yankee skirmish line melted away. Wilson's yipping troops hit the Union left. The Negroes broke and fled. Robinson's horsemen swept over the enemy right. The entire Federal line dissolved and within minutes it was a near rout. Many of the Yankees were captured, some run down by Confederate horsemen, and others chased into the muddy waters of the Rio Grande. The enemy commanders managed to rally part of the Thirty-Fourth Indiana and some of the Negro troops several hundred yards above the ruins of Palmetto Ranch. Robinson's

---

87. Ford's report of the Battle of Palmetto Ranch in Roberts, "Texas," *Confederate Military History*, XI, 126; Ford, Memoirs, V, 1031–1033.

88. Carrington's report in Brown, *Texas*, II, 432; Wooten, *Comprehensive History of Texas*, II, 560.

89. Branson's report, May 18, 1865, *Official Records*, ser. I, vol. XLVIII, pt. I, 268; Barrett's report, August 10, 1865, *ibid.*, 266; Ford, Memoirs, VII, 1180–1188.

90. Carrington's report in Brown, *Texas*, II, 436.

cavalry swooped around their left flank. Colonel Barrett ordered a retreat and the Yankees, throwing up skirmishers to check the Confederate pursuit, marched at quick time back toward Brazos Island.[91]

Ford's Texans followed the Federals for seven miles to Cobb's Ranch, just above Brazos Island. Knowing that his men and horses were much too exhausted to continue the pursuit, Ford said: "Boys, we have done finely. We will let well enough alone and retire."[92]

Just then a Confederate column riding at a gallop reached the scene—General Slaughter with Cater's battalion under Captain W. H. D. Carrington. Slaughter and Ford exchanged heated words as to whether or not the attack should be renewed. Ford insisted that his men were too tired to fight. Slaughter said that they were not and ordered Carrington's command to charge the Yankees as they attempted to cross the Boca Chica. By this time Brazos Island had been alerted and Barrett's command greatly reinforced. The Federals were strong enough to hold off any attack that Slaughter could muster.

As twilight fell the firing dwindled. An artillery shell burst near a youthful Confederate. Swearing loudly, the boy fired his rifle at the shadows of the island and the shooting part of the Civil War was over.[93]

The war between Ford and Slaughter, however, raged on. As the Confederates rode to an encampment near Palmetto Ranch, the two officers engaged in strenuous argument. Slaughter was highly irritated at Ford for refusing to obey orders and renew the attack. Ford was equally provoked. He denounced the general for giving such an order when it was obvious that the men, having fought hard that day, were almost too tired to shoulder their rifles.

At the Confederate encampment, officers and men stood around listening to a fiery discussion that ran from one difference of opinion to another. Finally, in exasperation, Slaughter sat down on a log, looked up at Ford and said: "You are going to camp here to-night, are you not?"

"No Sir."

---

91. Ford's report in Roberts, "Texas," *Confederate Military History*, XL, 127–128; Barrett's report, August 10, 1865, *Official Records*, ser. I, vol. XLVII, pt. I, 266; Bancroft, *History of North Mexican States and Texas*, II, 475; Wooten, *Comprehensive History of Texas*, II, 560.

92. Ford, Memoirs, V, 1032–1033.

93. Carrington's report in Brown, *Texas*, II, 433–435. With respect to the numbers engaged and the casualties, the accounts of the battle come nowhere near general agreement. Federal losses out of about 800 engaged were probably 30 killed and wounded and 113 taken prisoner. Confederate casualties must have been more than five slightly wounded, as reported. Carrington himself stated in his report (*ibid.*, 435) that after it was all over the Confederates took time out to bury their dead. It is likely that out of some 1,300 engaged all told, the Confederates lost about the same number in killed and wounded as the Federals.

The general frowned savagely. "I have ordered down several wagons loaded with subsistence and forage."

"I am not going to stop here in reach of the infantry forces at Brazos Island," Ford said stubbornly, "and allow them a chance to gobble me up before daylight."

"But remember the prisoners," the general said shaking his head.

"I do sir," Ford retorted, "if we Confederates were their prisoners, we would be compelled to march to a place of safety from attack by the Confederates."

It was too much for Slaughter. Fuming at such insubordination, he mounted and returned with his staff to Brownsville. Ford and his men took the prisoners to a safer camp eight miles to the north.[94]

The next day, Ford learned from a prisoner that Lee had surrendered over a month before and that the Federal officers at Brazos Island, having received the news, had moved toward Brownsville expecting Confederate capitulation. The skirmish with Robinson on May 12, the prisoner continued, had been an accident, the ensuing battle, a mistake. Ford and his lieutenants denied this story (the Yankee Army later advanced a similar view of the battle) and insisted that Union forces had come off Brazos Island looking for trouble, and certainly had found it.[95] This dispute has never been settled to the satisfaction of both sides but whatever brought about the last battle was actually insignificant as the final chapter of the Civil War came to a close. The Confederacy was no more and the South was faced with a long and dreary period of reconstruction. But to John Salmon Ford and thousands of other loyal Southerners the Confederacy never really died for it was something more than a government or an army: it symbolized a way of life that would continue even though the machinery that made it tangible had been destroyed.

A few days after Palmetto Ranch, Ford and his Texans, looking forward to civilian life with soft beds, good cooking, and honest work, rode north across the brush toward San Antonio.

---

94. Ford's report in Roberts, "Texas," *Confederate Military History*, XI, 128–129.

95. Ford's article in the San Antonio *Express*, October 10, 1890; Benson John Lossing, *Pictorial History of the Civil War in the United States of America* (3 vols.; Philadelphia, 1866–1868), III, 180.

Half-plate tintype of Privates Emzy Taylor and G. M. Taylor, Company E, "Lone Star Guards," 4th Texas Infantry, ca. 1861. Emzy Taylor was discharged for disability because of a "lung disease" in 1861. His brother, G. M. Taylor, was wounded in the Battle of Gaines' Mill in 1862 and served with the 4th Texas Infantry until being paroled at Appomattox Courthouse on April 12, 1865. *Courtesy Lawrence T. Jones III.*

Hood's Texas Brigade at Appomattox

COL. HAROLD B. SIMPSON*

Hood's Texas Brigade was the most famous Texas military unit in the Civil War. Made up of three Texas regiments, the First, Fourth, and Fifth Infantry, and a fourth regiment from Georgia (later replaced by the Third Arkansas), the brigade fought in the Seven Days, Second Manassas, Sharpsburg, Fredericksburg, Gettysburg, Chickamauga, Wilderness, Spotsylvania, Cold Harbor, and Petersburg campaigns. On most occasions the brigade was in the forefront of battle and gained the praise of commanding general Robert E. Lee for its courage and gallantry.

When the end came at Appomattox Courthouse in April 1865, only 617 men, or about 12 percent of those who served, were still with the brigade. Most of the others had been killed in battle, died of wounds or disease, or discharged because of injuries. The late Harold B. Simpson, a retired Air Force colonel and director of the Confederate Research Center at Hill Junior College, spent many years researching and writing about Hood's Texans. His four-volume Hood's Texas Brigade *(Waco: Texian Press, 1968–1977) is the definitive account of this proud Civil War unit.*

The following article, published in Texana, is a fitting tribute to the brigade and Colonel Simpson. An appendix to the article, listing all members of the brigade paroled at Appomattox, is not included here, but should be examined by those seeking names of individual members of the brigade at the time of surrender. Readers

---

* Harold B. Simpson, "Hood's Texas Brigade at Appomattox," *Texana,* III (Spring, 1965), 1–10.

wishing additional information on the brigade should see, in addition to Simpson's four volumes, J. B. Polley, Hood's Texas Brigade *(New York: Neale Publishing Co., 1910) and Nicholas A. Davis,* Chaplain Davis and Hood's Texas Brigade, *ed. Donald E. Everett (San Antonio: Principia Press of Trinity University, 1962).*

It was close to midnight on April 8, 1865, when Colonel Robert M. Powell led Hood's Texas Brigade into bivouac two miles east of Appomattox Court House.[1] Colonel Charles Marshall, Lee's military secretary, unable to sleep because of the noise and tension, heard the rear guard Texans chant as they moved into the Confederate lines:

> "The race is not to them that's got
> The longest legs to run,
> Nor the battle to that people
> That shoots the biggest gun."[2]

The day's march for the Texans along the north side of shallow, sparkling Appomattox River had been through an area marked by chaos, clutter, and confusion. Wagons were upended and burning on every side, and the deep-rutted road of retreat was strewn with all types of camp equipage—pots, pans, cups, and kettles. Medicine chests were split open and their contents spilled upon the ground. Disabled cannon with the spokes of their wheels chopped out and their caissons overturned blocked the roadway in many places.[3] Everything within sight, sound, and smell was characteristic of an army in hasty retreat and rapidly being brought to bay.

The retreat from Richmond and Petersburg had been a hellish nightmare for the struggling Army of Northern Virginia. Hounded relentlessly by Bulldog Grant and his seemingly endless blue infantry legions, nipped at on the flanks by Greyhound Sheridan and his dashing horse soldiers, with few rations and no rest, Robert E. Lee and his game veterans plodded westward toward Lynchburg. By April 9, the Federals effectively blocked Lee's retreat at a small, quiet Virginia village called Appomattox Court House, seat of Appomattox County, on the banks of Appomattox River.

After its boisterous entry into the lines the night before, the Texas Brigade, early on the morning of the ninth, marched to within one mile of Appomattox

---

1. Frank B. Chilton (ed.), *Official Minutes of Hood's Texas Brigade Monument Dedication* (Houston, 1911), 183.

2. Burk Davis, *To Appomattox, Nine Days, 1865* (New York, 1959), 341.

3. O. T. Hanks, *History of Captain B. F. Benton's Company, 1861–1865* (unpublished manuscript in the Texas Collection, Baylor University, Waco), 57.

Court House to take up their final combat position as the rear guard for Lee's Army.[4] This was the last operational march for Hood's Texas Brigade—the last mile of hundreds of miles that the Brigade had marched over the ravaged land from the tangled forests of Chickamauga to the rock strewn hills of Gettysburg. Never had the Lone Star Flag been carried so far and been served so well.

Assuming a defensive position on the outskirts of the village just north of the stream, the Texans built breastworks across the old stage road leading in from the northeast. The men were "ragged, starved and exhausted."[5] Except for a few scraps of hurriedly prepared bread and biscuits, they had not eaten for three days.[6] Fortunately, while gathering wood and breaking down fences to construct their breastworks, the Texans had found, in the dirt, a few small scatterings of corn that had been dropped where officers had fed their horses; this was eagerly gathered up, brushed off, and eaten.[7]

Regardless of their physical discomfiture and the hopelessness of their situation, the Texans, like the rest of Lee's 28,000 ragamuffins, dug in and determined to sell their lives dearly.

By mid-day on April 9, the ominous silence of an informal truce had settled over the valley of the Appomattox. The word spread rapidly that Lee had asked for and had been granted an interview with the Federal commander. As unbelievable as this seemed to the men, it could mean only one thing—General Lee was contemplating surrender.

Since April 7, when he was at Farmville, Lee had been negotiating surrender terms with Grant. Now, on April 9 at Appomattox Court House, almost completely surrounded by an adversary five times his number, Lee faced destruction or surrender. Although his old "War Horse," Pete Longstreet, and several other senior commanders wanted to try to fight their way through to Lynchburg and the mountains, General Lee had seen enough bloodshed. He dispatched a final note to Grant late on the morning of the ninth, requesting a meeting for the purpose of arranging surrender terms for the Army of Northern Virginia.

In the early afternoon of April 9, 1865, astride his favorite mount, "Traveller," and accompanied only by his military secretary, Lieutenant Colonel Charles Marshall, the great Virginian made his way toward Appomattox Court House and his pre-arranged rendezvous with Grant and destiny.

---

4. Chilton, *op. cit.*, 183.

5. D. H. Hamilton, *History of Company M, First Texas Regiment, Hood's Texas Brigade* (n.p., 1925), 69.

6. Hanks, *op. cit.*, 55.

7. *Ibid.*, 58.

The famous meeting of the two generals took place in the front parlor of Wilmer McLean's imposing brick home on Main Street not far from the Courthouse. Lee arrived first and sat down in a cane-backed chair near a marble-topped table. He was dressed elegantly in a new uniform of Confederate gray; his trousers were tucked inside of a handsome pair of jack boots that were adorned with gleaming spurs with large rowels. Lee carried long buckskin gauntlets and a beautiful saber with a gilt-wrapped hilt that had been presented to him by a Maryland admirer.

As Grant arrived at the meeting site, a Federal band outside struck up "Auld Lang Syne." The Union commander presented an entirely different appearance from that of Lee. Grant, who was suffering from a migraine headache and had just come in from field duty, was dressed in a private's uniform; only the three stars on his shoulder straps denoted his rank. His spurless boots as well as his blue uniform were spattered with mud, and he carried neither gloves nor saber. At forty-two, Grant was eighteen years Lee's junior; he lacked three inches of Lee's height of six feet, and his brown hair and beard had but a few traces of gray. Lee's hair and beard were almost white.

The two great Americans met at one-thirty in the afternoon—some two hours later agreement had been reached between the victor and the vanquished.[8] The terms were magnanimous—the officers could keep their sidearms; all men who owned horses could retain them; and rations were to be distributed immediately to the starving Confederates. Too, the officers and men were to be paroled and could return home unmolested. Grant didn't ask for Lee's sword, and Lee didn't offer it. As Lee departed the McLean House, Grant followed him as far as the stairs then tipped his hat in a salute as the Southern leader pensively rode away.

After the surrender, Lee, followed by Colonel Marshall rode slowly back across the shallow Appomattox to his headquarters. As he neared the Confederate lines, he was met by his old veterans who, with tears in their eyes, crowded round him trying to shake his hand, touch his person or even his horse, so great was their affection for their beloved commander. Tears filled Lee's eyes.

When word of the surrender reached the Texas Brigade in position at the rear of Longstreet's Corps, the men refused at first to believe the message. Finally convinced that the inevitable had taken place, one member of the Brigade dropping his hands despondently exclaimed, "I'd rather have died than surrendered,

---

8. While Lee had but one attendant at the McLean House, Colonel Marshall, eight Federal officers besides Grant were present at the surrender ceremony. Those Federal officers present were: Generals Phil Sheridan, O. C. Ord, Seth Williams and George A. Custer; Colonels Orville Babcock, Theodore Bowers, and Ely S. Parker, and Lieutenant Colonel Horace Porter.

but if 'Marse Bob' thinks that is best, then all that I have got to say is that 'Marse Bob' is bound to be right as usual."⁹

Other members of the Brigade didn't take the news of the surrender so philosophically. Many men of the 5th Texas, when they heard the news, bent the barrels of their guns in a convenient fork of a nearby red oak, others smashed their Enfields against rocks and trees determined that the Federals would not get an operating weapon. Captain W. T. Hill, Commander of the 5th Texas, counseled the men against such action; for the Federals had stated, he cautioned, "no good gun—no parole." This had the desired effect on several members who tried to reverse the bend in their gun barrels using the same fork in the red oak. Fortunately, the guns were not inspected when they were surrendered.¹⁰

There is little doubt that the men of Hood's Texas Brigade were among the most defiant of the remnant left of the once invincible Army of Northern Virginia. Only a few months before the surrender at Appomattox, a committee composed of representative members from all four regiments of the Brigade met to reaffirm their loyalty to the Confederacy and their unshaken belief in the Southern cause. A series of statements known as "The Resolutions of the Texas Brigade" came out of this meeting. The prologue to the Resolutions breathed fire and defiance and announced to the world that the Texans and Arkansans in Virginia were determined ". . . to maintain, at all hazards, and to the last extremity, the rights and liberties which a merciful God has been pleased to bestow upon them" and to seek ". . . a perpetual separation from the hated and despised foe, who have murdered our grey-haired fathers, insulted our women and children, and turned out thousands of helpless families to starve . . ."¹¹

The formal surrender of the Army of Northern Virginia took place on Monday morning, April 12, 1865. Both Lee and Grant had appointed three generals to work out the details for the surrender and the issuance of paroles for the Confederate Army.¹² Neither commander was present for the formal surrender ceremony. Lee had left his army the morning of April 12, for his Richmond home, and Grant had ridden to Burkeville on April 10, hoping to obtain train connections to City Point.

Before leaving for Richmond, General Lee issued one of the most famous military documents of the Civil War, General Order No. 9, commonly referred to as "Lee's Farewell to the Army of Northern Virginia." General Order No. 9

9. Mrs. A. V. Winkler, *The Confederate Capital and Hood's Texas Brigade* (Austin, 1894), 268.

10. Chilton, *op. cit.*, 183.

11. Harold B. Simpson (ed.), *Touched With Valor* (Hillsboro, Texas, 1964), Appendix V, 102–4.

12. Generals Gibbon, Griffin, and Merritt represented Grant and Generals Longstreet, Pendleton, and Gordon represented Lee.

was written by Colonel Marshall at Lee's request. Lee struck out a few words of Marshall's draft (which he deemed too harsh) and then had his military secretary make numerous copies of the "farewell" for his signature. Lee then had these signed copies distributed to his corps commanders and various members of his staff.[13] Lee's final message to his beloved army read as follows:

> After four years of arduous service, marked by unsurpassed courage and fortitude, the Army of Northern Virginia has been compelled to yield to overwhelming numbers and resources. I need not tell the survivors of so many hard fought battles, who have remained steadfast to the last, that I have consented to this result from no distrust of them, but, feeling that valor and devotion could accomplish nothing that could compensate for the loss that would have attended the continuation of the contest, I have determined to avoid the useless sacrifice of those whose past services have endeared them to their countrymen.
>
> By the terms of the agreement officers and men can return to their homes, and remain there until exchanged. You will take with you the satisfaction that proceeds from the consciousness of duty faithfully performed: And I earnestly pray that a merciful God will extend to you his blessing and protection.
>
> With an increasing admiration for your constancy and devotion to your country, and a grateful remembrance of your kind and generous consideration of myself I bid you an affectionate farewell.

The day of the formal surrender broke with low clinging clouds hiding the tops of the surrounding hills. A soft, misty spring rain fell in the morning, leaving the roads sticky and the grass wet. Of the 28,000 Confederates who surrendered and were paroled at Appomattox, only 8,000 were able to bear arms. The rest, weakened by hunger, wasted by sickness, and footsore from marching barefoot, were wholly unfit for duty and were a pitiful sight as they hobbled along with their regiments on April 12.

A few Confederate cavalry and artillery units had surrendered on April 11 and early on the morning of the twelfth, but the climax of the formal ceremonies came with the surrender of the veteran Confederate infantry corps—the men who had given the Army of Northern Virginia its aura of invincibility.[14] Joshua Lawrence Chamberlain, Brigadier General U.S.A., Congressional Medal of Honor winner (who after the war would be elected Governor of Maine and serve as president of Bowdoin College), commanded a Federal infantry division from the Fifth Corps. This division, which formed in a double line at order

---

13. Robert Underwood Johnson and Clarence Clough Buel (eds.), *Battles and Leaders of the Civil War* (New York, 1884–1888), 747; Douglas Southall Freeman, *Robert E. Lee* (New York, 1935), IV, 149–150, 154–155.

14. John J. Pullen, *The 20th Maine* (New York, 1957), 271.

arms along the Richmond to Lynchburg Stage Road east of the village, had been designated to take the surrender of Lee's army.

John Brown Gordon, Major General C.S.A. (who after the war would serve as Governor of Georgia and as a United States Senator), led the Confederate infantry brigades splashing across the shallow, murmuring Appomattox. Gordon, one of Lee's favorite commanders, had been selected to lead the last march of the Army of Northern Virginia.

As the Confederates approached the double ranked Federal division, Chamberlain gave the command, "Carry, arms" (the marching salute), as a show of respect for a worthy foe. Gordon in return, giving an honor for an honor, dropped the point of his saber toward the ground in acknowledgment of Chamberlain's courtesy, and, in turn, gave the command "Carry, arms" to his men.[15] Thus, two great American armies, the Army of the Potomac and the Army of Northern Virginia, meeting for the first and last time under conditions of non-violence, honored each other in a final soldier's salute.

Lee's ragged and gaunt veterans maintained their composure and stolidness until the time came to stack their arms and furl their battle-stained banners. At this moment finally came the realization that all they had been fighting for and had held dear through the bitter struggle—the comradeship forged on the anvil of bivouac and battle and the hope for an independent nation—had suddenly come to an end. Both Generals, Gordon and Chamberlain, describe this dramatic and heart-rending moment.

John B. Gordon in his "Reminiscences" portrayed this final touching act as follows:

At the formal surrender the veterans of the Army of Northern Virginia could no longer control their emotions, and tears ran like water down their shrunken faces. The flags which they still carried were objects of undisguised affection . . . as we reached the designated point [surrender site], the arms were stacked and the battle flags were folded. Those sad and suffering men, many of them weeping as they saw the old banners laid upon the stacked guns . . . began to tear the flags from the staffs and hide them in their shirts. . . .[16]

Joshua Lawrence Chamberlain, like Gordon, left an emotional picture of the Southern infantryman as the world and ideals he had been fighting for collapsed around him.

As each successive division masks our own, it halts, the men face inward towards us across the road, twelve feet away; then carefully "dress" their line, each captain taking

---

15. *Ibid.*, 273

16. John B. Gordon, *Reminiscences of the Civil War* (New York, 1904), 443–8.

pains for the good appearance of his company, worn and half starved as they were. . . . They fix bayonets, stack arms; then, hesitatingly, remove cartridge boxes and lay them down. Lastly,—reluctantly, with agony of expression,—they tenderly fold their flags, battle-worn and torn, blood-stained, heart-holding colors, and lay them down; some frenziedly rushing from the ranks, kneeling over them, clinging to them, pressing them to their lips with burning tears.[17]

The divisions of Longstreet's first Corps, the anchor rock of Lee's Army, surrendered last. Major General Charles Field, leading Hood's old division, brought up the rear, and with it, of course, marched the Texas Brigade. A member of the Twentieth Maine, one of the Federal units present at the surrender, thought that the brigades of Longstreet's Corps were the best marchers.[18]

In his famous four-volume work on Robert E. Lee, Douglas Southall Freeman, the dean of Confederate historians, wrote enthusiastically about the Texas Brigade on this final day. As he reviewed in retrospect the records of the brigades of the Army of Northern Virginia as each marched through the village to lay down its arms, Freeman said:

Of the Texas Brigade itself, perhaps the most renowned of all, 476 [473] officers and men marched up the road[19] and stacked the rifles that had been heard in all the army's [Army of Northern Virginia] great battles, except Chancellorsville. For absence from that action they had made atonement at Chickamauga and in Tennessee [and at Suffolk]. . . . Defeat, at the end of their military career, could not dim their record. 'I rely upon [the Texans] in all tight places', Lee had said.[20]

After the sorrowful ceremony was over, the Texans picked up their paroles and returned to their old bivouac area north of the Appomattox. By noon the formal surrender and the issuance of paroles to Hood's Texas Brigade had been completed.[21]

It is estimated that 5,300 men had enlisted during the war in the three Texas regiments and the one Arkansas regiment that composed the Texas Brigade at the time of the final surrender.[22] Of this number, only 617 (or about twelve per cent) were left to be paroled at Appomattox. Thus, some 4,700 members of the

---

17. Joshua Lawrence Chamberlain, *The Passing of the Armies, an Account of the final Campaign of the Army of the Potomac, Based Upon Personal Reminiscences of the Fifth Army Corps* (New York, 1915), 258–265.

18. Pullen, *op. cit.*, 275.

19. Freeman's figure included only the three Texas regiments. However the tough Third Arkansas Infantry was a bona fide member of Hood's Texas Brigade and should be included in all statistics.

20. Douglas Southall Freeman, *Lee's Lieutenants* (New York, 1946), 4 vols., 751.

21. Chilton, *op. cit.*, 183.

22. *Ibid.*, 184.

old Brigade had been killed in battle, had died of disease, had been invalided home due to sickness or crippling wounds, or had been discharged for being either over or under age—but few had deserted.

At Appomattox, the Texas Brigade, commanded by Colonel Robert M. Powell, surrendered a brigade headquarters contingent of five officers. The First Texas Infantry Regiment, commanded by Colonel Frederick S. Bass, surrendered sixteen officers and 133 enlisted men. The Fourth Texas, commanded by Lieutenant Colonel Clinton M. Winkler, surrendered fifteen officers and 143 enlisted men. The Fifth Texas, commanded by Captain William T. Hill, surrendered thirteen officers and 148 enlisted men, and the Third Arkansas Infantry Regiment, commanded by Lieutenant Colonel Robert S. Taylor, surrendered fifteen officers and 129 enlisted men.[23]

With the surrender over, the members of the Brigade made plans for their return home. Of the Texans, some decided to go to Yorktown and take a government steamer back to Galveston; a few decided to remain in Virginia and return to Texas at a later date; others decided to visit their relatives in the Southern states; but, by far the greatest number agreed to march back in one command to Texas. The plan of this latter group included marching to Danville, then by rail to Atlanta and Montgomery, and finally by steamer to Mobile, New Orleans, and Galveston.[24] The Arkansas regiment planned to return to "razorback country" by the way of Chattanooga and Memphis. Thus, with plans laid and the last farewells said, the veterans left the "pen" (as they called their four-day Appomattox encampment site) for their various destinations on the afternoon of April 12, 1865.[25]

One of the Texans, prior to his departure for home, journeyed to Richmond to pay General Lee a visit at his Franklin Street residence in that city. According to Custis Lee (the General's son), one day, soon after Appomattox when his father was busy answering a flood of correspondence, a tall Confederate soldier with one arm in a sling came to the door and asked to see General Lee. Custis, remarking that his father was very busy, turned the man away. As the wounded soldier turned to go, he said that he had fought with Hood's Texas Brigade and had followed Lee for four years, and that before he walked home to Texas he had hoped to shake his old commander's hand. Custis Lee couldn't refuse the soldier's simple request and so summoned his father. When the General came downstairs "the soldier took him by the hand, struggled to say something, and

---

23. Southern Historical Society Papers (Richmond), Vol. XV, Jan.–Dec., 1887.

24. Chilton, op. cit., 184

25. Ibid.

then burst into tears." He then covered his face with his good arm and walked out of the house.[26] Lee and "his Texans" had a great deal of affection for one another.

As mentioned previously, the greatest number of the Texas veterans decided to journey back to the Lone Star State in one command. Major "Howdy" Martin of the Fourth Texas and Captain T. T. Hill of the Fifth Texas led this group of some 300 on the trek back to the Lone Star State. One of the most valuable assets that Martin's group acquired as it made its way south through western North Carolina was Major George and his Durham cow. George had been General Hood's Quartermaster and had transferred with his commander to the Army of Tennessee. After Hood's disastrous Tennessee campaign George (accompanied by his cow) fought with Joe Johnston in the Carolinas. Hearing of Lee's surrender, he had started back to Texas when he accidentally came across the returning veterans of Hood's Brigade. Major George and his Durham cow were a welcomed addition. The cow had provided Hood's Headquarters with liquid refreshment for three years and was still giving milk.[27]

Traveling in such a large group had its disadvantages however, as food in quantity and suitable campsites were difficult to find. Hence, small groups splintered off as the main body traveled south. The trip back to Texas was tedious and trying. The hope of riding the railroad from Danville to Montgomery via Atlanta didn't materialize (Sherman and Wilson had done their work too well). The Texans were held up several days at Montgomery awaiting a steamer for Mobile, and then were offloaded at Selma to make way for a Federal Corps D'Afrique regiment that had a higher priority. Another delay at Mobile awaited Lee's veterans, who finally arrived at New Orleans on May 19. Here they were quartered in cotton sheds and guarded by another contingent of the Corps D'Afrique, who delighted in snipping off the C.S.A. buttons from the jackets of the Texans.

On June 2, 1865, Texas was reached, the first time in almost four years that many of the group had touched the soil of the Lone Star State. After a series of welcoming parties at Houston on June 3, this great Confederate fighting unit disbanded; north, south, east, and west they fanned out from the "Bayou City," singly and in small groups, bound for their home communities and into the shadows of history and legend.[28]

Although the sun of the Confederacy had set and the great experiment in

---

26. Richard M. Ketchum, "Faces From the Past," *American Heritage,* XII, No. 4 (June, 1961), 29.

27. Chilton, *op. cit.,* 184.

28. Harold B. Simpson, *Gaines' Mill to Appomattox* (Waco, 1963), 240–244.

states right's government had come to an end, the world would long remember Hood's Texas Brigade—few men in the history of warfare had fought so long and so well, with so little, and under such hardships.

Not for fame or reward, not for place or for rank,
Not lured by ambition or goaded by necessity,
But in simple obedience to duty as they understood it
These men suffered all, sacrificed all, endured all . . . and died.[29]

---

29. From the Confederate Memorial, Arlington National Cemetery.

Index

Designed and laid out by Martin Kohout using QuarkXPress software.
Set in Adobe Garamond, Adobe Garamond Expert, and
Adobe Garamond Alternate Italic.
Dustjacket designed by David Timmons, Timmons Willgren Design,
Austin, Texas.
Printed on fifty-five-pound Glatfelter paper and bound by
Edwards Brothers, Inc., Ann Arbor, Michigan.